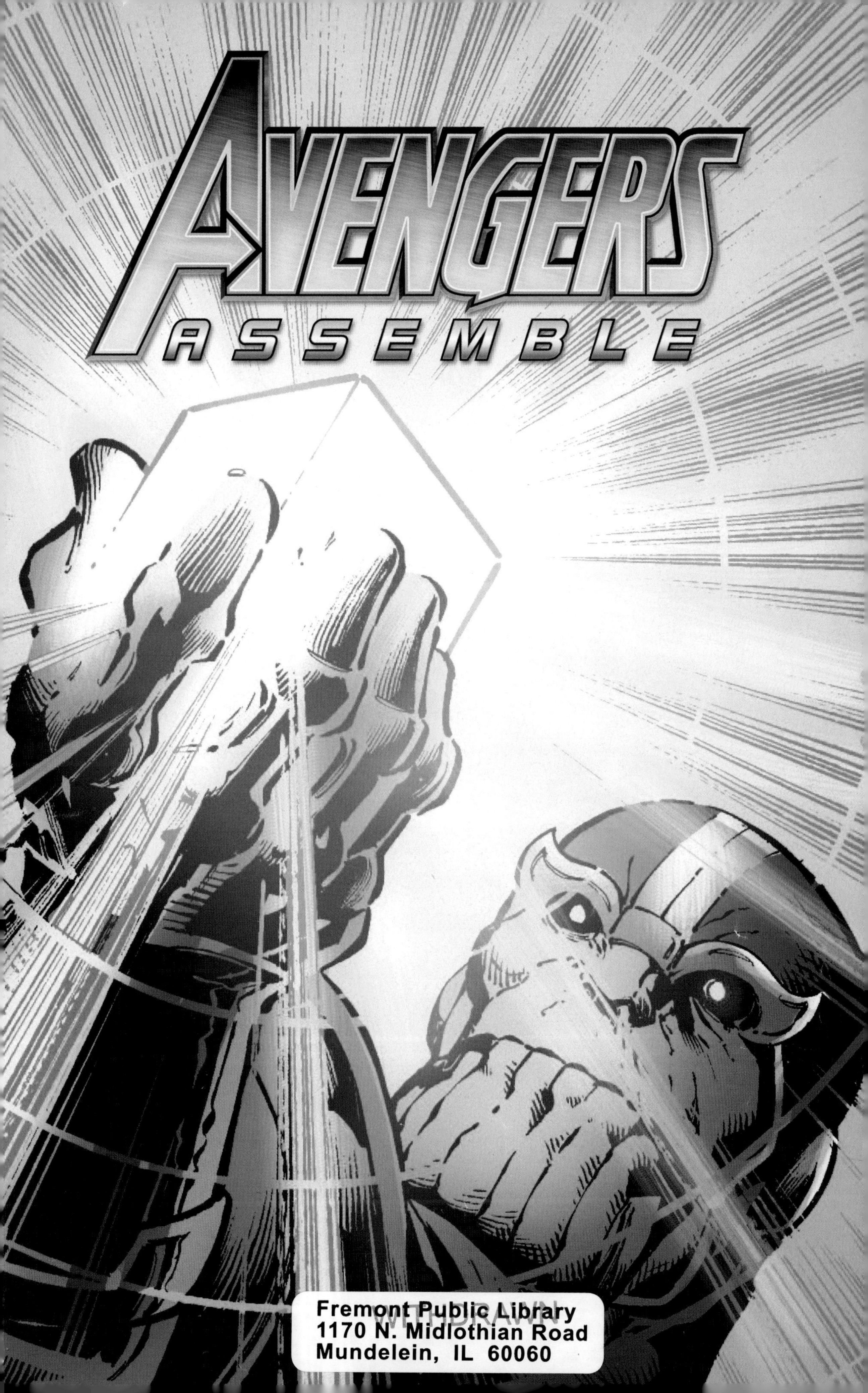
AVENGERS
ASSEMBLE

Collection Editor: Jennifer Grünwald
Assistant Editors: Alex Starbuck & Nelson Ribeiro
Editor, Special Projects: Mark D. Beazley
Senior Editor, Special Projects: Jeff Youngquist
Senior Vice President of Sales: David Gabriel
SVP of Brand Planning & Communications: Michael Pasciullo
Book Design: Jeff Powell

Editor in Chief: Axel Alonso
Chief Creative Officer: Joe Quesada
Publisher: Dan Buckley
Executive Producer: Alan Fine

AVENGERS ASSEMBLE BY BRIAN MICHAEL BENDIS. Contains material originally published in magazine form as AVENGERS ASSEMBLE #1-8. First printing 2013. ISBN# 978-0-7851-6327-5. Published by MARVEL WORLDWIDE, INC., a subsidiary of MARVEL ENTERTAINMENT, LLC. OFFICE OF PUBLICATION: 135 West 50th Street, New York, NY 10020. Copyright © 2012 and 2013 Marvel Characters, Inc. All rights reserved. All characters featured in this issue and the distinctive names and likenesses thereof, and all related indicia are trademarks of Marvel Characters, Inc. No similarity between any of the names, characters, persons, and/or institutions in this magazine with those of any living or dead person or institution is intended, and any such similarity which may exist is purely coincidental. Printed in the U.S.A. ALAN FINE, EVP - Office of the President, Marvel Worldwide, Inc. and EVP & CMO Marvel Characters B.V.; DAN BUCKLEY, Publisher & President - Print, Animation & Digital Divisions; JOE QUESADA, Chief Creative Officer; TOM BREVOORT, SVP of Publishing; DAVID BOGART, SVP of Operations & Procurement, Publishing; RUWAN JAYATILLEKE, SVP & Associate Publisher, Publishing; C.B. CEBULSKI, SVP of Creator & Content Development; DAVID GABRIEL, SVP of Publishing Sales & Circulation; MICHAEL PASCIULLO, SVP of Brand Planning & Communications; JIM O'KEEFE, VP of Operations & Logistics; DAN CARR, Executive Director of Publishing Technology; SUSAN CRESPI, Editorial Operations Manager; ALEX MORALES, Publishing Operations Manager; STAN LEE, Chairman Emeritus. For information regarding advertising in Marvel Comics or on Marvel.com, please contact Niza Disla, Director of Marvel Partnerships, at ndisla@marvel.com. For Marvel subscription inquiries, please call 800-217-9158. Manufactured between 11/12/2012 and 12/31/2012 by R.R. DONNELLEY, INC., SALEM, VA, USA.

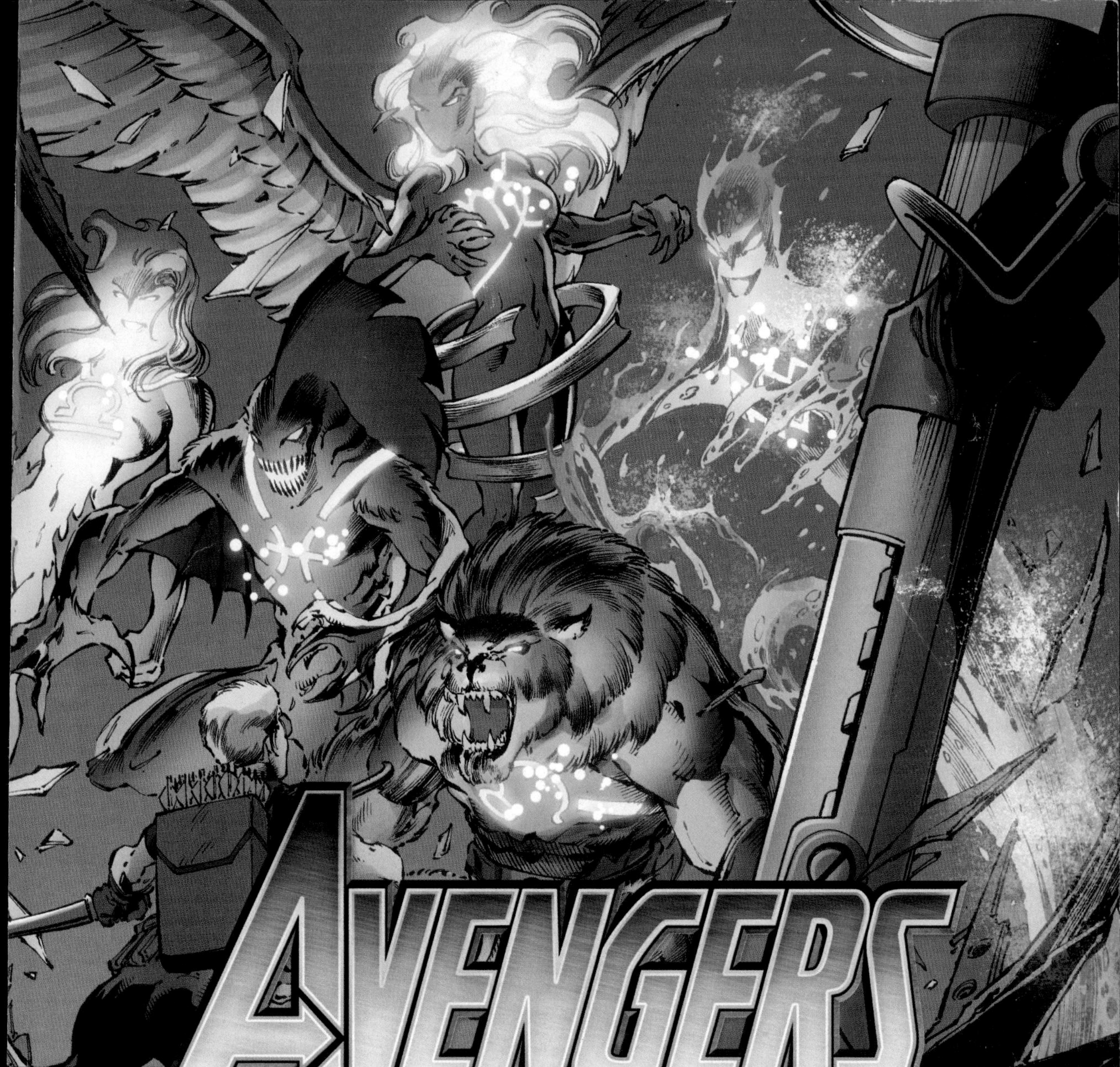

AVENGERS ASSEMBLE

WRITER
BRIAN MICHAEL BENDIS

PENCILER
MARK BAGLEY

INKER
DANNY MIKI

COLORIST
PAUL MOUNTS

LETTERER
VC'S CLAYTON COWLES

COVER ART
MARK BAGLEY, DANNY MIKI WITH **JUSTIN PONSOR** (#1-2)
& PAUL MOUNTS (#3-8)

ASSISTANT EDITORS
JOHN DENNING & JAKE THOMAS

ASSOCIATE EDITOR
LAUREN SANKOVITCH

EDITOR
TOM BREVOORT

SPECIAL THANKS TO KI TAE KIM

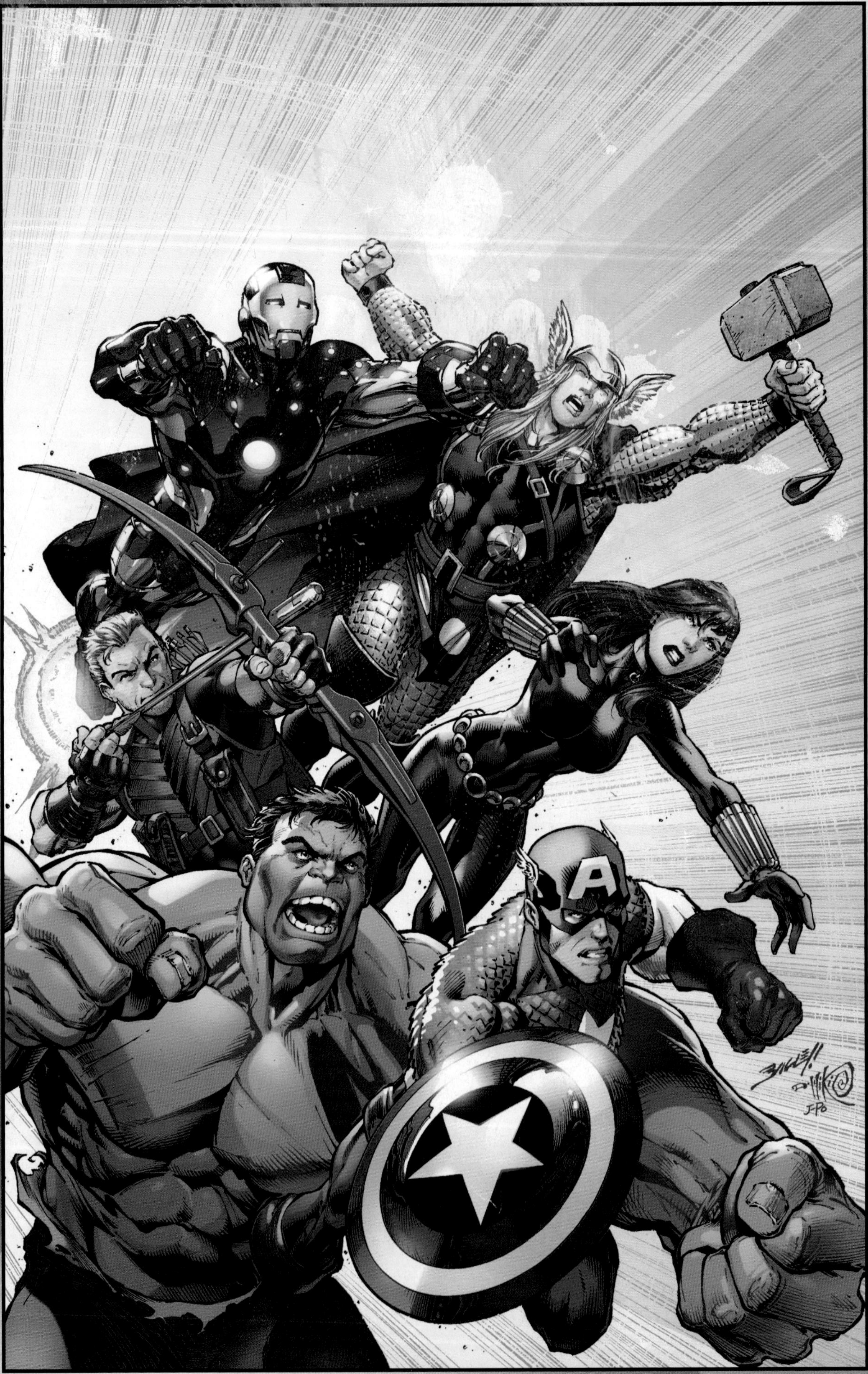

ONE

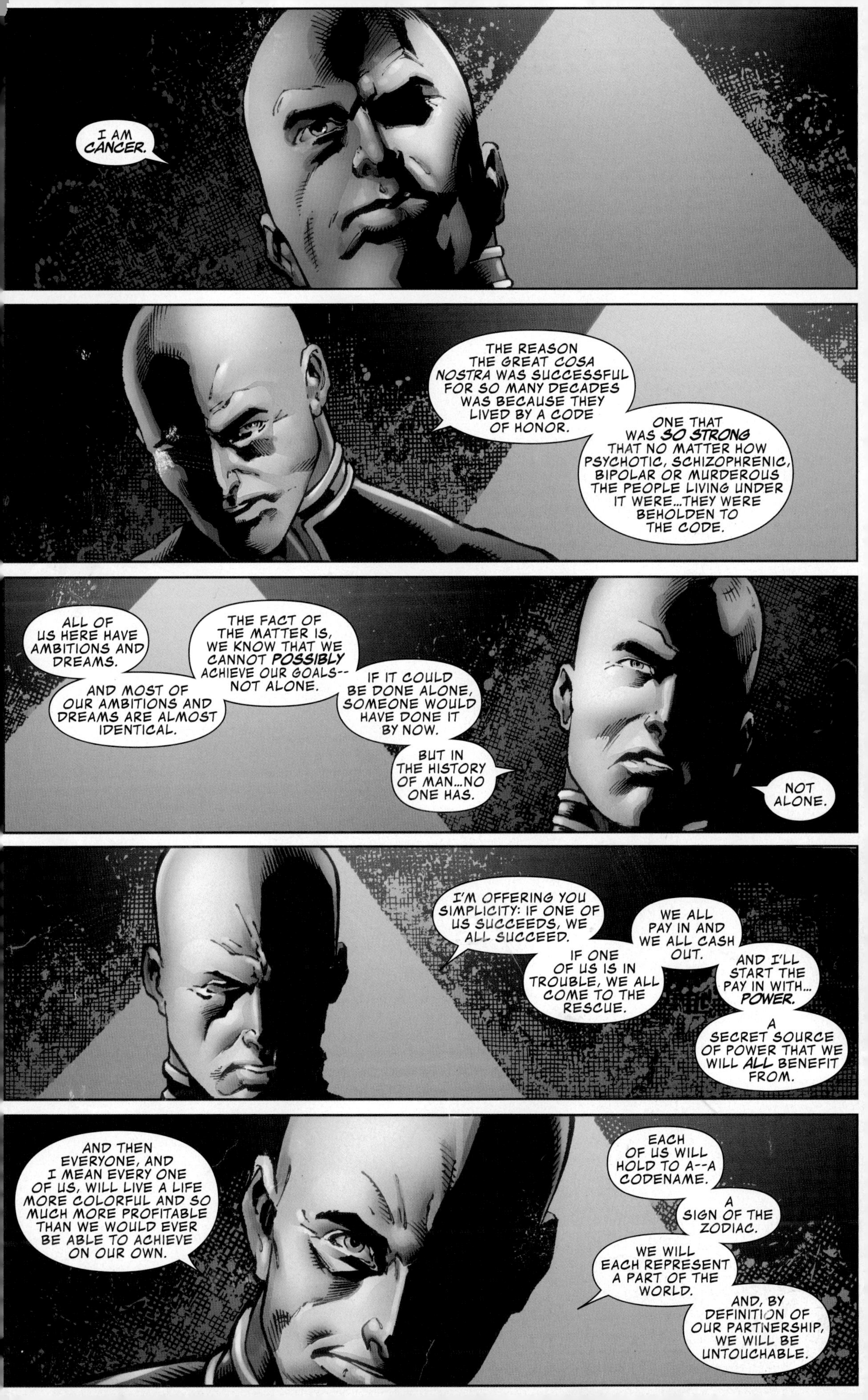
I AM *CANCER.*
THE REASON THE GREAT COSA NOSTRA WAS SUCCESSFUL FOR SO MANY DECADES WAS BECAUSE THEY LIVED BY A CODE OF HONOR.
ONE THAT WAS ***SO STRONG*** THAT NO MATTER HOW PSYCHOTIC, SCHIZOPHRENIC, BIPOLAR OR MURDEROUS THE PEOPLE LIVING UNDER IT WERE...THEY WERE BEHOLDEN TO THE CODE.
ALL OF US HERE HAVE AMBITIONS AND DREAMS.
AND MOST OF OUR AMBITIONS AND DREAMS ARE ALMOST IDENTICAL.
THE FACT OF THE MATTER IS, WE KNOW THAT WE CANNOT ***POSSIBLY*** ACHIEVE OUR GOALS-- NOT ALONE.
IF IT COULD BE DONE ALONE, SOMEONE WOULD HAVE DONE IT BY NOW.
BUT IN THE HISTORY OF MAN...NO ONE HAS.
NOT ALONE.
I'M OFFERING YOU SIMPLICITY: IF ONE OF US SUCCEEDS, WE ALL SUCCEED.
WE ALL PAY IN AND WE ALL CASH OUT.
IF ONE OF US IS IN TROUBLE, WE ALL COME TO THE RESCUE.
AND I'LL START THE PAY IN WITH... ***POWER.***
A SECRET SOURCE OF POWER THAT WE WILL ***ALL*** BENEFIT FROM.
AND THEN EVERYONE, AND I MEAN EVERY ONE OF US, WILL LIVE A LIFE MORE COLORFUL AND SO MUCH MORE PROFITABLE THAN WE WOULD EVER BE ABLE TO ACHIEVE ON OUR OWN.
EACH OF US WILL HOLD TO A--A CODENAME.
A SIGN OF THE ZODIAC.
WE WILL EACH REPRESENT A PART OF THE WORLD.
AND, BY DEFINITION OF OUR PARTNERSHIP, WE WILL BE UNTOUCHABLE.

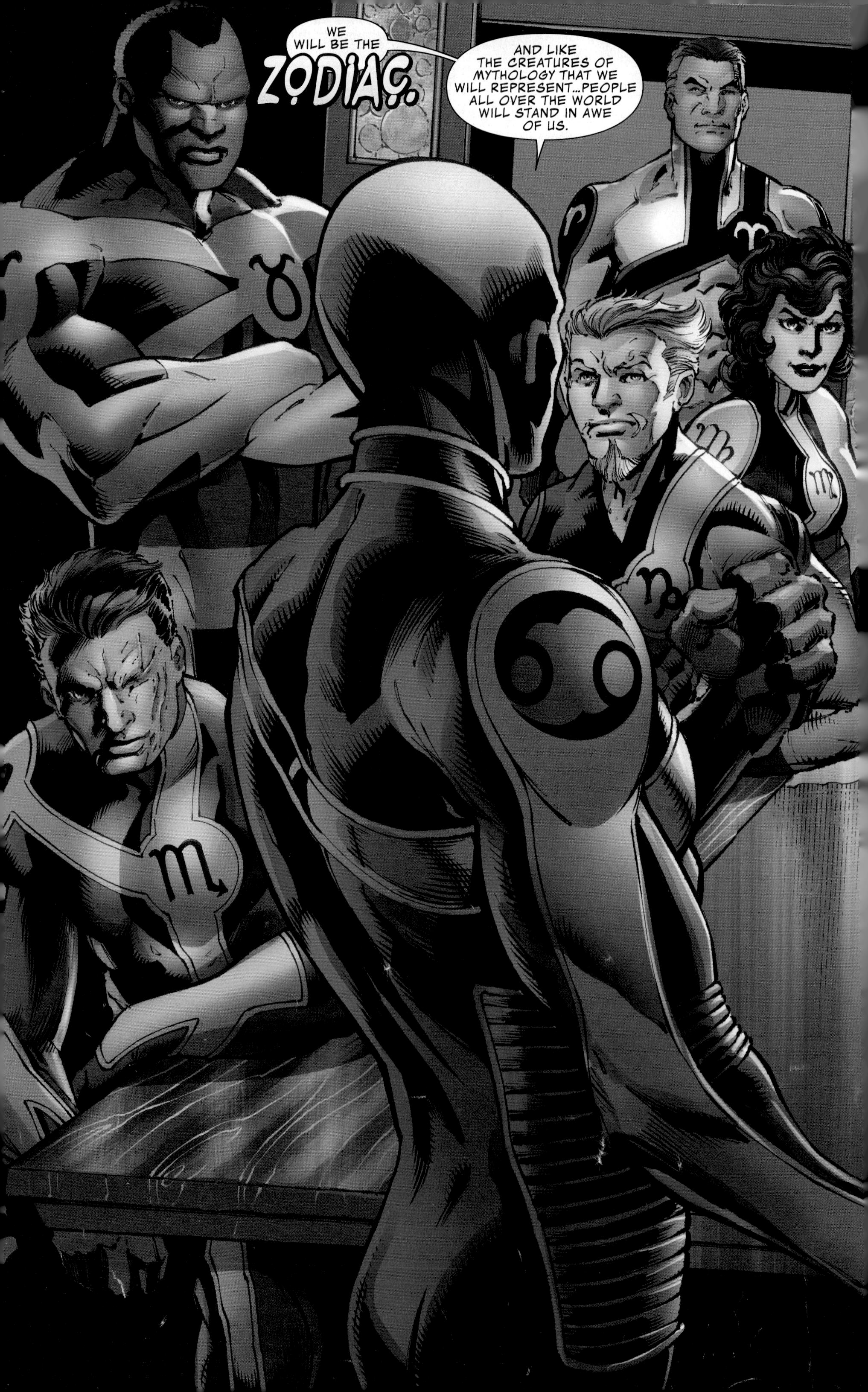
WE WILL BE THE ZODIAC.
AND LIKE THE CREATURES OF MYTHOLOGY THAT WE WILL REPRESENT...PEOPLE ALL OVER THE WORLD WILL STAND IN AWE OF US.

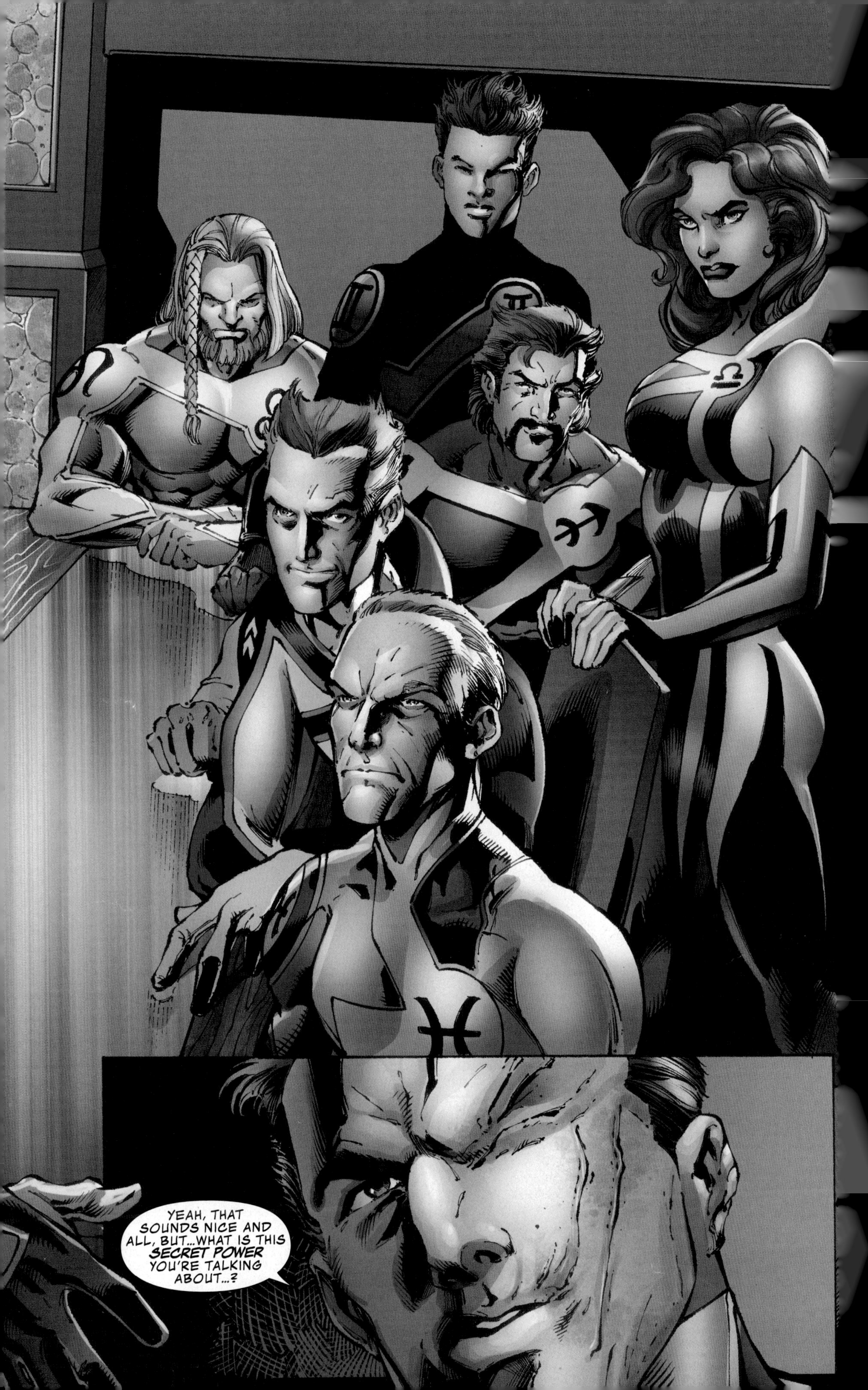
YEAH, THAT SOUNDS NICE AND ALL, BUT...WHAT IS THIS SECRET POWER YOU'RE TALKING ABOUT...?

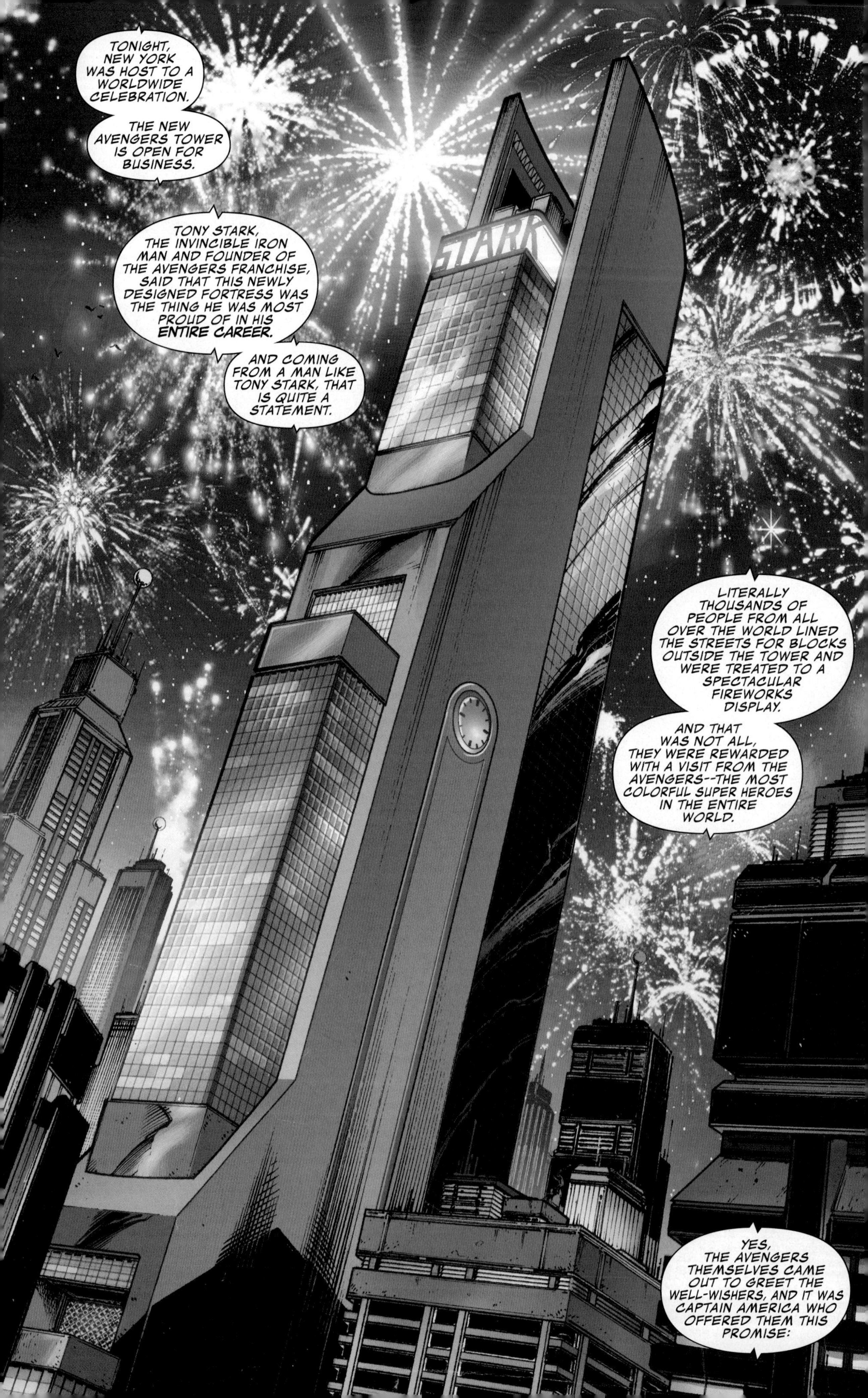
TONIGHT, NEW YORK WAS HOST TO A WORLDWIDE CELEBRATION.
THE NEW AVENGERS TOWER IS OPEN FOR BUSINESS.
TONY STARK, THE INVINCIBLE IRON MAN AND FOUNDER OF THE AVENGERS FRANCHISE, SAID THAT THIS NEWLY DESIGNED FORTRESS WAS THE THING HE WAS MOST PROUD OF IN HIS **ENTIRE CAREER.**
AND COMING FROM A MAN LIKE TONY STARK, THAT IS QUITE A STATEMENT.
STARK
LITERALLY THOUSANDS OF PEOPLE FROM ALL OVER THE WORLD LINED THE STREETS FOR BLOCKS OUTSIDE THE TOWER AND WERE TREATED TO A SPECTACULAR FIREWORKS DISPLAY.
AND THAT WAS NOT ALL, THEY WERE REWARDED WITH A VISIT FROM THE AVENGERS--THE MOST COLORFUL SUPER HEROES IN THE ENTIRE WORLD.
YES, THE AVENGERS THEMSELVES CAME OUT TO GREET THE WELL-WISHERS, AND IT WAS CAPTAIN AMERICA WHO OFFERED THEM THIS PROMISE:

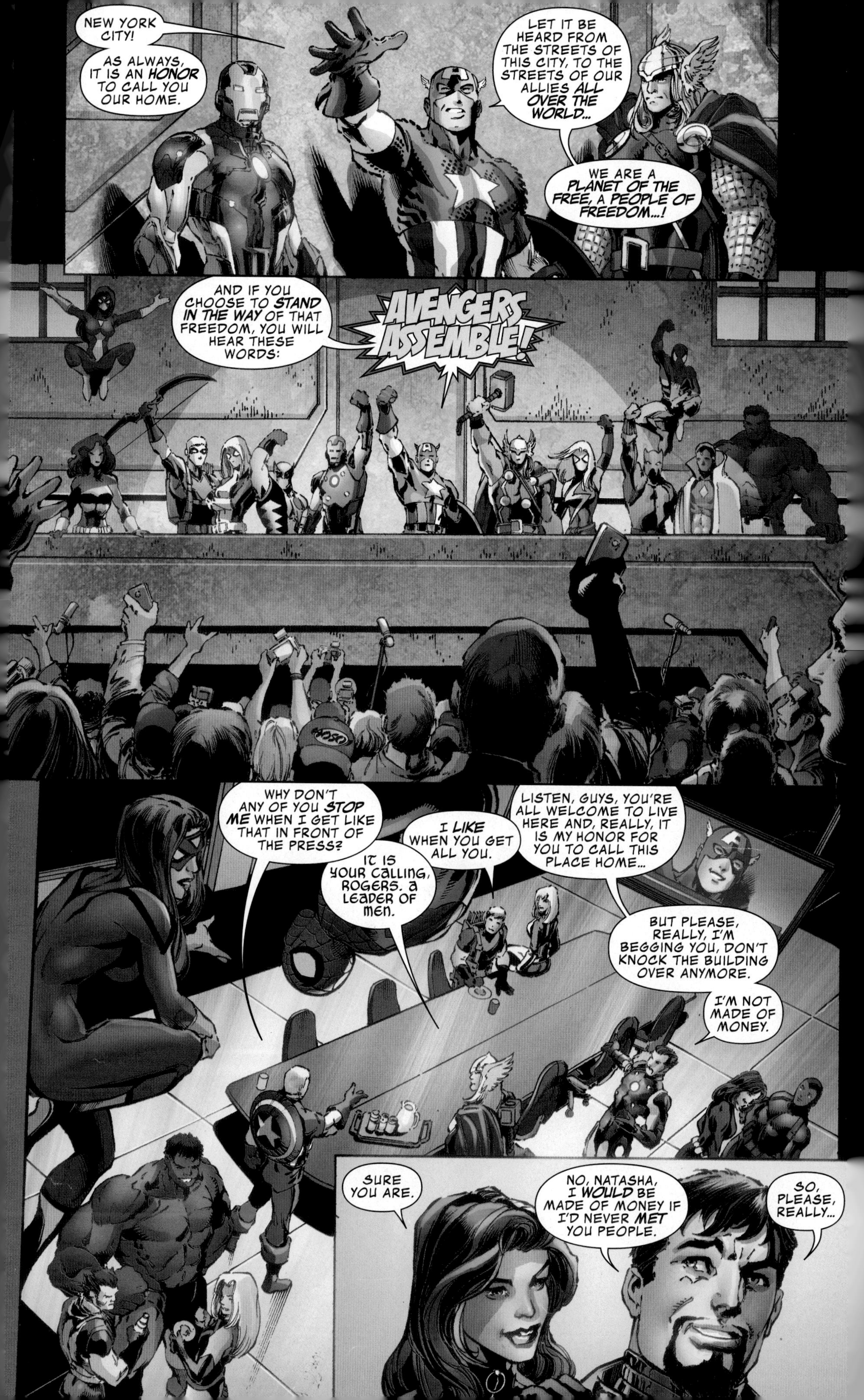
NEW YORK CITY!
AS ALWAYS, IT IS AN HONOR TO CALL YOU OUR HOME.
LET IT BE HEARD FROM THE STREETS OF THIS CITY, TO THE STREETS OF OUR ALLIES ALL OVER THE WORLD...
WE ARE A PLANET OF THE FREE, A PEOPLE OF FREEDOM...!
AND IF YOU CHOOSE TO STAND IN THE WAY OF THAT FREEDOM, YOU WILL HEAR THESE WORDS:
AVENGERS ASSEMBLE!
WHY DON'T ANY OF YOU STOP ME WHEN I GET LIKE THAT IN FRONT OF THE PRESS?
IT IS YOUR CALLING, ROGERS. A LEADER OF MEN.
I LIKE WHEN YOU GET ALL YOU.
LISTEN, GUYS, YOU'RE ALL WELCOME TO LIVE HERE AND, REALLY, IT IS MY HONOR FOR YOU TO CALL THIS PLACE HOME...
BUT PLEASE, REALLY, I'M BEGGING YOU, DON'T KNOCK THE BUILDING OVER ANYMORE.
I'M NOT MADE OF MONEY.
SURE YOU ARE.
NO, NATASHA, I WOULD BE MADE OF MONEY IF I'D NEVER MET YOU PEOPLE.
SO, PLEASE, REALLY...

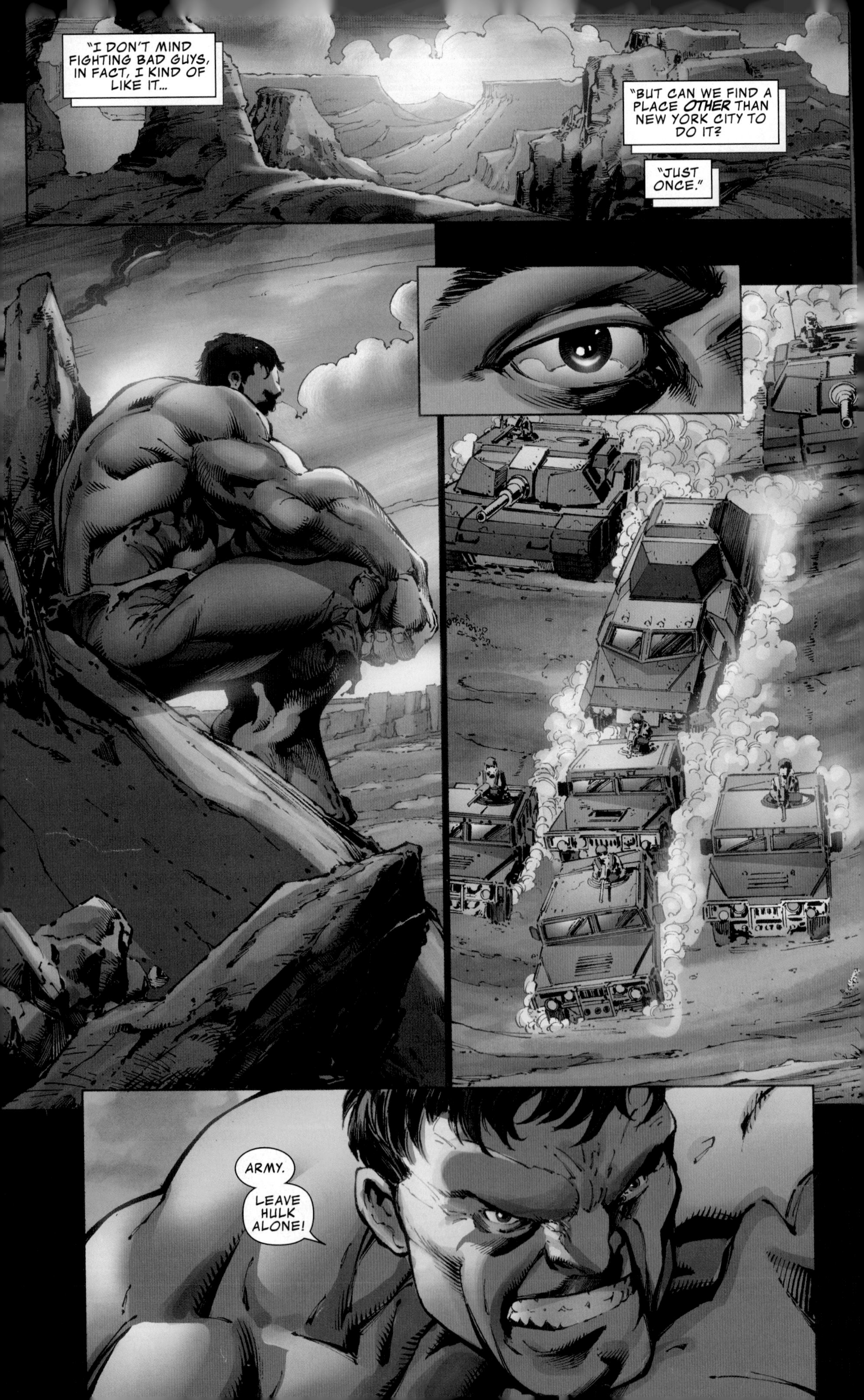
"I DON'T MIND FIGHTING BAD GUYS, IN FACT, I KIND OF LIKE IT...
"BUT CAN WE FIND A PLACE *OTHER* THAN NEW YORK CITY TO DO IT?
"JUST ONCE."
ARMY.
LEAVE HULK ALONE!

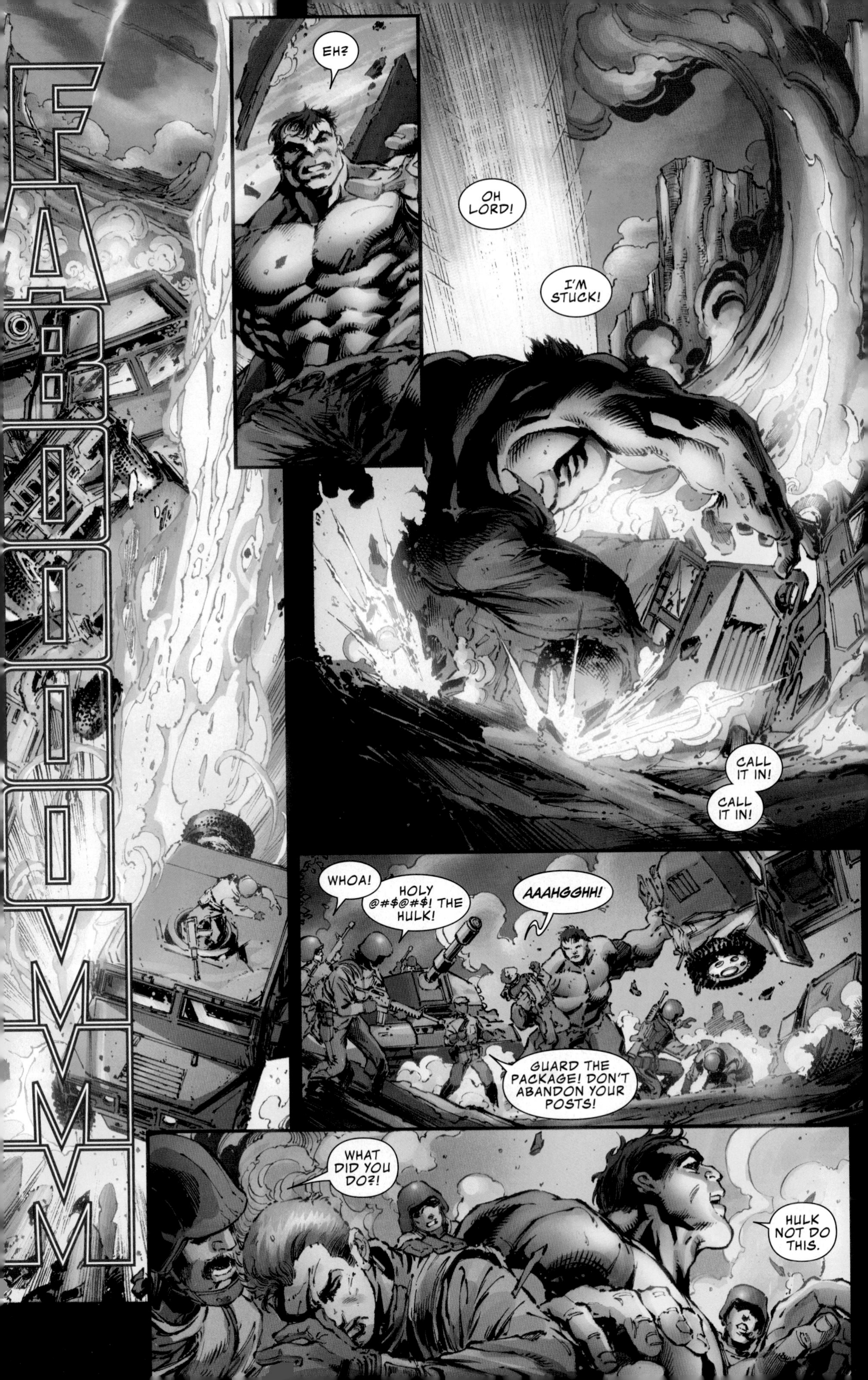
FA-BOOOMMM
EH?
OH LORD!
I'M STUCK!
CALL IT IN!
CALL IT IN!
WHOA!
HOLY @#$@#$! THE HULK!
AAAHGGHH!
GUARD THE PACKAGE! DON'T ABANDON YOUR POSTS!
WHAT DID YOU DO?!
HULK NOT DO THIS.

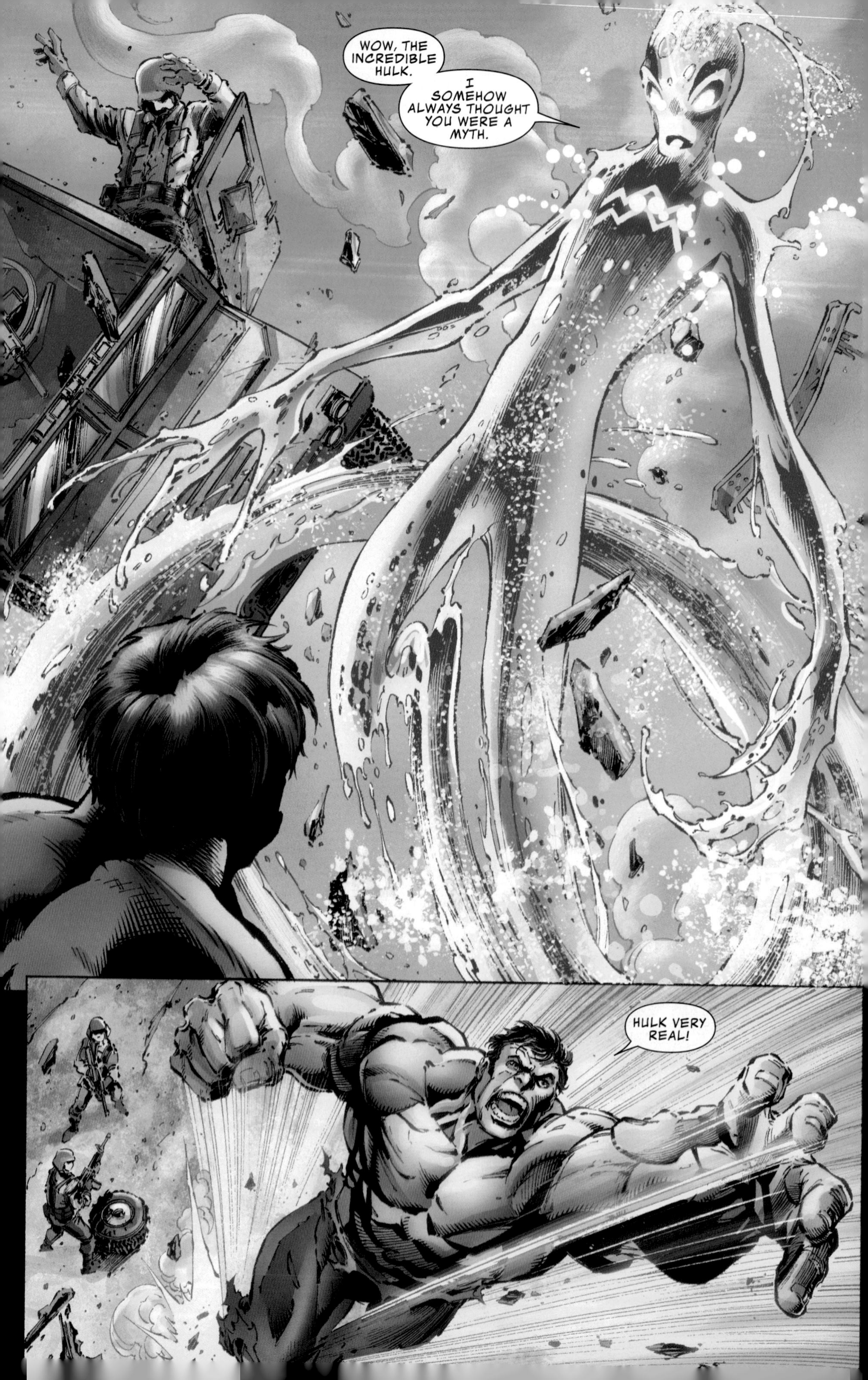
WOW, THE INCREDIBLE HULK.
I SOMEHOW ALWAYS THOUGHT YOU WERE A MYTH.
HULK VERY REAL!

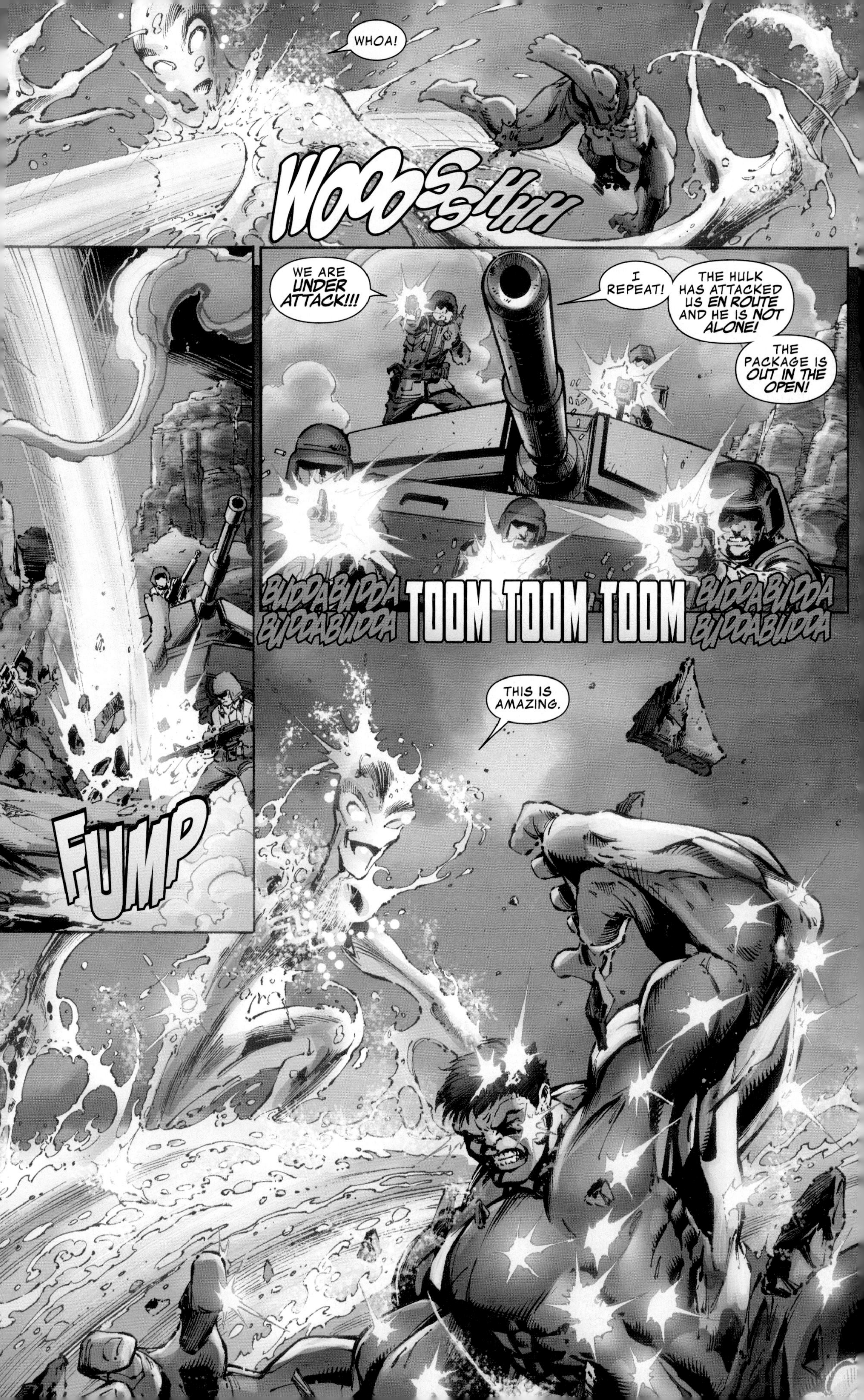
WHOA!
WOOOSHHH
WE ARE UNDER ATTACK!!!
I REPEAT!
THE HULK HAS ATTACKED US EN ROUTE AND HE IS NOT ALONE!
THE PACKAGE IS OUT IN THE OPEN!
BUDDABUDDA BUDDABUDDA
TOOM TOOM TOOM
BUDDABUDDA BUDDABUDDA
FUMP
THIS IS AMAZING.

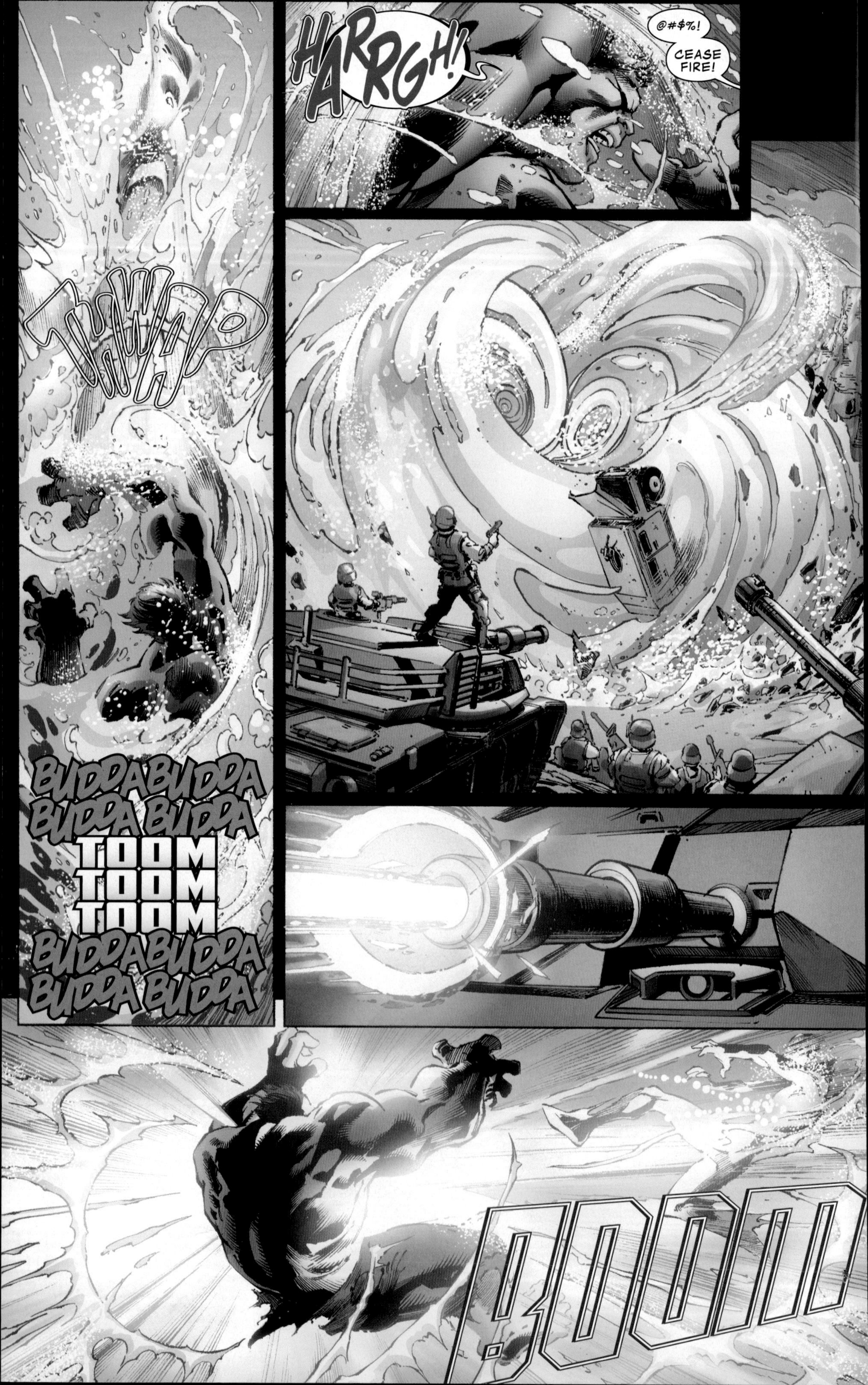
HARRGH!
@#$%!
CEASE FIRE!
BUDDABUDDA
BUDDA BUDDA
TOOM
TOOM
TOOM
BUDDABUDDA
BUDDA BUDDA

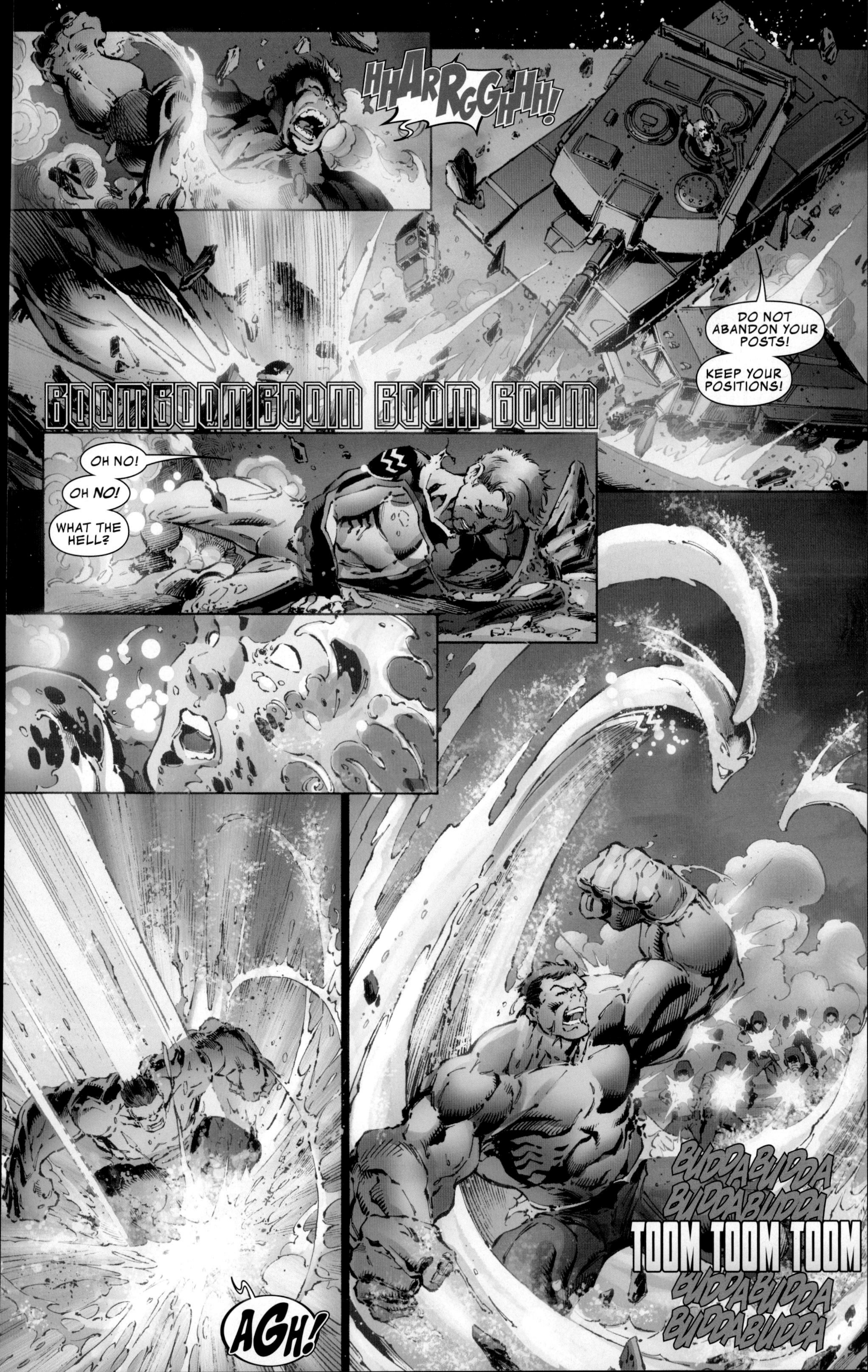
HHARRGGHHH!
DO NOT ABANDON YOUR POSTS!
KEEP YOUR POSITIONS!
BOOMBOOMBOOM BOOM BOOM
OH NO!
OH NO!
WHAT THE HELL?
BUDDABUDDA
BUDDABUDDA
TOOM TOOM TOOM
BUDDABUDDA
BUDDABUDDA
AGH!

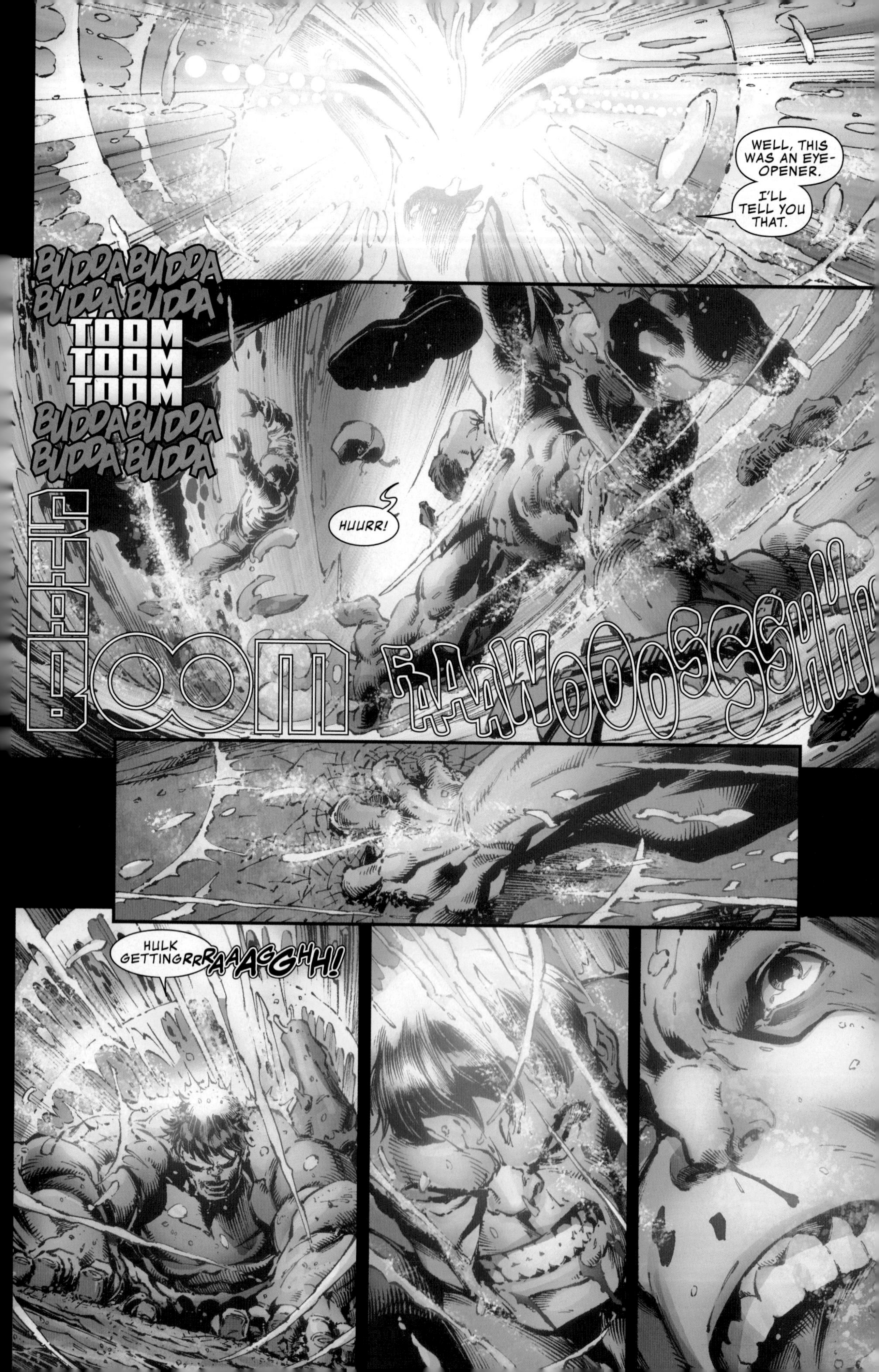
WELL, THIS WAS AN EYE-OPENER.
I'LL TELL YOU THAT.
BUDDABUDDA BUDDA BUDDA
TOOM TOOM TOOM
BUDDABUDDA BUDDA BUDDA
HUURR!
HULK GETTINGRRRAAAGGHH!

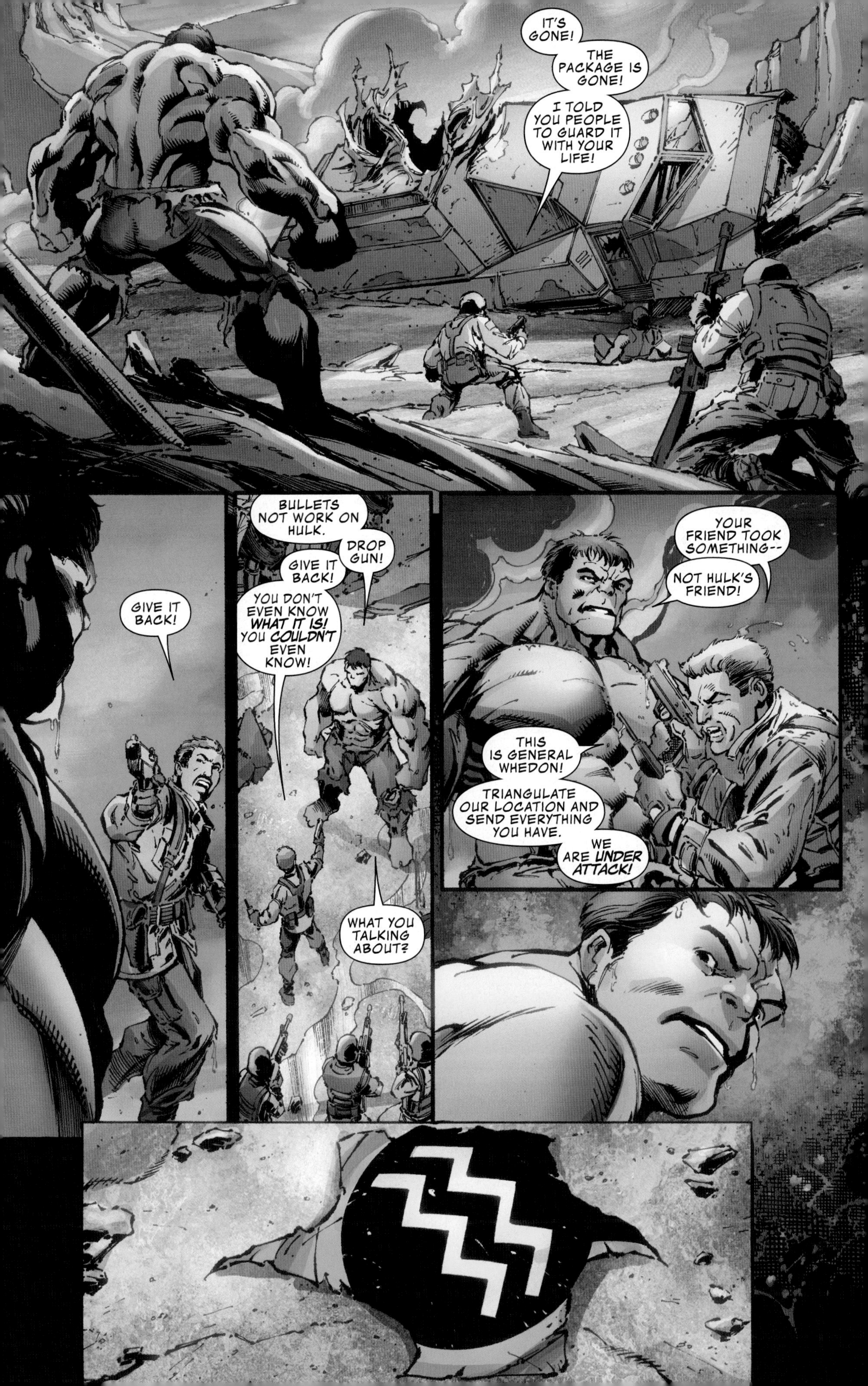
IT'S GONE!
THE PACKAGE IS GONE!
I TOLD YOU PEOPLE TO GUARD IT WITH YOUR LIFE!
GIVE IT BACK!
BULLETS NOT WORK ON HULK.
DROP GUN!
GIVE IT BACK!
YOU DON'T EVEN KNOW WHAT IT IS! YOU COULDN'T EVEN KNOW!
WHAT YOU TALKING ABOUT?
YOUR FRIEND TOOK SOMETHING--
NOT HULK'S FRIEND!
THIS IS GENERAL WHEDON!
TRIANGULATE OUR LOCATION AND SEND EVERYTHING YOU HAVE.
WE ARE UNDER ATTACK!

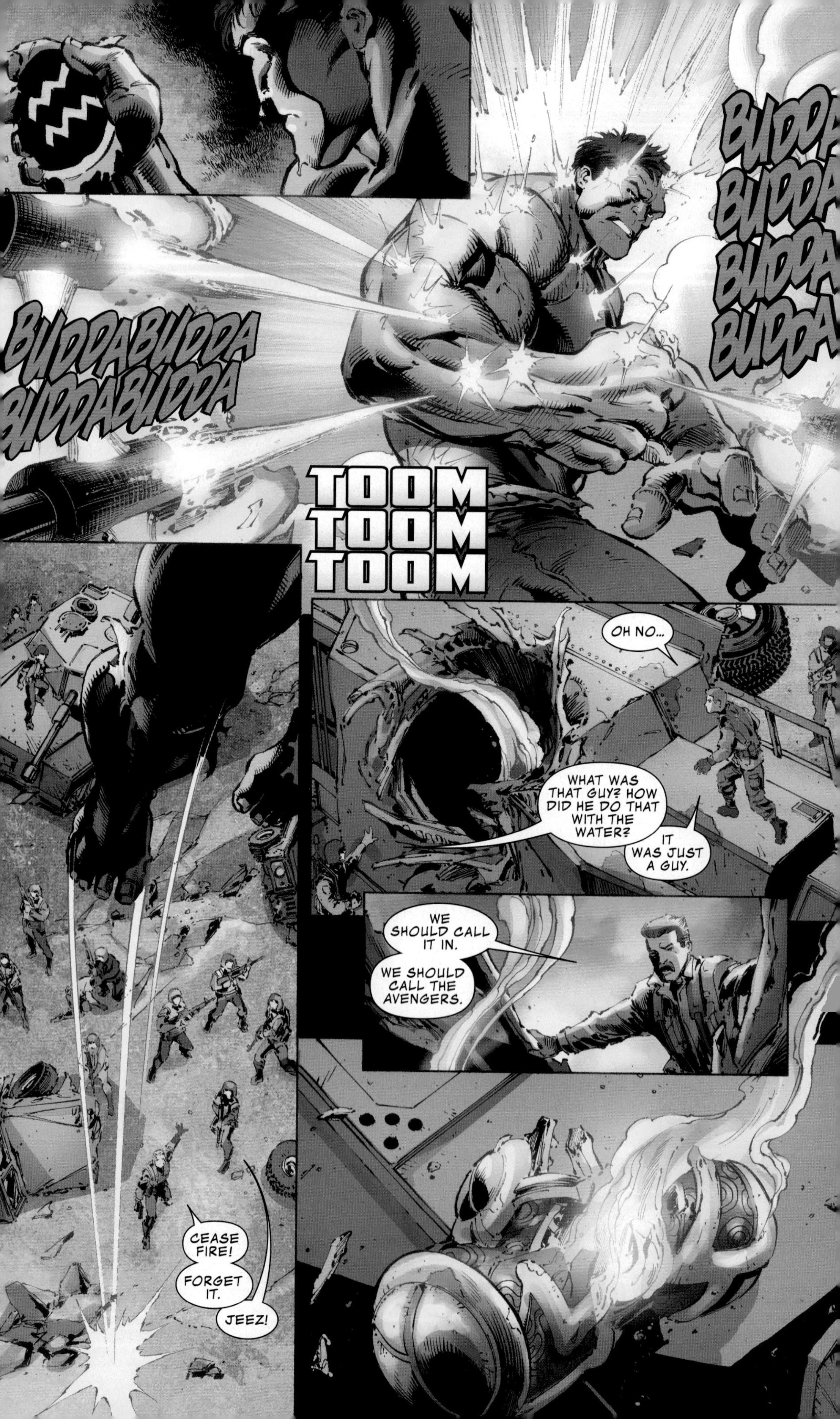
BUDDA
BUDDA
BUDDA
BUDDA
BUDDABUDDA
BUDDABUDDA
TOOM
TOOM
TOOM
OH NO...
WHAT WAS THAT GUY? HOW DID HE DO THAT WITH THE WATER?
IT WAS JUST A GUY.
WE SHOULD CALL IT IN.
WE SHOULD CALL THE AVENGERS.
CEASE FIRE!
FORGET IT.
JEEZ!

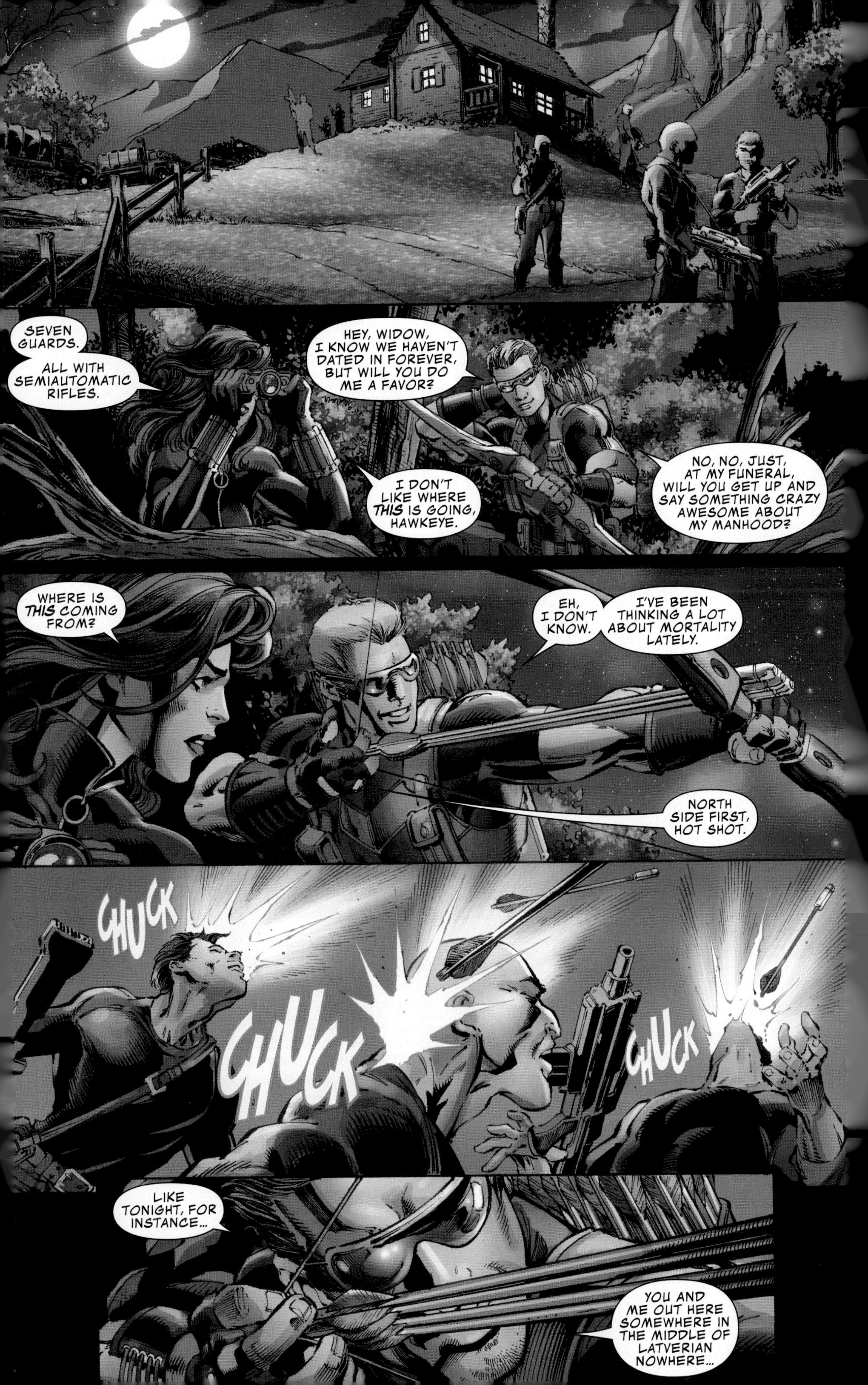
SEVEN GUARDS.
ALL WITH SEMIAUTOMATIC RIFLES.
HEY, WIDOW, I KNOW WE HAVEN'T DATED IN FOREVER, BUT WILL YOU DO ME A FAVOR?
I DON'T LIKE WHERE THIS IS GOING, HAWKEYE.
NO, NO, JUST, AT MY FUNERAL, WILL YOU GET UP AND SAY SOMETHING CRAZY AWESOME ABOUT MY MANHOOD?
WHERE IS THIS COMING FROM?
EH, I DON'T KNOW.
I'VE BEEN THINKING A LOT ABOUT MORTALITY LATELY.
NORTH SIDE FIRST, HOT SHOT.
CHUCK
CHUCK
CHUCK
LIKE TONIGHT, FOR INSTANCE...
YOU AND ME OUT HERE SOMEWHERE IN THE MIDDLE OF LATVERIAN NOWHERE...

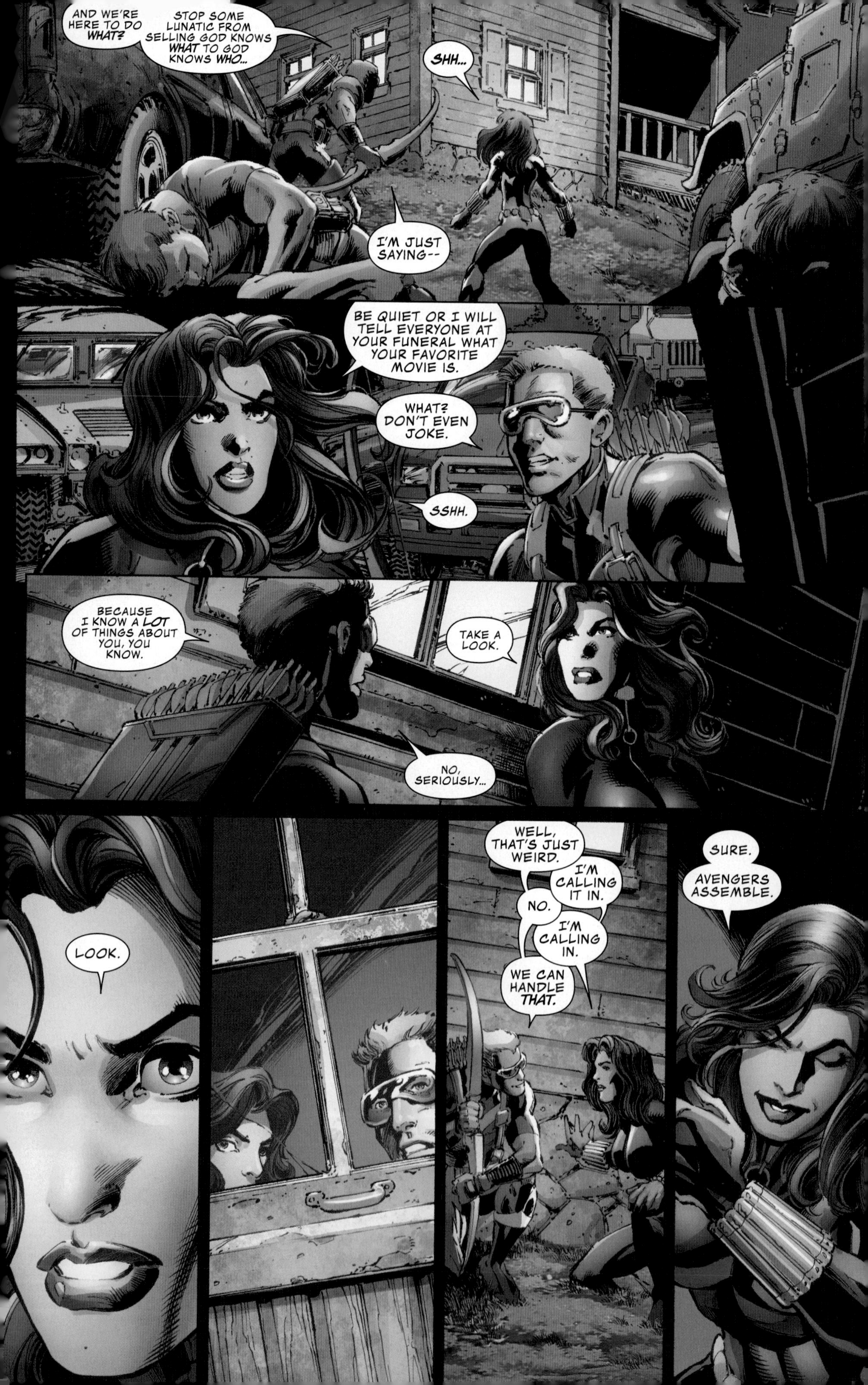
AND WE'RE HERE TO DO WHAT?
STOP SOME LUNATIC FROM SELLING GOD KNOWS WHAT TO GOD KNOWS WHO...
SHH...
I'M JUST SAYING--
BE QUIET OR I WILL TELL EVERYONE AT YOUR FUNERAL WHAT YOUR FAVORITE MOVIE IS.
WHAT? DON'T EVEN JOKE.
SSHH.
BECAUSE I KNOW A LOT OF THINGS ABOUT YOU, YOU KNOW.
TAKE A LOOK.
NO, SERIOUSLY...
LOOK.
WELL, THAT'S JUST WEIRD.
I'M CALLING IT IN.
NO.
I'M CALLING IN.
WE CAN HANDLE THAT.
SURE.
AVENGERS ASSEMBLE.

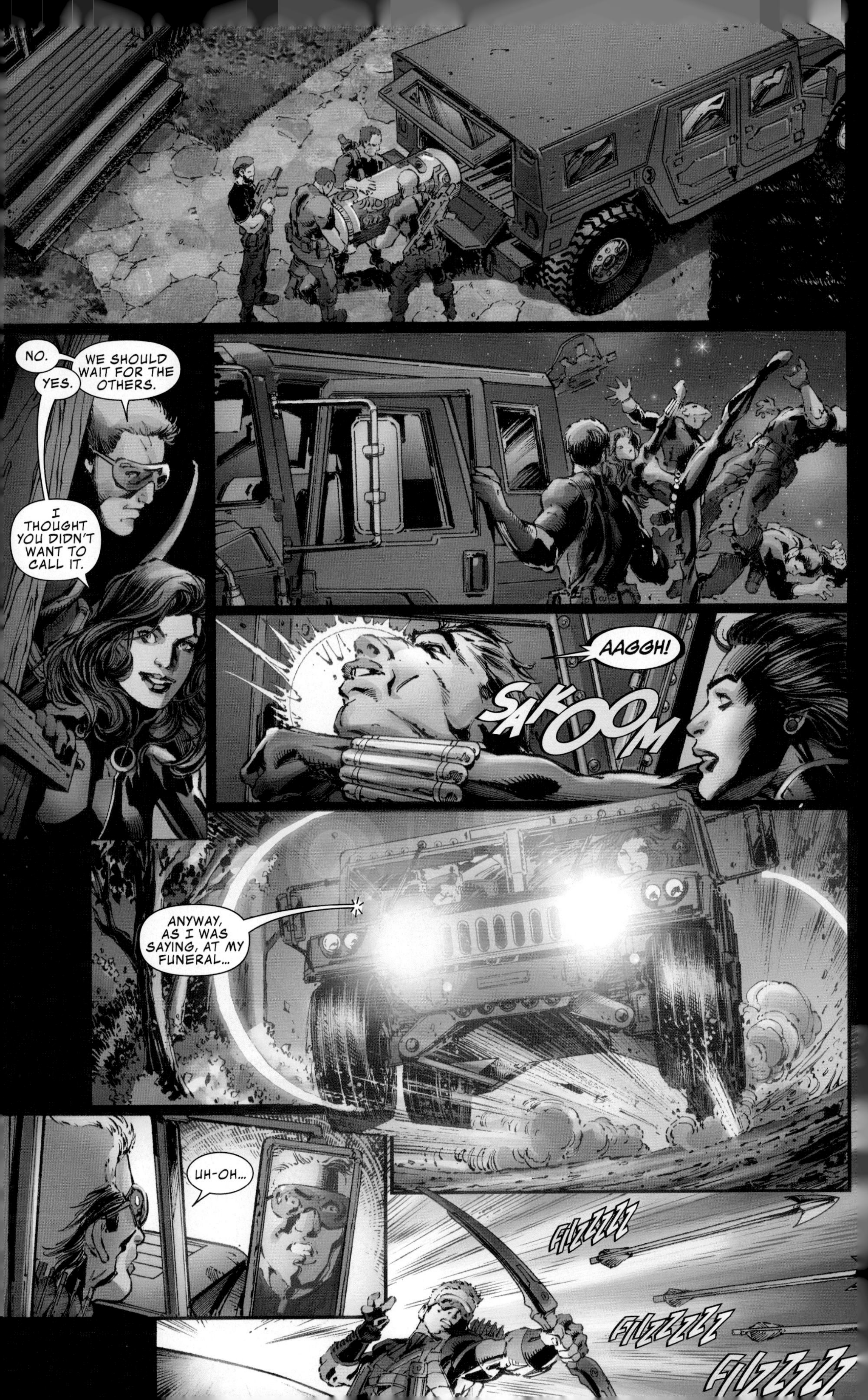
NO.
YES.
WE SHOULD WAIT FOR THE OTHERS.
I THOUGHT YOU DIDN'T WANT TO CALL IT.
AAGGH!
SAKOOM
ANYWAY, AS I WAS SAYING, AT MY FUNERAL...
UH-OH...
FIZZZZZ
FIZZZZZZ
FIZZZZZ

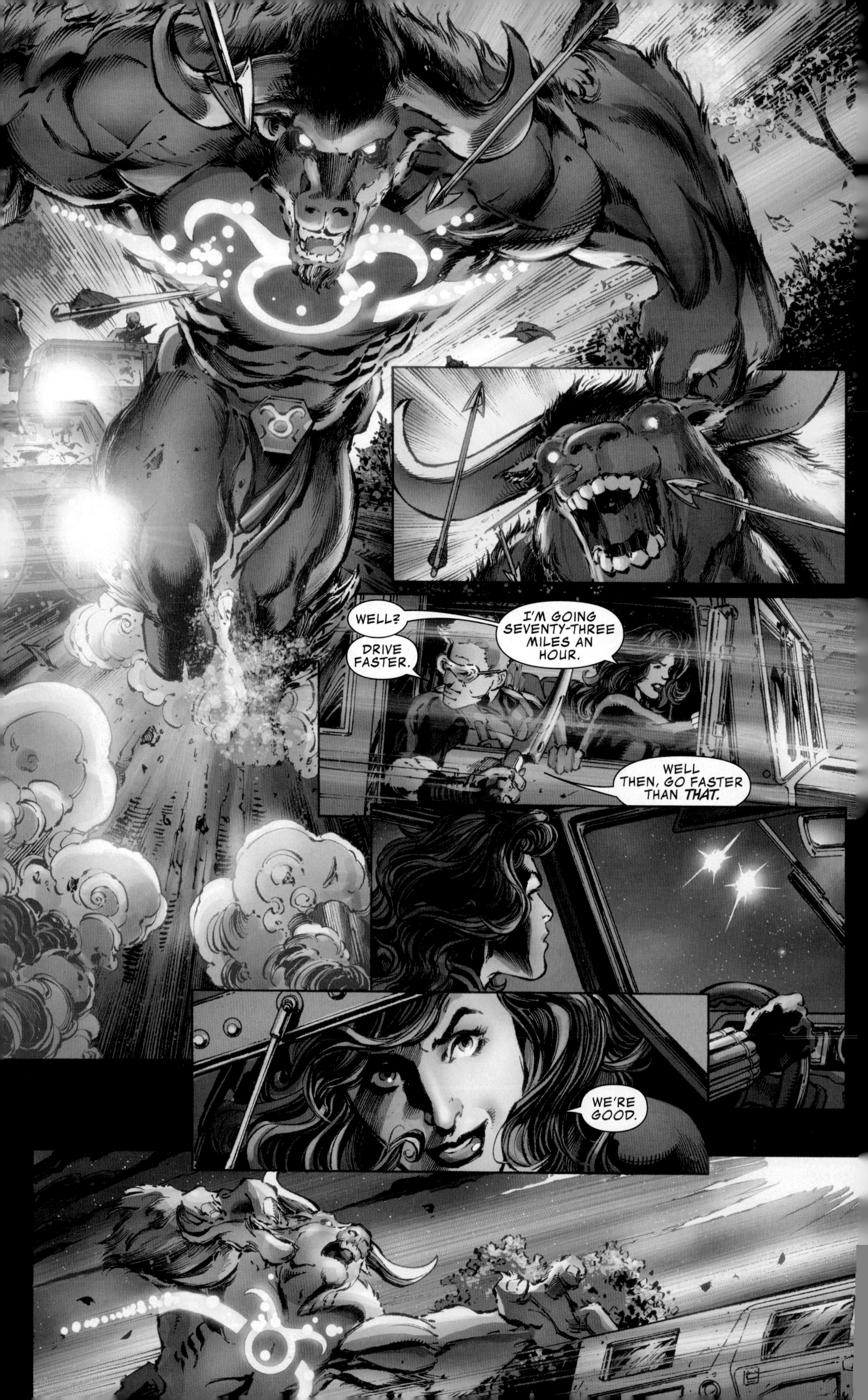
WELL?
I'M GOING SEVENTY-THREE MILES AN HOUR.
DRIVE FASTER.
WELL THEN, GO FASTER THAN *THAT.*
WE'RE GOOD.

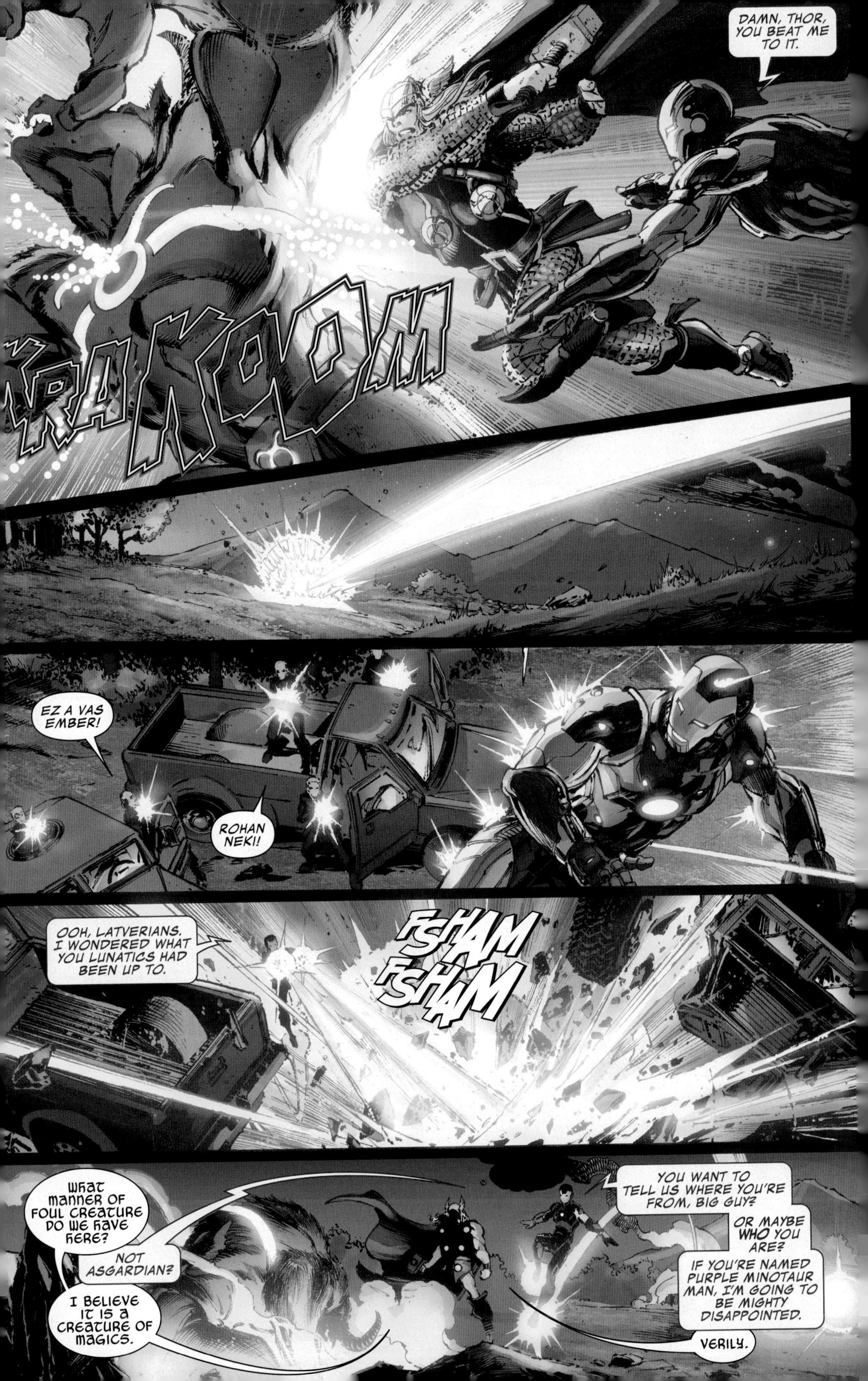
DAMN, THOR, YOU BEAT ME TO IT.
KRAKOOM
EZ A VAS EMBER!
ROHAN NEKI!
OOH, LATVERIANS. I WONDERED WHAT YOU LUNATICS HAD BEEN UP TO.
FSHAM FSHAM
WHAT MANNER OF FOUL CREATURE DO WE HAVE HERE?
NOT ASGARDIAN?
I BELIEVE IT IS A CREATURE OF MAGICS.
YOU WANT TO TELL US WHERE YOU'RE FROM, BIG GUY?
OR MAYBE WHO YOU ARE?
IF YOU'RE NAMED PURPLE MINOTAUR MAN, I'M GOING TO BE MIGHTY DISAPPOINTED.
VERILY.

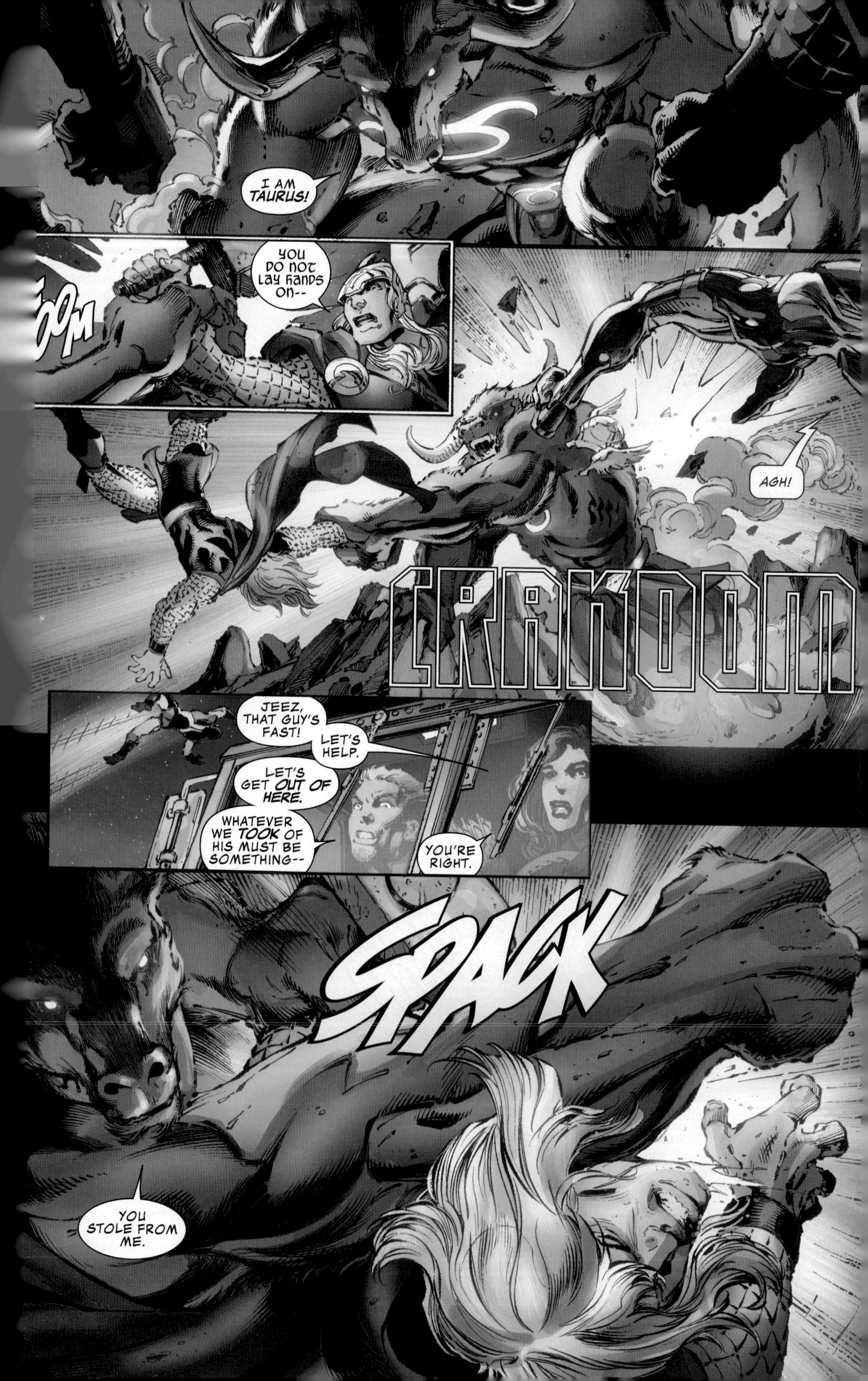
I AM TAURUS!
OOM
YOU DO NOT LAY HANDS ON--
AGH!
CRAKOOM
JEEZ, THAT GUY'S FAST!
LET'S HELP.
LET'S GET OUT OF HERE.
WHATEVER WE TOOK OF HIS MUST BE SOMETHING--
YOU'RE RIGHT.
SPACK
YOU STOLE FROM ME.

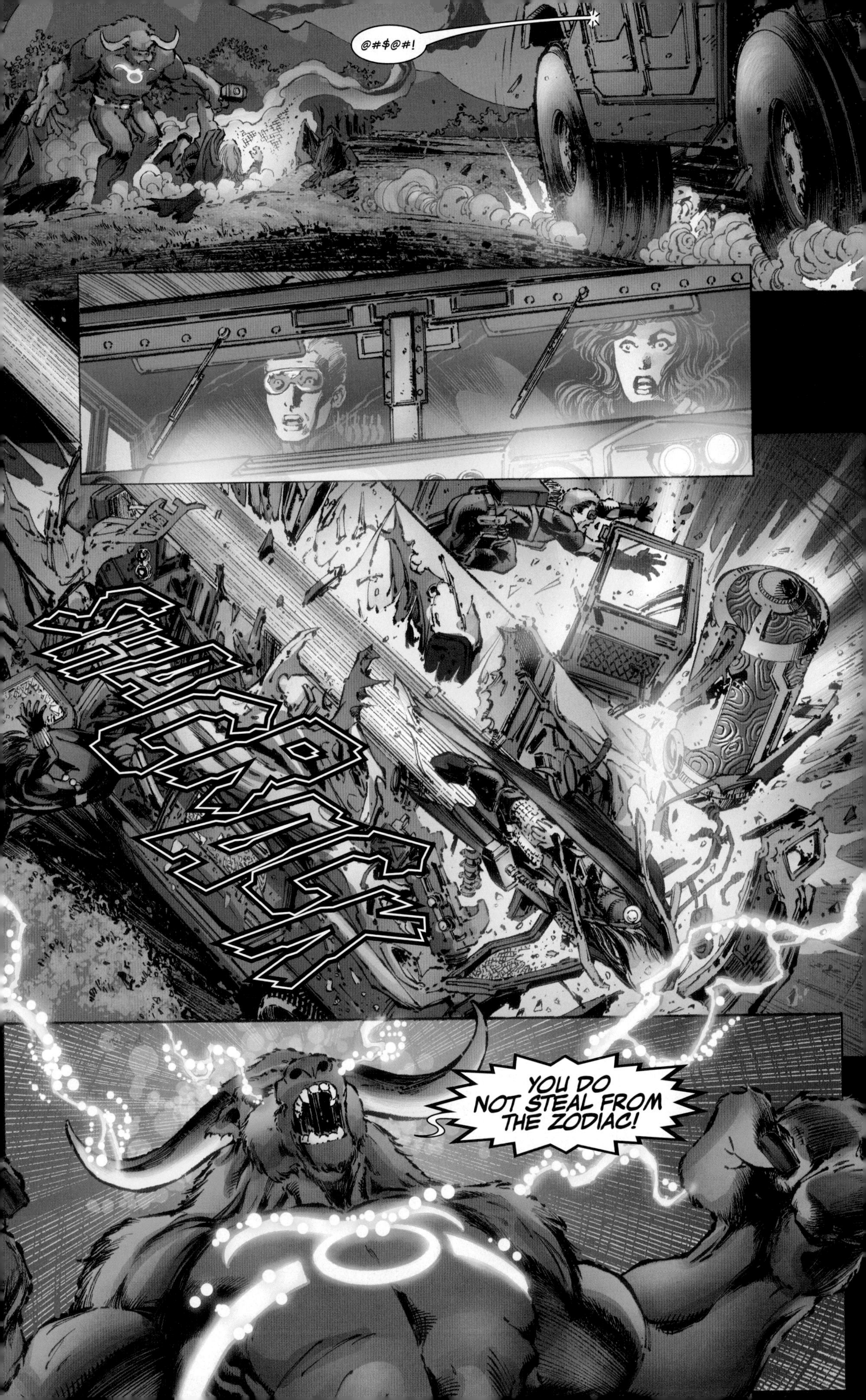
@#$@#!
YOU DO NOT STEAL FROM THE ZODIAC!

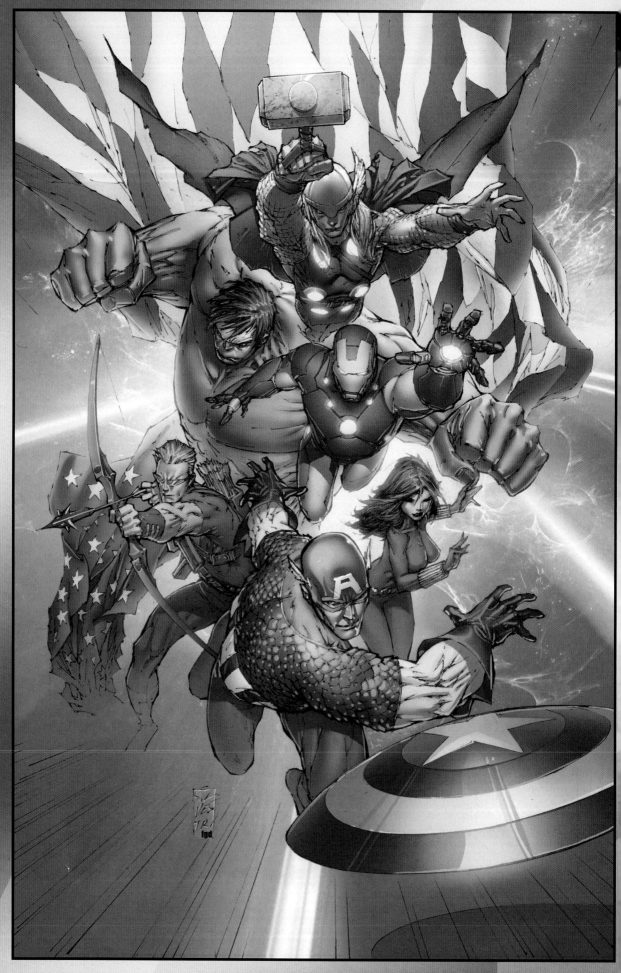

#1 VARIANT BY MARC SILVESTRI & FRANK D'ARMATA

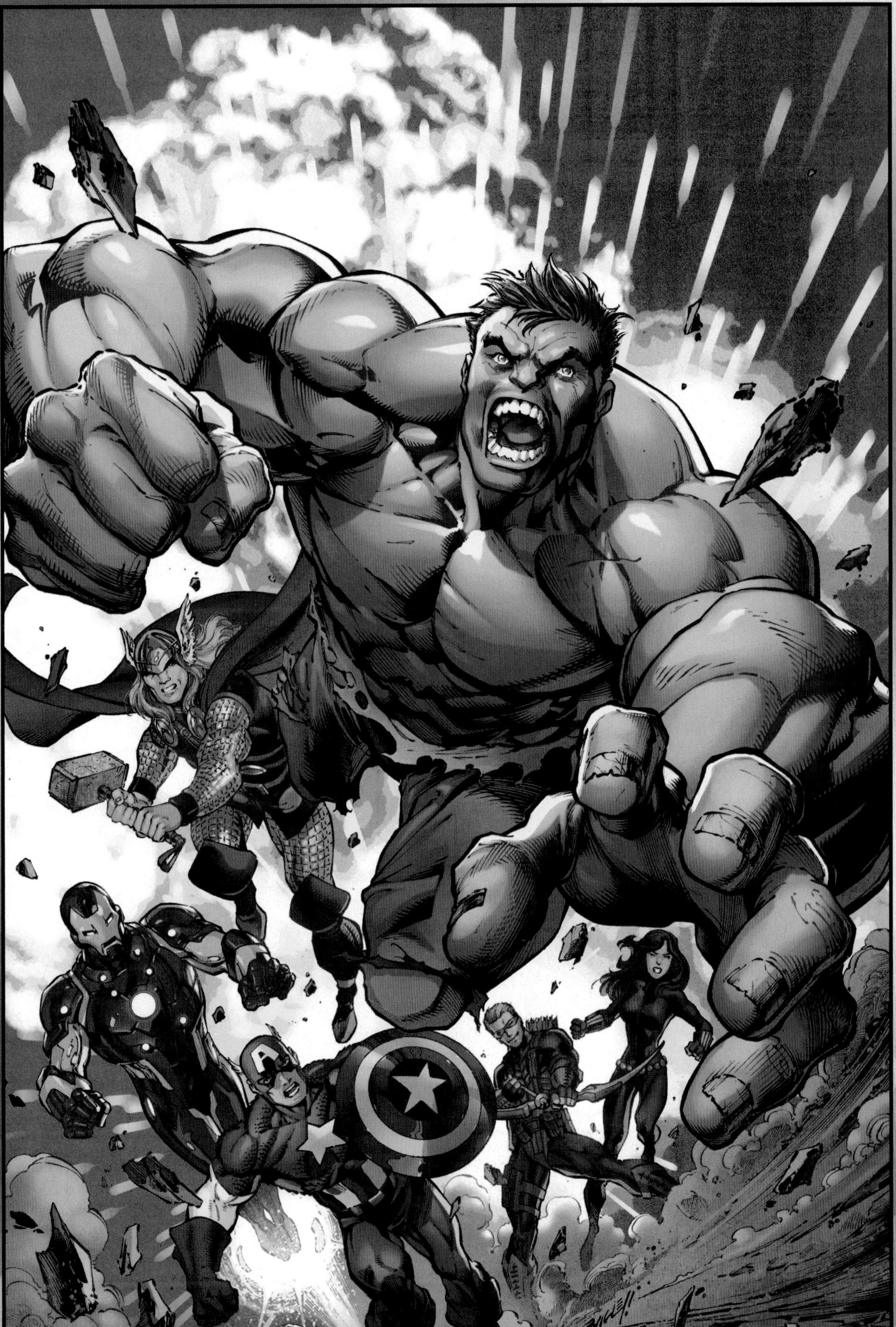

TWO

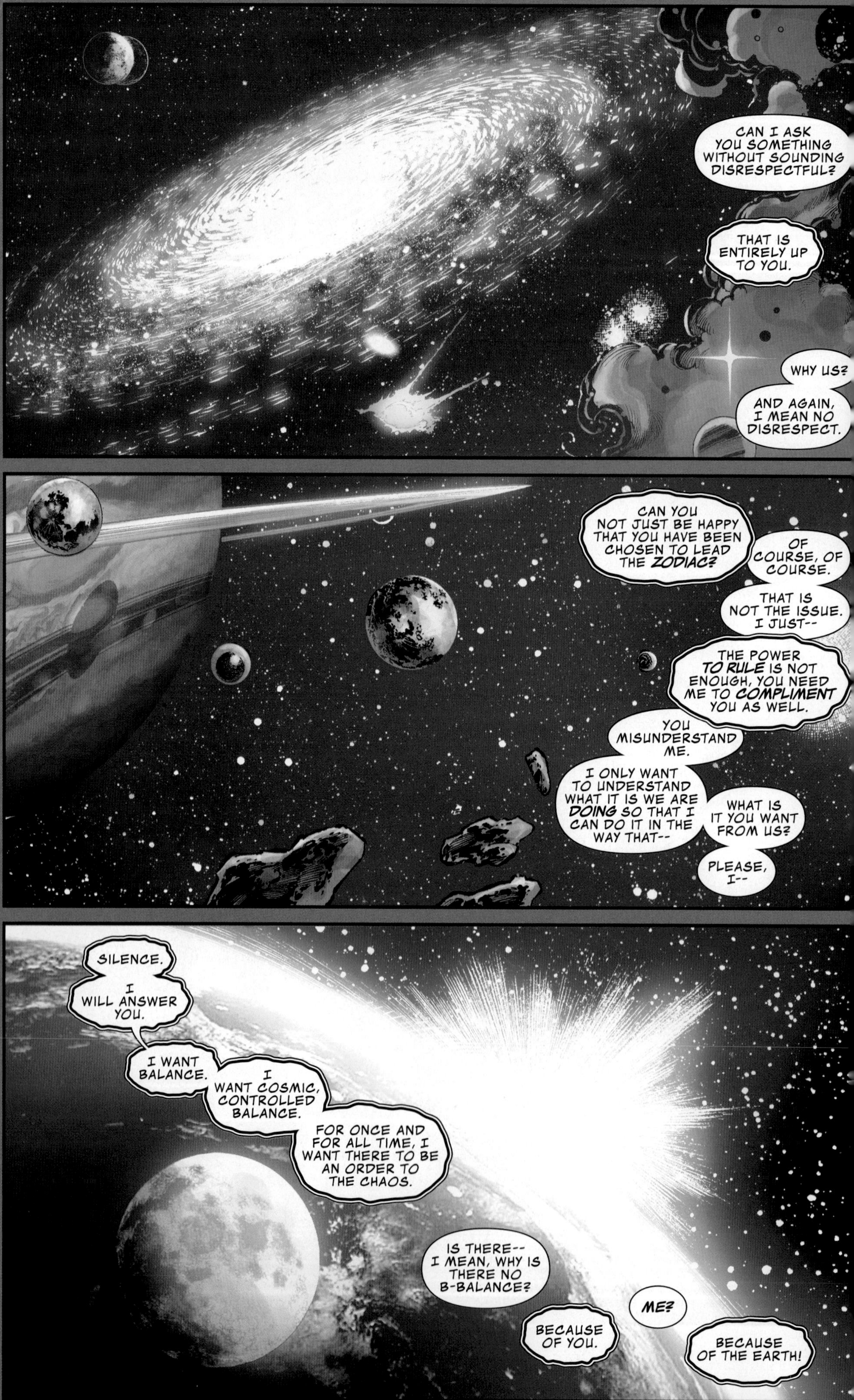

CAN I ASK YOU SOMETHING WITHOUT SOUNDING DISRESPECTFUL?
THAT IS ENTIRELY UP TO YOU.
WHY US?
AND AGAIN, I MEAN NO DISRESPECT.
CAN YOU NOT JUST BE HAPPY THAT YOU HAVE BEEN CHOSEN TO LEAD THE ZODIAC?
OF COURSE, OF COURSE.
THAT IS NOT THE ISSUE. I JUST--
THE POWER TO RULE IS NOT ENOUGH, YOU NEED ME TO COMPLIMENT YOU AS WELL.
YOU MISUNDERSTAND ME.
I ONLY WANT TO UNDERSTAND WHAT IT IS WE ARE DOING SO THAT I CAN DO IT IN THE WAY THAT--
WHAT IS IT YOU WANT FROM US?
PLEASE, I--
SILENCE.
I WILL ANSWER YOU.
I WANT BALANCE.
I WANT COSMIC, CONTROLLED BALANCE.
FOR ONCE AND FOR ALL TIME, I WANT THERE TO BE AN ORDER TO THE CHAOS.
IS THERE-- I MEAN, WHY IS THERE NO B-BALANCE?
BECAUSE OF YOU.
ME?
BECAUSE OF THE EARTH!

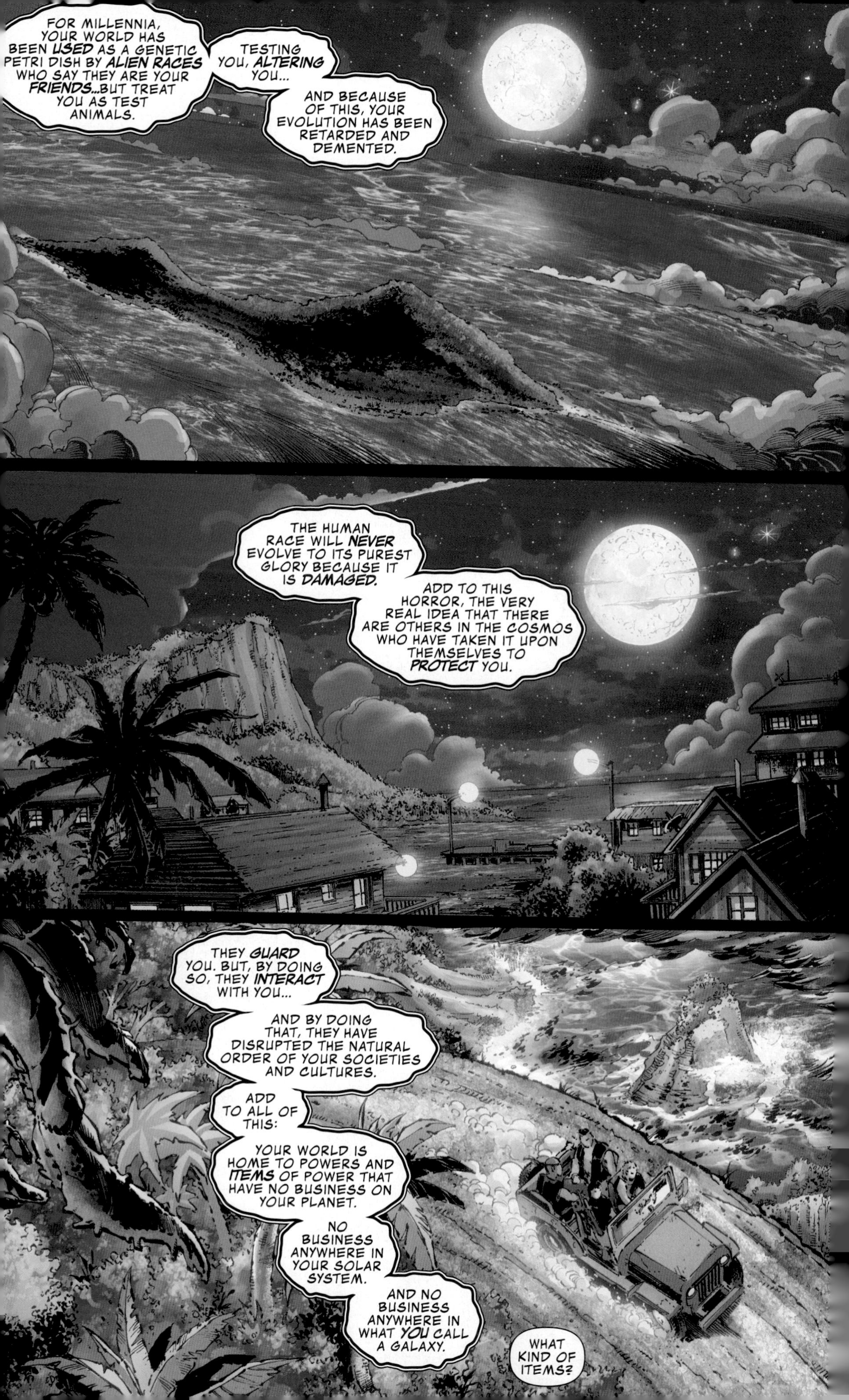
FOR MILLENNIA, YOUR WORLD HAS BEEN USED AS A GENETIC PETRI DISH BY ALIEN RACES WHO SAY THEY ARE YOUR FRIENDS...BUT TREAT YOU AS TEST ANIMALS.
TESTING YOU, ALTERING YOU...
AND BECAUSE OF THIS, YOUR EVOLUTION HAS BEEN RETARDED AND DEMENTED.
THE HUMAN RACE WILL NEVER EVOLVE TO ITS PUREST GLORY BECAUSE IT IS DAMAGED.
ADD TO THIS HORROR, THE VERY REAL IDEA THAT THERE ARE OTHERS IN THE COSMOS WHO HAVE TAKEN IT UPON THEMSELVES TO PROTECT YOU.
THEY GUARD YOU. BUT, BY DOING SO, THEY INTERACT WITH YOU...
AND BY DOING THAT, THEY HAVE DISRUPTED THE NATURAL ORDER OF YOUR SOCIETIES AND CULTURES.
ADD TO ALL OF THIS:
YOUR WORLD IS HOME TO POWERS AND ITEMS OF POWER THAT HAVE NO BUSINESS ON YOUR PLANET.
NO BUSINESS ANYWHERE IN YOUR SOLAR SYSTEM.
AND NO BUSINESS ANYWHERE IN WHAT YOU CALL A GALAXY.
WHAT KIND OF ITEMS?

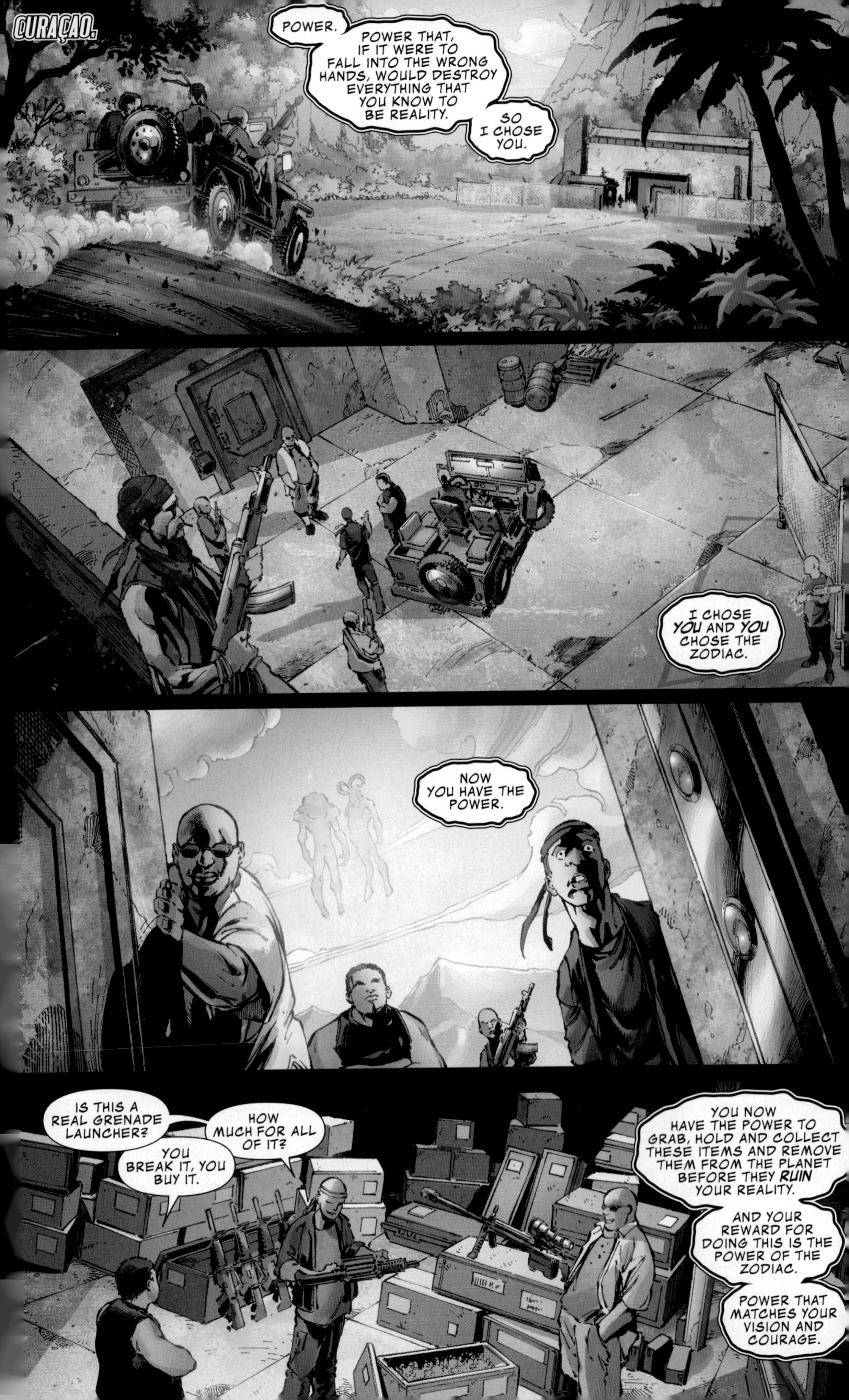
CURAÇAO.
POWER.
POWER THAT, IF IT WERE TO FALL INTO THE WRONG HANDS, WOULD DESTROY EVERYTHING THAT YOU KNOW TO BE REALITY.
SO I CHOSE YOU.
I CHOSE YOU AND YOU CHOSE THE ZODIAC.
NOW YOU HAVE THE POWER.
IS THIS A REAL GRENADE LAUNCHER?
YOU BREAK IT, YOU BUY IT.
HOW MUCH FOR ALL OF IT?
YOU NOW HAVE THE POWER TO GRAB, HOLD AND COLLECT THESE ITEMS AND REMOVE THEM FROM THE PLANET BEFORE THEY RUIN YOUR REALITY.
AND YOUR REWARD FOR DOING THIS IS THE POWER OF THE ZODIAC.
POWER THAT MATCHES YOUR VISION AND COURAGE.

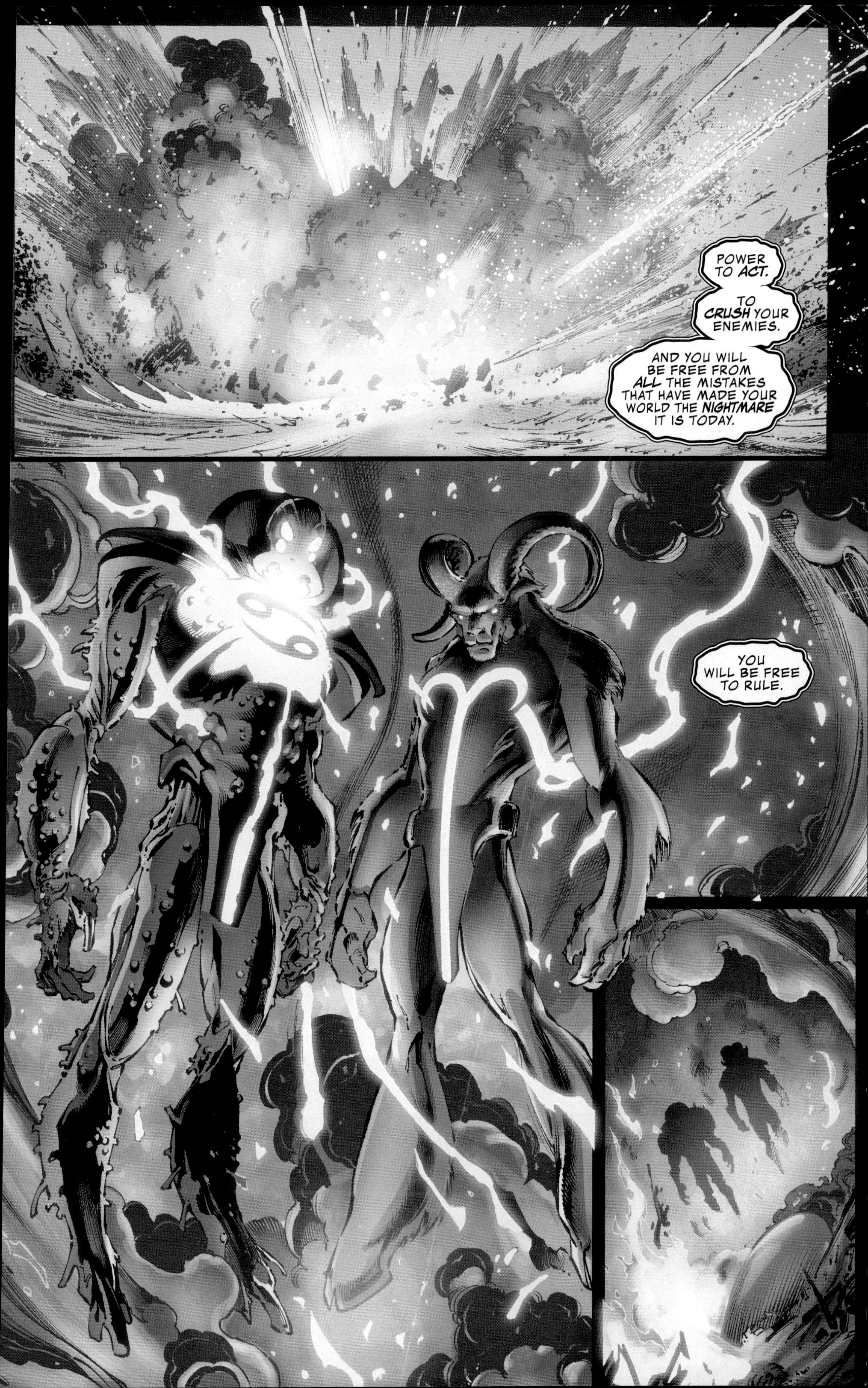
POWER TO ACT.
TO CRUSH YOUR ENEMIES.
AND YOU WILL BE FREE FROM ALL THE MISTAKES THAT HAVE MADE YOUR WORLD THE NIGHTMARE IT IS TODAY.
YOU WILL BE FREE TO RULE.

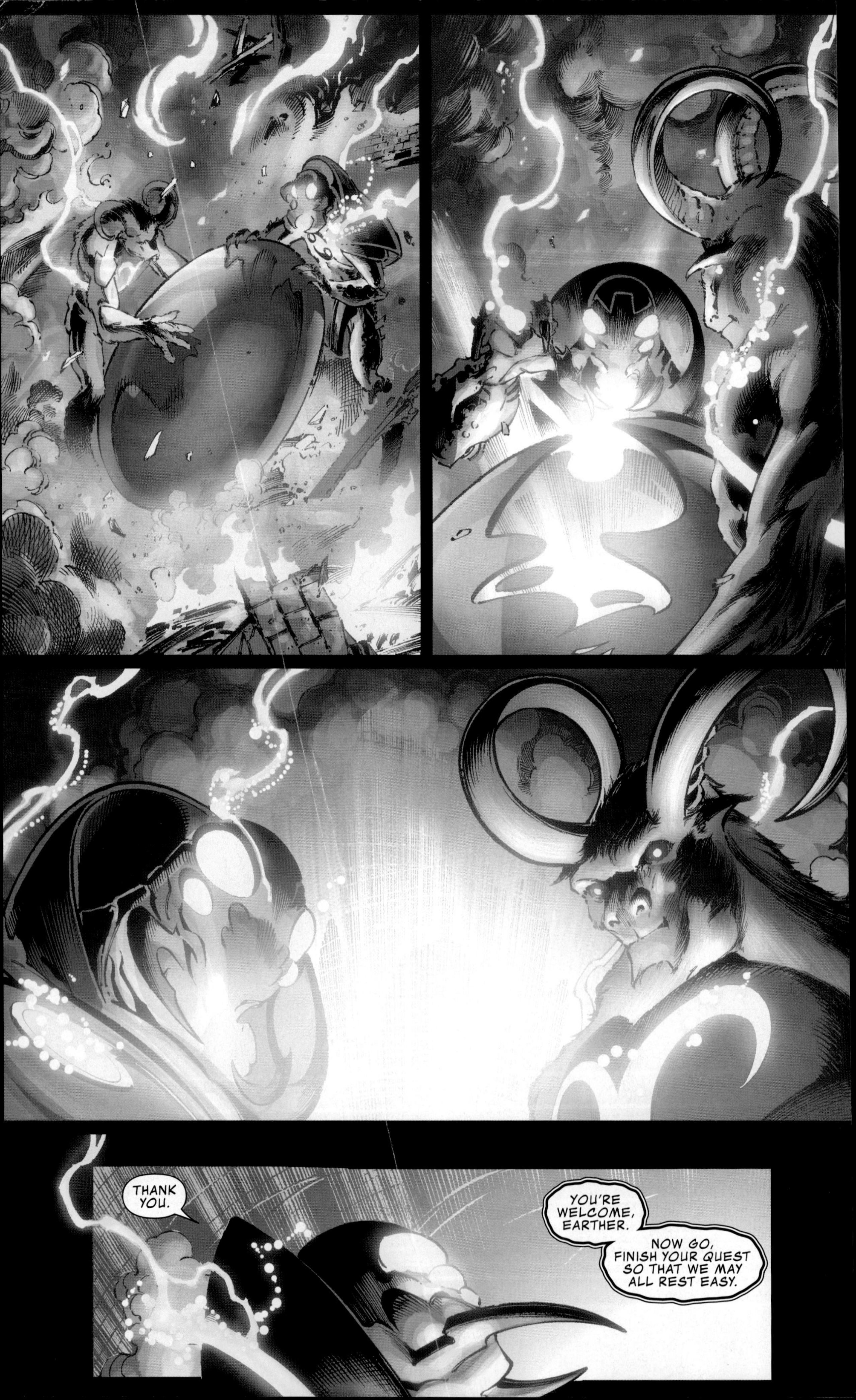
THANK YOU.
YOU'RE WELCOME, EARTHER.
NOW GO, FINISH YOUR QUEST SO THAT WE MAY ALL REST EASY.

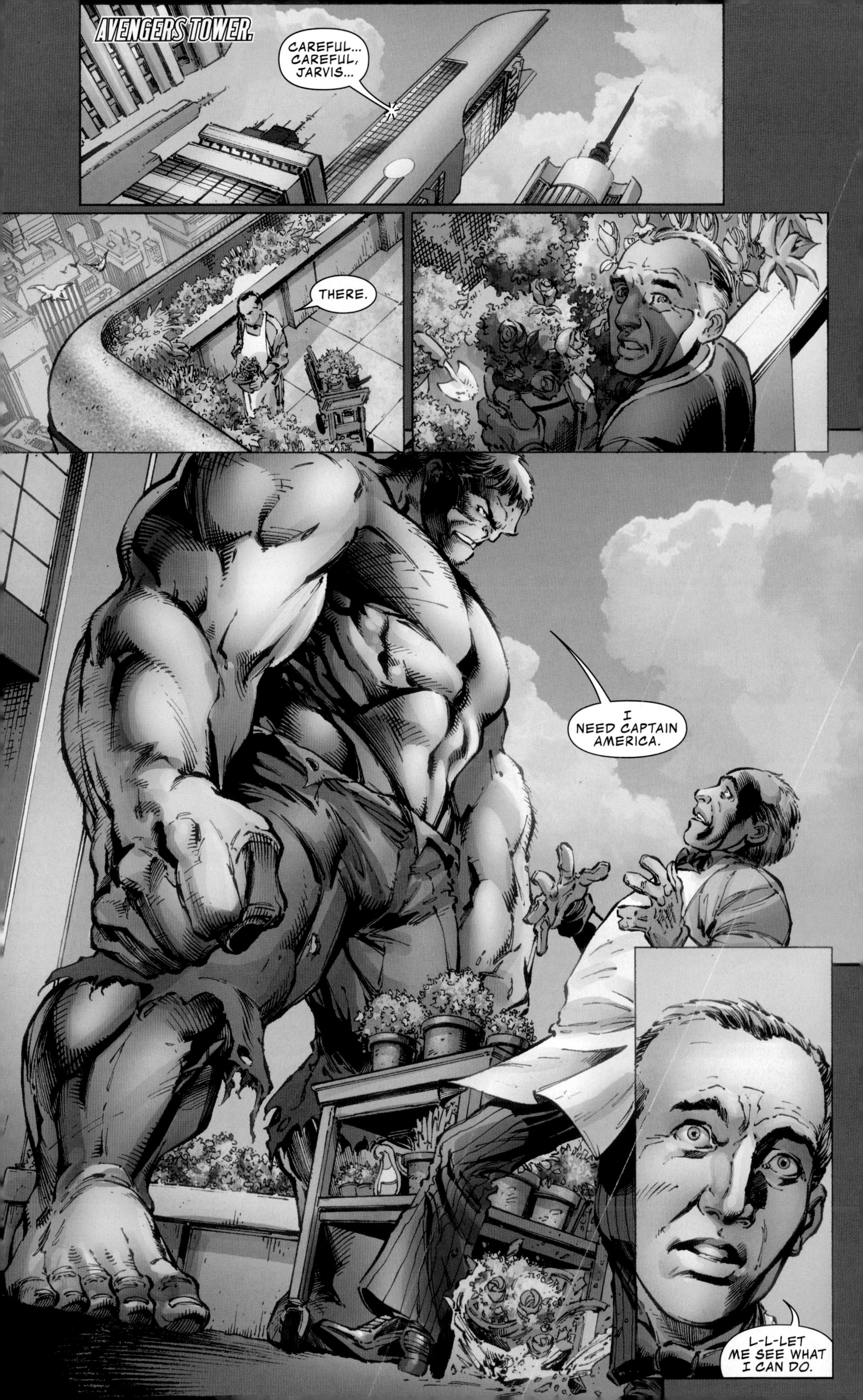
AVENGERS TOWER.
CAREFUL... CAREFUL, JARVIS...
THERE.
I NEED CAPTAIN AMERICA.
L-L-LET ME SEE WHAT I CAN DO.

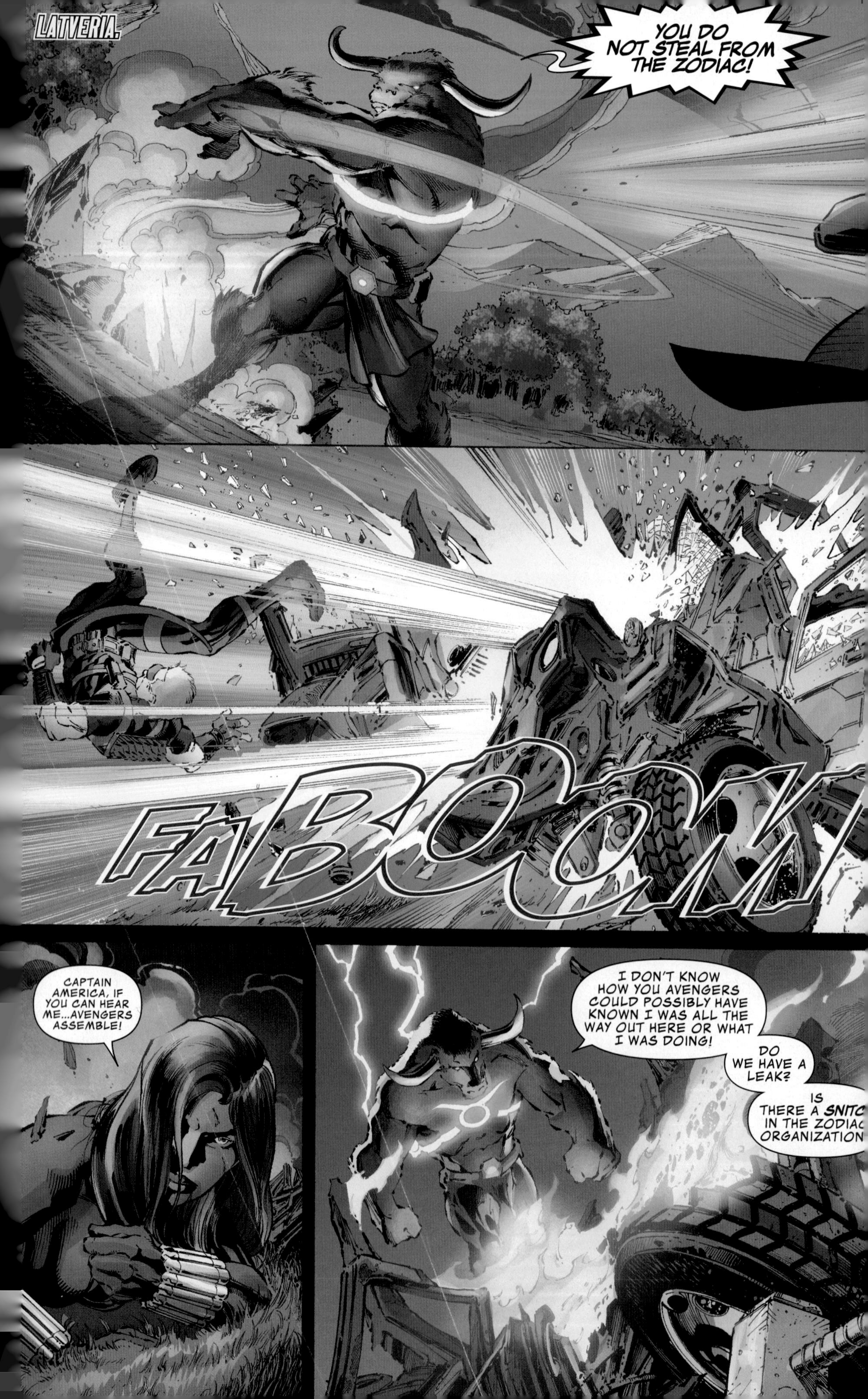
LATVERIA.
YOU DO NOT STEAL FROM THE ZODIAC!
FABOOM
CAPTAIN AMERICA, IF YOU CAN HEAR ME...AVENGERS ASSEMBLE!
I DON'T KNOW HOW YOU AVENGERS COULD POSSIBLY HAVE KNOWN I WAS ALL THE WAY OUT HERE OR WHAT I WAS DOING!
DO WE HAVE A LEAK?

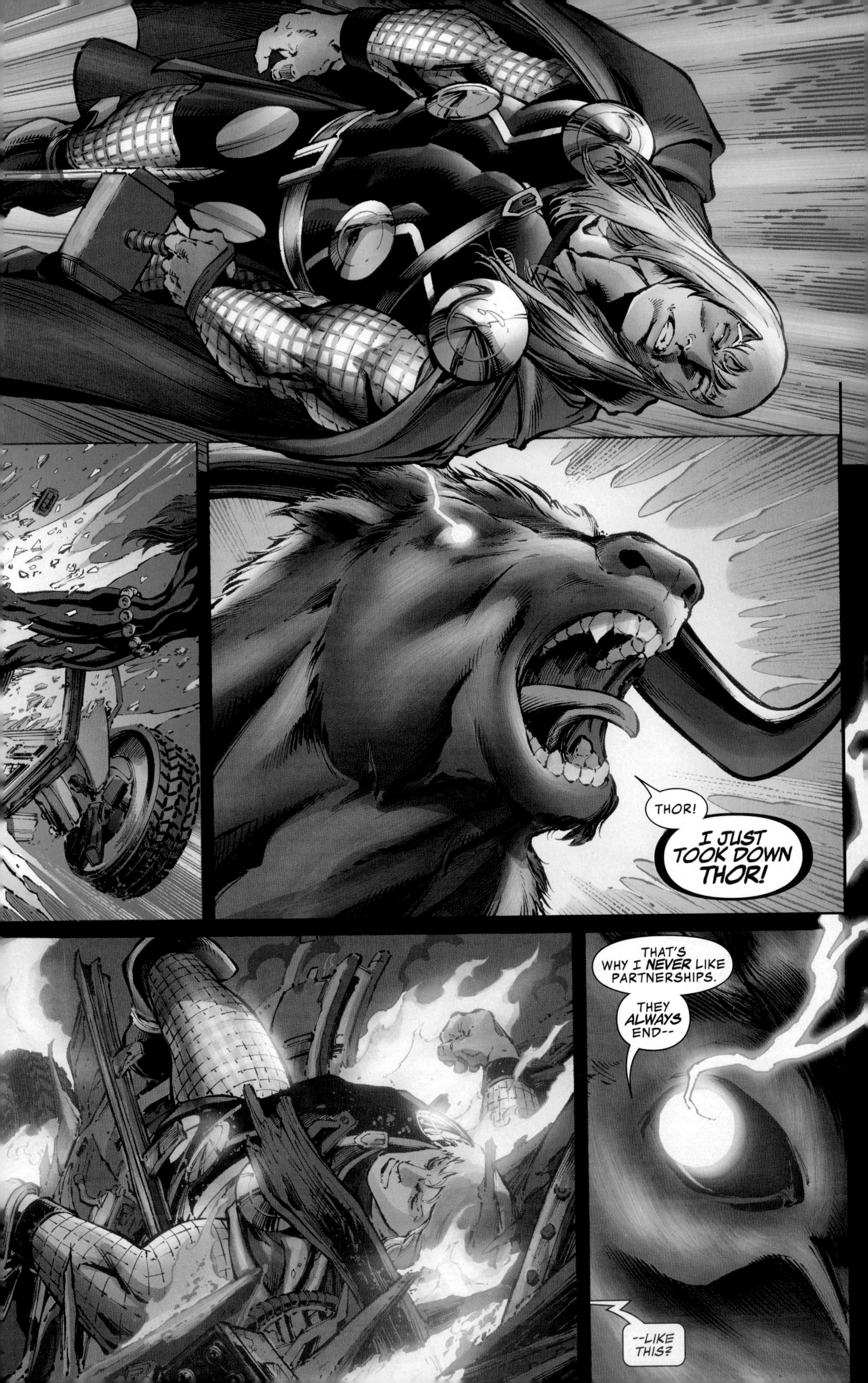
THOR!
I JUST TOOK DOWN THOR!
THAT'S WHY I NEVER LIKE PARTNERSHIPS.
THEY ALWAYS END--
--LIKE THIS?

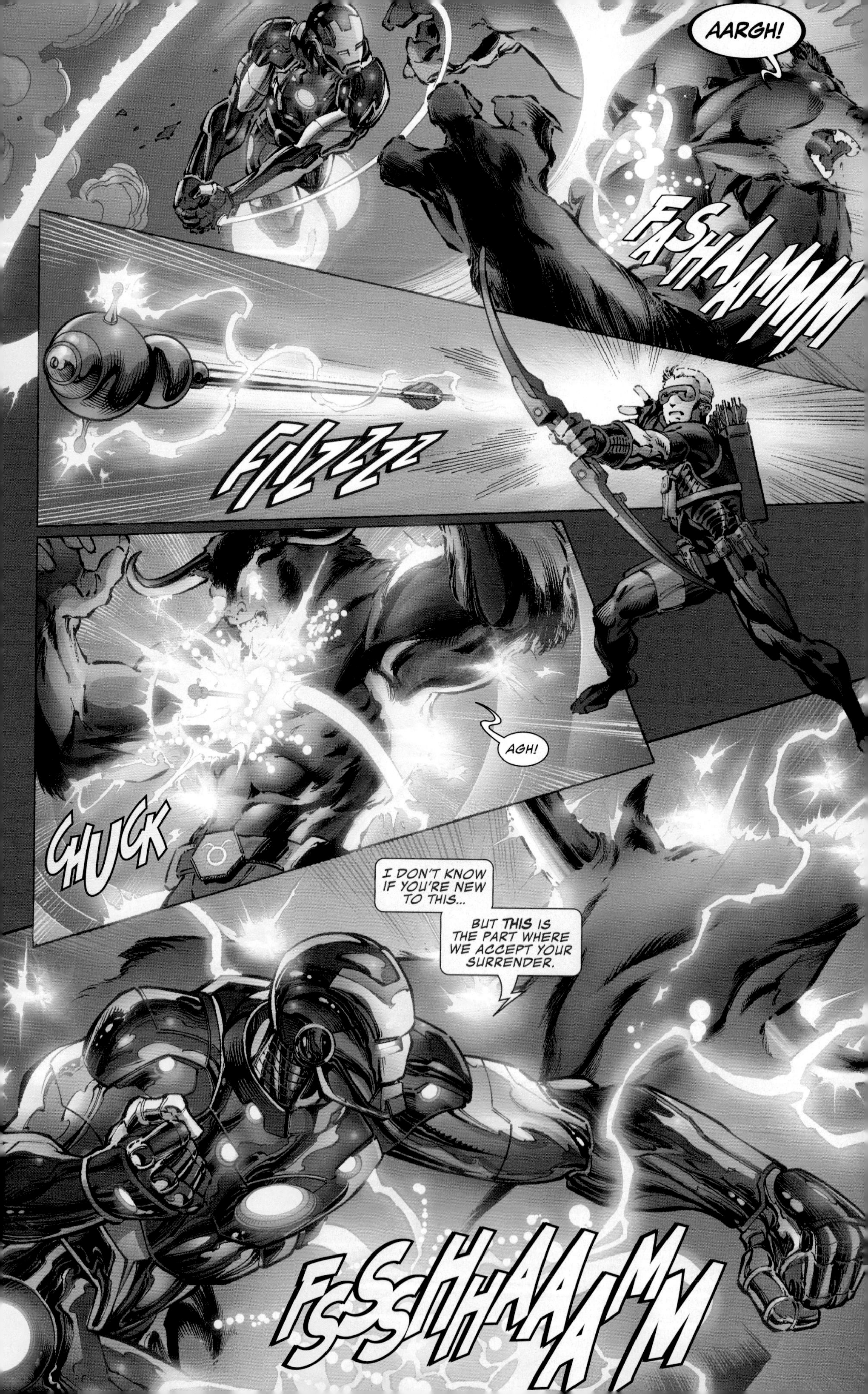
AARGH!
FASHAMMM
FIZZZZZ
AGH!
CHUCK
I DON'T KNOW IF YOU'RE NEW TO THIS...
BUT THIS IS THE PART WHERE WE ACCEPT YOUR SURRENDER.
FSSHHAAAMM

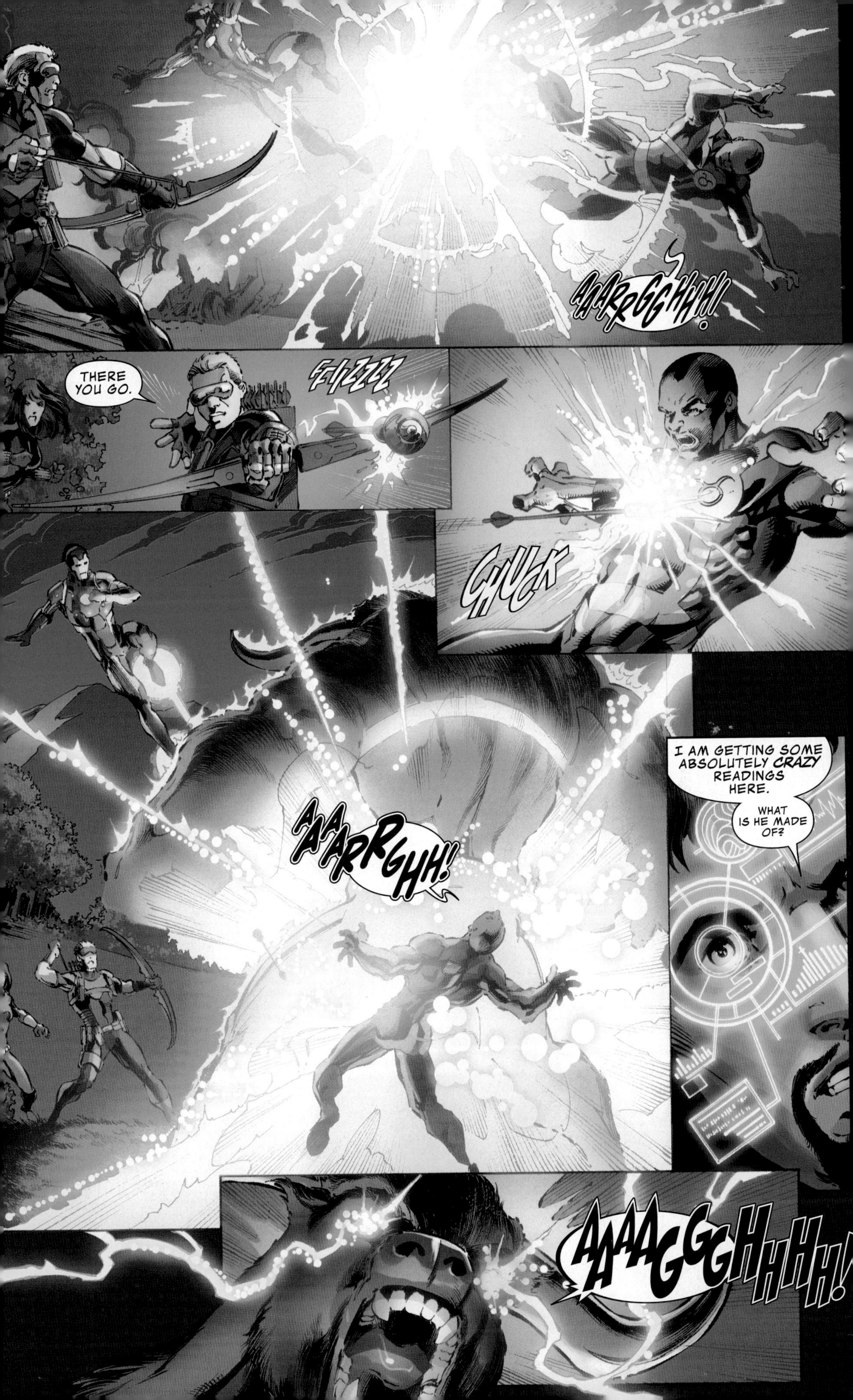
AAARRGGHHH!
THERE YOU GO.
FFFIZZZZZ
CHUCK
AAARRGHH!
I AM GETTING SOME ABSOLUTELY CRAZY READINGS HERE.
WHAT IS HE MADE OF?
AAAAGGGHHHHH!

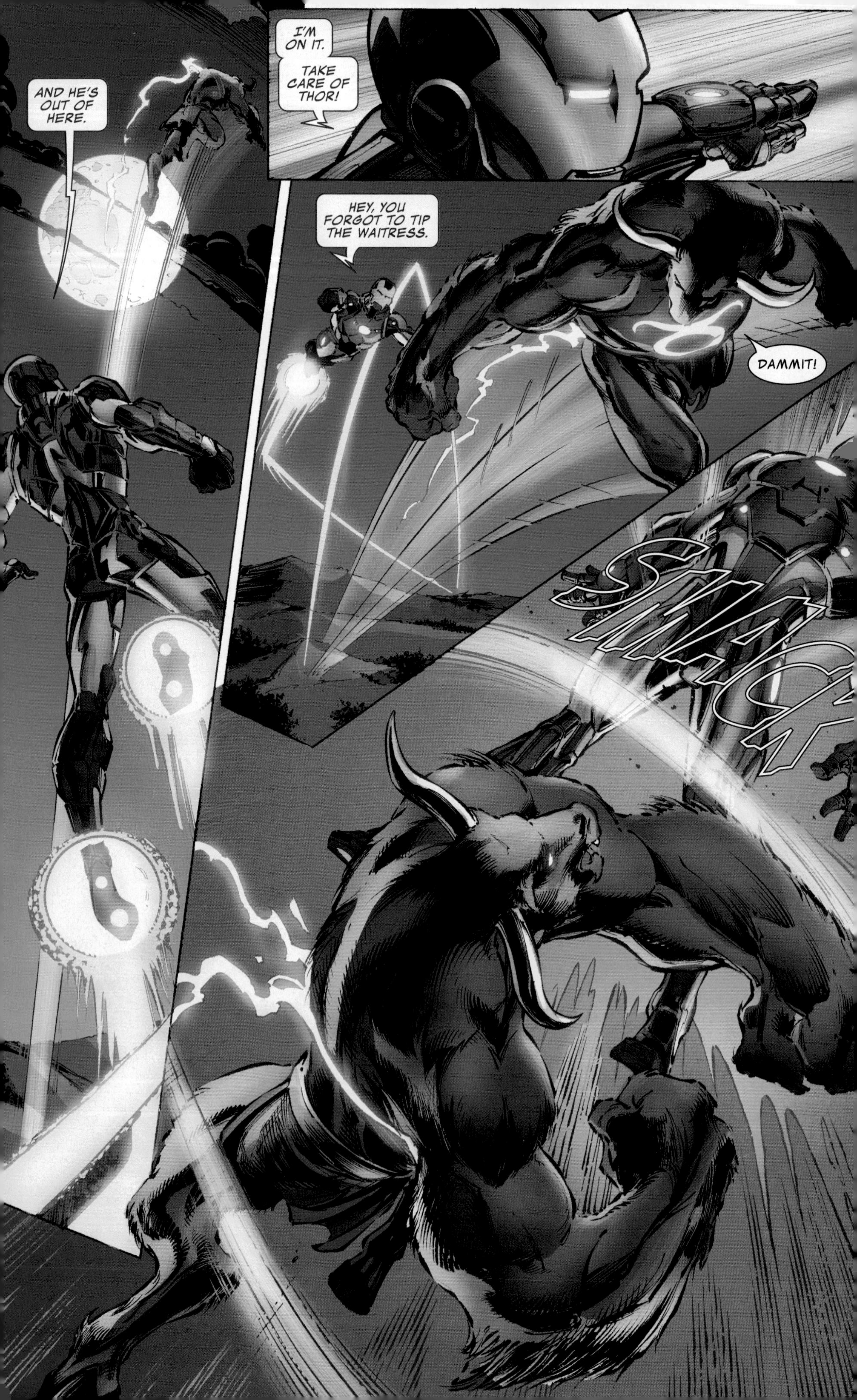
AND HE'S OUT OF HERE.
I'M ON IT.
TAKE CARE OF THOR!
HEY, YOU FORGOT TO TIP THE WAITRESS.
DAMMIT!
SMACK

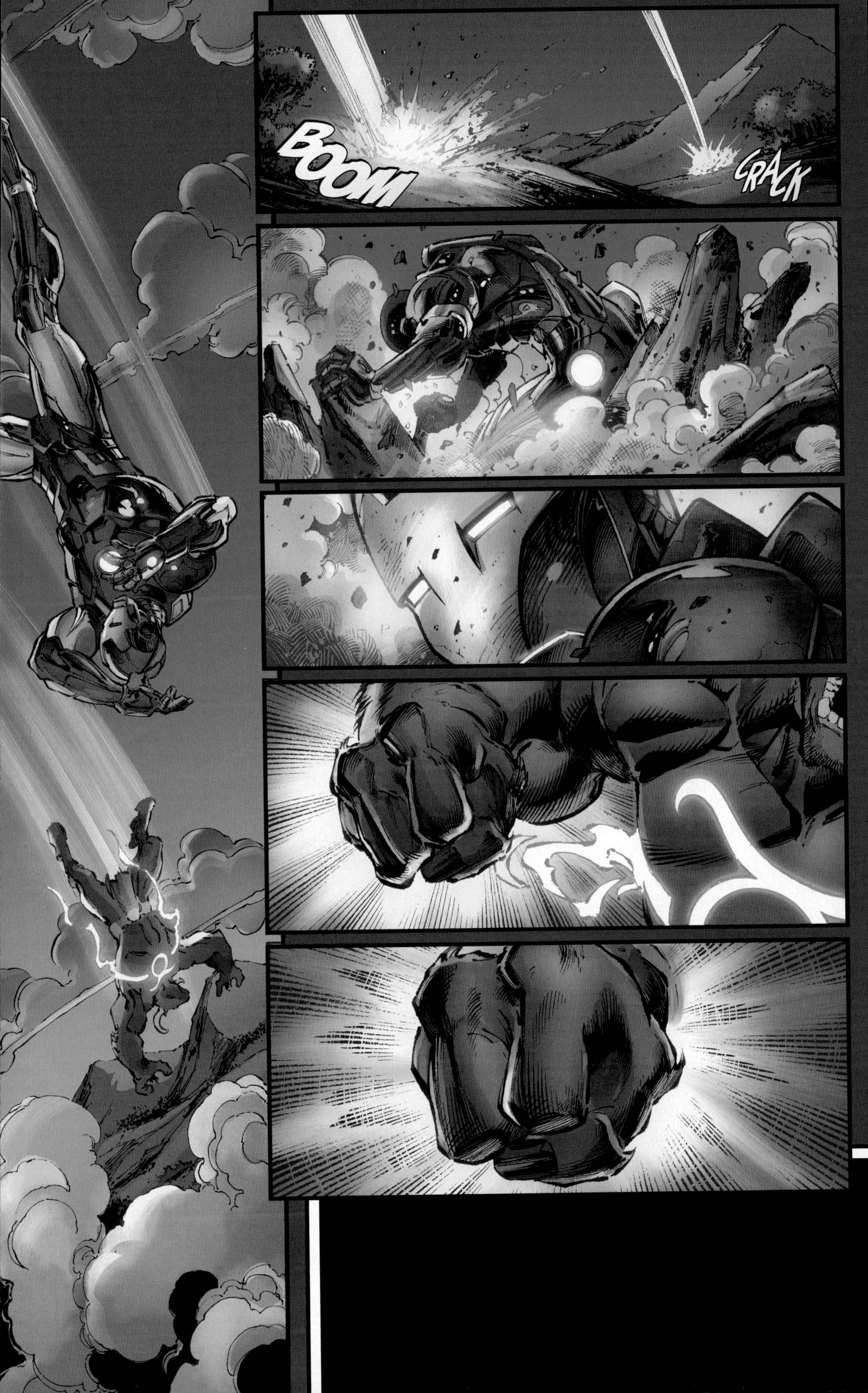
BOOM
CRACK

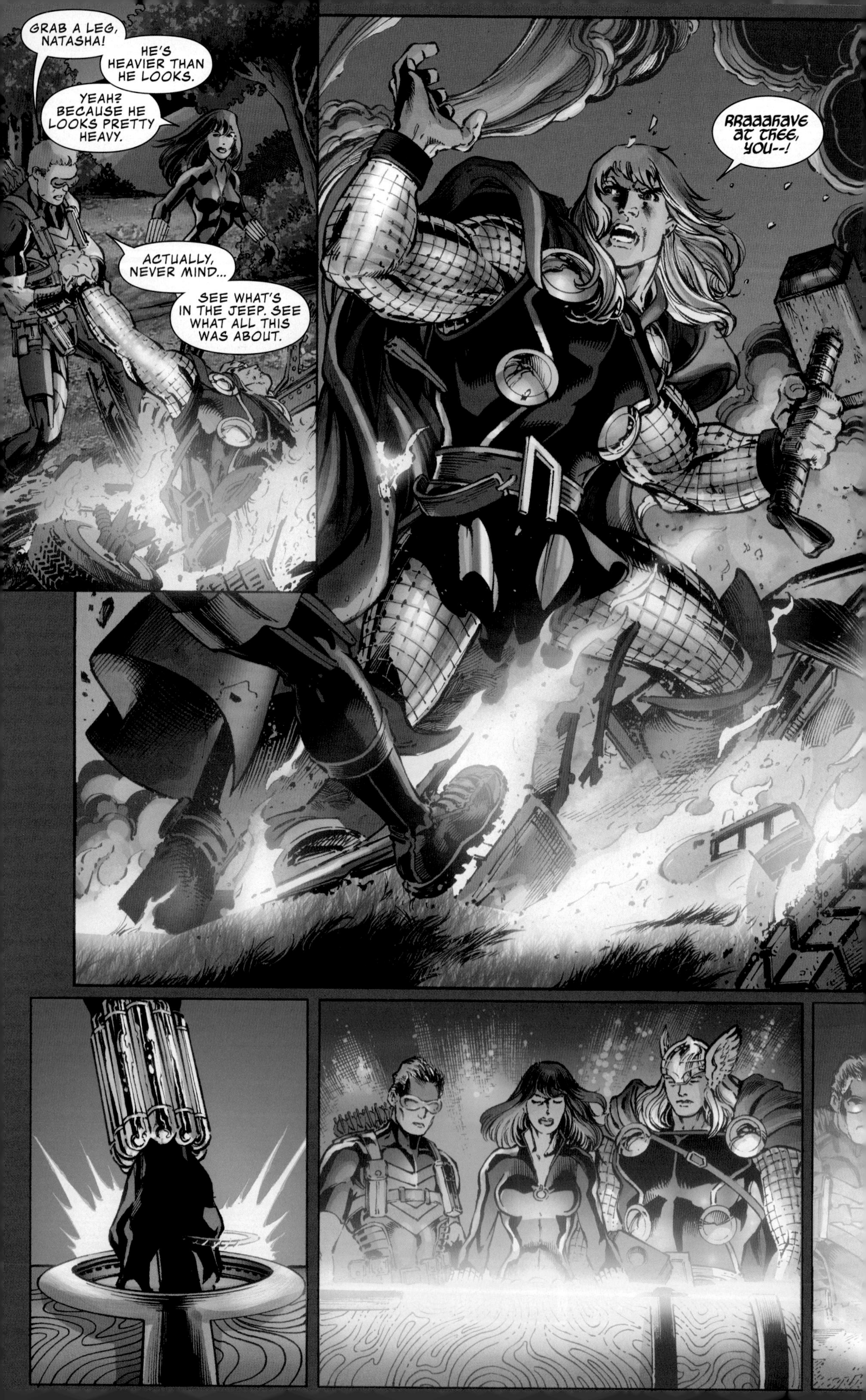
GRAB A LEG, NATASHA!
HE'S HEAVIER THAN HE LOOKS.
YEAH? BECAUSE HE LOOKS PRETTY HEAVY.
ACTUALLY, NEVER MIND...
SEE WHAT'S IN THE JEEP. SEE WHAT ALL THIS WAS ABOUT.
RRAAAHAVE AT THEE, YOU--!

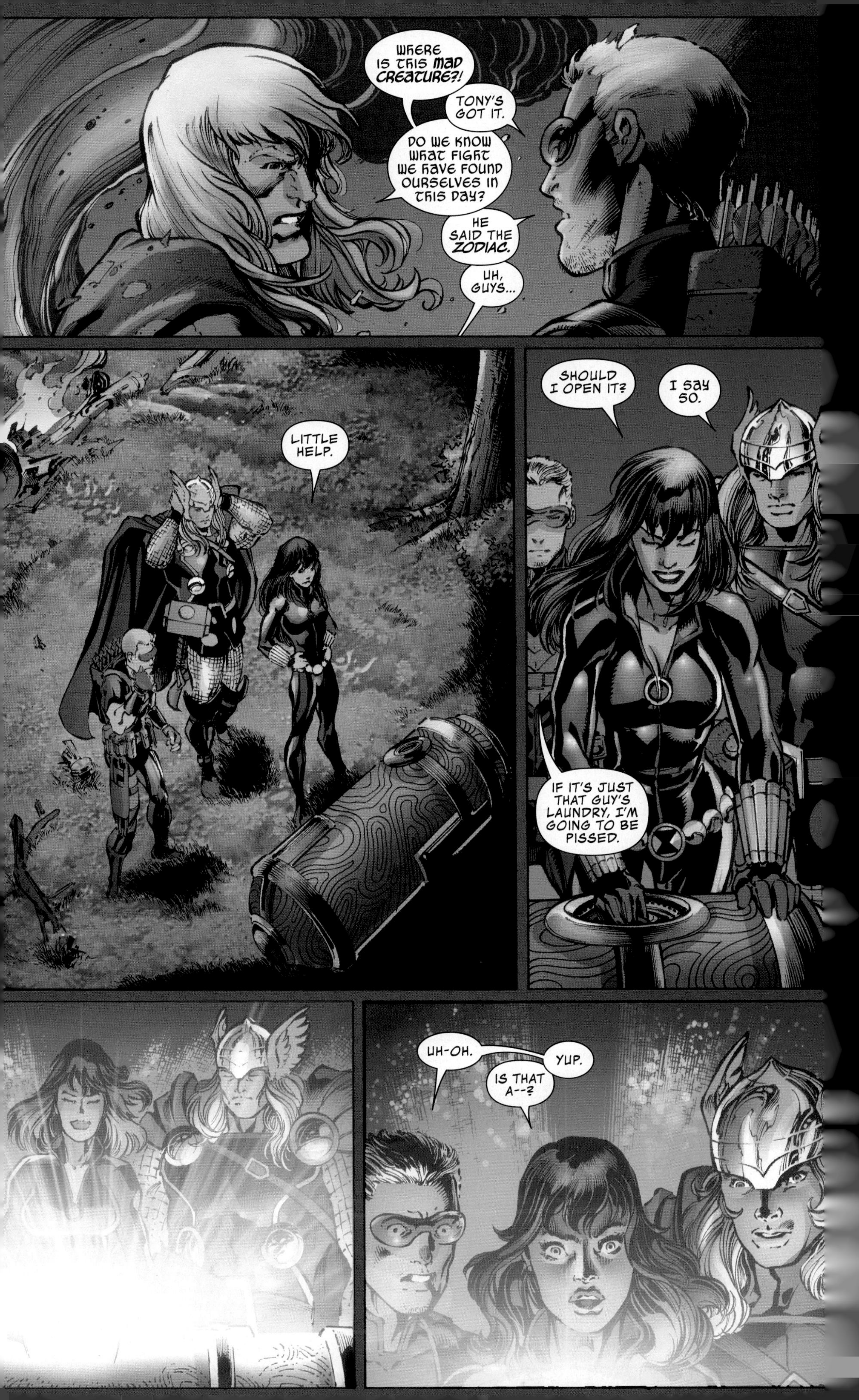
WHERE IS THIS MAD CREATURE?!
TONY'S GOT IT.
DO WE KNOW WHAT FIGHT WE HAVE FOUND OURSELVES IN THIS DAY?
HE SAID THE ZODIAC.
UH, GUYS...
LITTLE HELP.
SHOULD I OPEN IT?
I SAY SO.
IF IT'S JUST THAT GUY'S LAUNDRY, I'M GOING TO BE PISSED.
UH-OH.
YUP.
IS THAT A--?

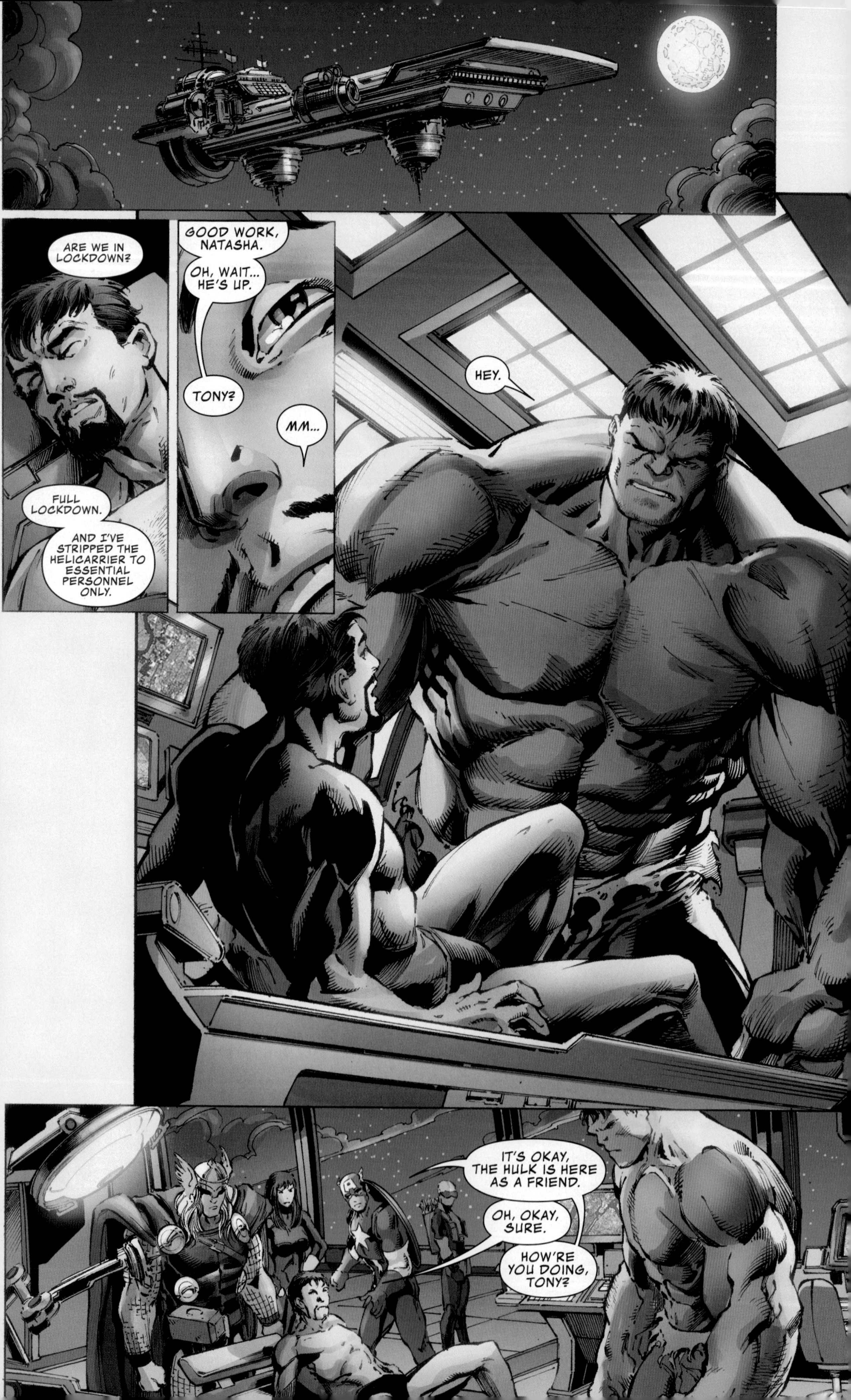
ARE WE IN LOCKDOWN?
GOOD WORK, NATASHA.
OH, WAIT... HE'S UP.
TONY?
MM...
HEY.
FULL LOCKDOWN.
AND I'VE STRIPPED THE HELICARRIER TO ESSENTIAL PERSONNEL ONLY.
IT'S OKAY, THE HULK IS HERE AS A FRIEND.
OH, OKAY, SURE.
HOW'RE YOU DOING, TONY?

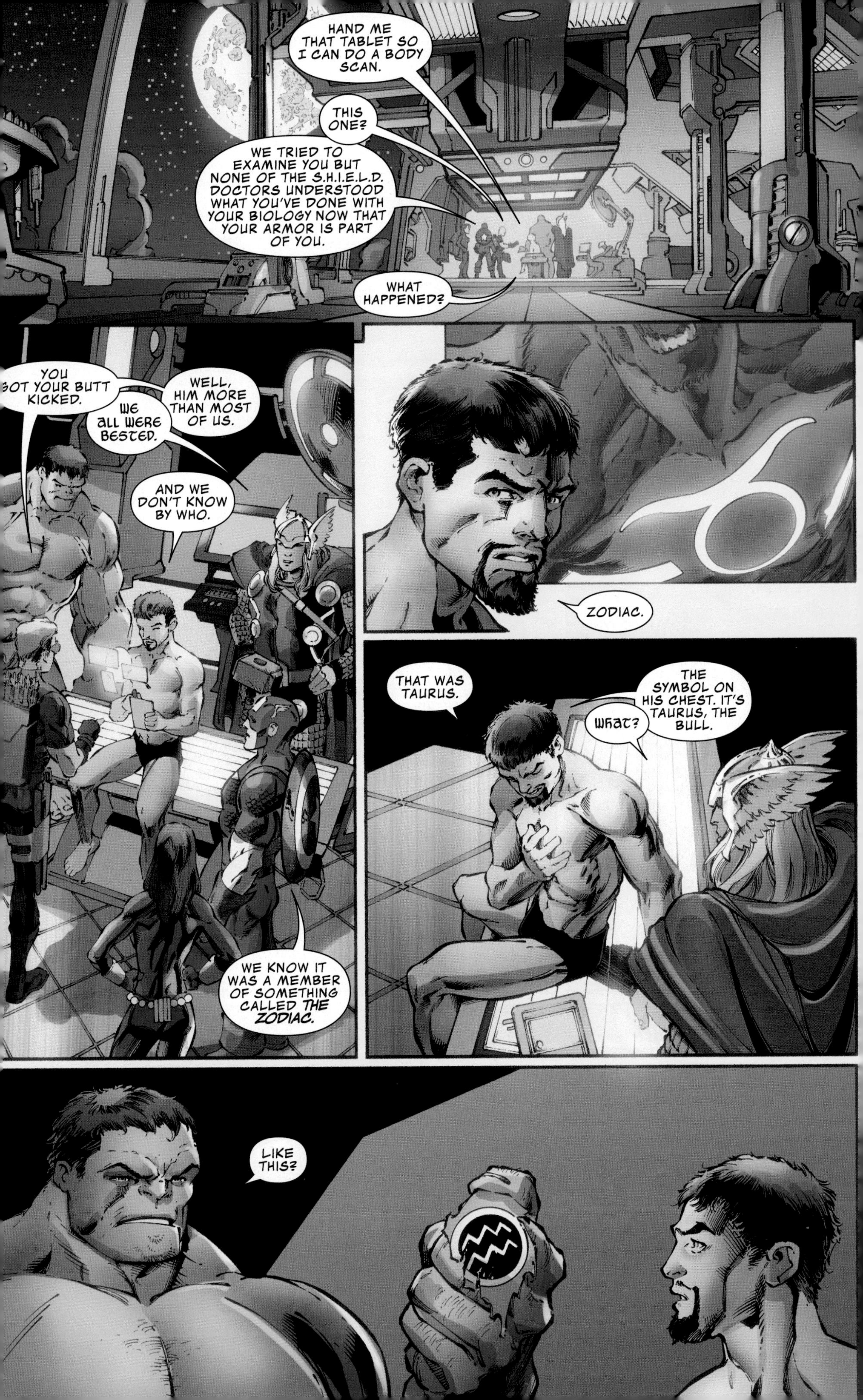

HAND ME THAT TABLET SO I CAN DO A BODY SCAN.
THIS ONE?
WE TRIED TO EXAMINE YOU BUT NONE OF THE S.H.I.E.L.D. DOCTORS UNDERSTOOD WHAT YOU'VE DONE WITH YOUR BIOLOGY NOW THAT YOUR ARMOR IS PART OF YOU.
WHAT HAPPENED?
YOU GOT YOUR BUTT KICKED.
WE ALL WERE BESTED.
WELL, HIM MORE THAN MOST OF US.
AND WE DON'T KNOW BY WHO.
WE KNOW IT WAS A MEMBER OF SOMETHING CALLED THE ZODIAC.
ZODIAC.
THAT WAS TAURUS.
WHAT?
THE SYMBOL ON HIS CHEST. IT'S TAURUS, THE BULL.
LIKE THIS?

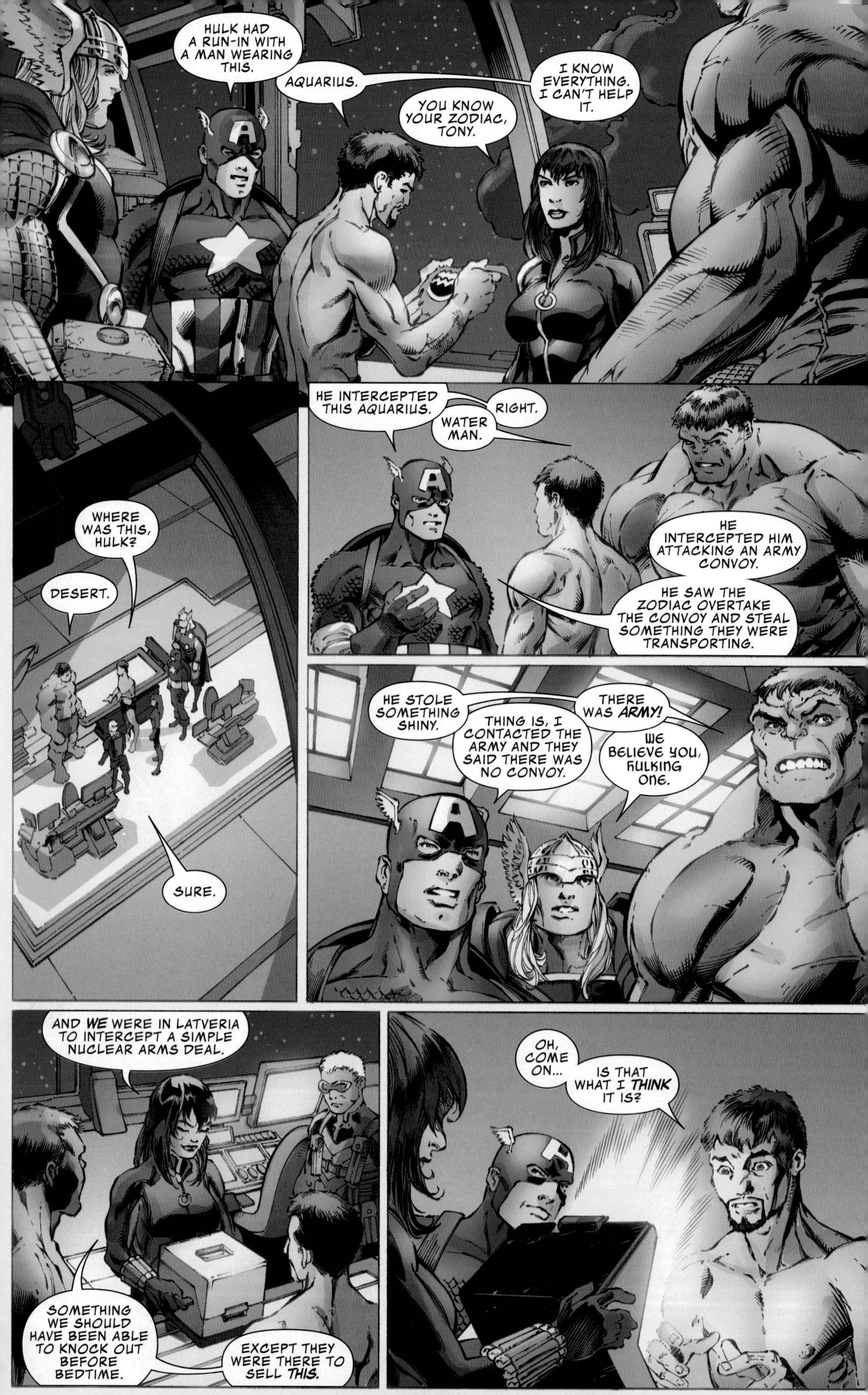
HULK HAD A RUN-IN WITH A MAN WEARING THIS.
AQUARIUS.
YOU KNOW YOUR ZODIAC, TONY.
I KNOW EVERYTHING. I CAN'T HELP IT.
WHERE WAS THIS, HULK?
DESERT.
SURE.
HE INTERCEPTED THIS AQUARIUS.
WATER MAN.
RIGHT.
HE INTERCEPTED HIM ATTACKING AN ARMY CONVOY.
HE SAW THE ZODIAC OVERTAKE THE CONVOY AND STEAL SOMETHING THEY WERE TRANSPORTING.
HE STOLE SOMETHING SHINY.
THERE WAS ARMY!
THING IS, I CONTACTED THE ARMY AND THEY SAID THERE WAS NO CONVOY.
WE BELIEVE YOU, HULKING ONE.
AND WE WERE IN LATVERIA TO INTERCEPT A SIMPLE NUCLEAR ARMS DEAL.
SOMETHING WE SHOULD HAVE BEEN ABLE TO KNOCK OUT BEFORE BEDTIME.
EXCEPT THEY WERE THERE TO SELL THIS.
OH, COME ON...
IS THAT WHAT I THINK IT IS?

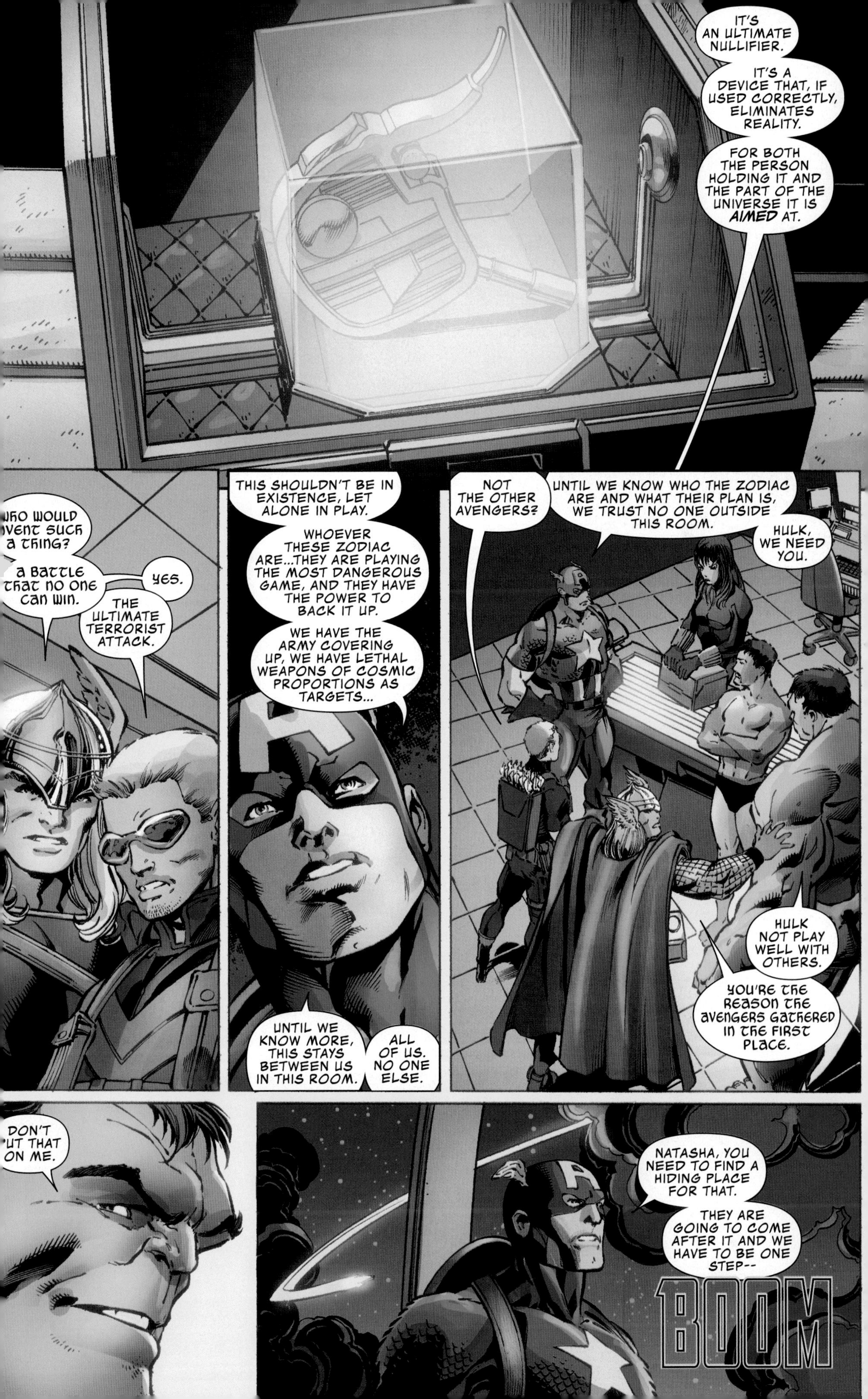

IT'S AN ULTIMATE NULLIFIER.
IT'S A DEVICE THAT, IF USED CORRECTLY, ELIMINATES REALITY.
FOR BOTH THE PERSON HOLDING IT AND THE PART OF THE UNIVERSE IT IS AIMED AT.
WHO WOULD ...VENT SUCH A THING?
A BATTLE THAT NO ONE CAN WIN.
YES.
THE ULTIMATE TERRORIST ATTACK.
THIS SHOULDN'T BE IN EXISTENCE, LET ALONE IN PLAY.
WHOEVER THESE ZODIAC ARE...THEY ARE PLAYING THE MOST DANGEROUS GAME, AND THEY HAVE THE POWER TO BACK IT UP.
WE HAVE THE ARMY COVERING UP, WE HAVE LETHAL WEAPONS OF COSMIC PROPORTIONS AS TARGETS...
UNTIL WE KNOW MORE, THIS STAYS BETWEEN US IN THIS ROOM.
ALL OF US. NO ONE ELSE.
NOT THE OTHER AVENGERS?
UNTIL WE KNOW WHO THE ZODIAC ARE AND WHAT THEIR PLAN IS, WE TRUST NO ONE OUTSIDE THIS ROOM.
HULK, WE NEED YOU.
HULK NOT PLAY WELL WITH OTHERS.
YOU'RE THE REASON THE AVENGERS GATHERED IN THE FIRST PLACE.
DON'T ...UT THAT ON ME.
NATASHA, YOU NEED TO FIND A HIDING PLACE FOR THAT.
THEY ARE GOING TO COME AFTER IT AND WE HAVE TO BE ONE STEP--
BOOM

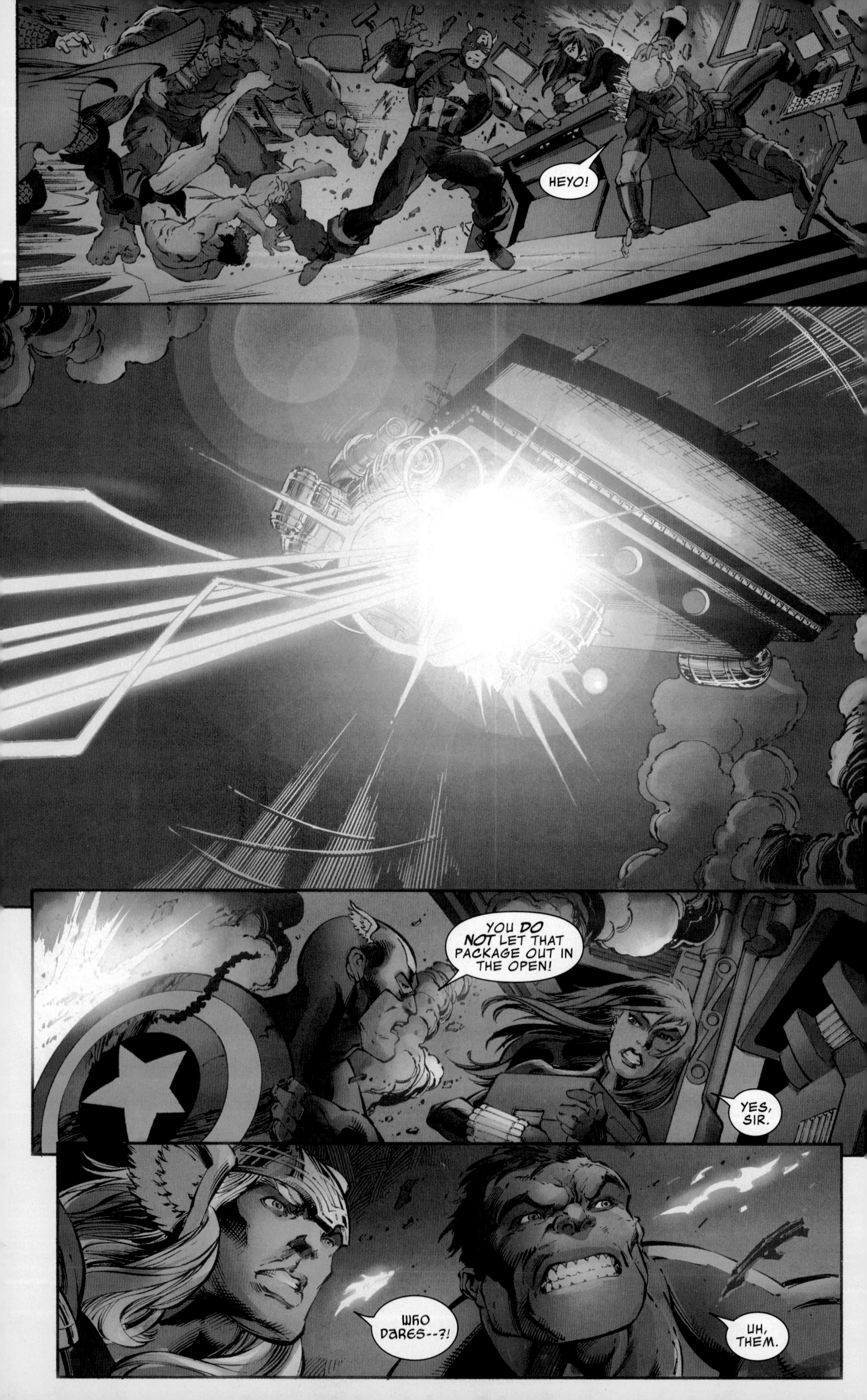
HEYO!
YOU DO NOT LET THAT PACKAGE OUT IN THE OPEN!
YES, SIR.
WHO DARES--?!
UH, THEM.

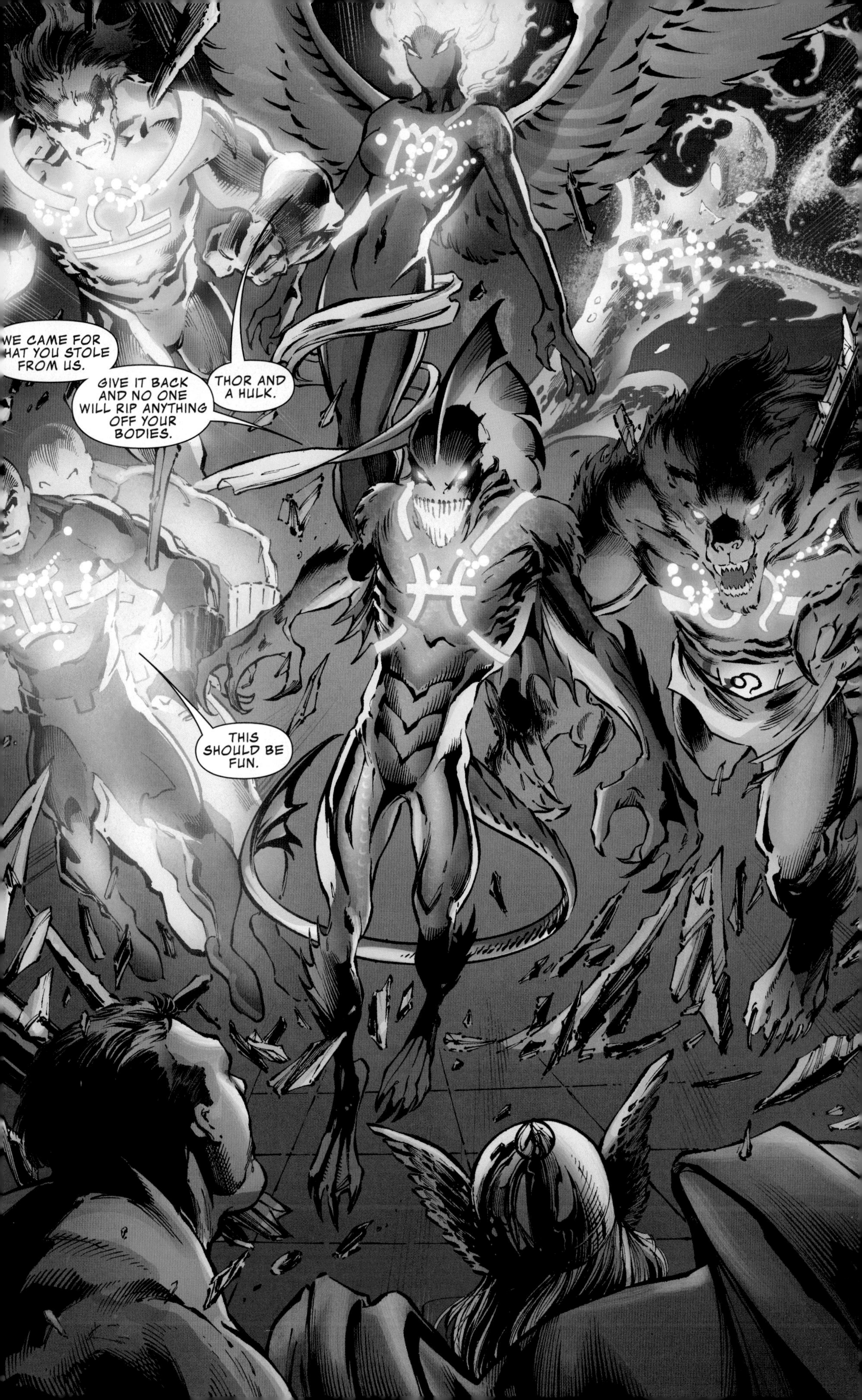
WE CAME FOR
HAT YOU STOLE
FROM US.
GIVE IT BACK
AND NO ONE
WILL RIP ANYTHING
OFF YOUR
BODIES.
THOR AND
A HULK.
THIS
SHOULD BE
FUN.

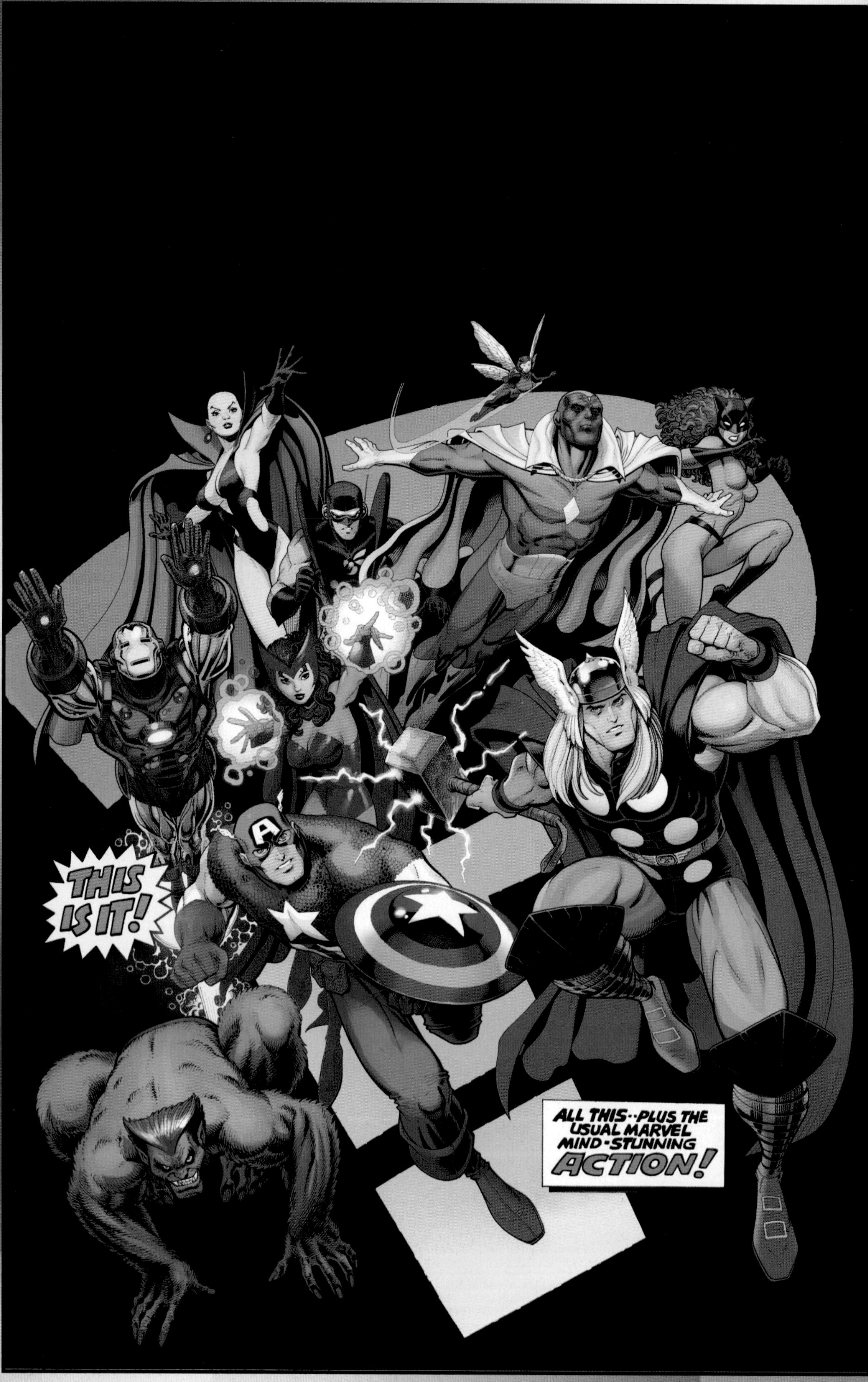
THIS IS IT!
ALL THIS--PLUS THE USUAL MARVEL MIND-STUNNING ACTION!

#1 VARIANT BY ARTHUR ADAMS & JASON KEITH

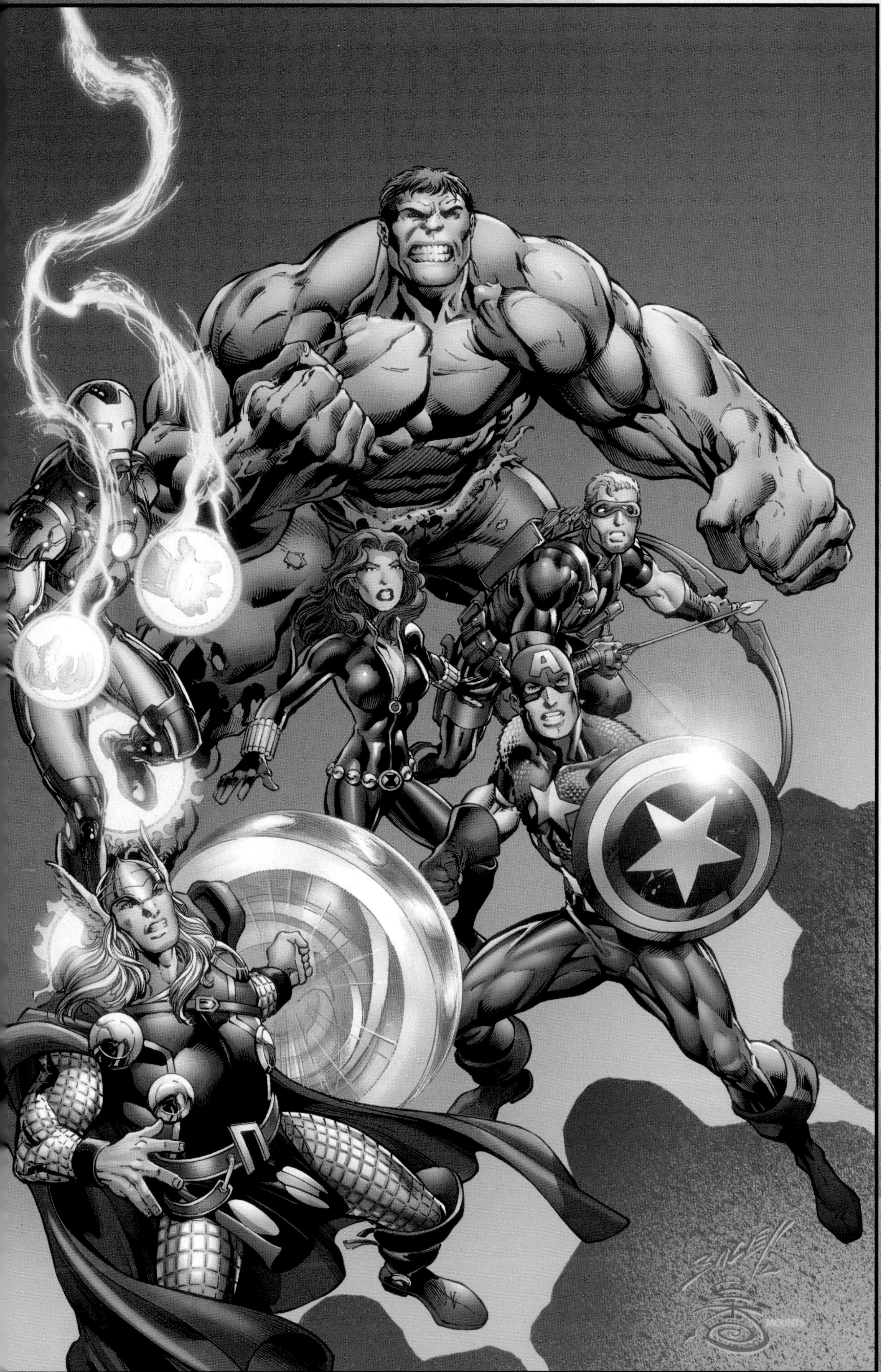
MOUNTS

THREE

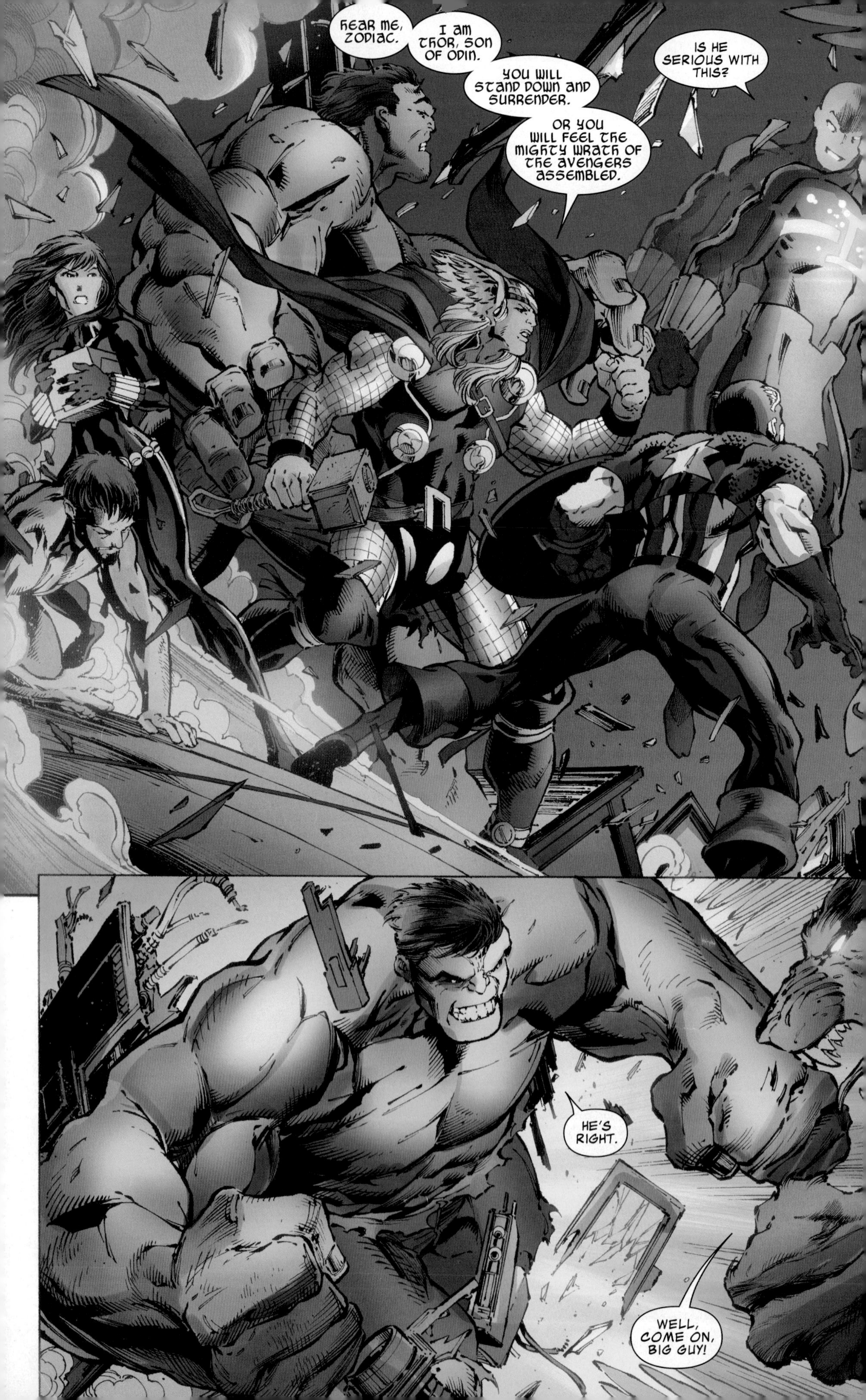
HEAR ME, ZODIAC.
I AM THOR, SON OF ODIN.
YOU WILL STAND DOWN AND SURRENDER.
OR YOU WILL FEEL THE MIGHTY WRATH OF THE AVENGERS ASSEMBLED.
IS HE SERIOUS WITH THIS?
HE'S RIGHT.
WELL, COME ON, BIG GUY!

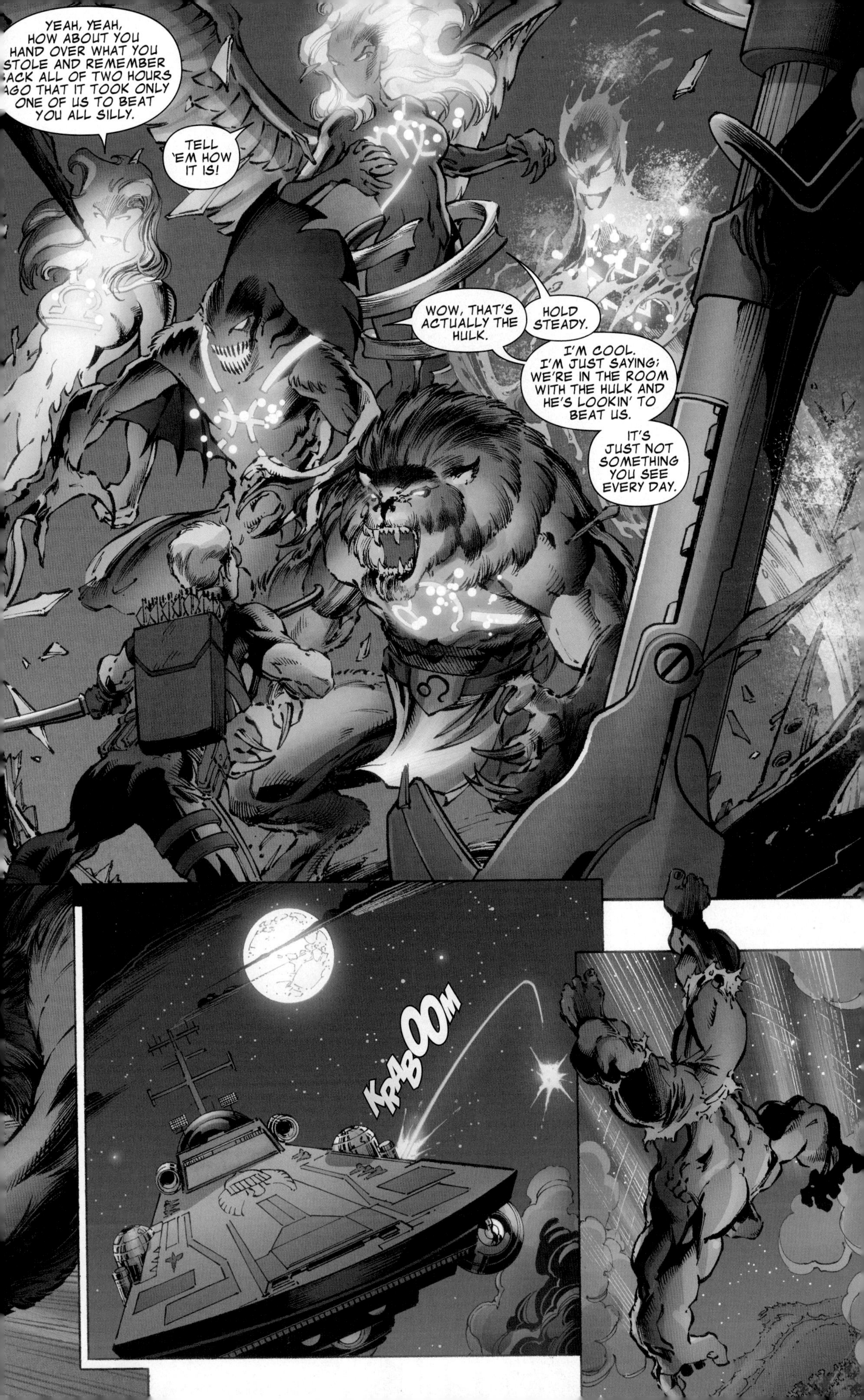
YEAH, YEAH, HOW ABOUT YOU HAND OVER WHAT YOU STOLE AND REMEMBER BACK ALL OF TWO HOURS AGO THAT IT TOOK ONLY ONE OF US TO BEAT YOU ALL SILLY.
TELL 'EM HOW IT IS!
WOW, THAT'S ACTUALLY THE HULK.
HOLD STEADY.
I'M COOL. I'M JUST SAYING; WE'RE IN THE ROOM WITH THE HULK AND HE'S LOOKIN' TO BEAT US.
IT'S JUST NOT SOMETHING YOU SEE EVERY DAY.
KRABOOM

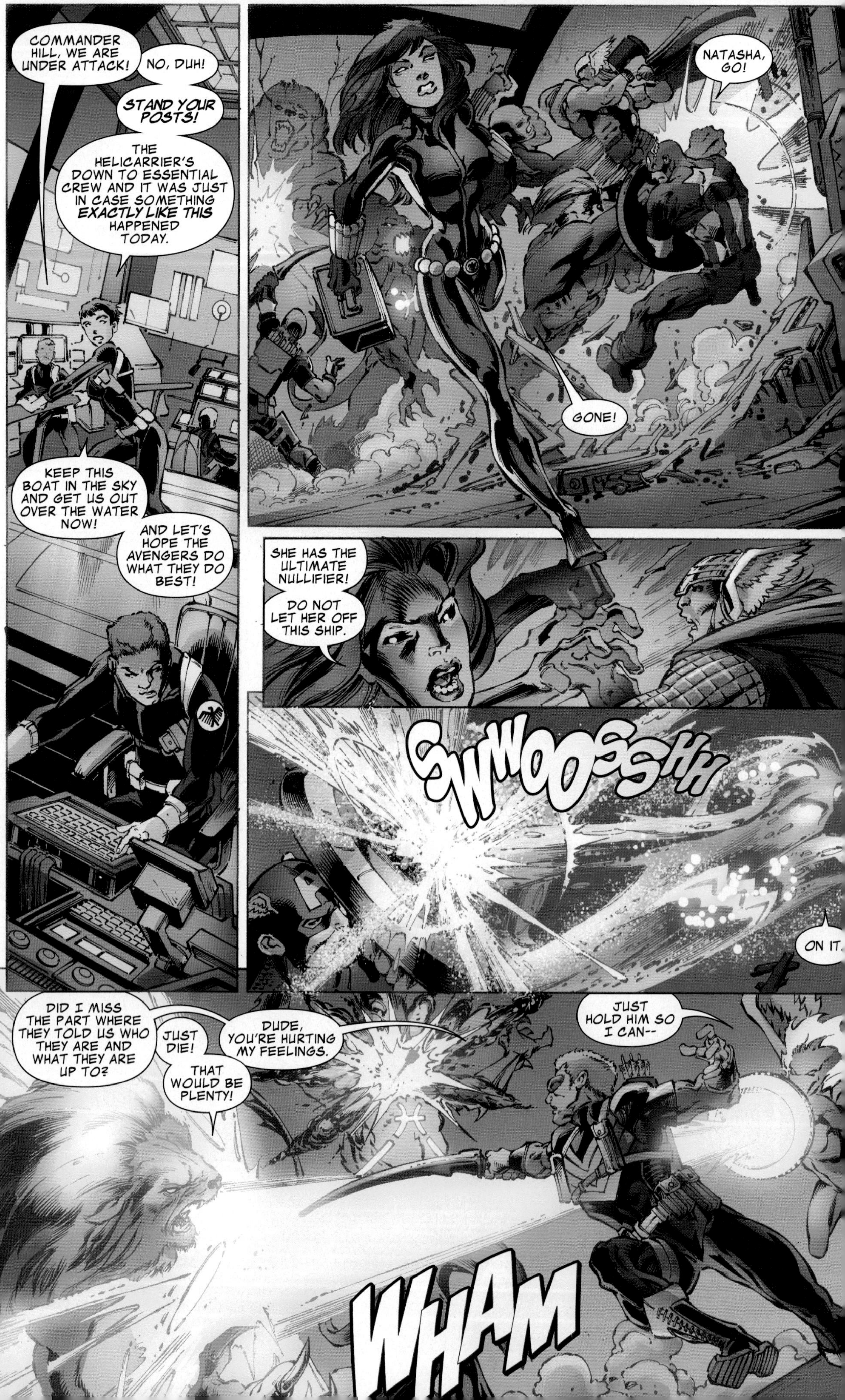
COMMANDER HILL, WE ARE UNDER ATTACK!
NO, DUH!
STAND YOUR POSTS!
THE HELICARRIER'S DOWN TO ESSENTIAL CREW AND IT WAS JUST IN CASE SOMETHING EXACTLY LIKE THIS HAPPENED TODAY.
KEEP THIS BOAT IN THE SKY AND GET US OUT OVER THE WATER NOW!
AND LET'S HOPE THE AVENGERS DO WHAT THEY DO BEST!
NATASHA, GO!
GONE!
SHE HAS THE ULTIMATE NULLIFIER!
DO NOT LET HER OFF THIS SHIP.
SWWOOSSHH
ON IT.
DID I MISS THE PART WHERE THEY TOLD US WHO THEY ARE AND WHAT THEY ARE UP TO?
JUST DIE!
THAT WOULD BE PLENTY!
DUDE, YOU'RE HURTING MY FEELINGS.
JUST HOLD HIM SO I CAN--
WHAM

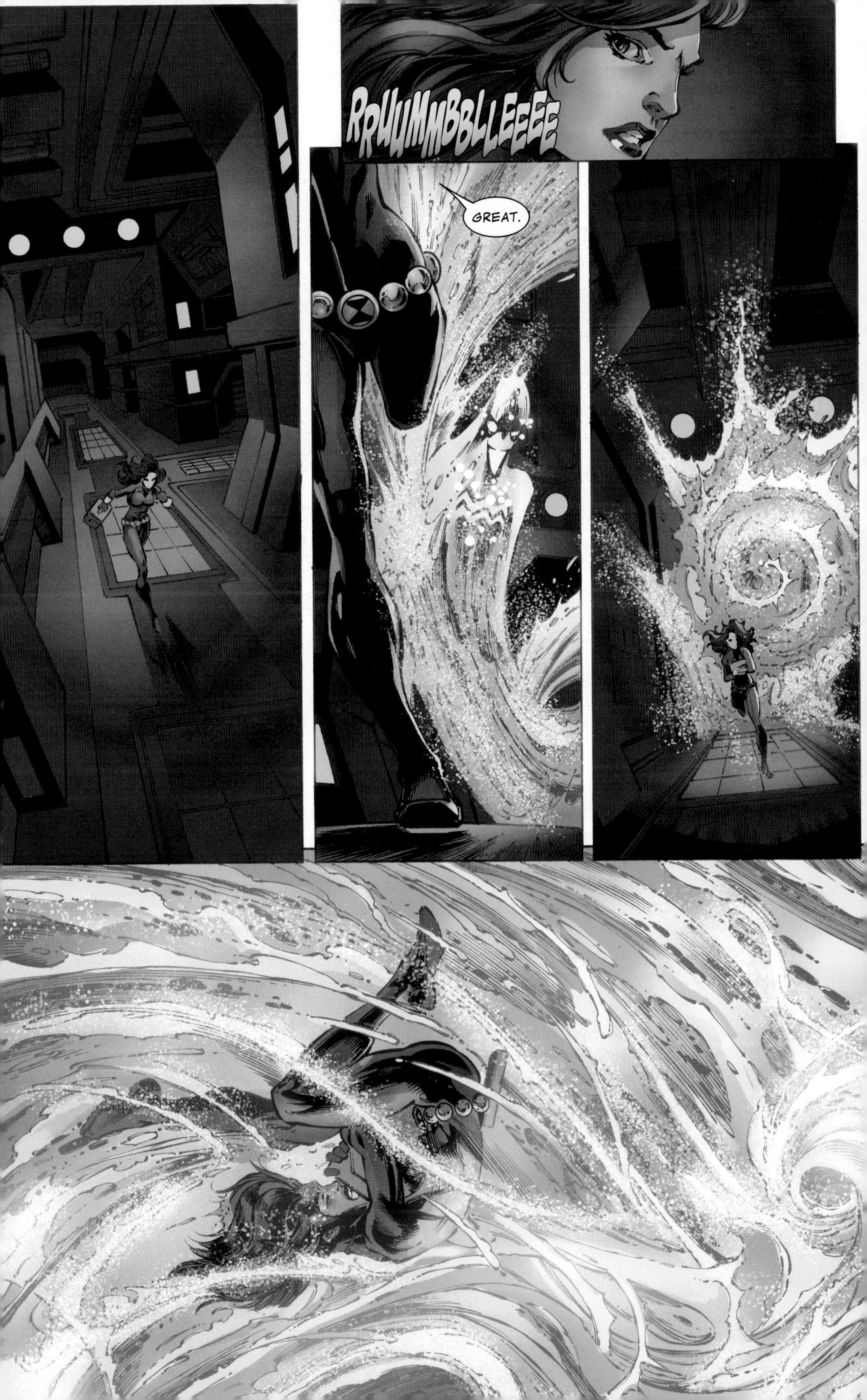
RRUUMMBBLLEEEE
GREAT.

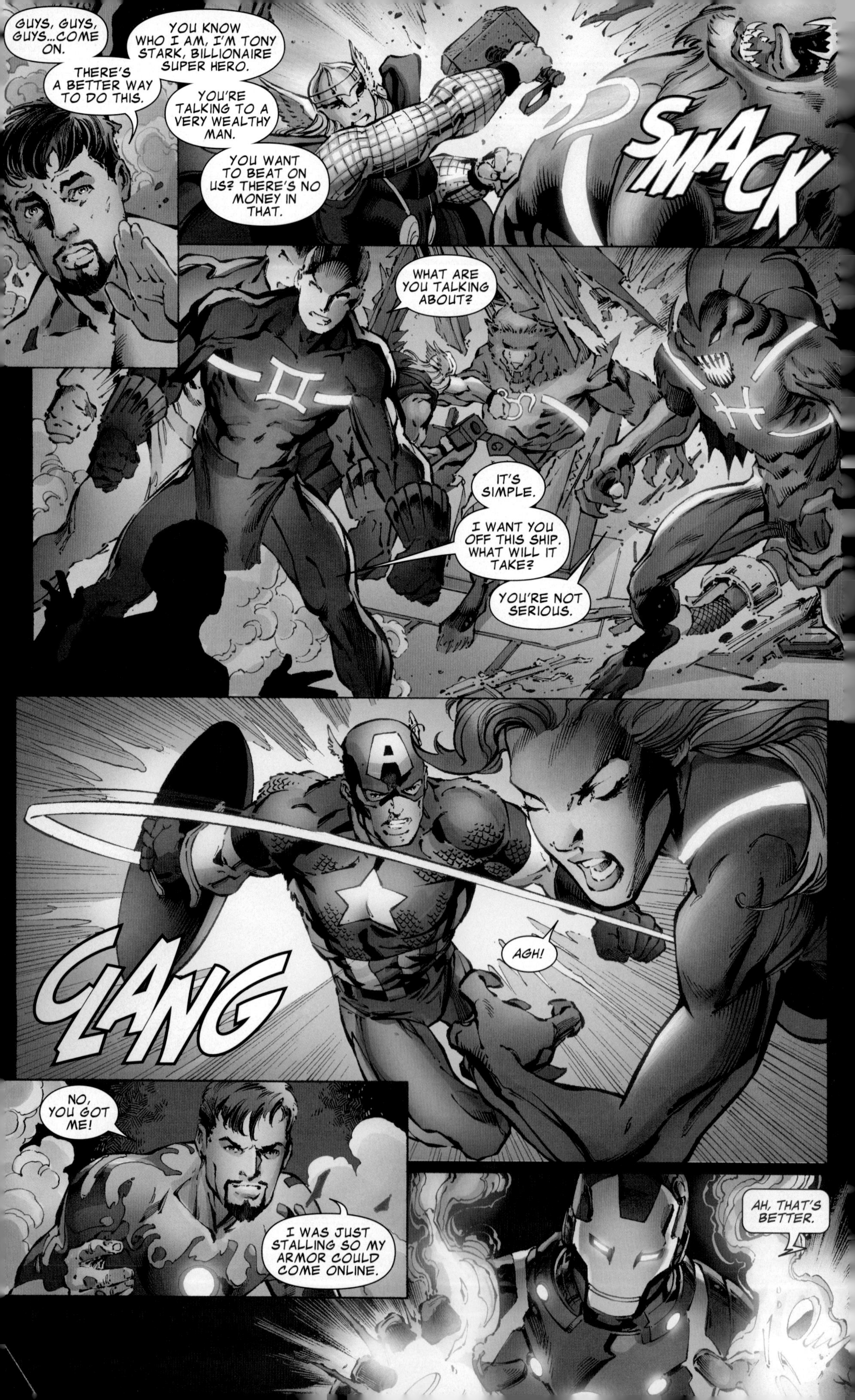
GUYS, GUYS, GUYS...COME ON.
THERE'S A BETTER WAY TO DO THIS.
YOU KNOW WHO I AM, I'M TONY STARK, BILLIONAIRE SUPER HERO.
YOU'RE TALKING TO A VERY WEALTHY MAN.
YOU WANT TO BEAT ON US? THERE'S NO MONEY IN THAT.
SMACK
WHAT ARE YOU TALKING ABOUT?
IT'S SIMPLE.
I WANT YOU OFF THIS SHIP. WHAT WILL IT TAKE?
YOU'RE NOT SERIOUS.
CLANG
AGH!
NO, YOU GOT ME!
I WAS JUST STALLING SO MY ARMOR COULD COME ONLINE.
AH, THAT'S BETTER.

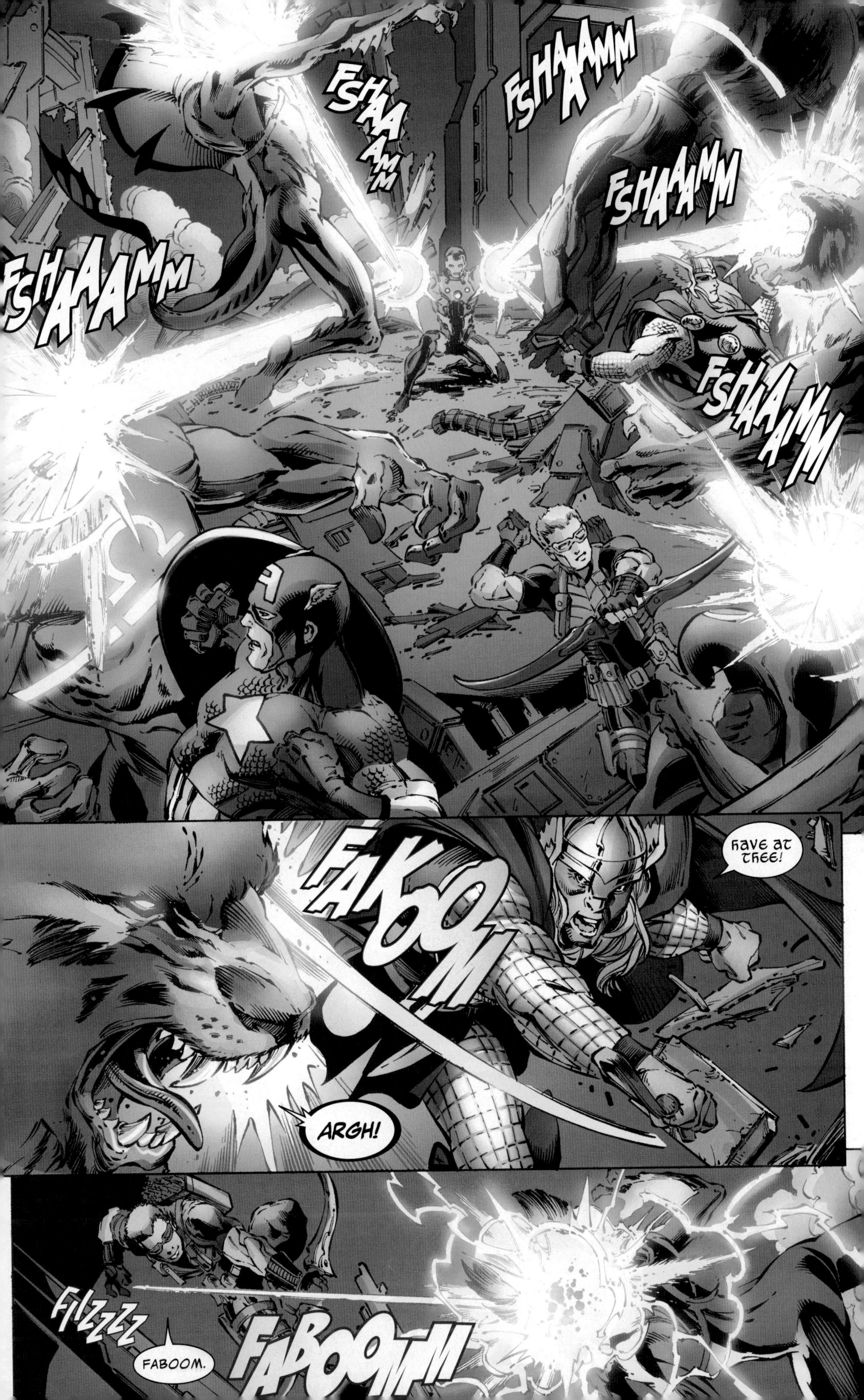
FSHAAAMM
FSHAAAMM
FSHAAAMM
FSHAAAMM
FSHAAAMM
FAKOOM
HAVE AT THEE!
ARGH!
FTZZZZ
FABOOM.
FABOOMM

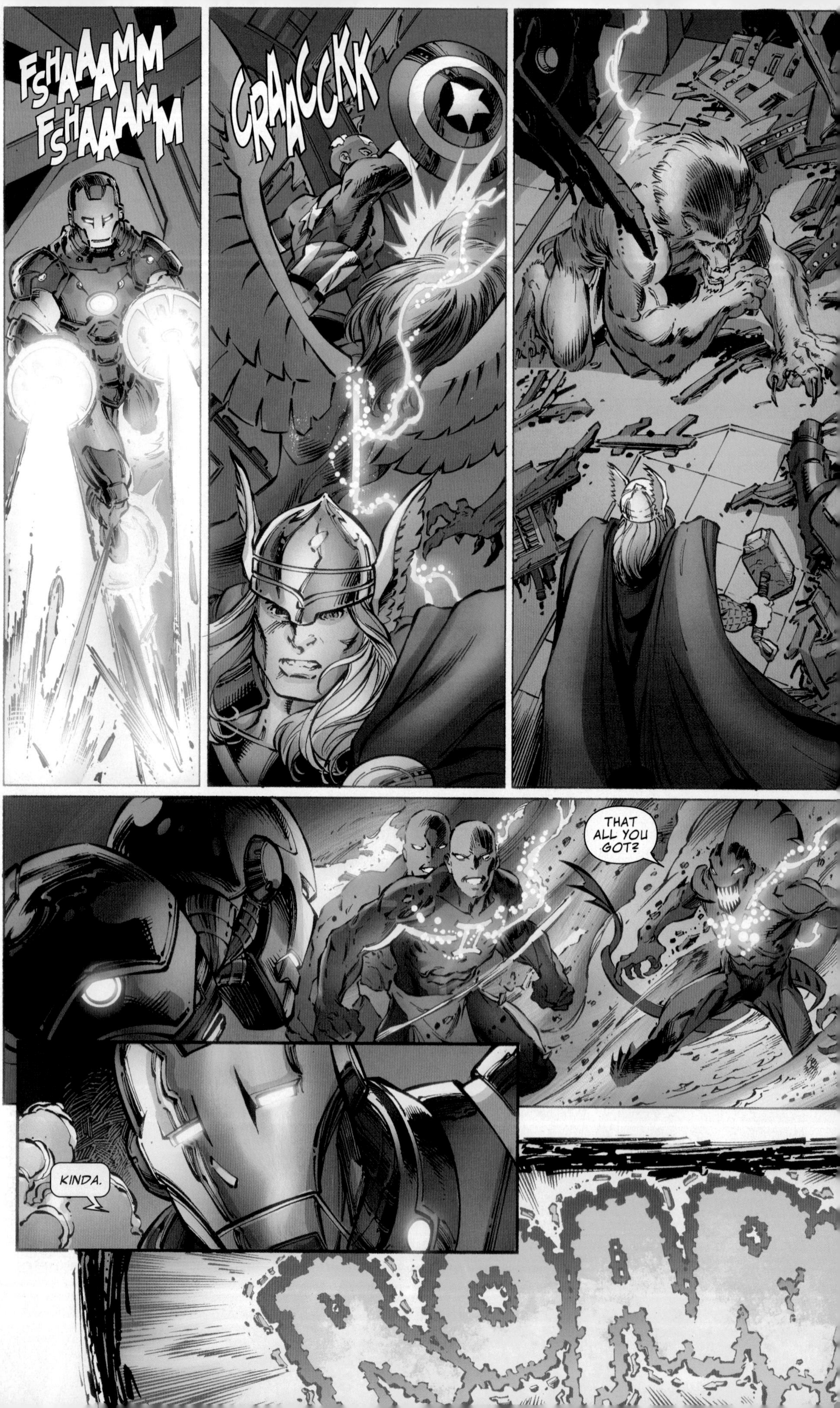
FSHAAAMM
FSHAAAMM
CRAACCKK
THAT ALL YOU GOT?
KINDA.

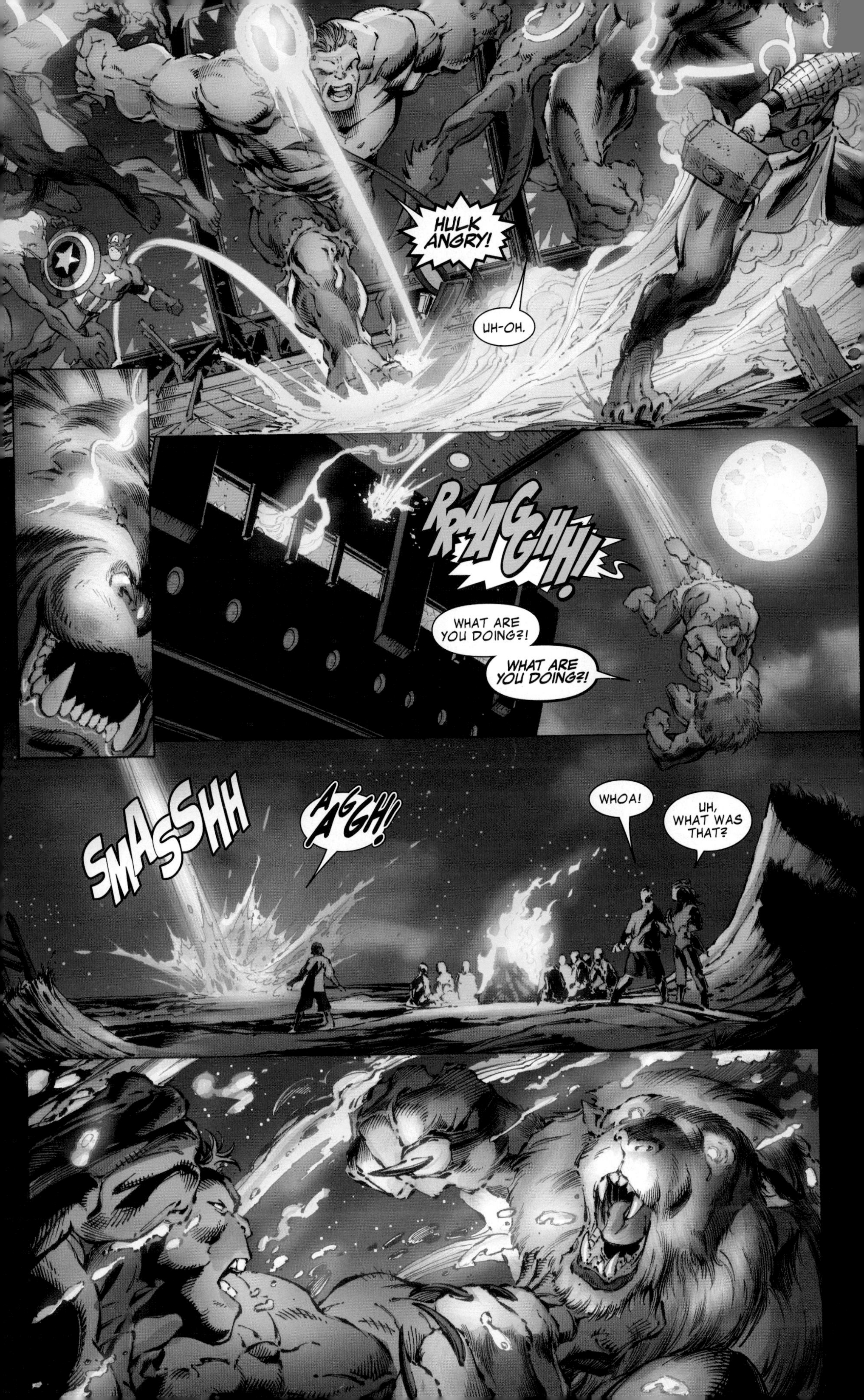
HULK ANGRY!
UH-OH.
RRAAGGHH!
WHAT ARE YOU DOING?!
WHAT ARE YOU DOING?!
SMASSHH
AAGH!
WHOA!
UH, WHAT WAS THAT?

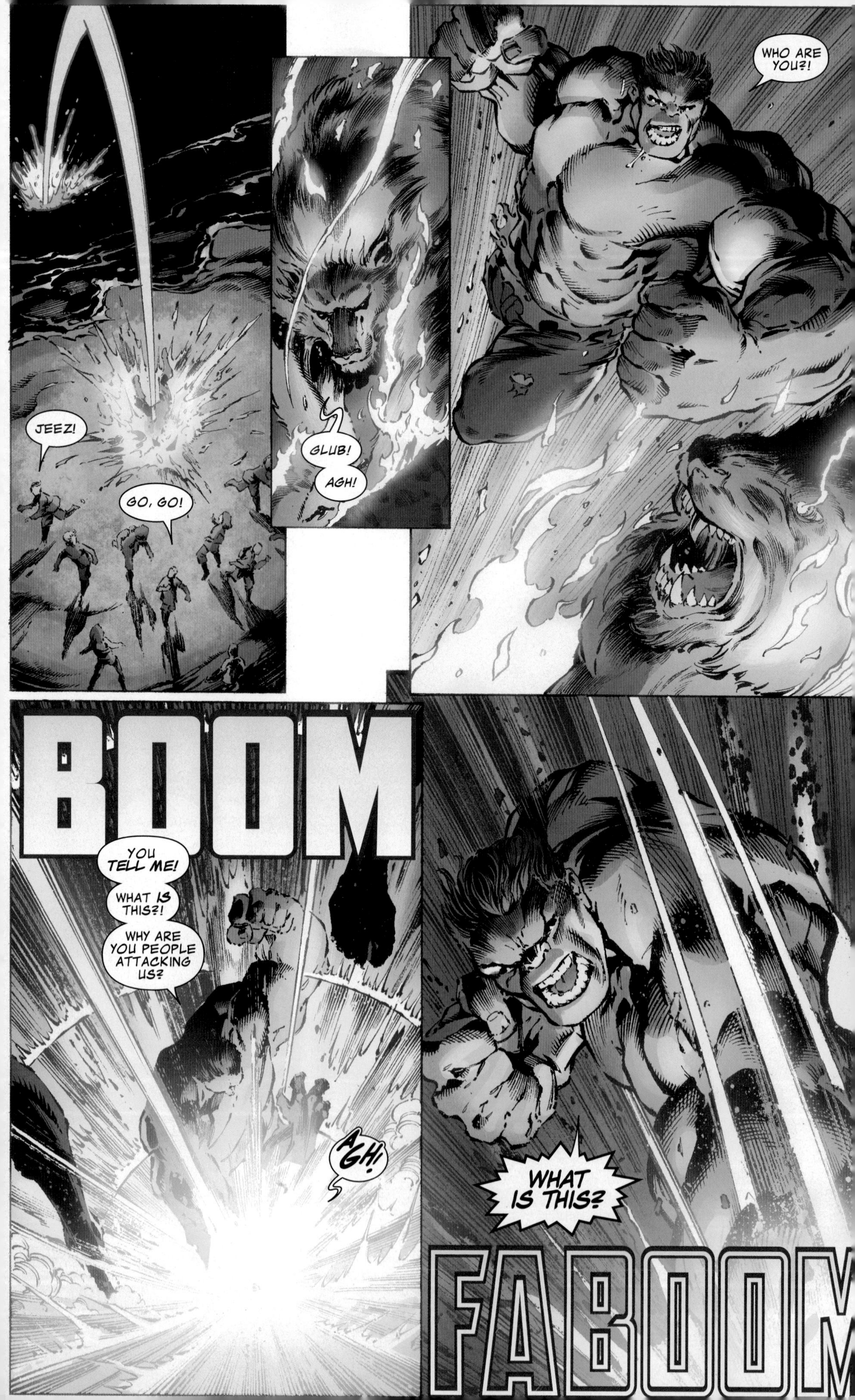
JEEZ!
GO, GO!
GLUB!
AGH!
WHO ARE YOU?!
BOOM
YOU TELL ME!
WHAT IS THIS?!
WHY ARE YOU PEOPLE ATTACKING US?
AGH!
WHAT IS THIS?
FABOOM

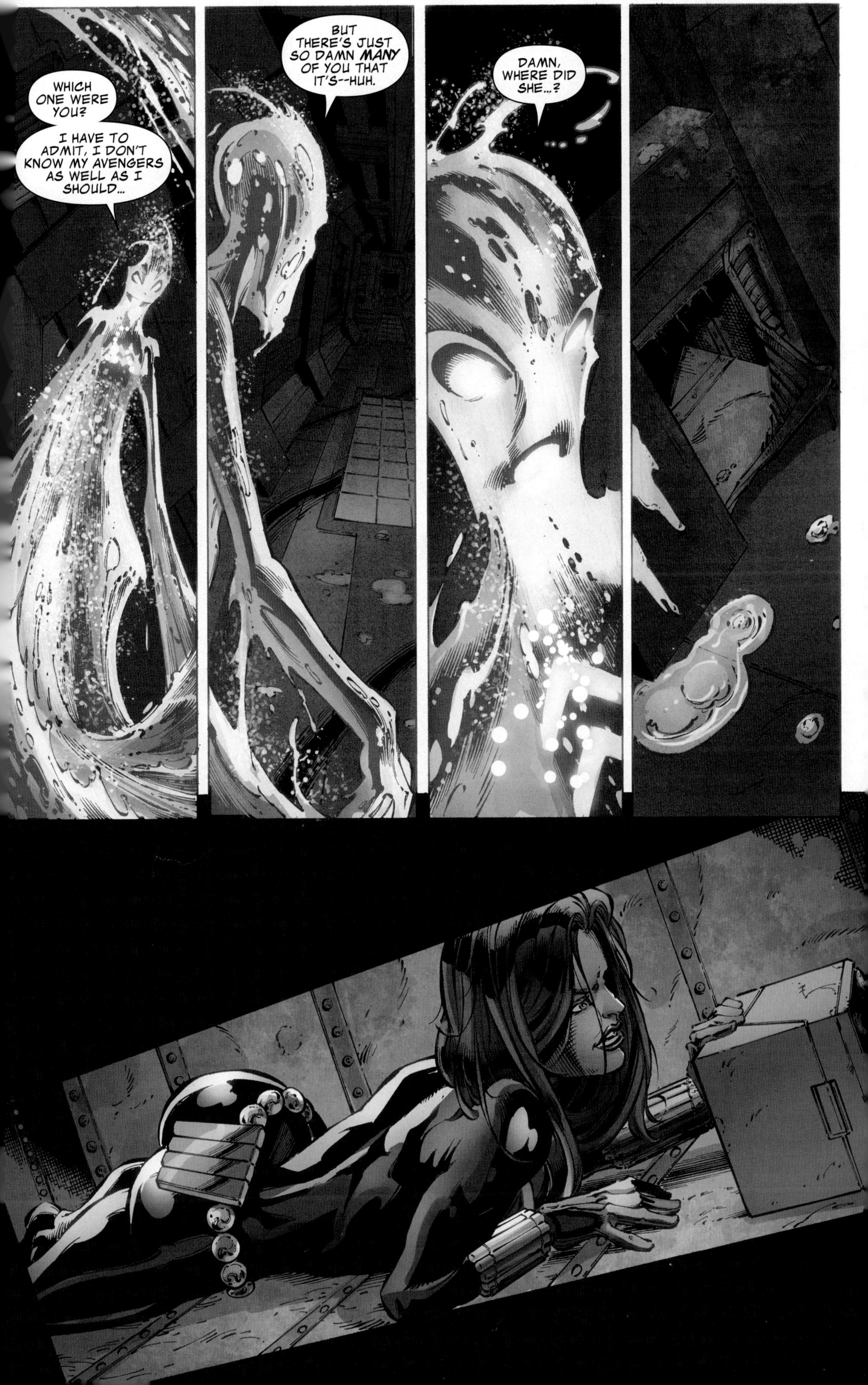
WHICH ONE WERE YOU?
I HAVE TO ADMIT, I DON'T KNOW MY AVENGERS AS WELL AS I SHOULD...
BUT THERE'S JUST SO DAMN MANY OF YOU THAT IT'S--HUH.
DAMN, WHERE DID SHE...?

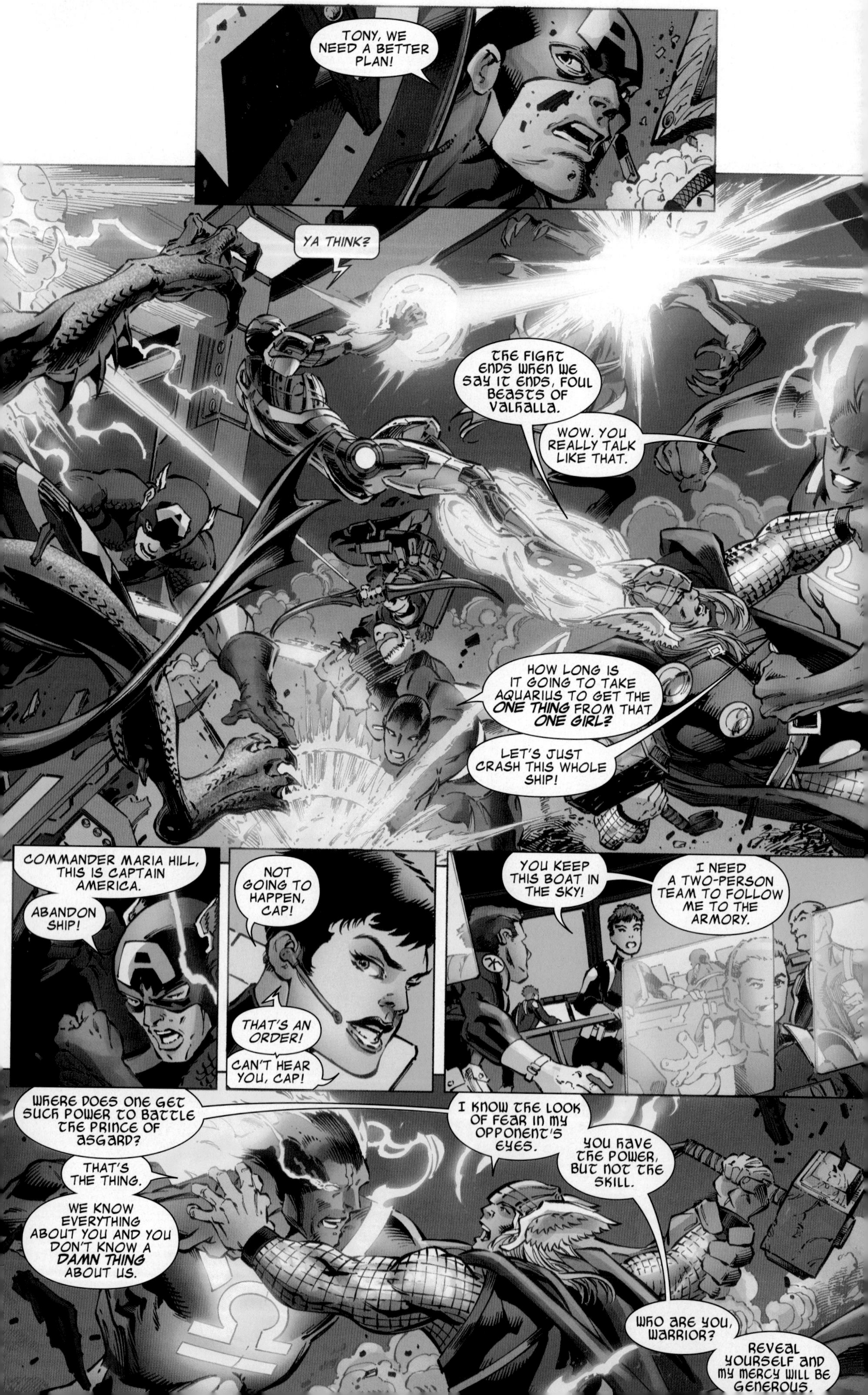
TONY, WE NEED A BETTER PLAN!
YA THINK?
THE FIGHT ENDS WHEN WE SAY IT ENDS, FOUL BEASTS OF VALHALLA.
WOW. YOU REALLY TALK LIKE THAT.
HOW LONG IS IT GOING TO TAKE AQUARIUS TO GET THE ONE THING FROM THAT ONE GIRL?
LET'S JUST CRASH THIS WHOLE SHIP!
COMMANDER MARIA HILL, THIS IS CAPTAIN AMERICA.
ABANDON SHIP!
NOT GOING TO HAPPEN, CAP!
THAT'S AN ORDER!
CAN'T HEAR YOU, CAP!
YOU KEEP THIS BOAT IN THE SKY!
I NEED A TWO-PERSON TEAM TO FOLLOW ME TO THE ARMORY.
WHERE DOES ONE GET SUCH POWER TO BATTLE THE PRINCE OF ASGARD?
THAT'S THE THING.
WE KNOW EVERYTHING ABOUT YOU AND YOU DON'T KNOW A DAMN THING ABOUT US.
I KNOW THE LOOK OF FEAR IN MY OPPONENT'S EYES.
YOU HAVE THE POWER, BUT NOT THE SKILL.
WHO ARE YOU, WARRIOR?
REVEAL YOURSELF AND MY MERCY WILL BE GENEROUS.

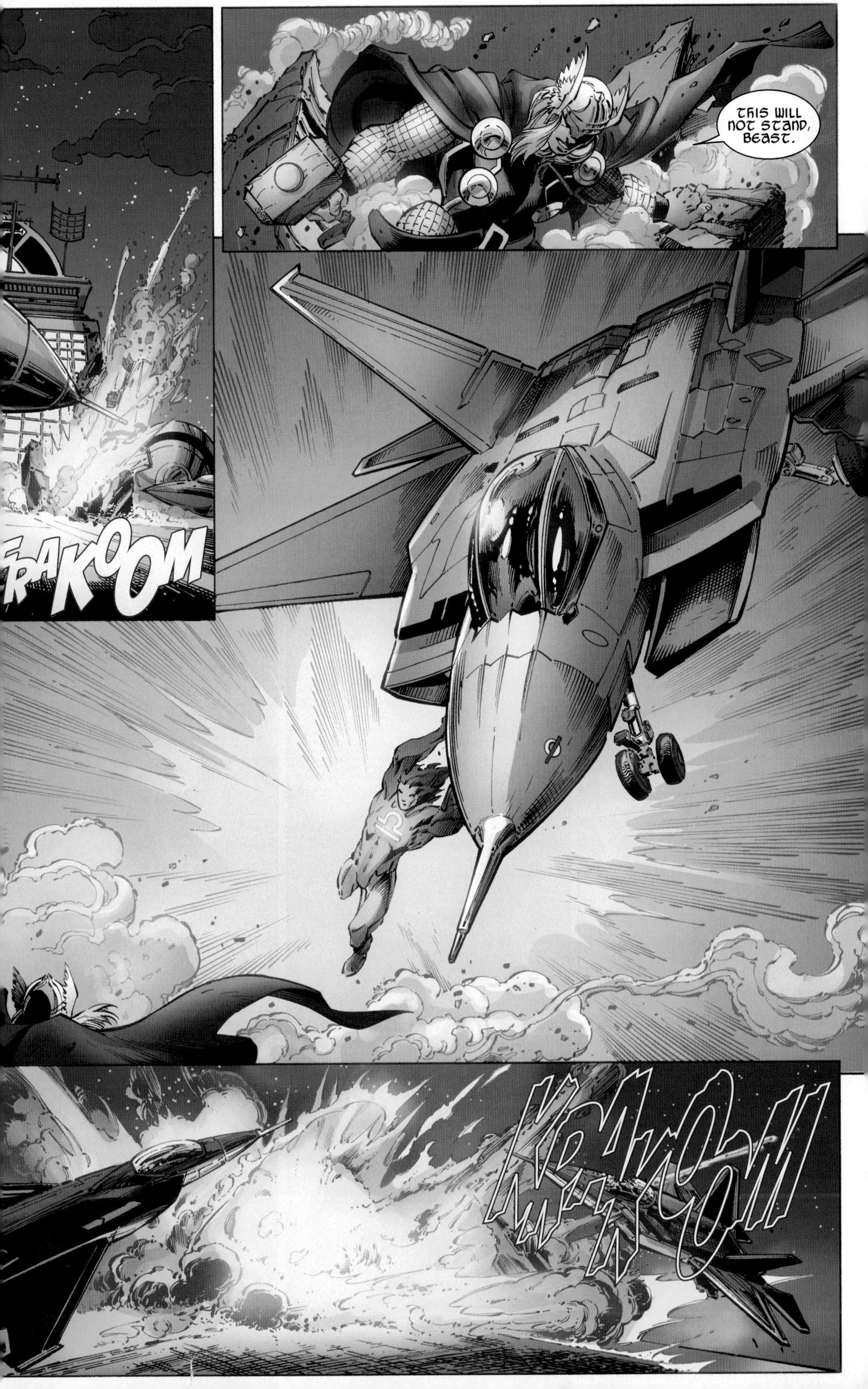
THIS WILL NOT STAND, BEAST.

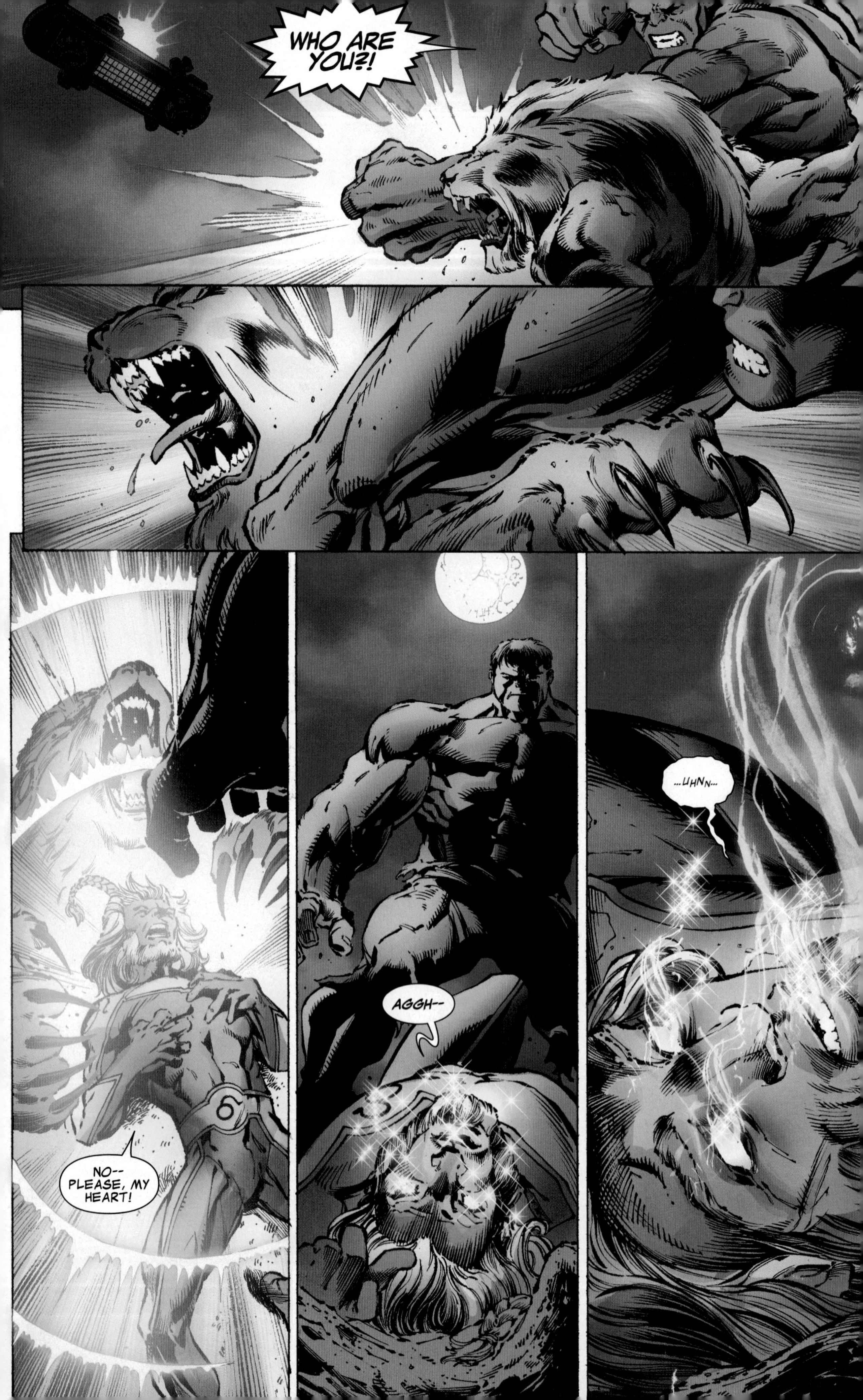
WHO ARE YOU?!
NO-- PLEASE, MY HEART!
AGGH--
...UHNN...

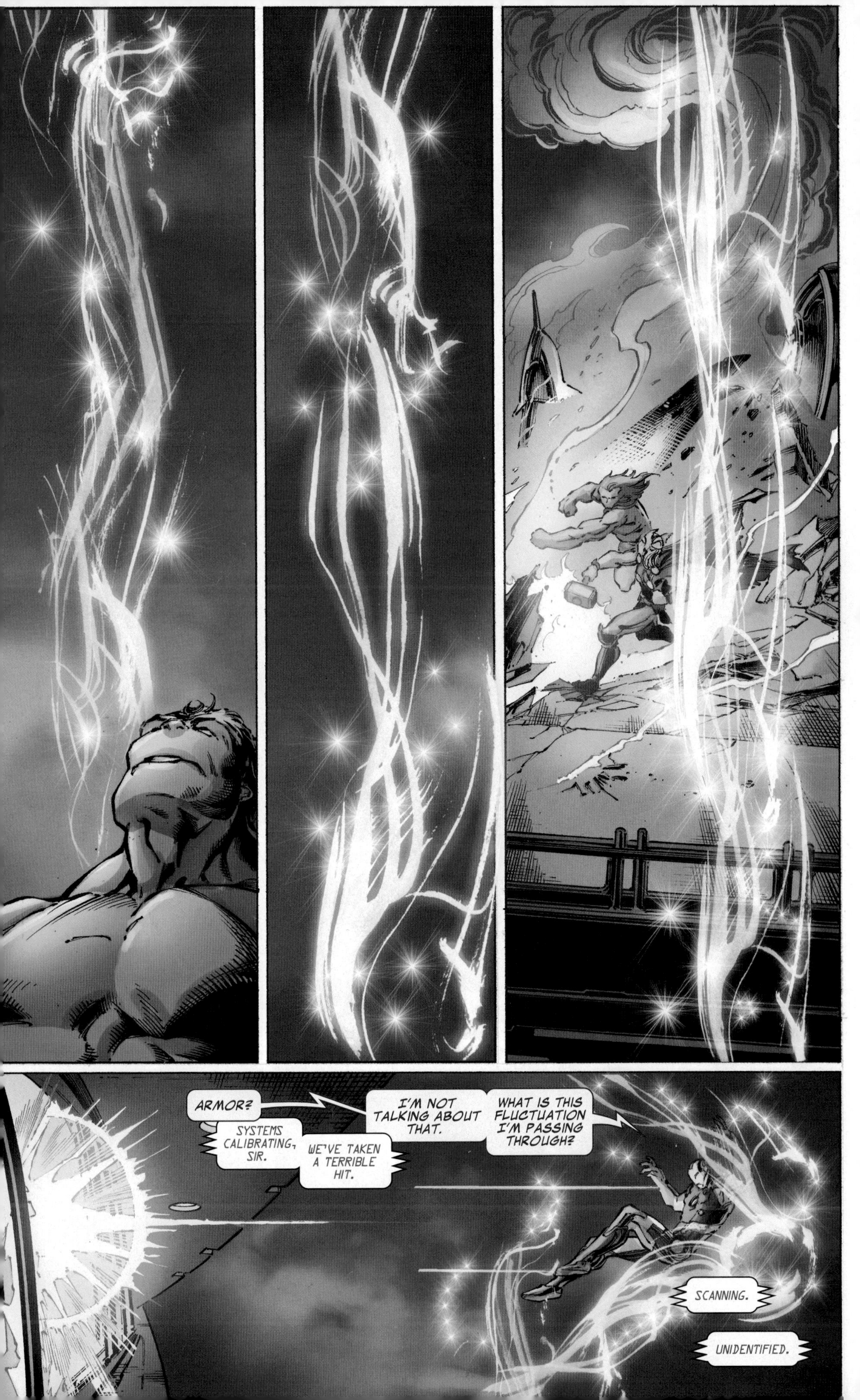
ARMOR?
SYSTEMS CALIBRATING, SIR.
WE'VE TAKEN A TERRIBLE HIT.
I'M NOT TALKING ABOUT THAT.
WHAT IS THIS FLUCTUATION I'M PASSING THROUGH?
SCANNING.
UNIDENTIFIED.

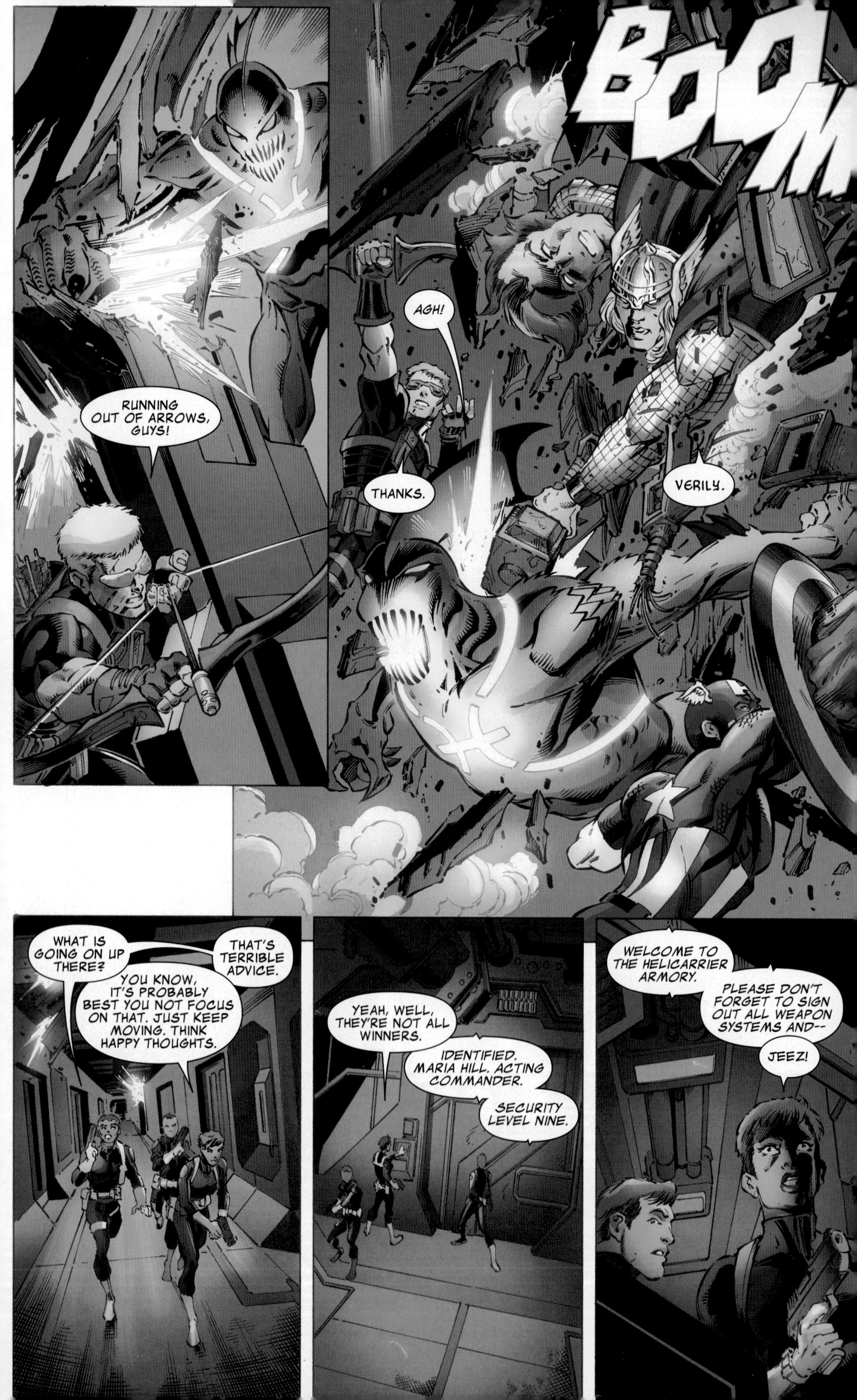
BOOM
RUNNING OUT OF ARROWS, GUYS!
AGH!
THANKS.
VERILY.
WHAT IS GOING ON UP THERE?
YOU KNOW, IT'S PROBABLY BEST YOU NOT FOCUS ON THAT. JUST KEEP MOVING. THINK HAPPY THOUGHTS.
THAT'S TERRIBLE ADVICE.
YEAH, WELL, THEY'RE NOT ALL WINNERS.
IDENTIFIED. MARIA HILL. ACTING COMMANDER.
SECURITY LEVEL NINE.
WELCOME TO THE HELICARRIER ARMORY.
PLEASE DON'T FORGET TO SIGN OUT ALL WEAPON SYSTEMS AND--
JEEZ!

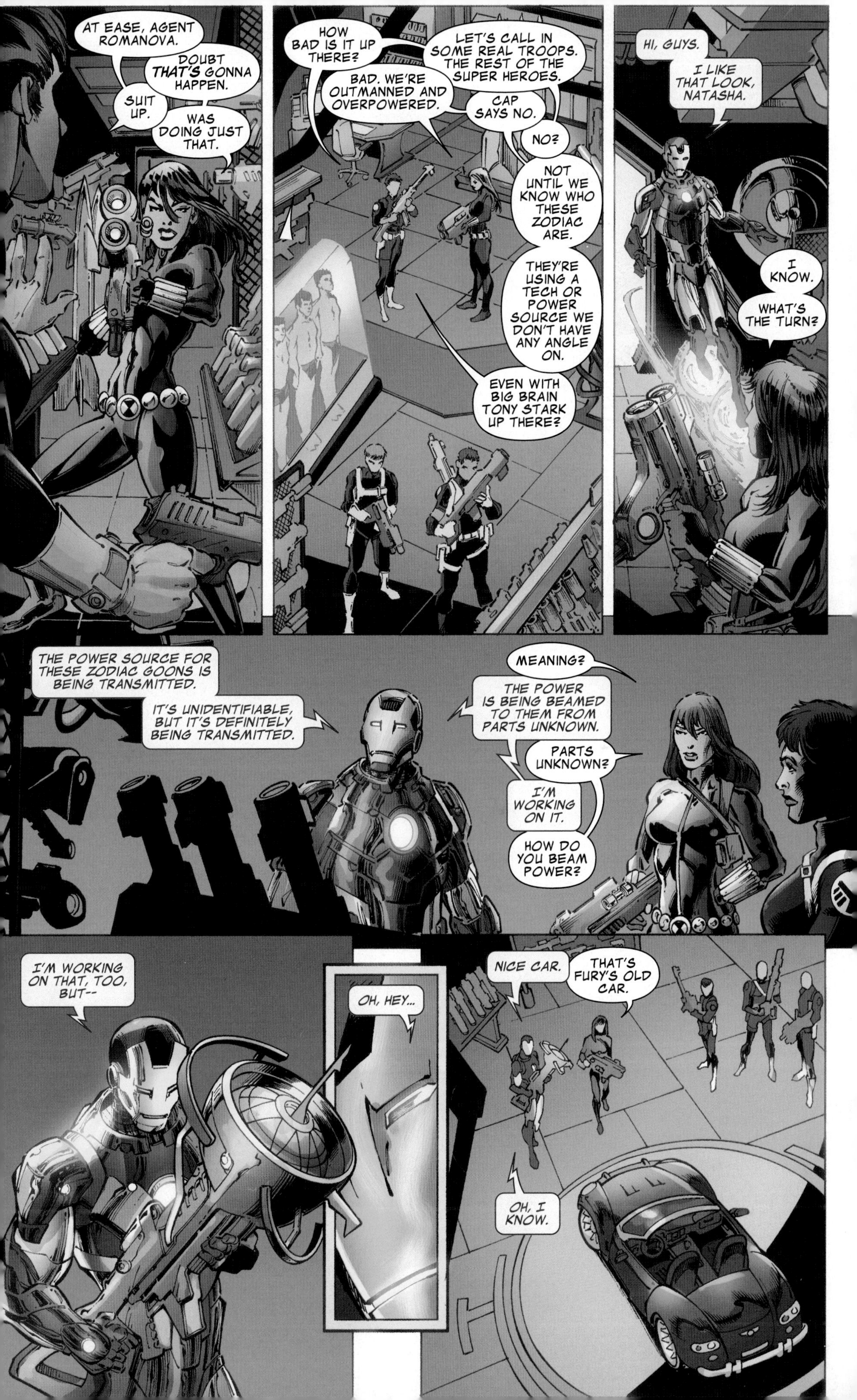
AT EASE, AGENT ROMANOVA.
DOUBT THAT'S GONNA HAPPEN.
SUIT UP.
WAS DOING JUST THAT.
HOW BAD IS IT UP THERE?
LET'S CALL IN SOME REAL TROOPS. THE REST OF THE SUPER HEROES.
BAD. WE'RE OUTMANNED AND OVERPOWERED.
CAP SAYS NO.
NO?
NOT UNTIL WE KNOW WHO THESE ZODIAC ARE.
THEY'RE USING A TECH OR POWER SOURCE WE DON'T HAVE ANY ANGLE ON.
EVEN WITH BIG BRAIN TONY STARK UP THERE?
HI, GUYS.
I LIKE THAT LOOK, NATASHA.
I KNOW.
WHAT'S THE TURN?
THE POWER SOURCE FOR THESE ZODIAC GOONS IS BEING TRANSMITTED.
IT'S UNIDENTIFIABLE, BUT IT'S DEFINITELY BEING TRANSMITTED.
MEANING?
THE POWER IS BEING BEAMED TO THEM FROM PARTS UNKNOWN.
PARTS UNKNOWN?
I'M WORKING ON IT.
HOW DO YOU BEAM POWER?
I'M WORKING ON THAT, TOO, BUT--
OH, HEY...
NICE CAR.
THAT'S FURY'S OLD CAR.
OH, I KNOW.

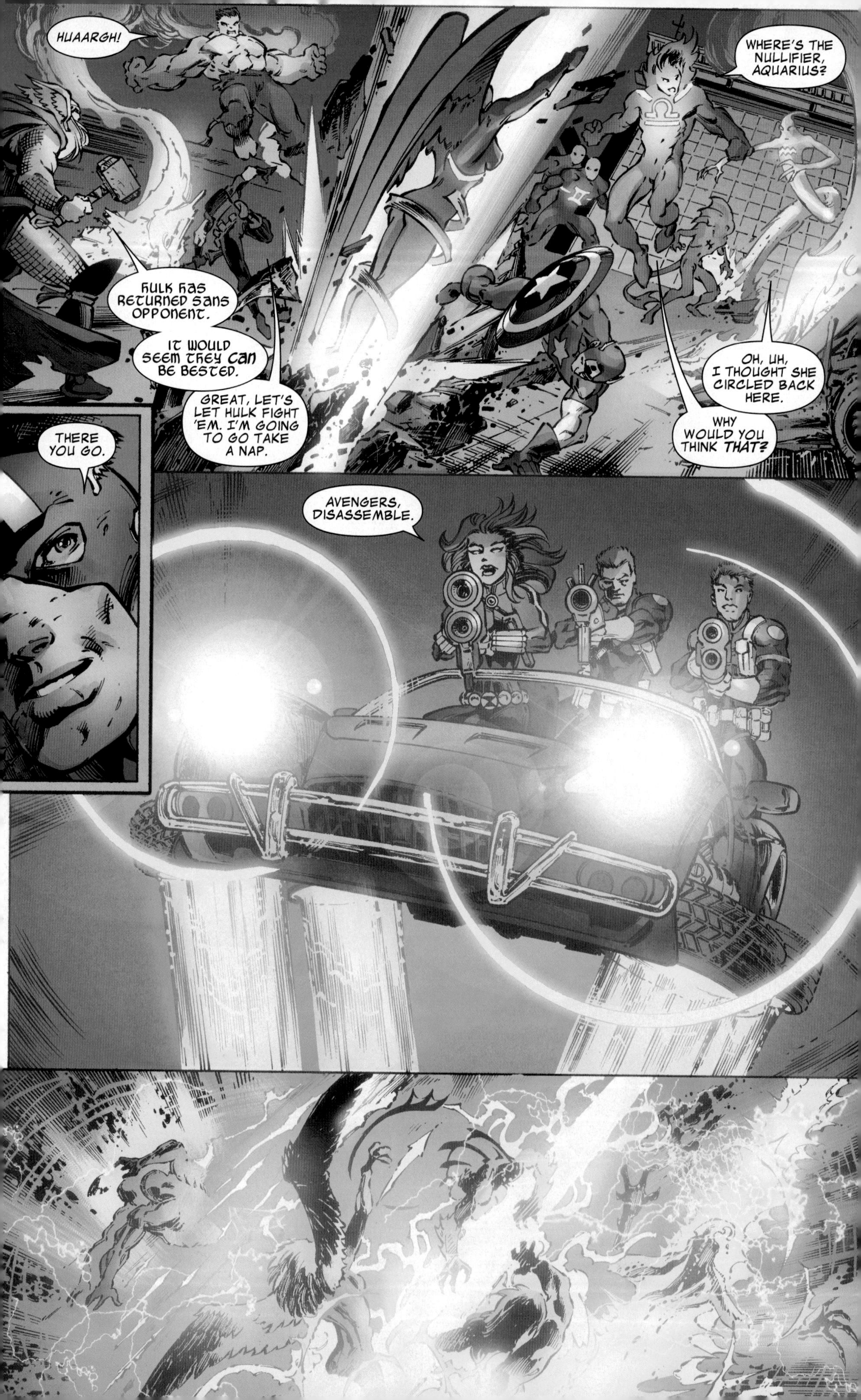
HUAARGH!
WHERE'S THE NULLIFIER, AQUARIUS?
HULK HAS RETURNED SANS OPPONENT.
IT WOULD SEEM THEY CAN BE BESTED.
GREAT, LET'S LET HULK FIGHT 'EM. I'M GOING TO GO TAKE A NAP.
OH, UH, I THOUGHT SHE CIRCLED BACK HERE.
WHY WOULD YOU THINK THAT?
THERE YOU GO.
AVENGERS, DISASSEMBLE.

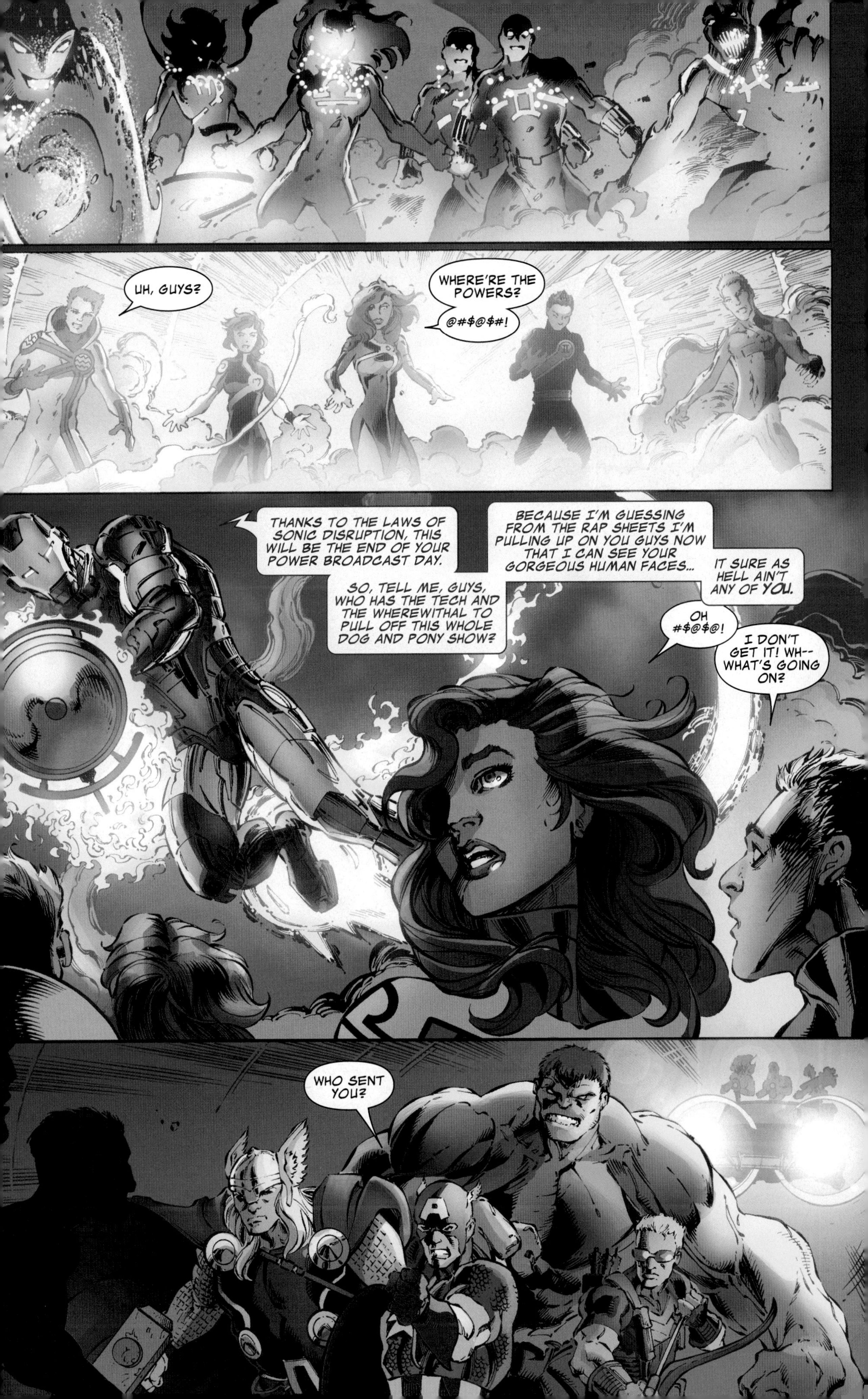
UH, GUYS?
WHERE'RE THE POWERS?
@#$@$#!
THANKS TO THE LAWS OF SONIC DISRUPTION, THIS WILL BE THE END OF YOUR POWER BROADCAST DAY.
SO, TELL ME, GUYS, WHO HAS THE TECH AND THE WHEREWITHAL TO PULL OFF THIS WHOLE DOG AND PONY SHOW?
BECAUSE I'M GUESSING FROM THE RAP SHEETS I'M PULLING UP ON YOU GUYS NOW THAT I CAN SEE YOUR GORGEOUS HUMAN FACES...
IT SURE AS HELL AIN'T ANY OF YOU.
OH #$@$@!
I DON'T GET IT! WH-- WHAT'S GOING ON?
WHO SENT YOU?

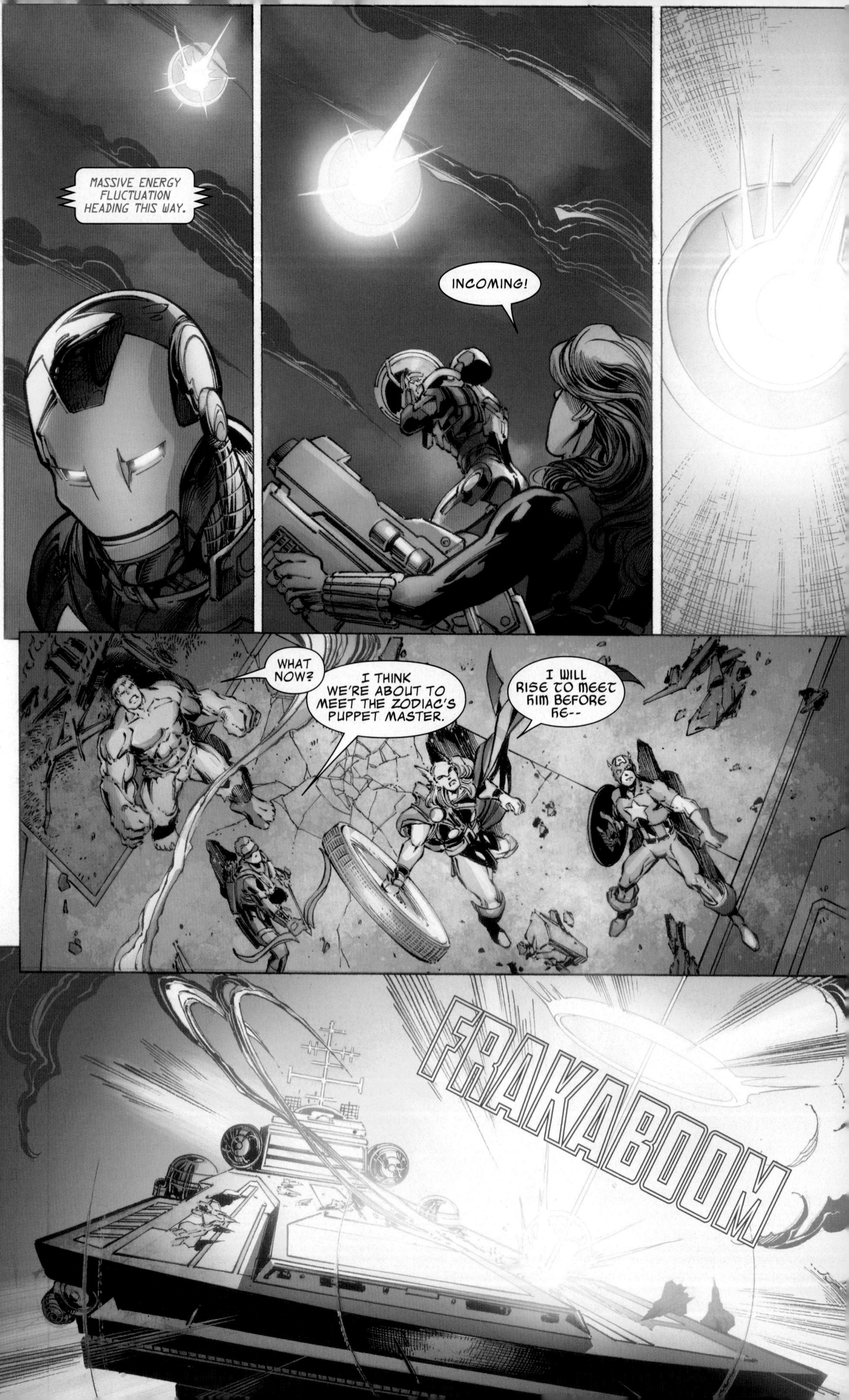
MASSIVE ENERGY FLUCTUATION HEADING THIS WAY.
INCOMING!
WHAT NOW?
I THINK WE'RE ABOUT TO MEET THE ZODIAC'S PUPPET MASTER.
I WILL RISE TO MEET HIM BEFORE HE--
FRAKABOOM

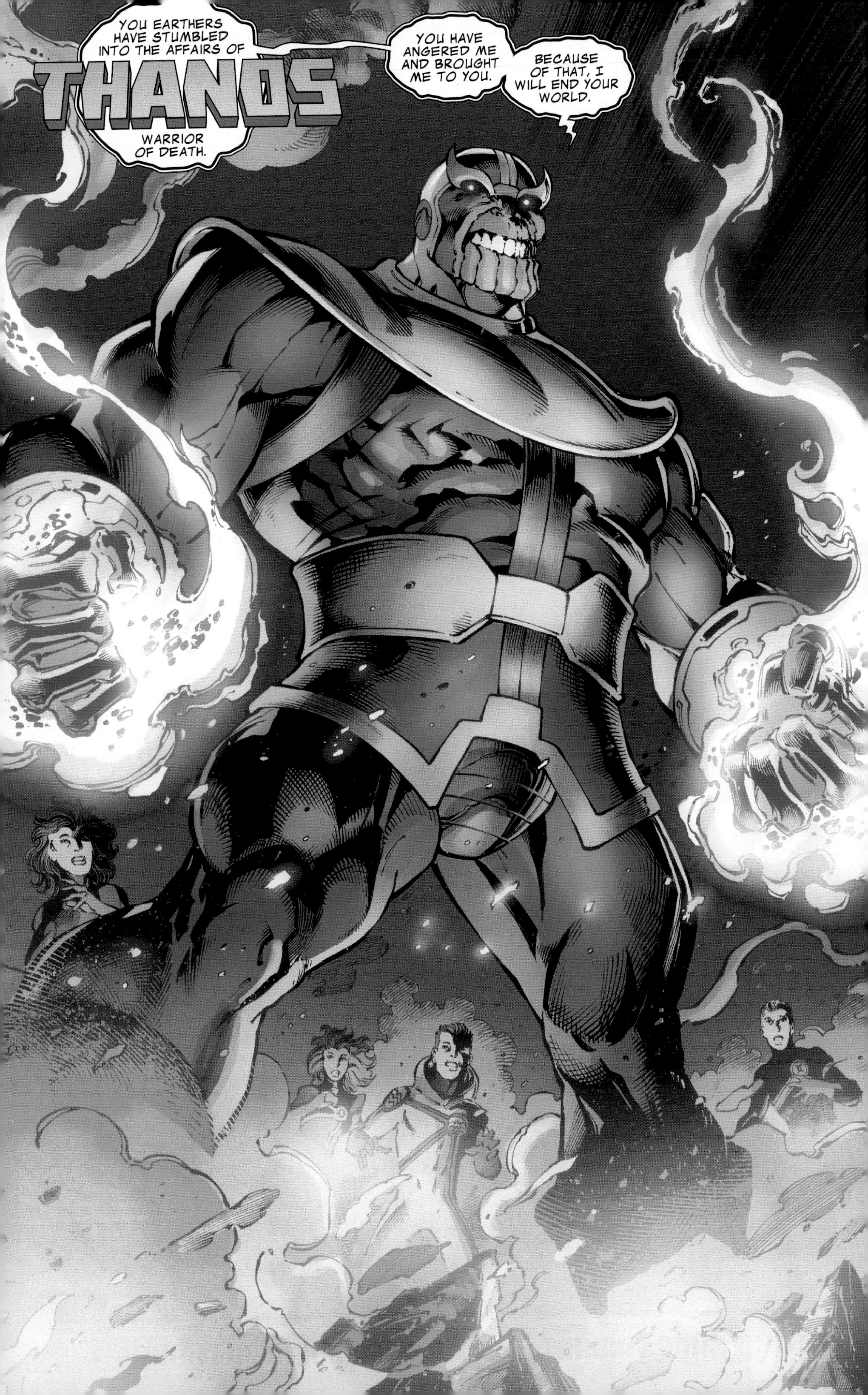
YOU EARTHERS HAVE STUMBLED INTO THE AFFAIRS OF
THANOS
WARRIOR OF DEATH.
YOU HAVE ANGERED ME AND BROUGHT ME TO YOU.
BECAUSE OF THAT, I WILL END YOUR WORLD.

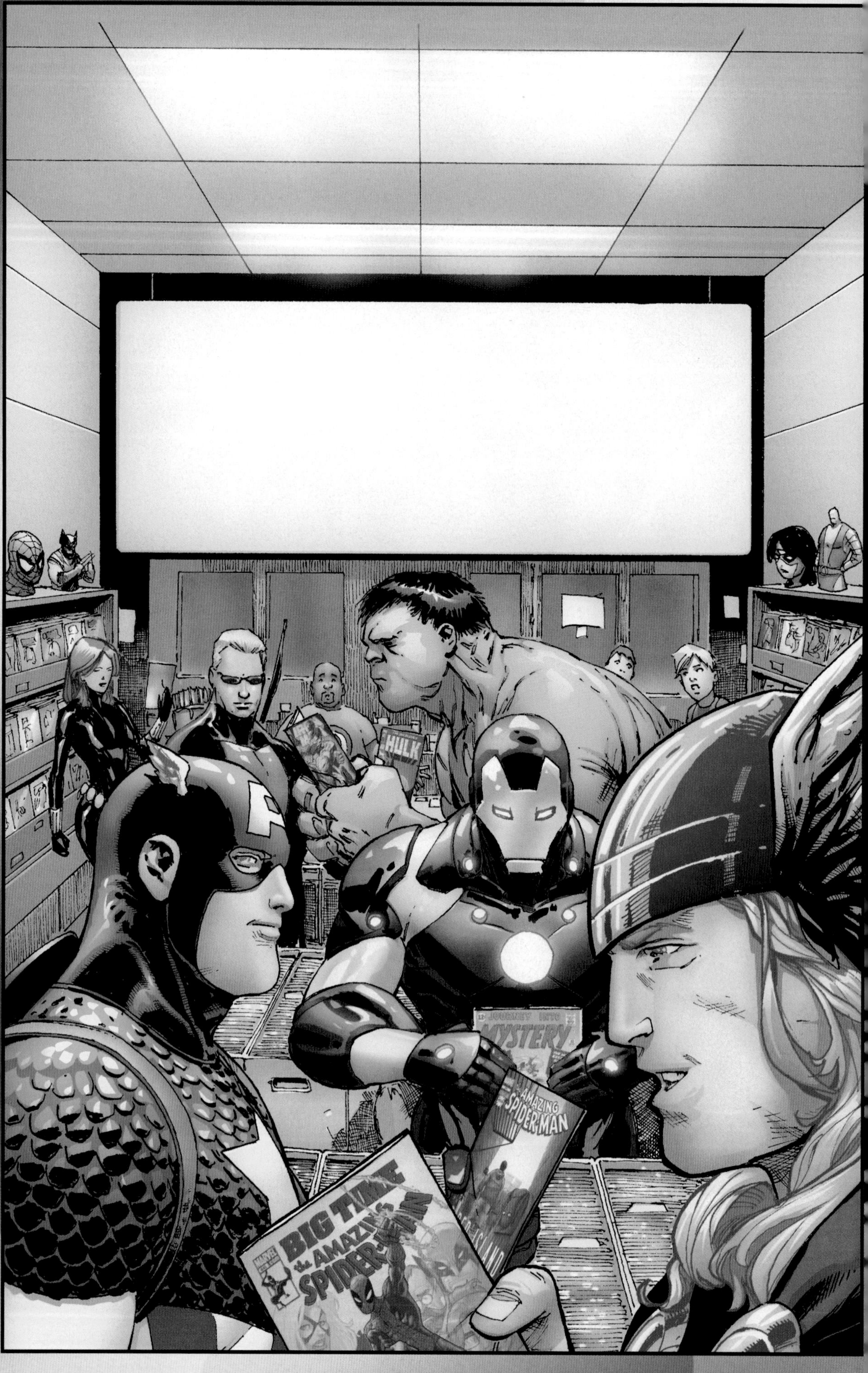
HULK
JOURNEY INTO MYSTERY
AMAZING SPIDER-MAN
BIG TIME
the AMAZING SPIDER-MAN

#1 COMIC SHOP VARIANT BY KOI PHAM & EDGAR DELGADO

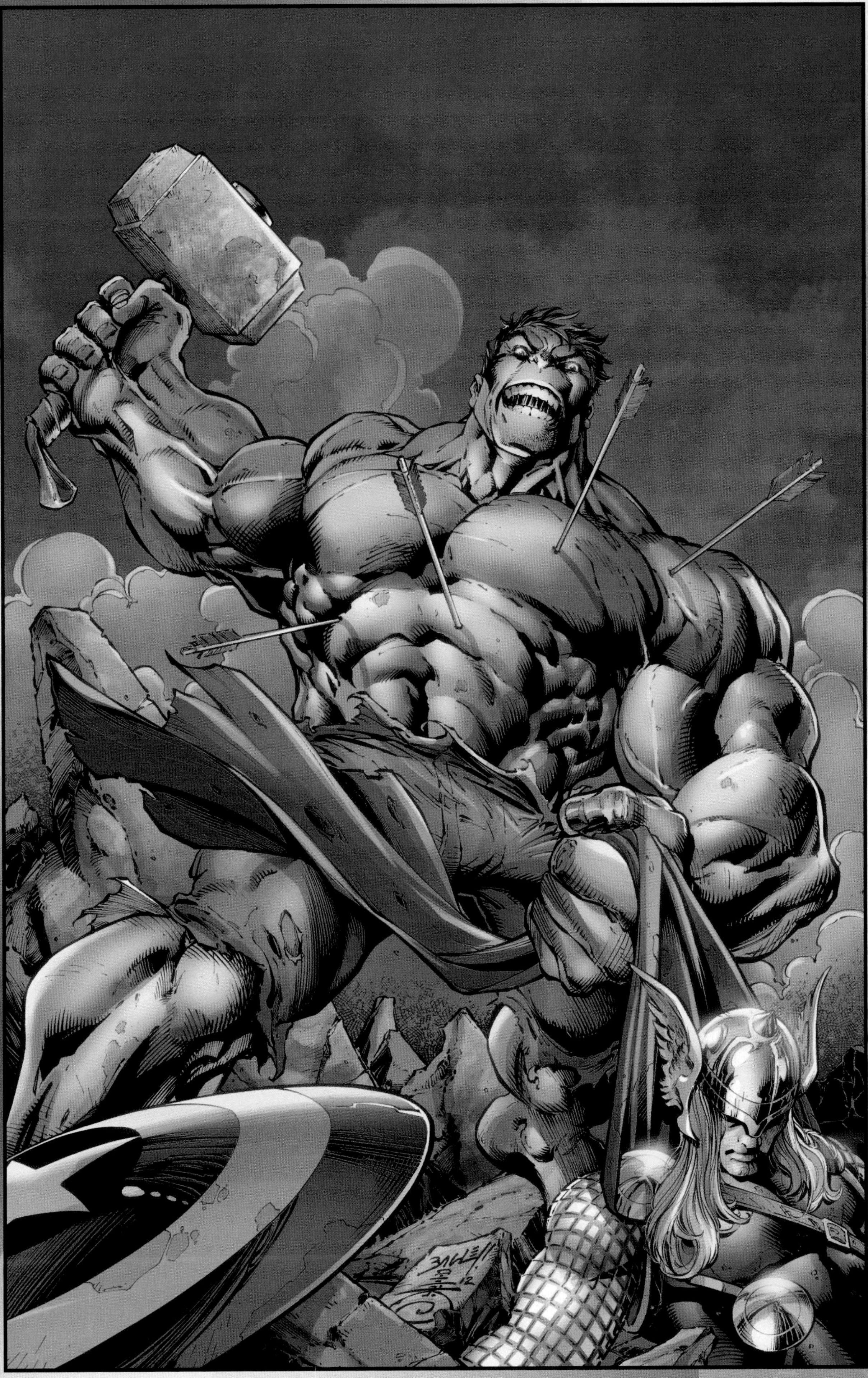

FOUR

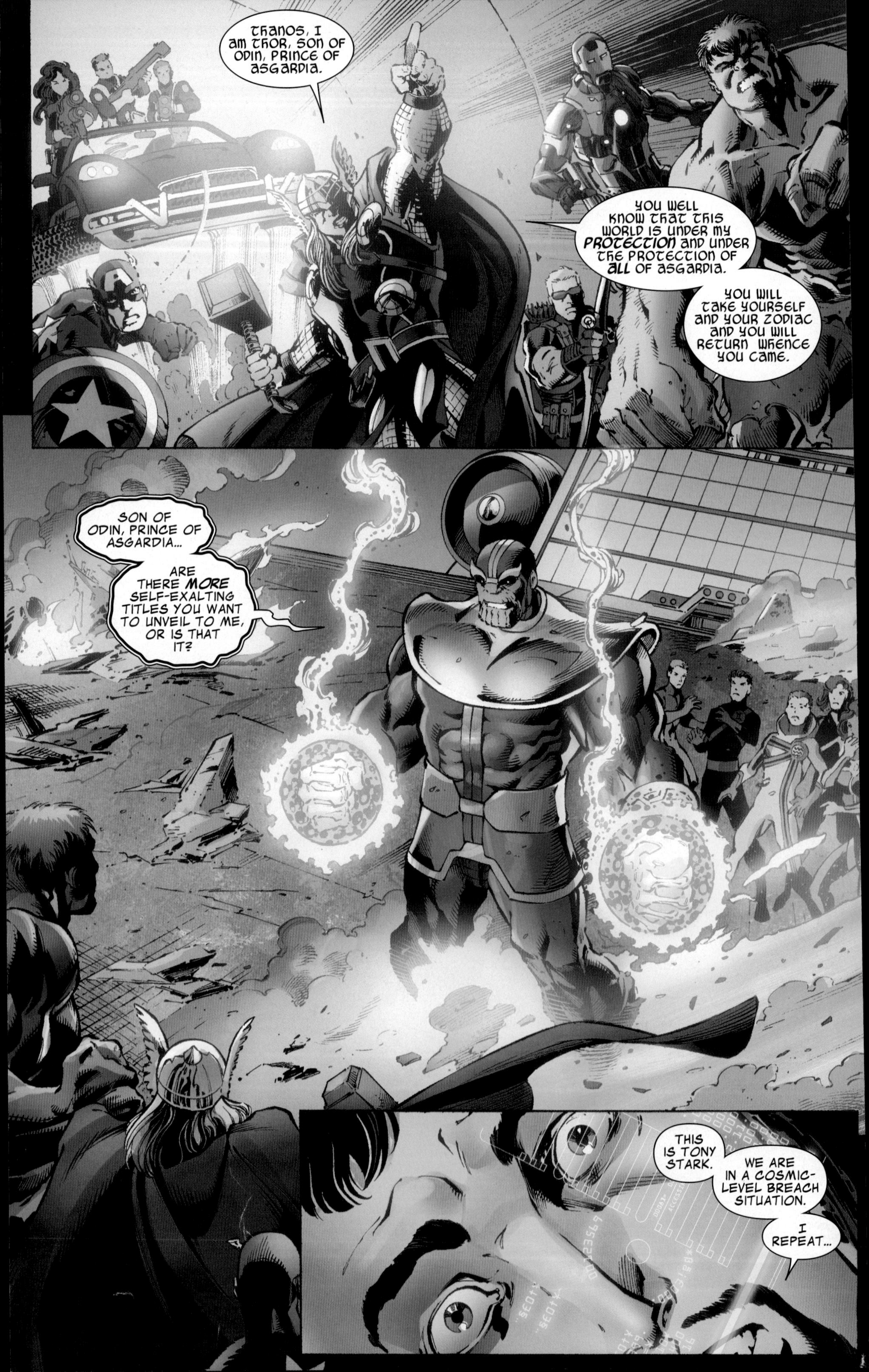
THANOS, I AM THOR, SON OF ODIN, PRINCE OF ASGARDIA.
YOU WELL KNOW THAT THIS WORLD IS UNDER MY PROTECTION AND UNDER THE PROTECTION OF ALL OF ASGARDIA.
YOU WILL TAKE YOURSELF AND YOUR ZODIAC AND YOU WILL RETURN WHENCE YOU CAME.
SON OF ODIN, PRINCE OF ASGARDIA...
ARE THERE MORE SELF-EXALTING TITLES YOU WANT TO UNVEIL TO ME, OR IS THAT IT?
THIS IS TONY STARK.
WE ARE IN A COSMIC-LEVEL BREACH SITUATION.
I REPEAT...

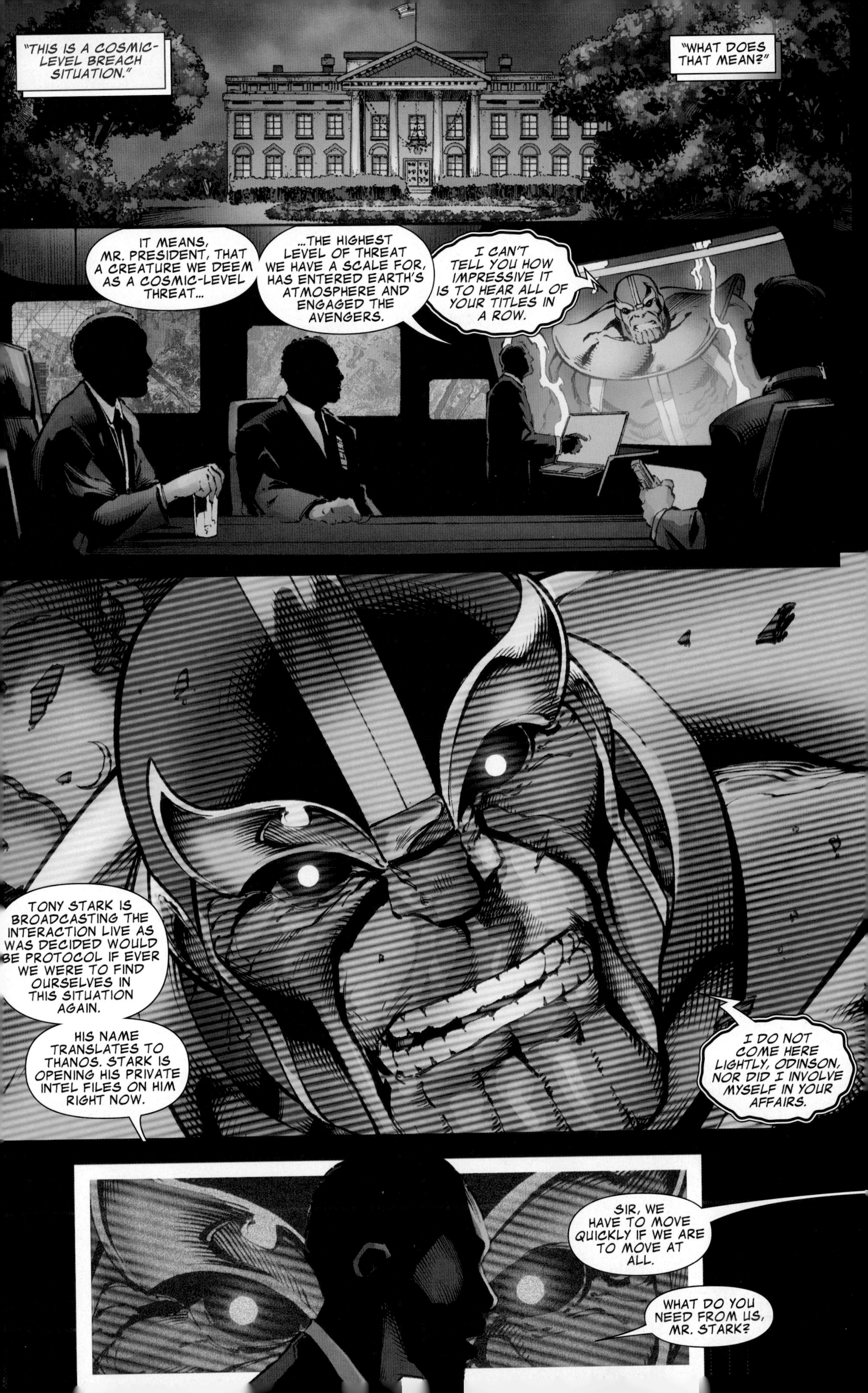
"THIS IS A COSMIC-LEVEL BREACH SITUATION."
"WHAT DOES THAT MEAN?"
IT MEANS, MR. PRESIDENT, THAT A CREATURE WE DEEM AS A COSMIC-LEVEL THREAT...
...THE HIGHEST LEVEL OF THREAT WE HAVE A SCALE FOR, HAS ENTERED EARTH'S ATMOSPHERE AND ENGAGED THE AVENGERS.
I CAN'T TELL YOU HOW IMPRESSIVE IT IS TO HEAR ALL OF YOUR TITLES IN A ROW.
TONY STARK IS BROADCASTING THE INTERACTION LIVE AS WAS DECIDED WOULD BE PROTOCOL IF EVER WE WERE TO FIND OURSELVES IN THIS SITUATION AGAIN.
HIS NAME TRANSLATES TO THANOS. STARK IS OPENING HIS PRIVATE INTEL FILES ON HIM RIGHT NOW.
I DO NOT COME HERE LIGHTLY, ODINSON, NOR DID I INVOLVE MYSELF IN YOUR AFFAIRS.
SIR, WE HAVE TO MOVE QUICKLY IF WE ARE TO MOVE AT ALL.
WHAT DO YOU NEED FROM US, MR. STARK?

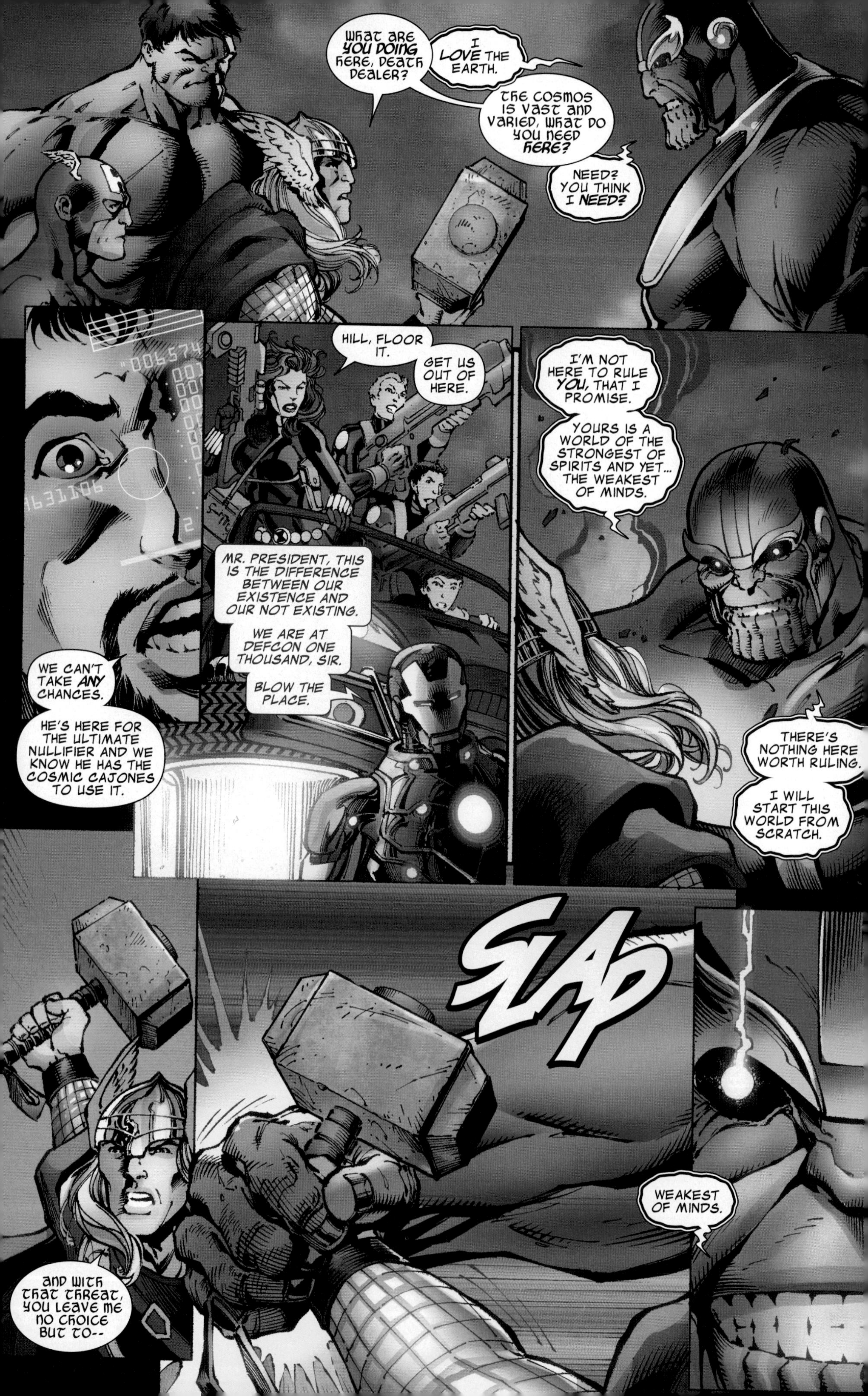

WHAT ARE YOU DOING HERE, DEATH DEALER?
I LOVE THE EARTH.
THE COSMOS IS VAST AND VARIED, WHAT DO YOU NEED HERE?
NEED? YOU THINK I NEED?
HILL, FLOOR IT.
GET US OUT OF HERE.
I'M NOT HERE TO RULE YOU, THAT I PROMISE.
YOURS IS A WORLD OF THE STRONGEST OF SPIRITS AND YET... THE WEAKEST OF MINDS.
MR. PRESIDENT, THIS IS THE DIFFERENCE BETWEEN OUR EXISTENCE AND OUR NOT EXISTING.
WE ARE AT DEFCON ONE THOUSAND, SIR.
BLOW THE PLACE.
WE CAN'T TAKE ANY CHANCES.
HE'S HERE FOR THE ULTIMATE NULLIFIER AND WE KNOW HE HAS THE COSMIC CAJONES TO USE IT.
THERE'S NOTHING HERE WORTH RULING.
I WILL START THIS WORLD FROM SCRATCH.
SLAP
WEAKEST OF MINDS.
AND WITH THAT THREAT, YOU LEAVE ME NO CHOICE BUT TO--

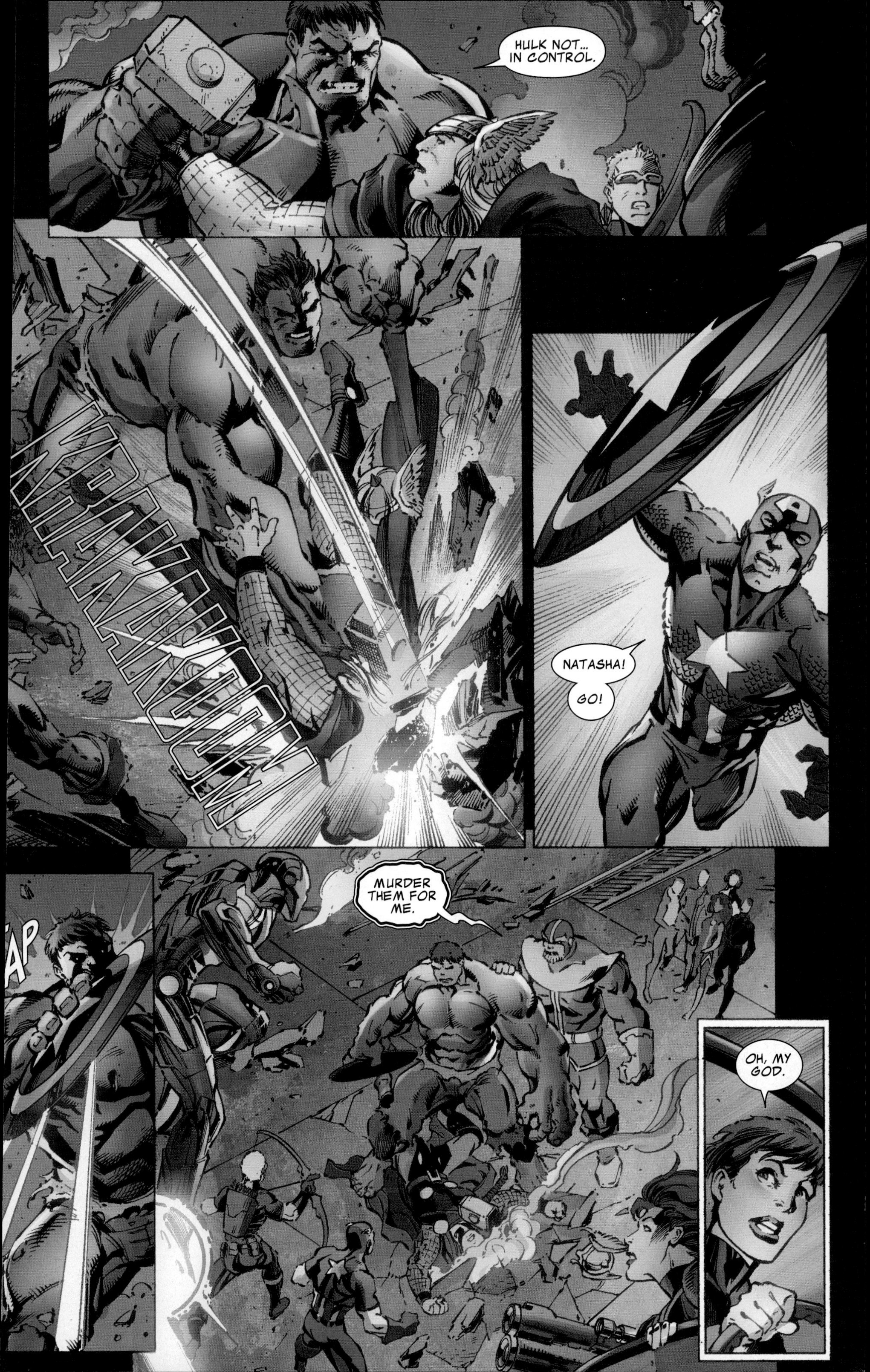
HULK NOT... IN CONTROL.
NATASHA!
GO!
MURDER THEM FOR ME.
OH, MY GOD.

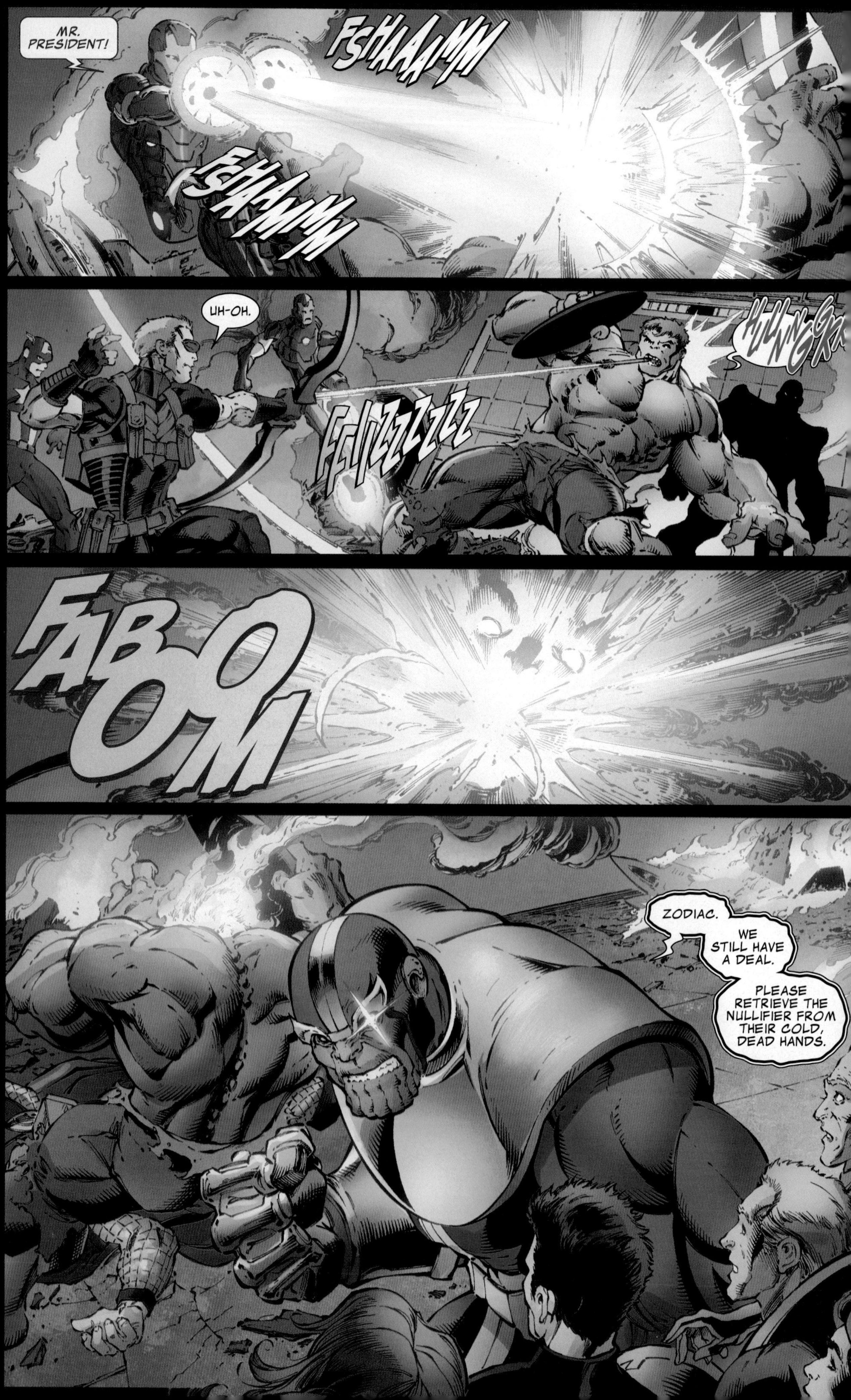
MR. PRESIDENT!
FSHAAAMM
FSHAAMMM
UH-OH.
HUUNNGRR
FFTZZZZZZ
FABOOM
ZODIAC.
WE STILL HAVE A DEAL.
PLEASE RETRIEVE THE NULLIFIER FROM THEIR COLD, DEAD HANDS.

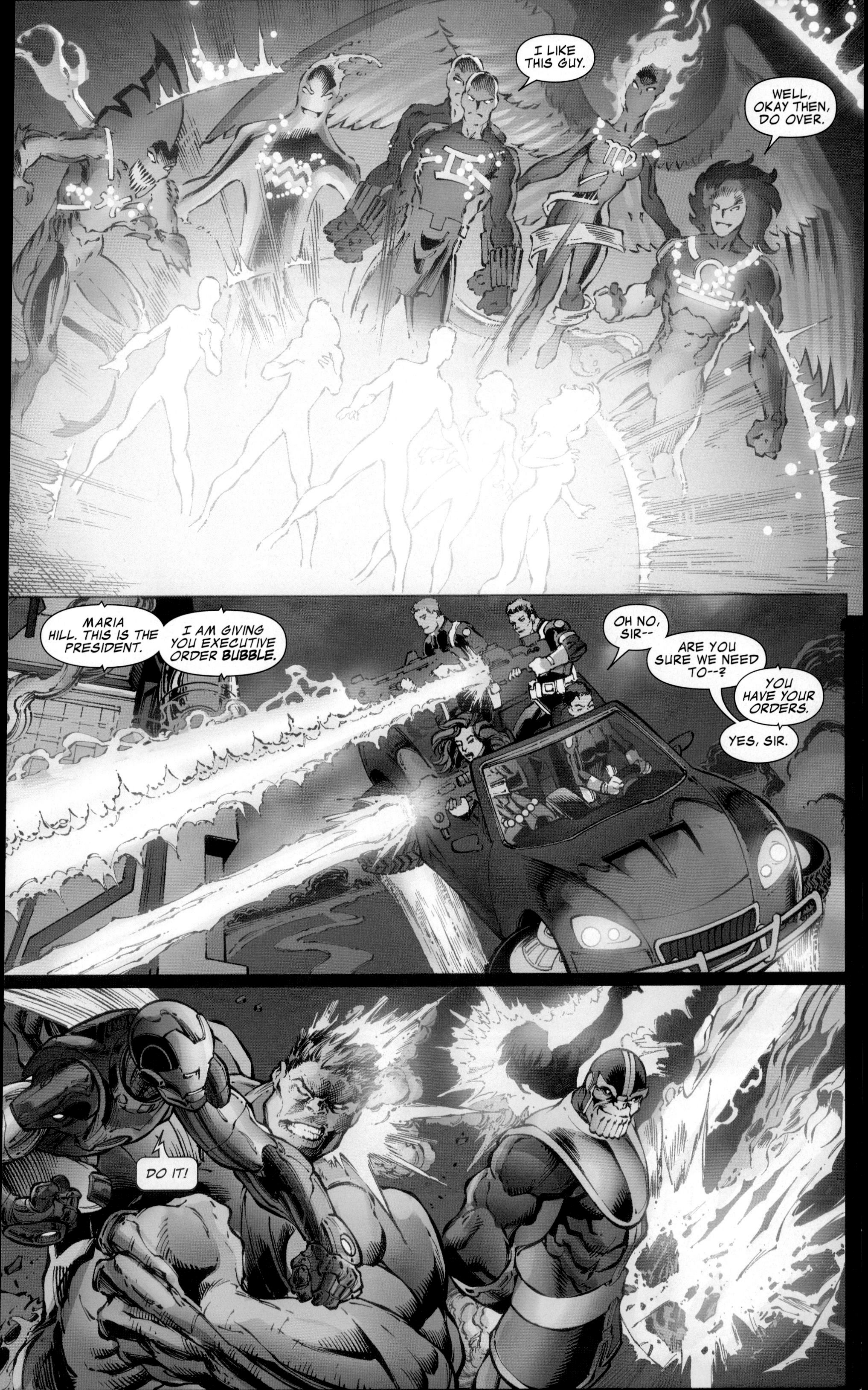
I LIKE THIS GUY.
WELL, OKAY THEN, DO OVER.
MARIA HILL. THIS IS THE PRESIDENT.
I AM GIVING YOU EXECUTIVE ORDER BUBBLE.
OH NO, SIR--
ARE YOU SURE WE NEED TO--?
YOU HAVE YOUR ORDERS.
YES, SIR.
DO IT!

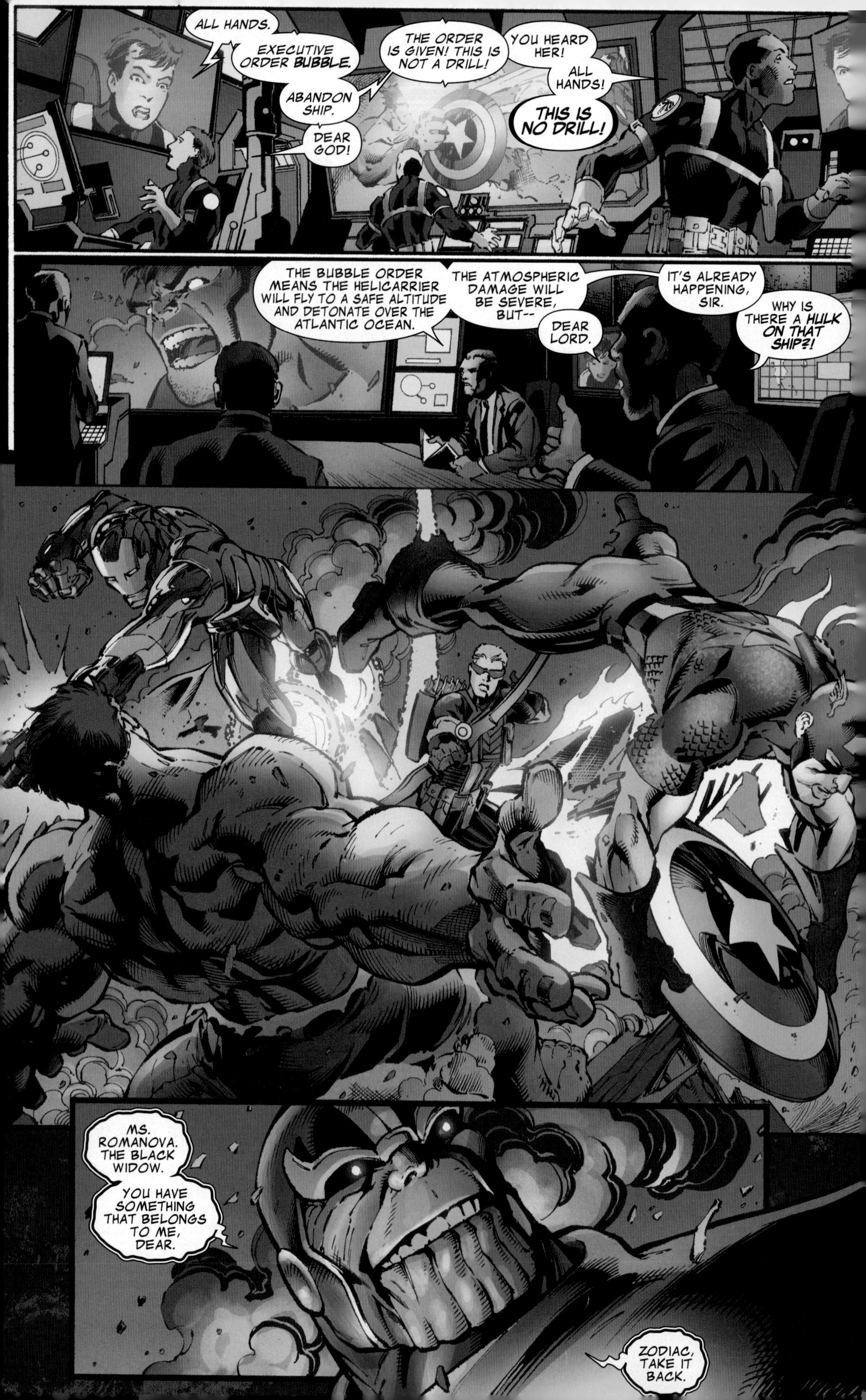
ALL HANDS.
EXECUTIVE ORDER BUBBLE.
ABANDON SHIP.
DEAR GOD!
THE ORDER IS GIVEN! THIS IS NOT A DRILL!
YOU HEARD HER!
ALL HANDS!
THIS IS NO DRILL!
THE BUBBLE ORDER MEANS THE HELICARRIER WILL FLY TO A SAFE ALTITUDE AND DETONATE OVER THE ATLANTIC OCEAN.
THE ATMOSPHERIC DAMAGE WILL BE SEVERE, BUT--
DEAR LORD.
IT'S ALREADY HAPPENING, SIR.
WHY IS THERE A HULK ON THAT SHIP?!
MS. ROMANOVA. THE BLACK WIDOW.
YOU HAVE SOMETHING THAT BELONGS TO ME, DEAR.
ZODIAC, TAKE IT BACK.

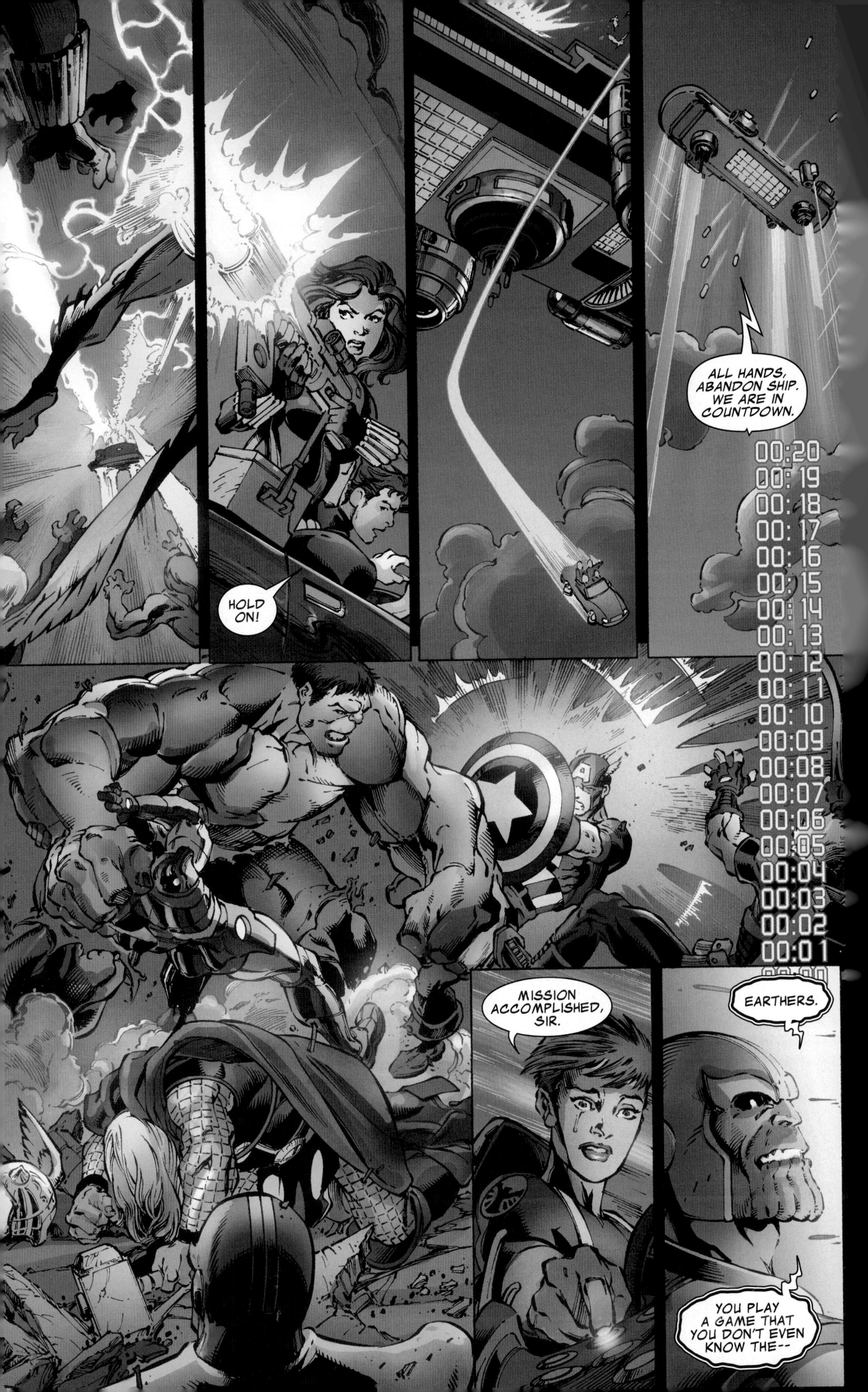
HOLD ON!
ALL HANDS, ABANDON SHIP. WE ARE IN COUNTDOWN.
00:20
00: 19
00: 18
00: 17
00: 16
00: 15
00: 14
00: 13
00: 12
00: 11
00: 10
00:09
00:08
00:07
00:06
00:05
00:04
00:03
00:02
00:01
MISSION ACCOMPLISHED, SIR.
EARTHERS.
YOU PLAY A GAME THAT YOU DON'T EVEN KNOW THE--

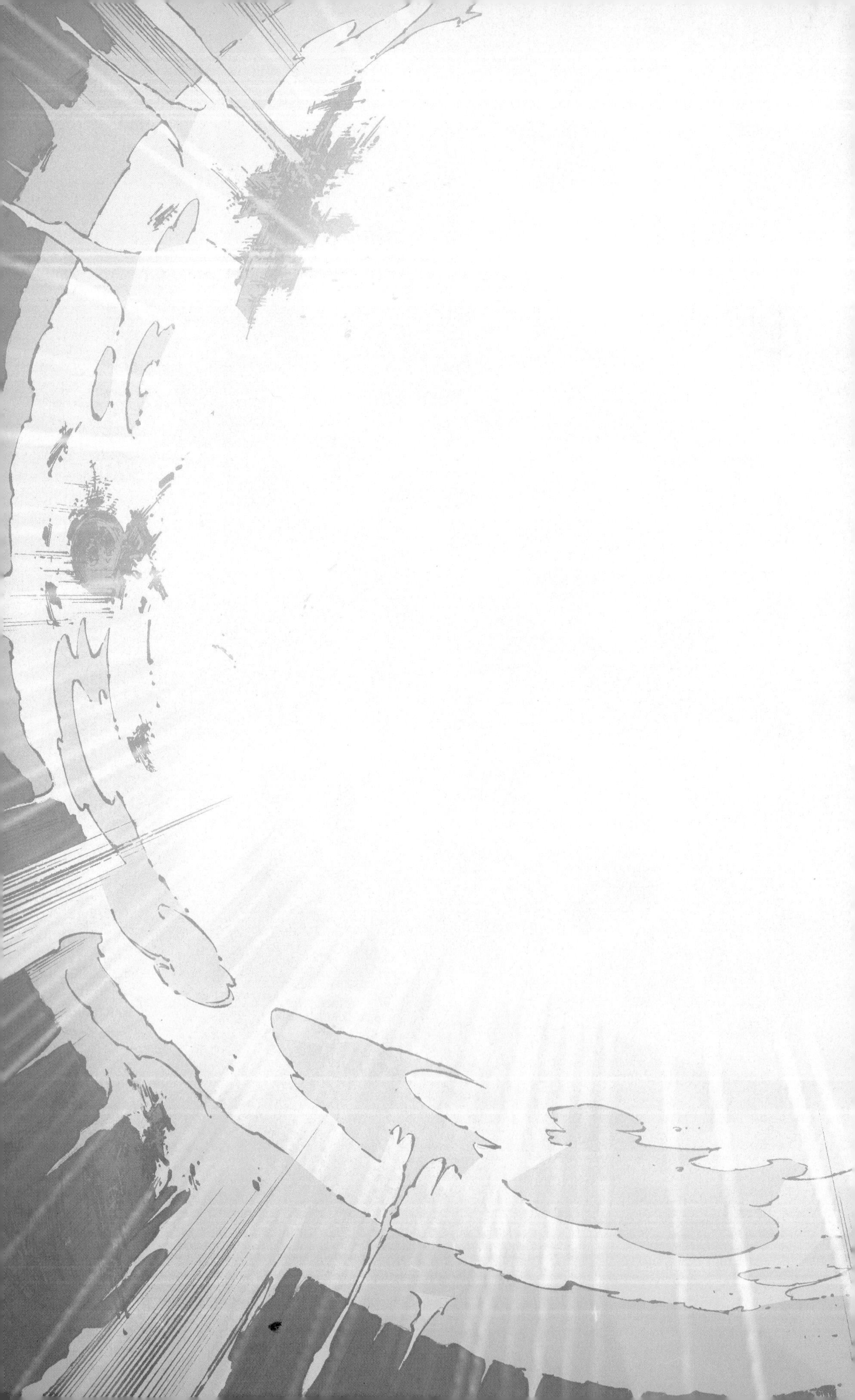

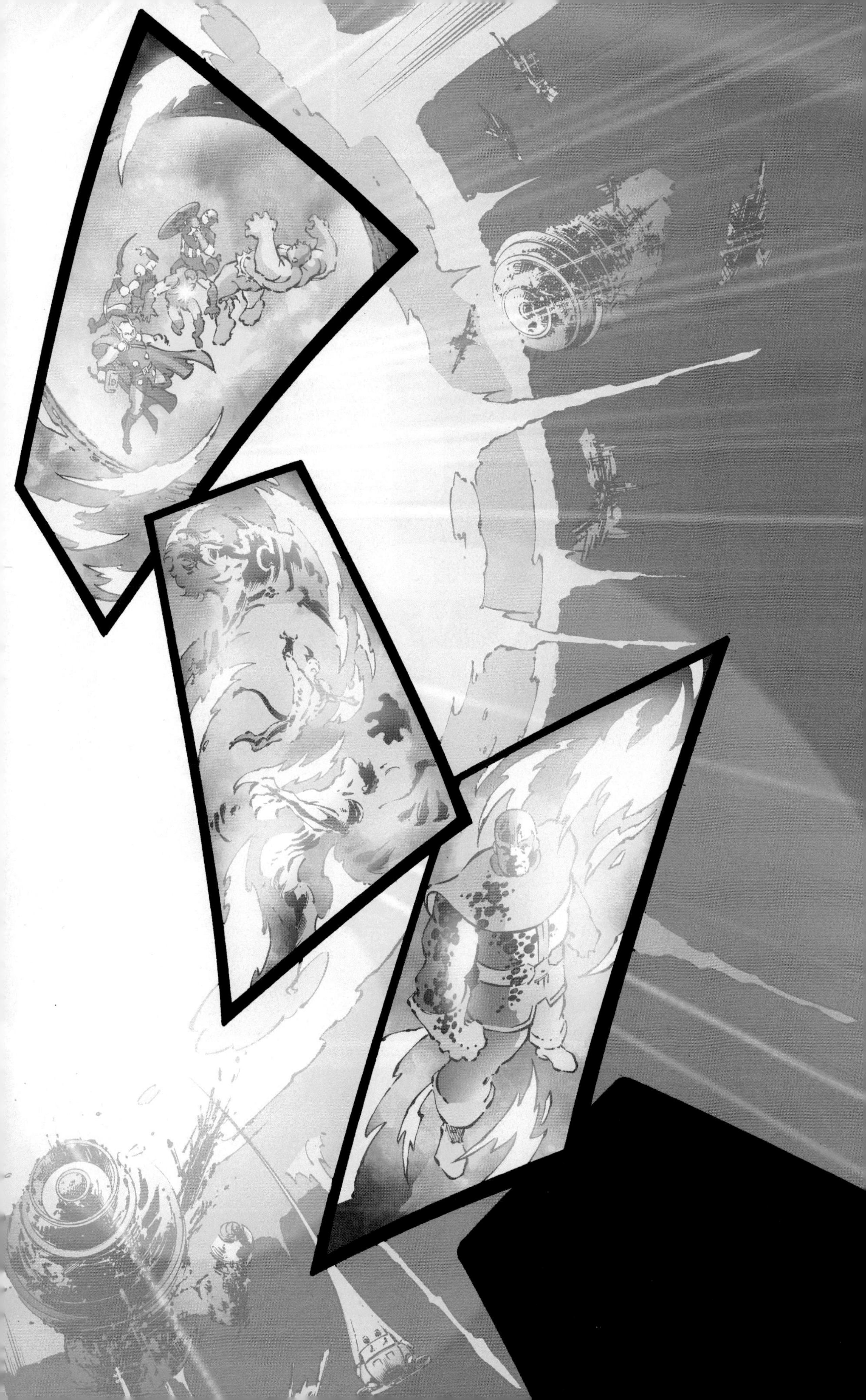

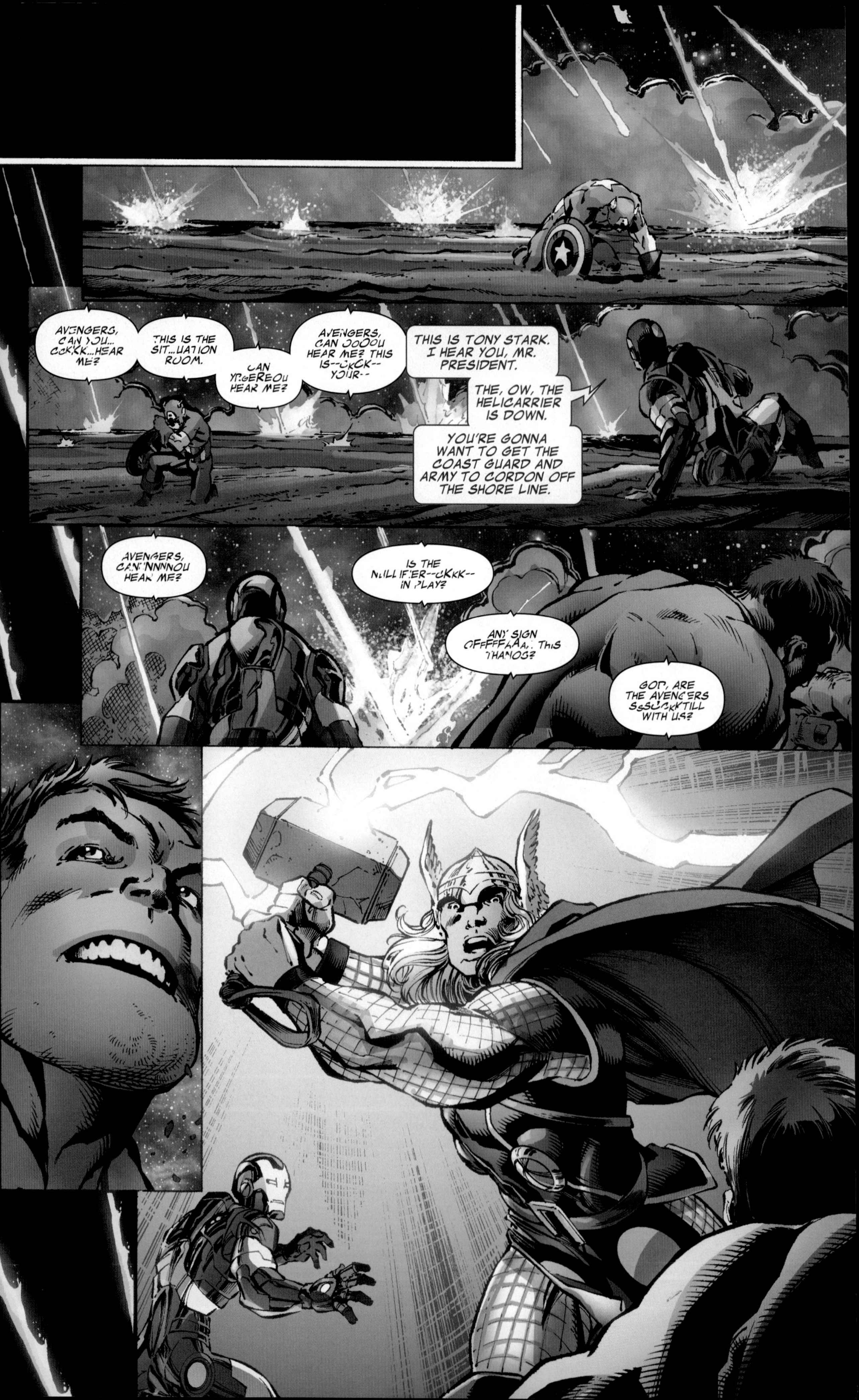
AVENGERS, CAN YOU... CCKKK...HEAR ME?
THIS IS THE SIT...UATION ROOM.
CAN YRGEREOU HEAR ME?
AVENGERS, CAN JOOOOU HEAR ME? THIS IS--CKCK--YOUR--
THIS IS TONY STARK. I HEAR YOU, MR. PRESIDENT.
THE, OW, THE HELICARRIER IS DOWN.
YOU'RE GONNA WANT TO GET THE COAST GUARD AND ARMY TO CORDON OFF THE SHORE LINE.
AVENGERS, CANNNNNOU HEAR ME?
IS THE NULLIFIER--CKKK--IN PLAY?
ANY SIGN OFFFFFAAA. THIS THANOS?
GOD, ARE THE AVENGERS SSSCKKTILL WITH US?

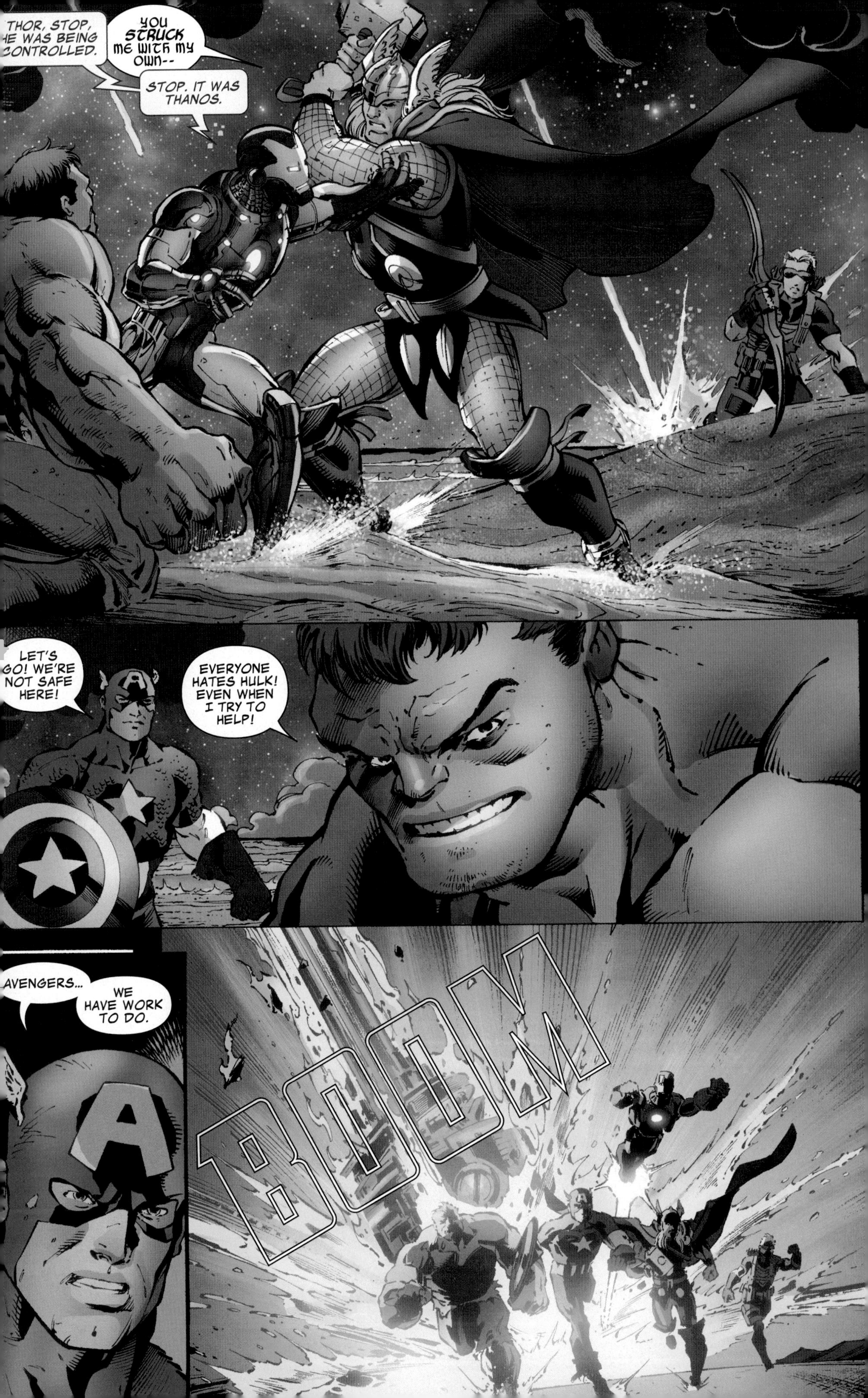
THOR, STOP, HE WAS BEING CONTROLLED.
YOU STRUCK ME WITH MY OWN--
STOP. IT WAS THANOS.
LET'S GO! WE'RE NOT SAFE HERE!
EVERYONE HATES HULK! EVEN WHEN I TRY TO HELP!
AVENGERS...
WE HAVE WORK TO DO.
BOOM

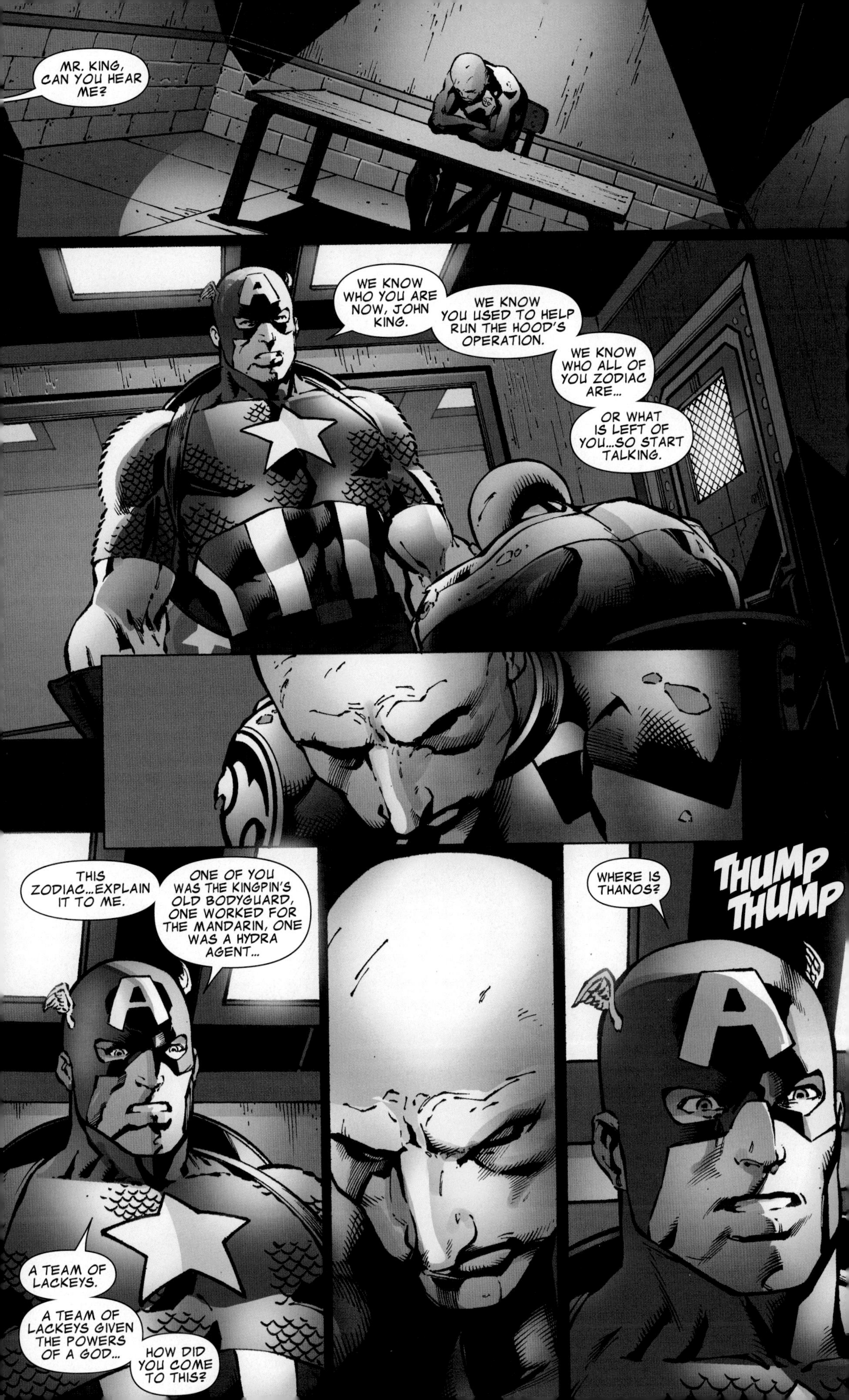
MR. KING, CAN YOU HEAR ME?
WE KNOW WHO YOU ARE NOW, JOHN KING.
WE KNOW YOU USED TO HELP RUN THE HOOD'S OPERATION.
WE KNOW WHO ALL OF YOU ZODIAC ARE...
OR WHAT IS LEFT OF YOU...SO START TALKING.
THIS ZODIAC...EXPLAIN IT TO ME.
ONE OF YOU WAS THE KINGPIN'S OLD BODYGUARD, ONE WORKED FOR THE MANDARIN, ONE WAS A HYDRA AGENT...
A TEAM OF LACKEYS.
A TEAM OF LACKEYS GIVEN THE POWERS OF A GOD...
HOW DID YOU COME TO THIS?
WHERE IS THANOS?
THUMP THUMP

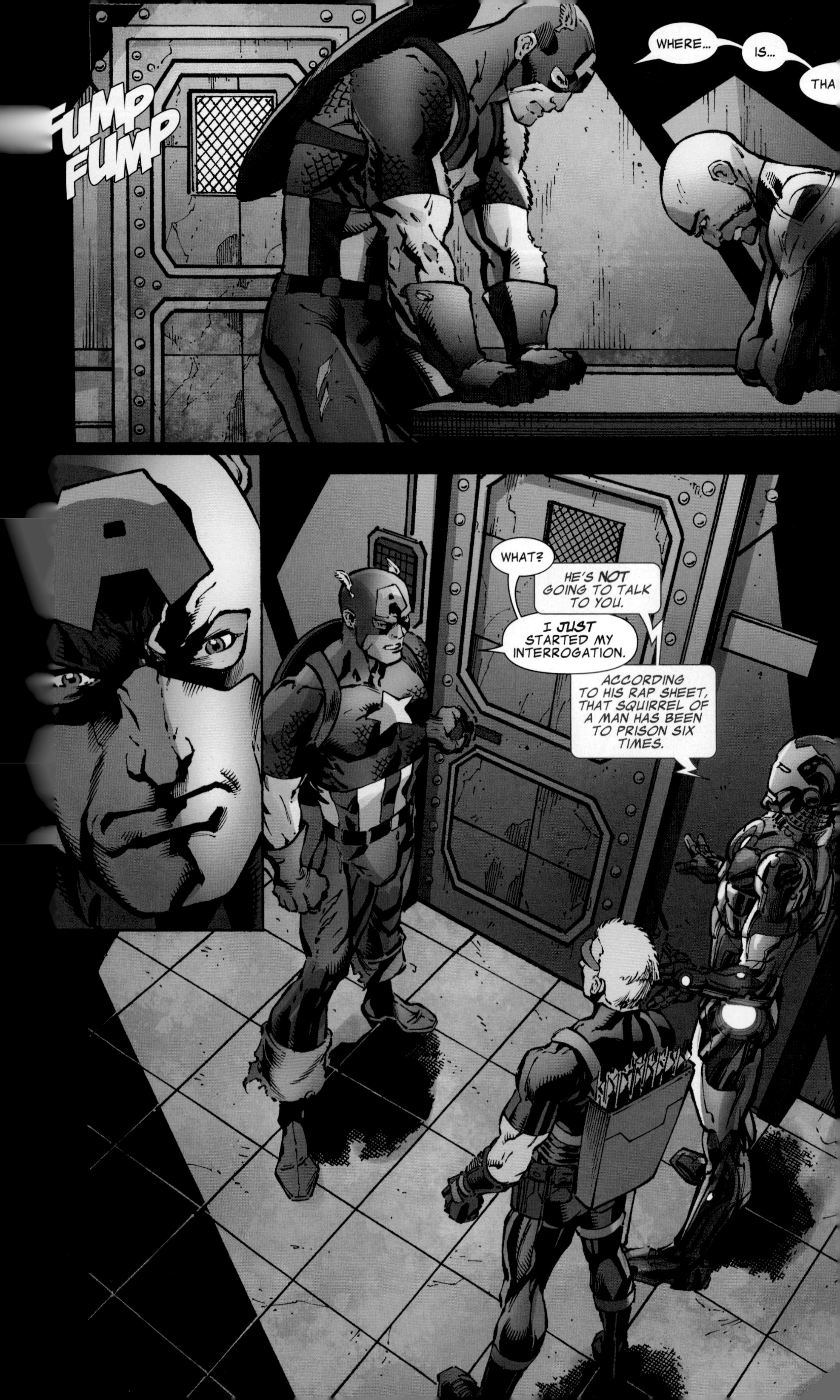
FUMP FUMP
WHERE...
IS...
THA
WHAT?
HE'S NOT GOING TO TALK TO YOU.
I JUST STARTED MY INTERROGATION.
ACCORDING TO HIS RAP SHEET, THAT SQUIRREL OF A MAN HAS BEEN TO PRISON SIX TIMES.

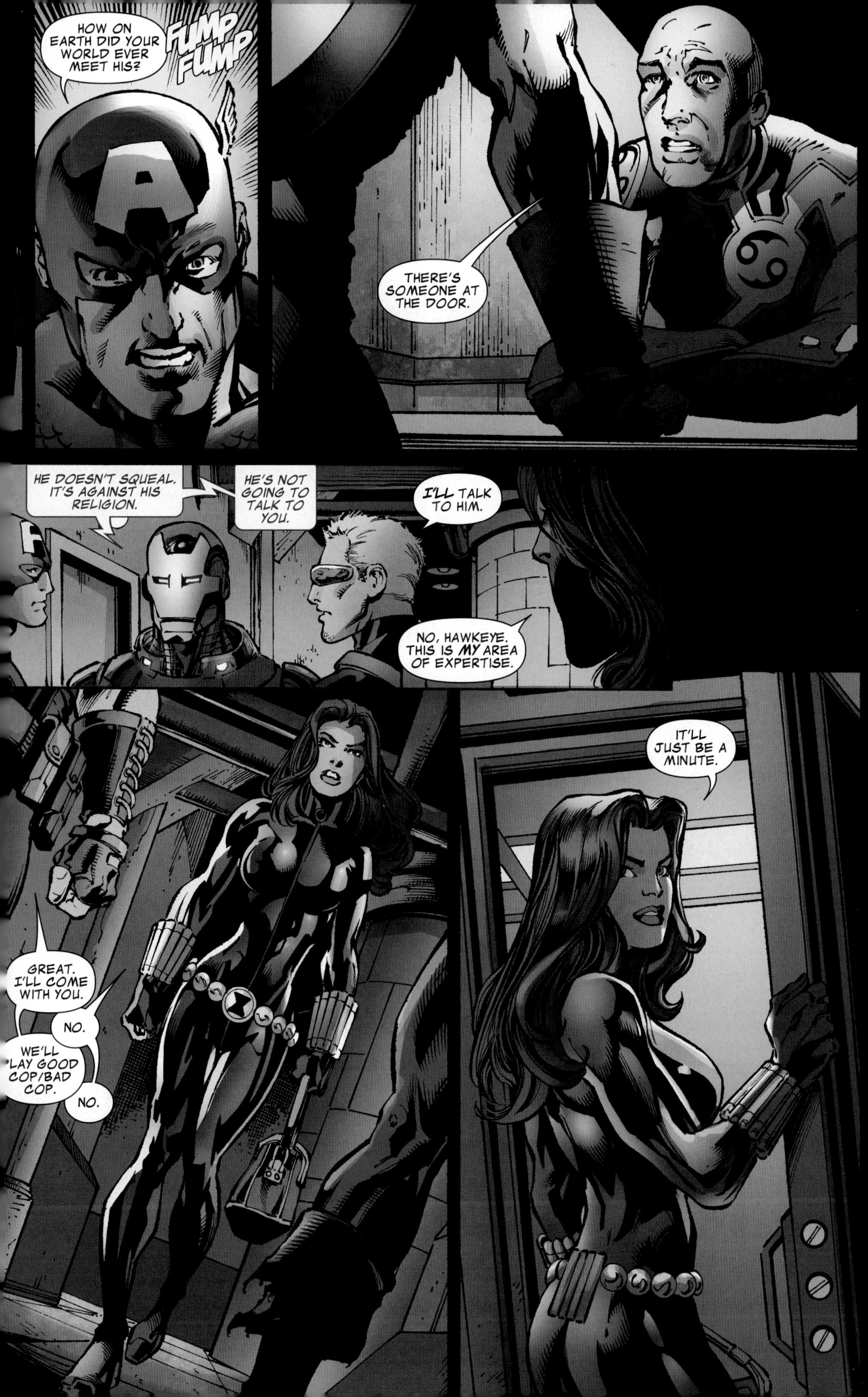
HOW ON EARTH DID YOUR WORLD EVER MEET HIS?
FUMP FUMP
THERE'S SOMEONE AT THE DOOR.
HE DOESN'T SQUEAL. IT'S AGAINST HIS RELIGION.
HE'S NOT GOING TO TALK TO YOU.
I'LL TALK TO HIM.
NO, HAWKEYE. THIS IS MY AREA OF EXPERTISE.
GREAT. I'LL COME WITH YOU.
NO.
WE'LL 'LAY GOOD COP/BAD COP.
NO.
IT'LL JUST BE A MINUTE.

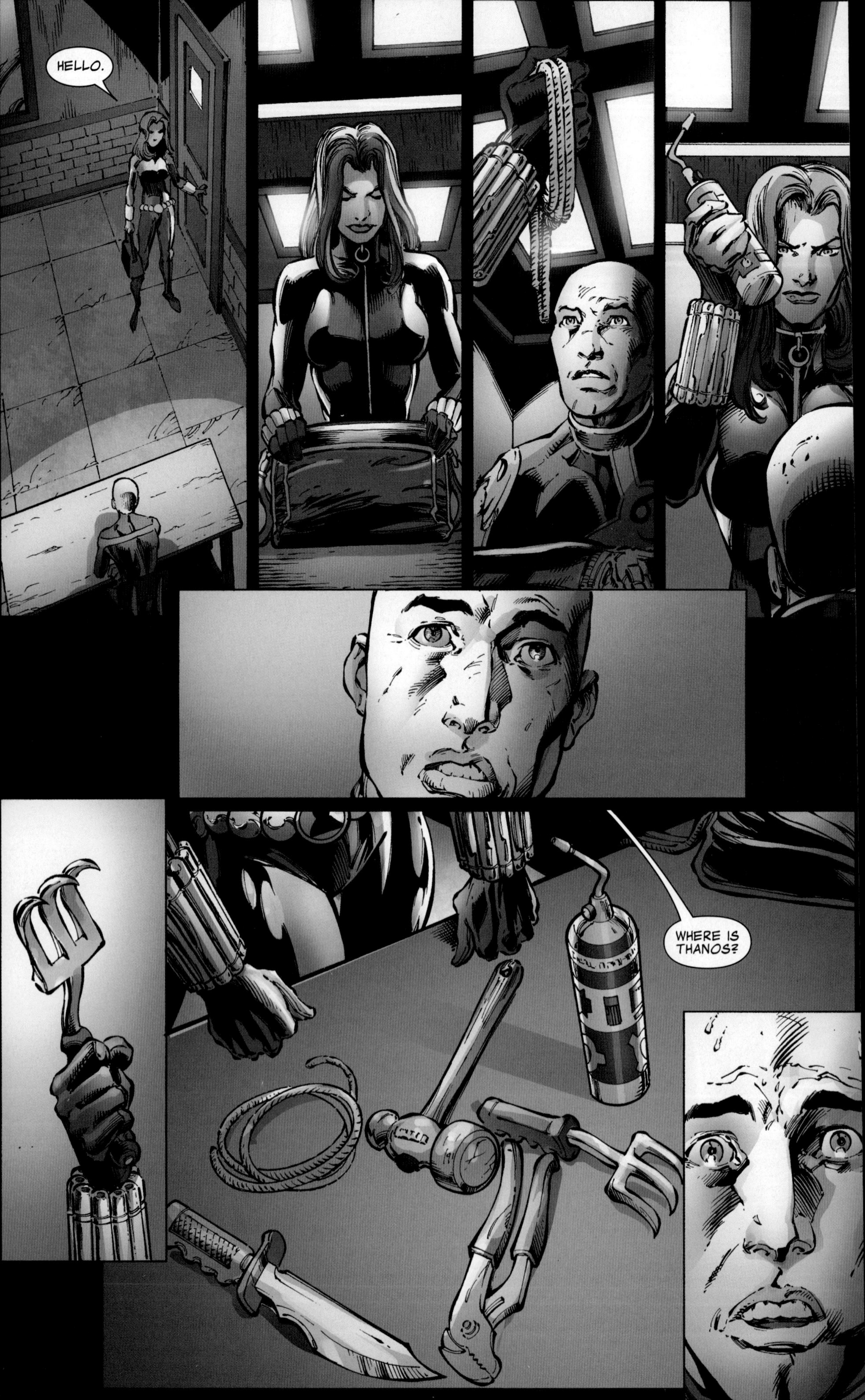
HELLO.
WHERE IS THANOS?

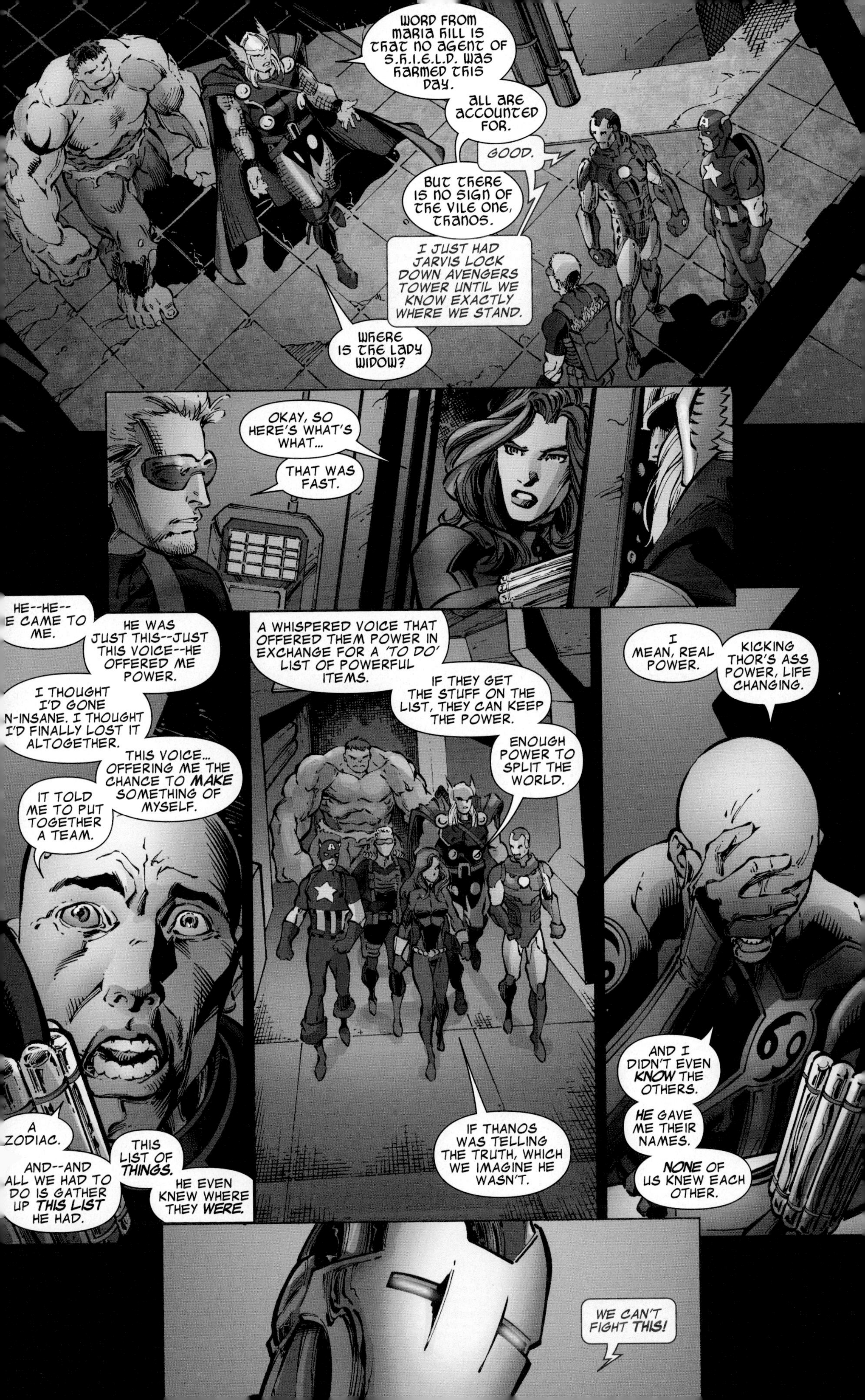
WORD FROM MARIA HILL IS THAT NO AGENT OF S.H.I.E.L.D. WAS HARMED THIS DAY.
ALL ARE ACCOUNTED FOR.
GOOD.
BUT THERE IS NO SIGN OF THE VILE ONE, THANOS.
I JUST HAD JARVIS LOCK DOWN AVENGERS TOWER UNTIL WE KNOW EXACTLY WHERE WE STAND.
WHERE IS THE LADY WIDOW?
OKAY, SO HERE'S WHAT'S WHAT...
THAT WAS FAST.
HE--HE-- E CAME TO ME.
HE WAS JUST THIS--JUST THIS VOICE--HE OFFERED ME POWER.
I THOUGHT I'D GONE N-INSANE. I THOUGHT I'D FINALLY LOST IT ALTOGETHER.
THIS VOICE... OFFERING ME THE CHANCE TO MAKE SOMETHING OF MYSELF.
IT TOLD ME TO PUT TOGETHER A TEAM.
A ZODIAC.
AND--AND ALL WE HAD TO DO IS GATHER UP THIS LIST HE HAD.
THIS LIST OF THINGS.
HE EVEN KNEW WHERE THEY WERE.
A WHISPERED VOICE THAT OFFERED THEM POWER IN EXCHANGE FOR A 'TO DO' LIST OF POWERFUL ITEMS.
IF THEY GET THE STUFF ON THE LIST, THEY CAN KEEP THE POWER.
ENOUGH POWER TO SPLIT THE WORLD.
IF THANOS WAS TELLING THE TRUTH, WHICH WE IMAGINE HE WASN'T.
I MEAN, REAL POWER.
KICKING THOR'S ASS POWER, LIFE CHANGING.
AND I DIDN'T EVEN KNOW THE OTHERS.
HE GAVE ME THEIR NAMES.
NONE OF US KNEW EACH OTHER.
WE CAN'T FIGHT THIS!

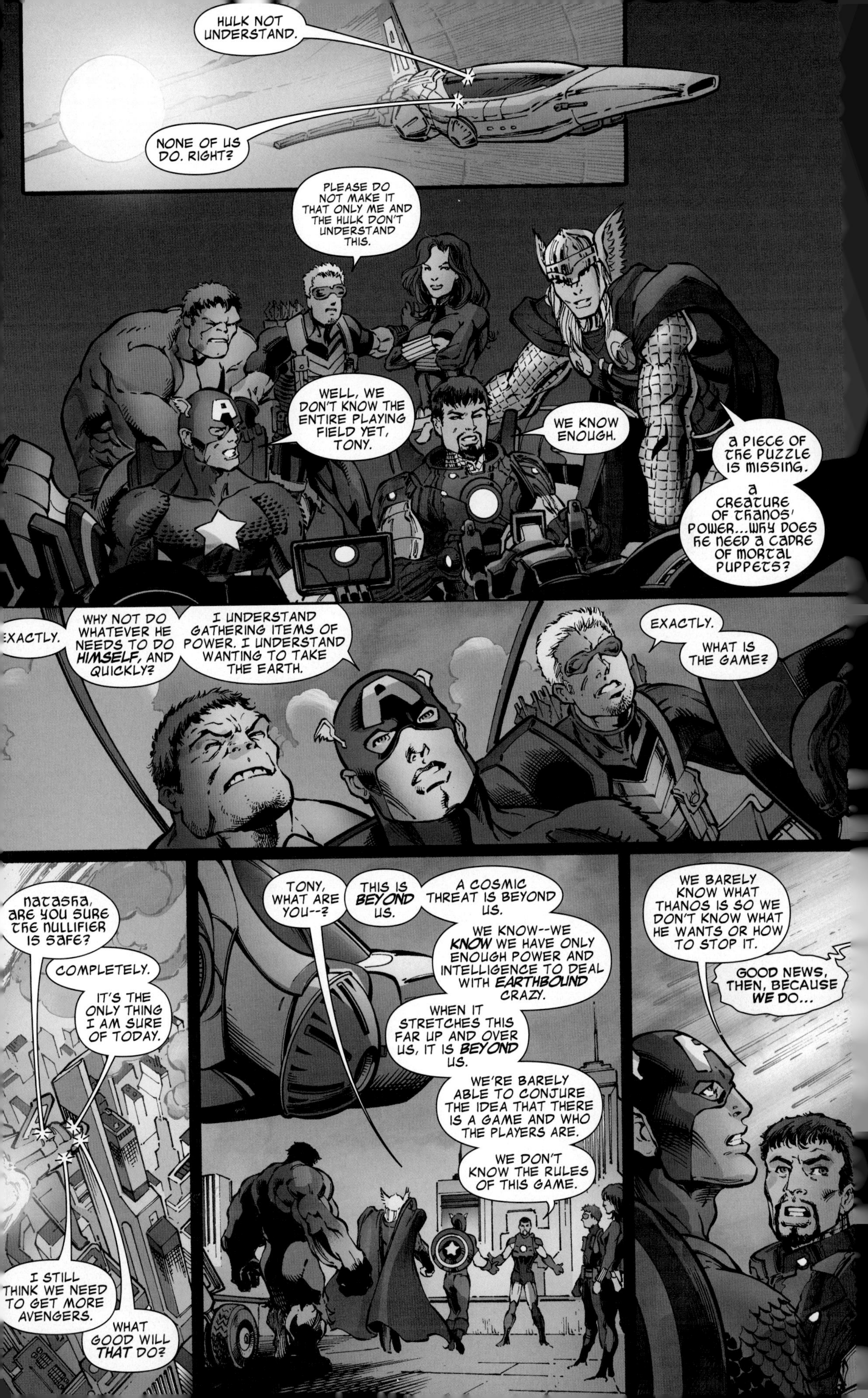
HULK NOT UNDERSTAND.
NONE OF US DO. RIGHT?
PLEASE DO NOT MAKE IT THAT ONLY ME AND THE HULK DON'T UNDERSTAND THIS.
WELL, WE DON'T KNOW THE ENTIRE PLAYING FIELD YET, TONY.
WE KNOW ENOUGH.
A PIECE OF THE PUZZLE IS MISSING.
A CREATURE OF THANOS' POWER...WHY DOES HE NEED A CADRE OF MORTAL PUPPETS?
EXACTLY.
WHY NOT DO WHATEVER HE NEEDS TO DO *HIMSELF*, AND QUICKLY?
I UNDERSTAND GATHERING ITEMS OF POWER. I UNDERSTAND WANTING TO TAKE THE EARTH.
EXACTLY.
WHAT IS THE GAME?
NATASHA, ARE YOU SURE THE NULLIFIER IS SAFE?
COMPLETELY.
IT'S THE ONLY THING I AM SURE OF TODAY.
I STILL THINK WE NEED TO GET MORE AVENGERS.
WHAT GOOD WILL *THAT* DO?
TONY, WHAT ARE YOU--?
THIS IS *BEYOND* US.
A COSMIC THREAT IS BEYOND US.
WE KNOW--WE *KNOW* WE HAVE ONLY ENOUGH POWER AND INTELLIGENCE TO DEAL WITH *EARTHBOUND* CRAZY.
WHEN IT STRETCHES THIS FAR UP AND OVER US, IT IS *BEYOND* US.
WE'RE BARELY ABLE TO CONJURE THE IDEA THAT THERE IS A GAME AND WHO THE PLAYERS ARE.
WE DON'T KNOW THE RULES OF THIS GAME.
WE BARELY KNOW WHAT THANOS IS SO WE DON'T KNOW WHAT HE WANTS OR HOW TO STOP IT.
GOOD NEWS, THEN, BECAUSE *WE DO*...

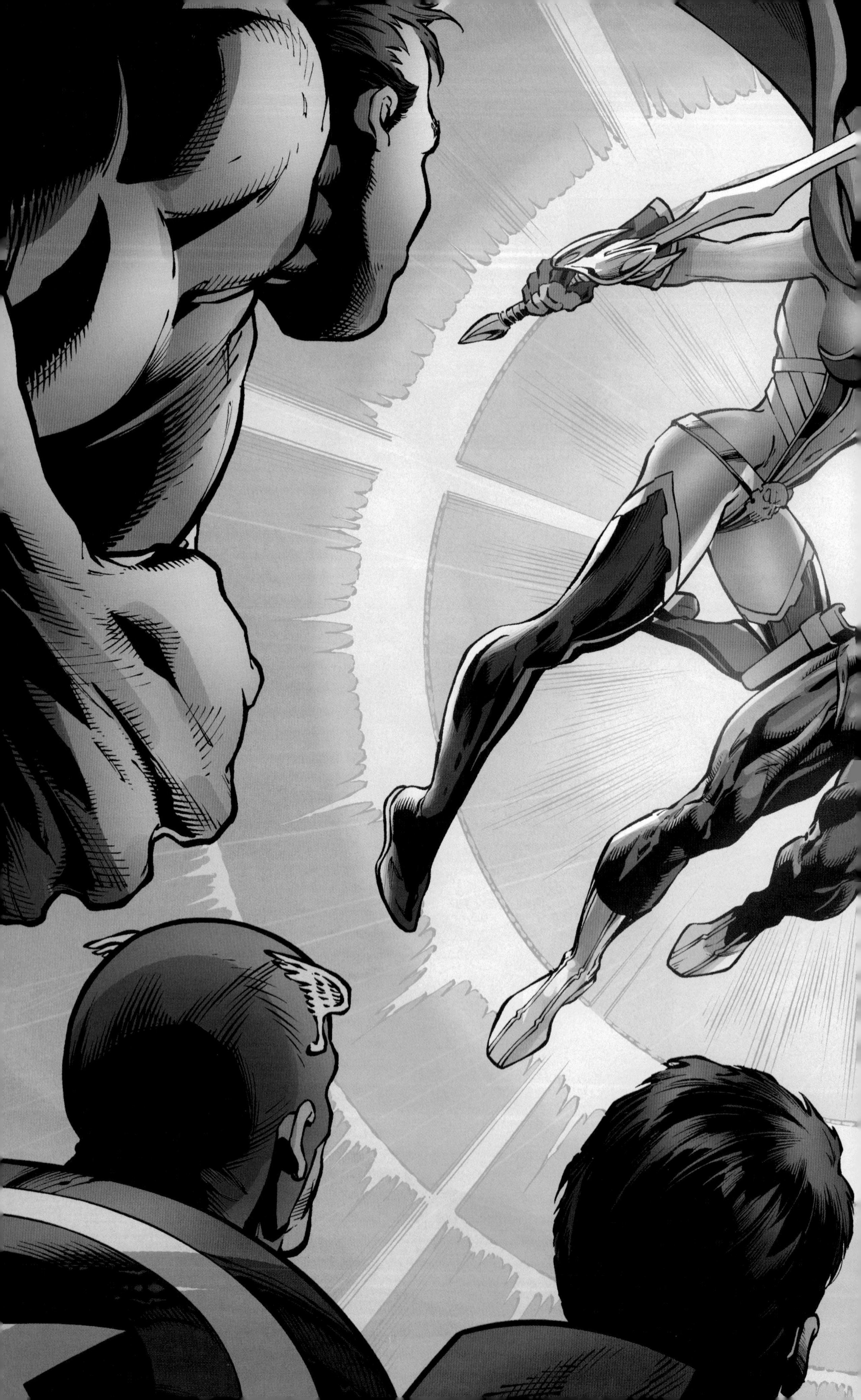

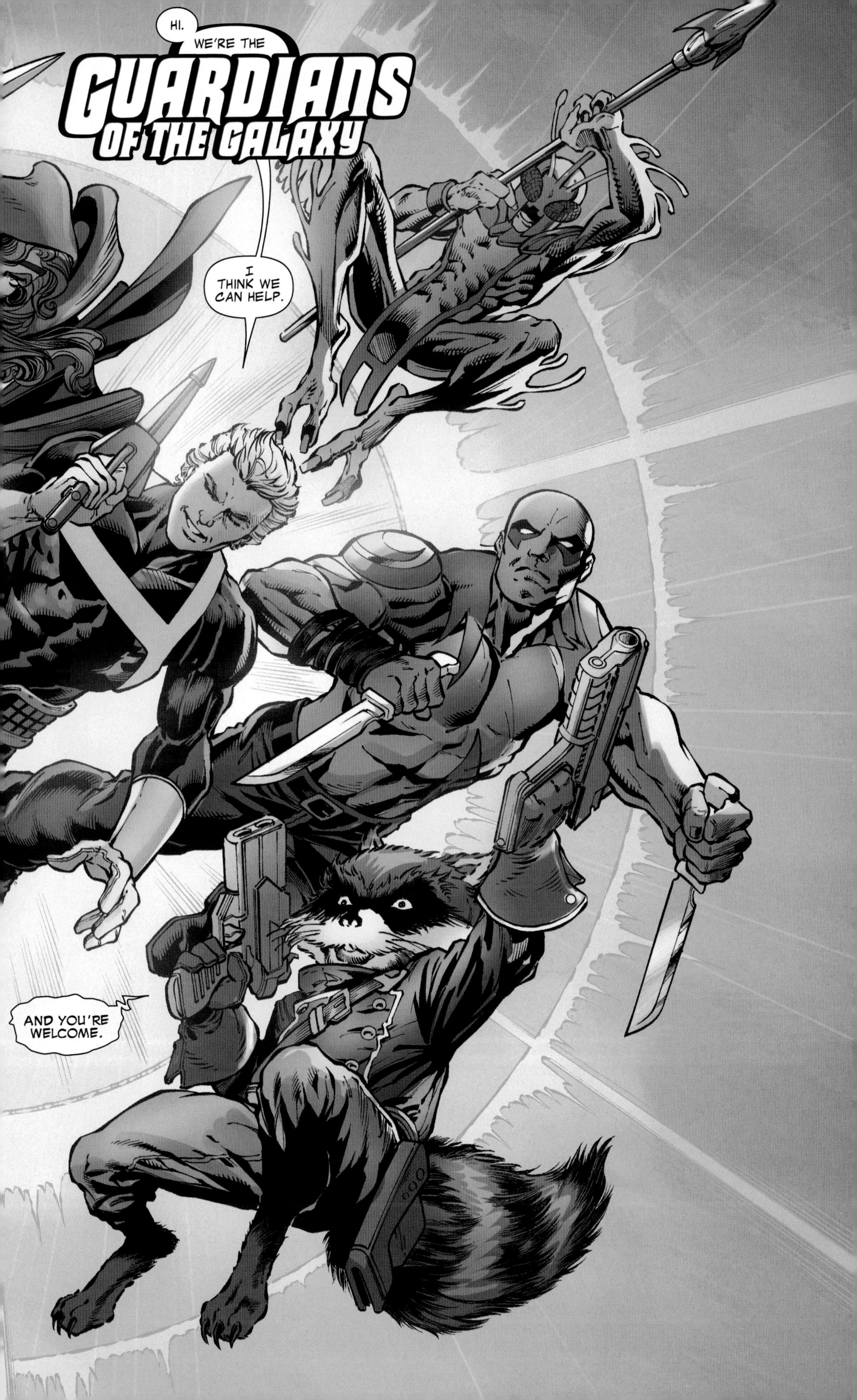
HI.
WE'RE THE
GUARDIANS OF THE GALAXY
I THINK WE CAN HELP.
AND YOU'RE WELCOME.

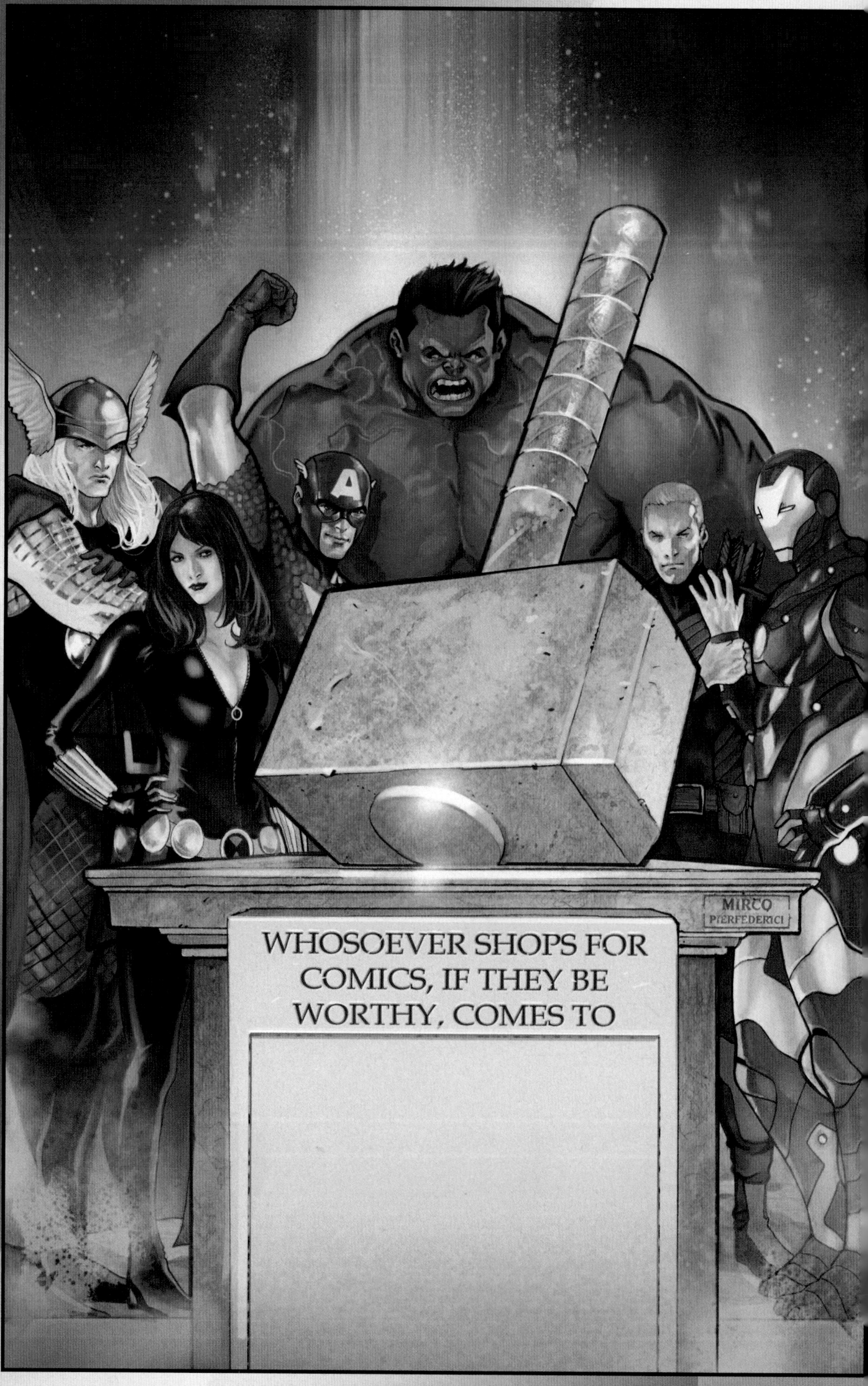
MIRCO PIERFEDERICI
WHOSOEVER SHOPS FOR COMICS, IF THEY BE WORTHY, COMES TO

#1 COMIC SHOP VARIANT BY MIRCO PIERFEDERICI

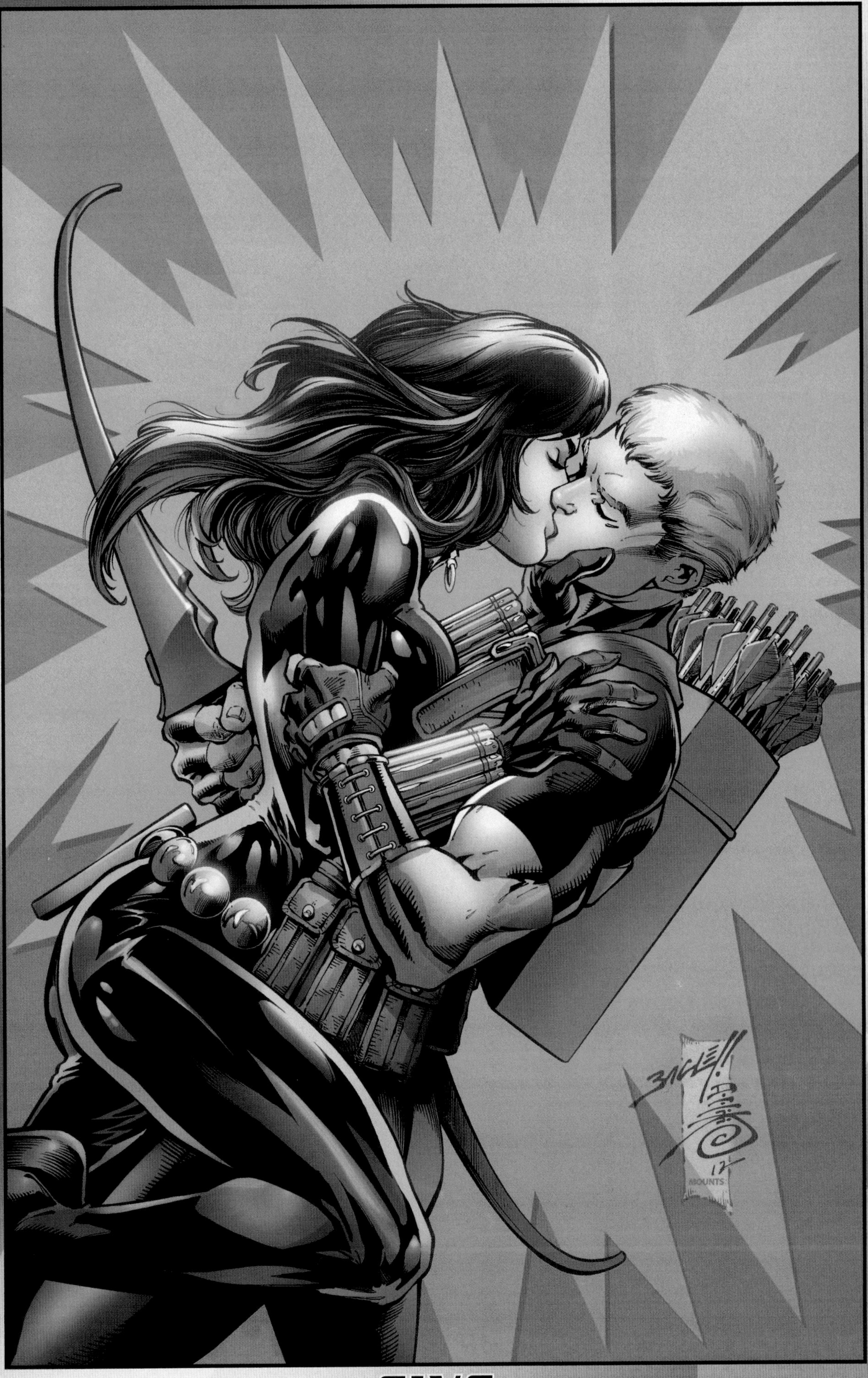

FIVE

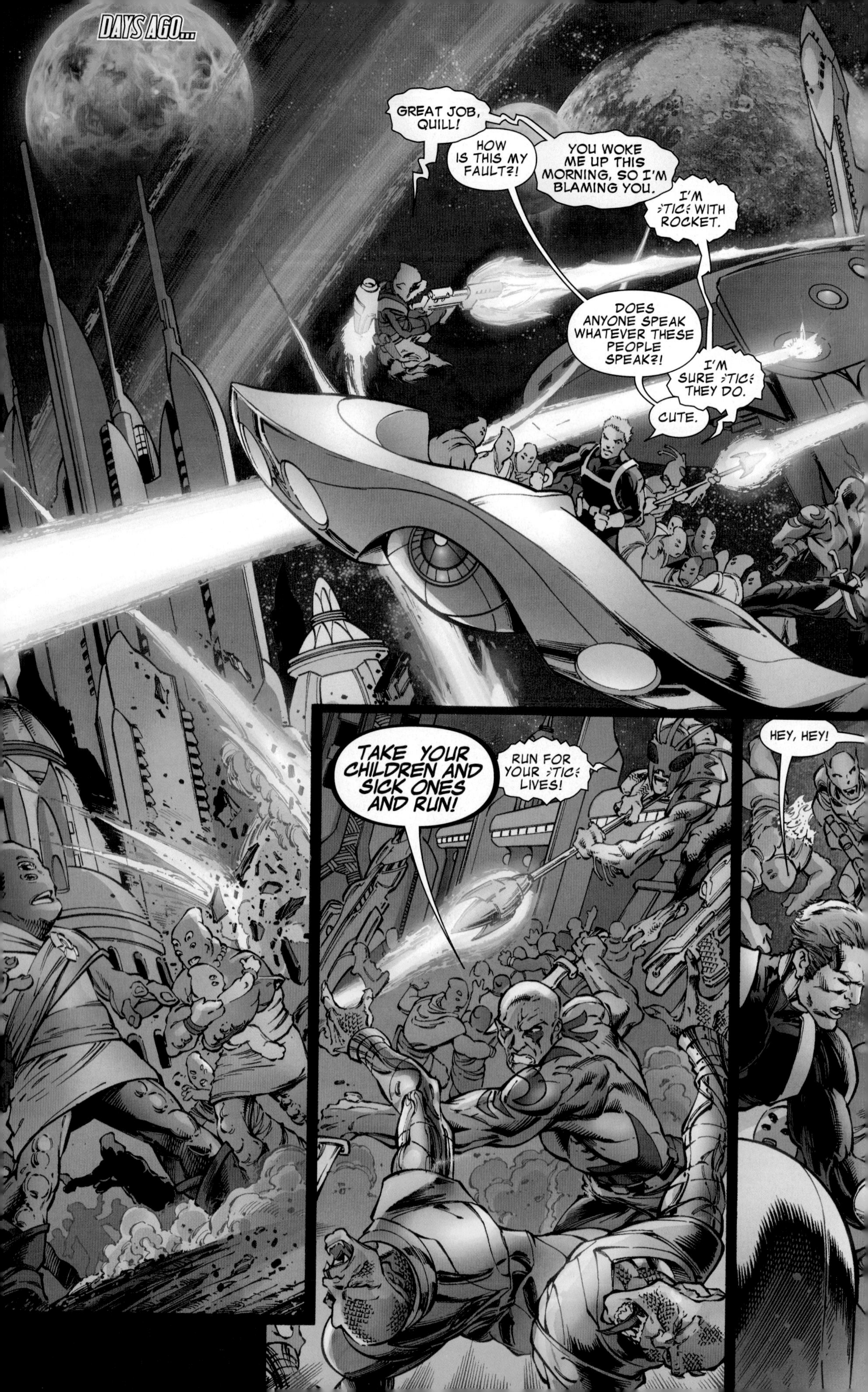
DAYS AGO...
GREAT JOB, QUILL!
HOW IS THIS MY FAULT?!
YOU WOKE ME UP THIS MORNING, SO I'M BLAMING YOU.
I'M ≈TIC≈ WITH ROCKET.
DOES ANYONE SPEAK WHATEVER THESE PEOPLE SPEAK?!
I'M SURE ≈TIC≈ THEY DO.
CUTE.
TAKE YOUR CHILDREN AND SICK ONES AND RUN!
RUN FOR YOUR ≈TIC≈ LIVES!
HEY, HEY!

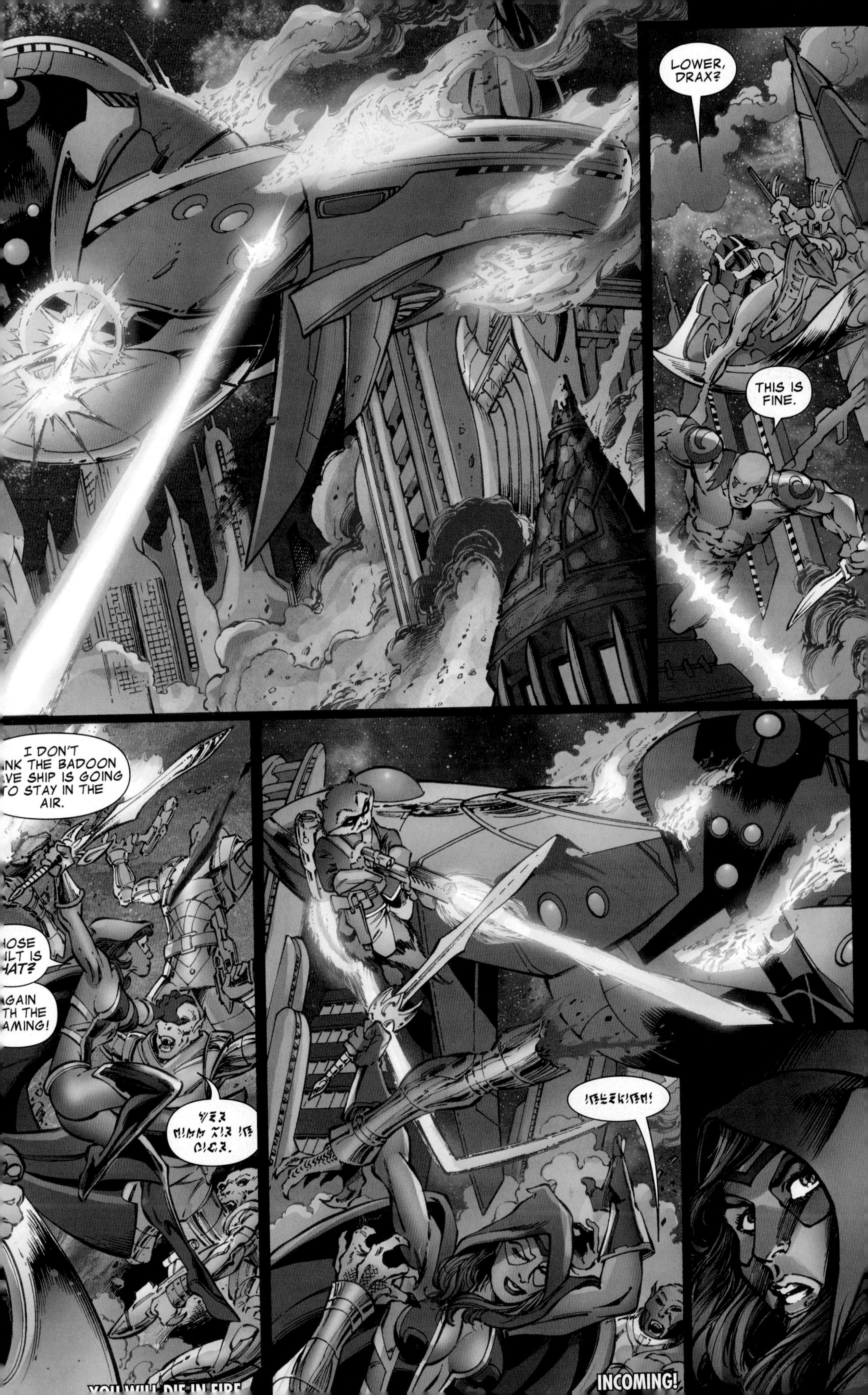

LOWER, DRAX?
THIS IS FINE.
I DON'T NK THE BADOON VE SHIP IS GOING TO STAY IN THE AIR.
HOSE ILT IS HAT?
AGAIN TH THE AMING!
INCOMING!

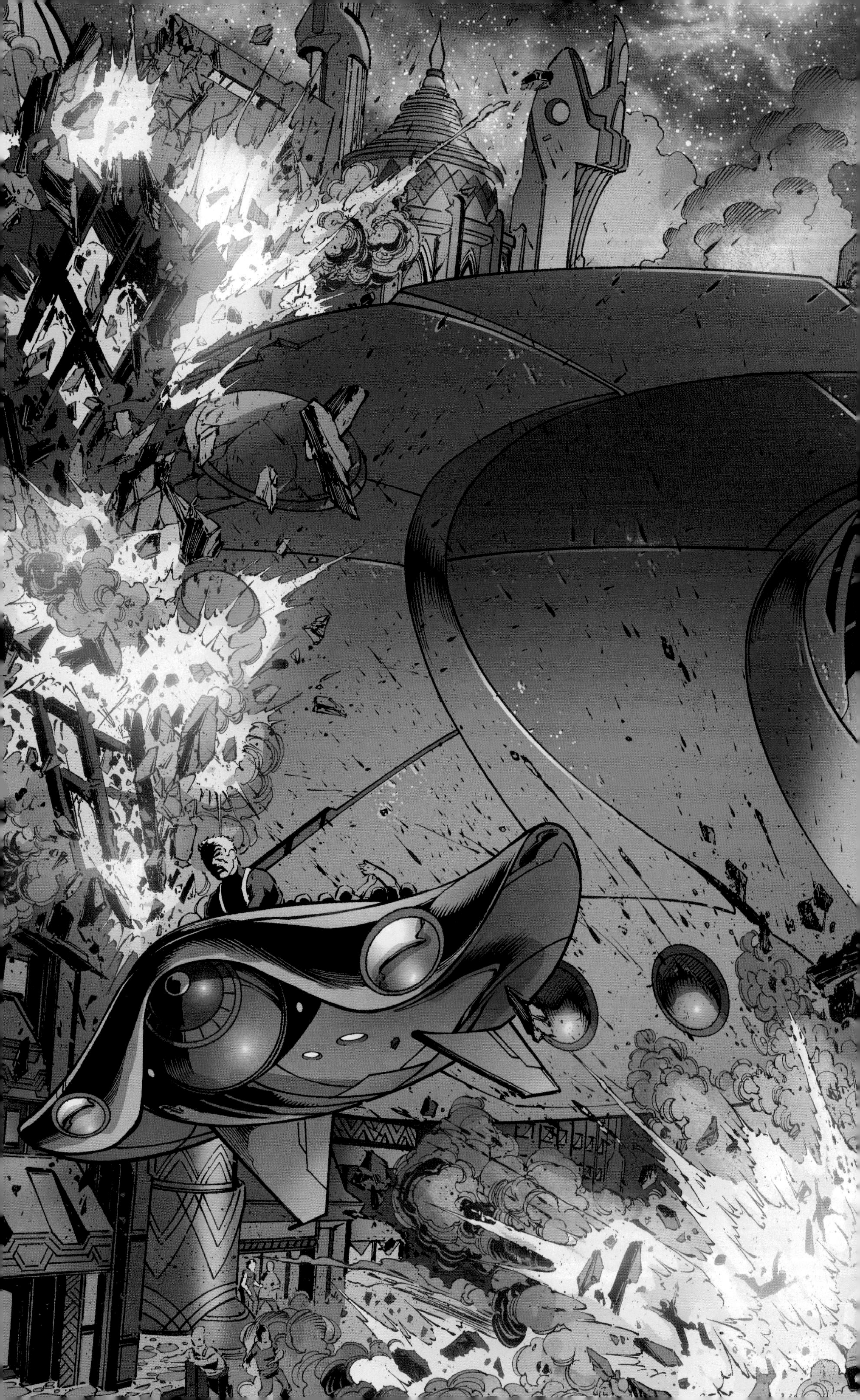

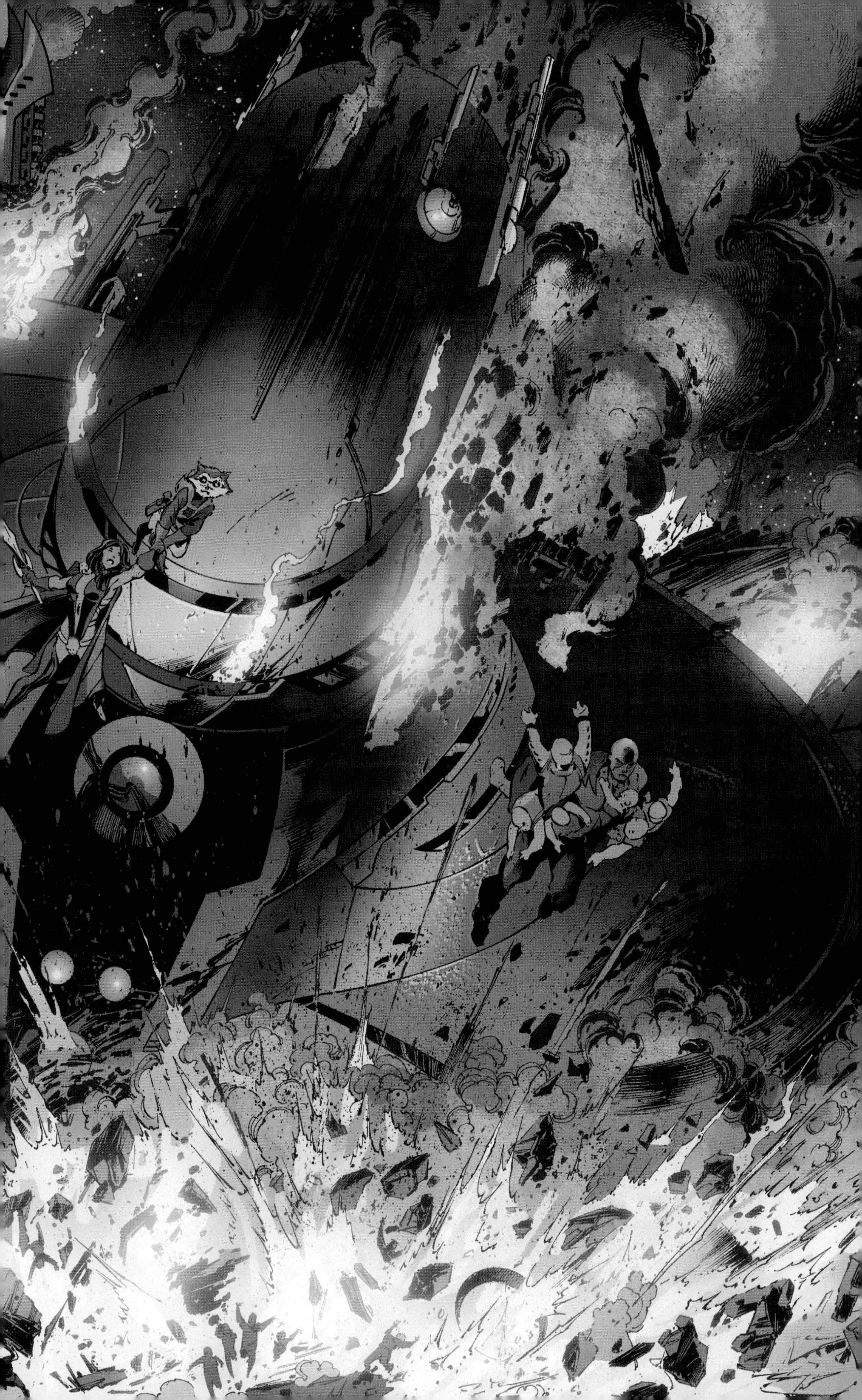

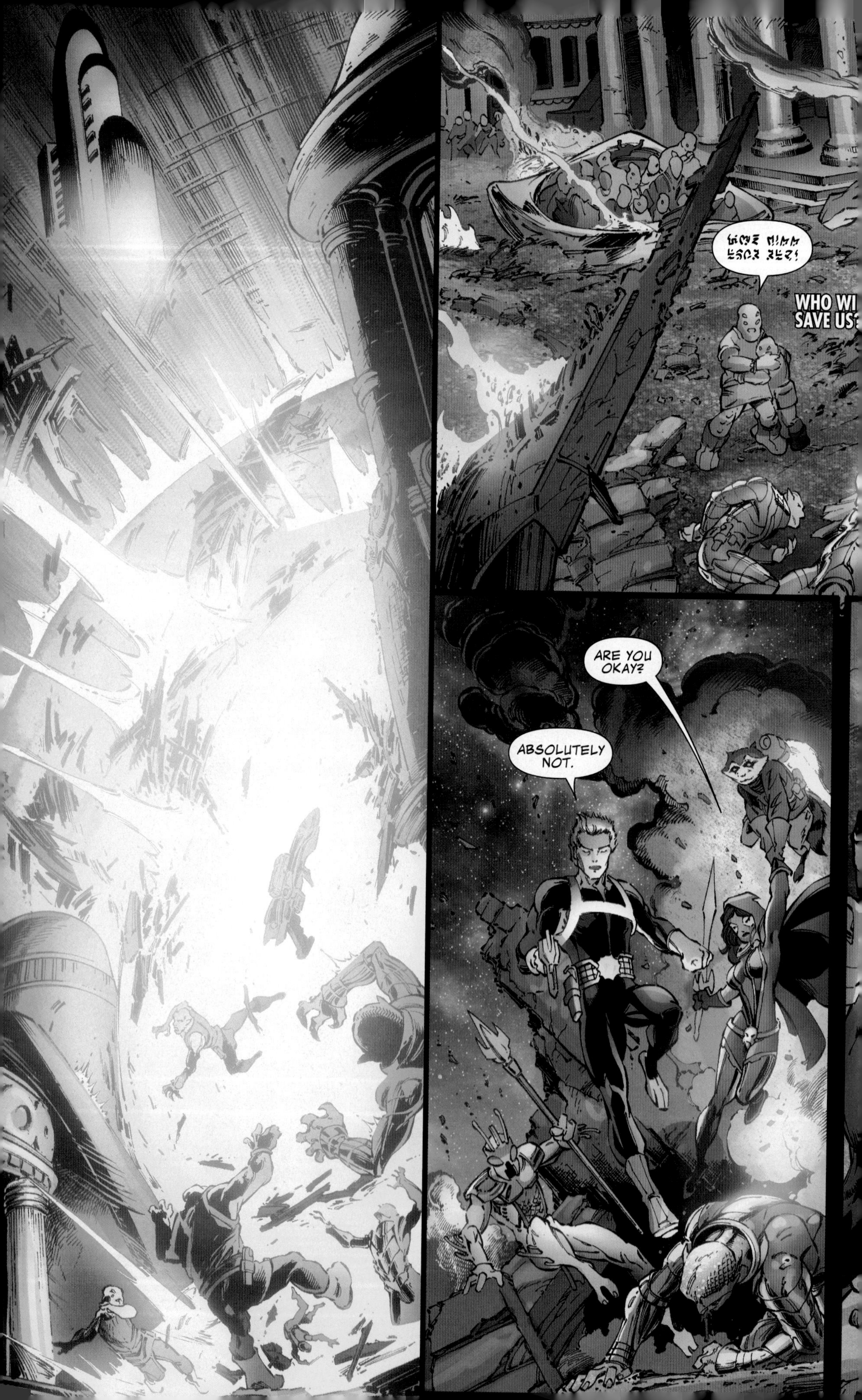
WHO WI
SAVE US
ARE YOU OKAY?
ABSOLUTELY NOT.

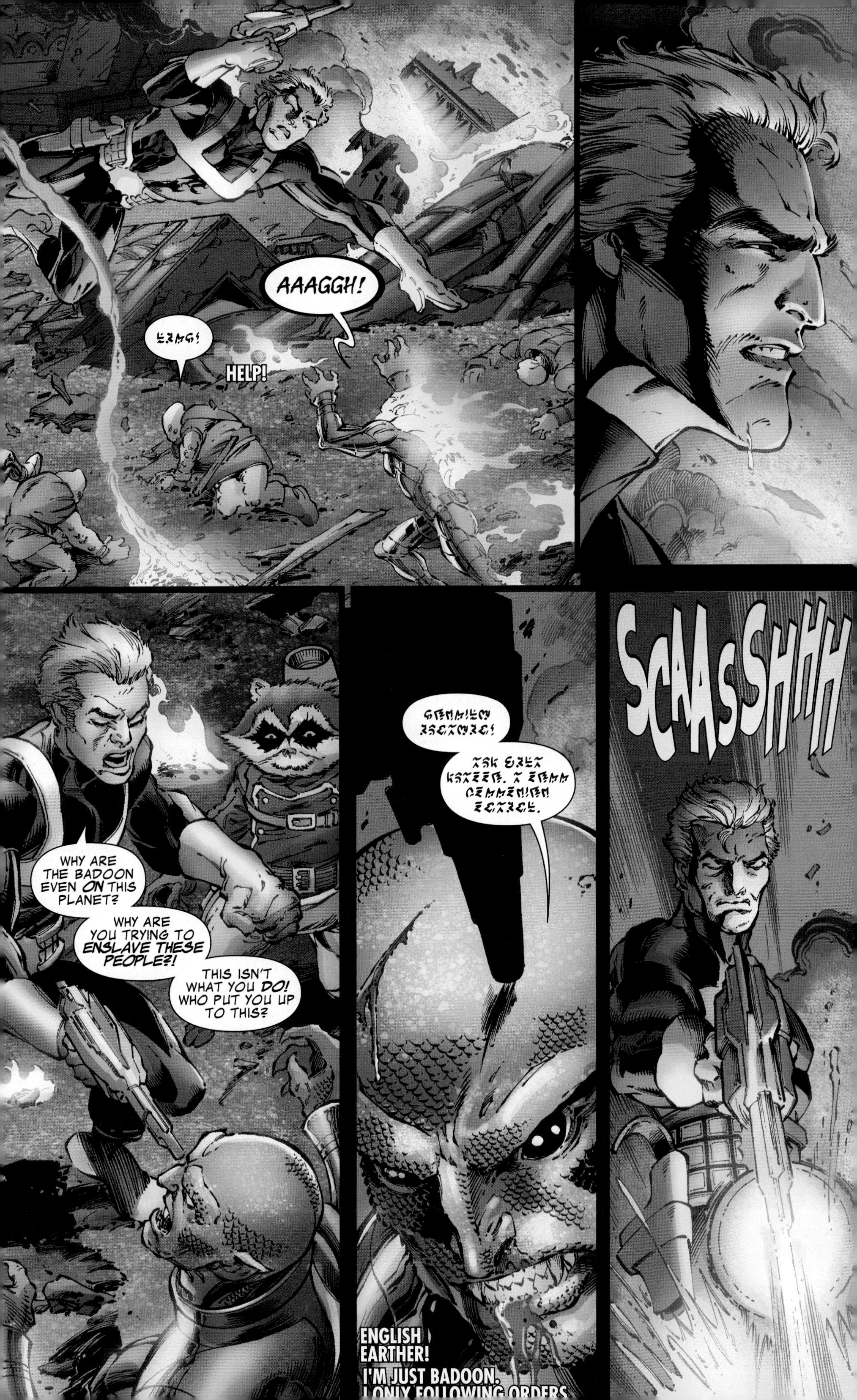

AAAGGH!
HELP!
WHY ARE THE BADOON EVEN ON THIS PLANET?
WHY ARE YOU TRYING TO ENSLAVE THESE PEOPLE?!
THIS ISN'T WHAT YOU DO! WHO PUT YOU UP TO THIS?
ENGLISH EARTHER!
I'M JUST BADOON. I ONLY FOLLOWING ORDERS
SCAASHHH

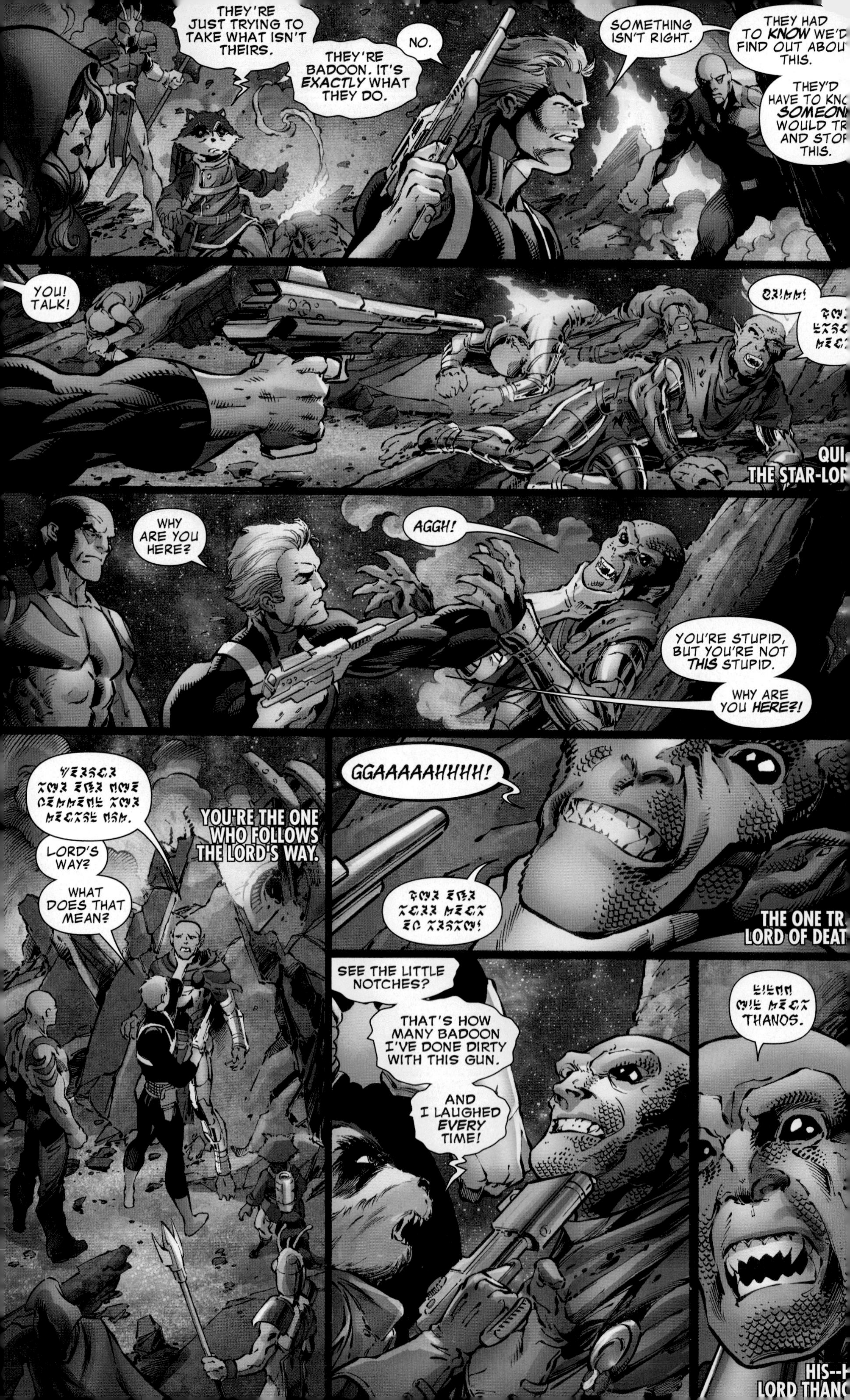
THEY'RE JUST TRYING TO TAKE WHAT ISN'T THEIRS.
NO.
THEY'RE BADOON. IT'S EXACTLY WHAT THEY DO.
SOMETHING ISN'T RIGHT.
THEY HAD TO KNOW WE'D FIND OUT ABOU THIS.
THEY'D HAVE TO KNO SOMEON WOULD TR AND STOF THIS.
YOU! TALK!
QUI THE STAR-LOR
WHY ARE YOU HERE?
AGGH!
YOU'RE STUPID, BUT YOU'RE NOT THIS STUPID.
WHY ARE YOU HERE?!
YOU'RE THE ONE WHO FOLLOWS THE LORD'S WAY.
LORD'S WAY?
WHAT DOES THAT MEAN?
GGAAAAAHHHH!
THE ONE TR LORD OF DEAT
SEE THE LITTLE NOTCHES?
THAT'S HOW MANY BADOON I'VE DONE DIRTY WITH THIS GUN.
AND I LAUGHED EVERY TIME!
THANOS.
HIS--H LORD THANO

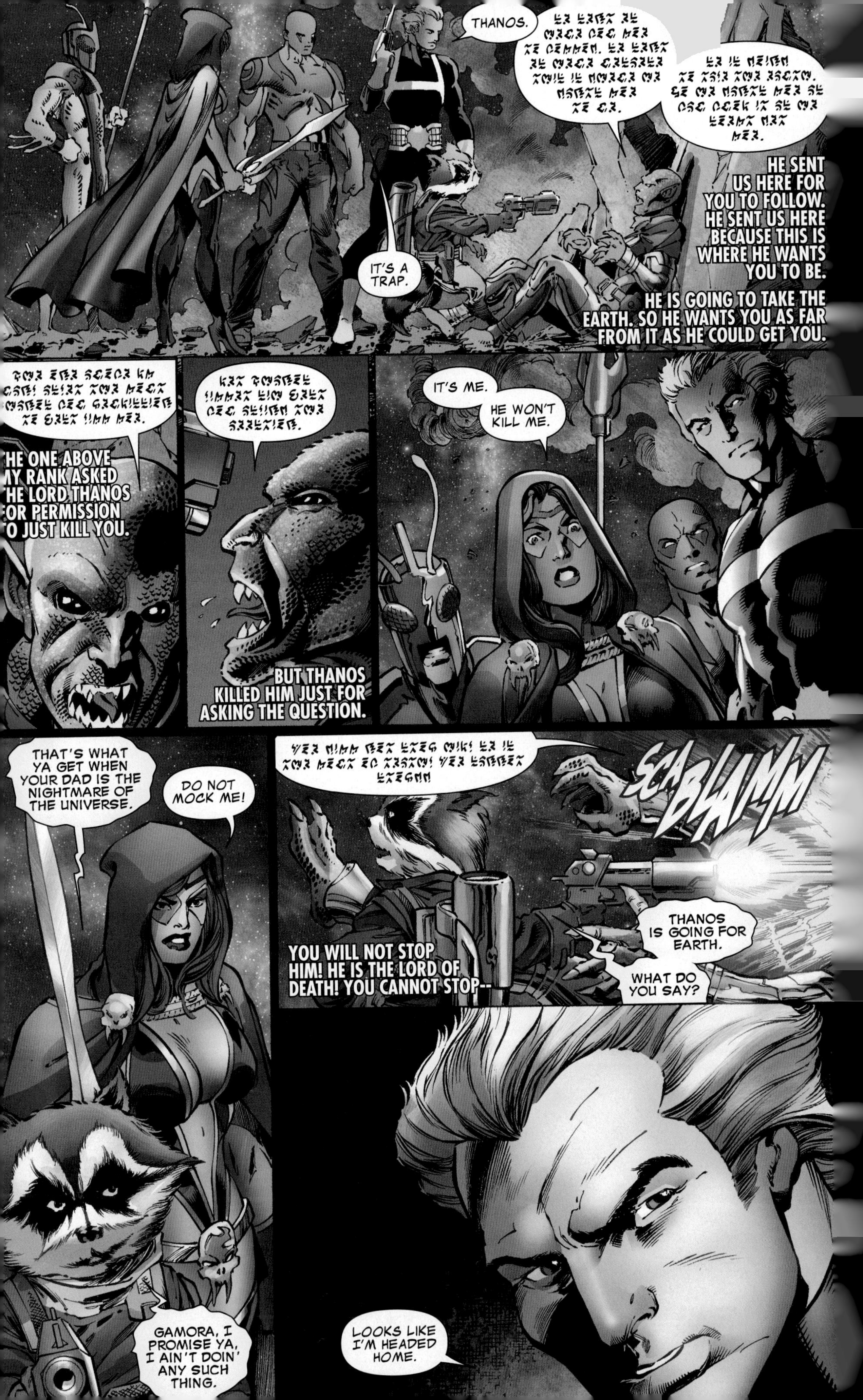
THANOS.
IT'S A TRAP.
HE SENT US HERE FOR YOU TO FOLLOW. HE SENT US HERE BECAUSE THIS IS WHERE HE WANTS YOU TO BE.
HE IS GOING TO TAKE THE EARTH. SO HE WANTS YOU AS FAR FROM IT AS HE COULD GET YOU.
HE ONE ABOVE MY RANK ASKED HE LORD THANOS FOR PERMISSION TO JUST KILL YOU.
BUT THANOS KILLED HIM JUST FOR ASKING THE QUESTION.
IT'S ME.
HE WON'T KILL ME.
THAT'S WHAT YA GET WHEN YOUR DAD IS THE NIGHTMARE OF THE UNIVERSE.
DO NOT MOCK ME!
SCA-BLAMM
YOU WILL NOT STOP HIM! HE IS THE LORD OF DEATH! YOU CANNOT STOP--
THANOS IS GOING FOR EARTH.
WHAT DO YOU SAY?
GAMORA, I PROMISE YA, I AIN'T DOIN' ANY SUCH THING.
LOOKS LIKE I'M HEADED HOME.

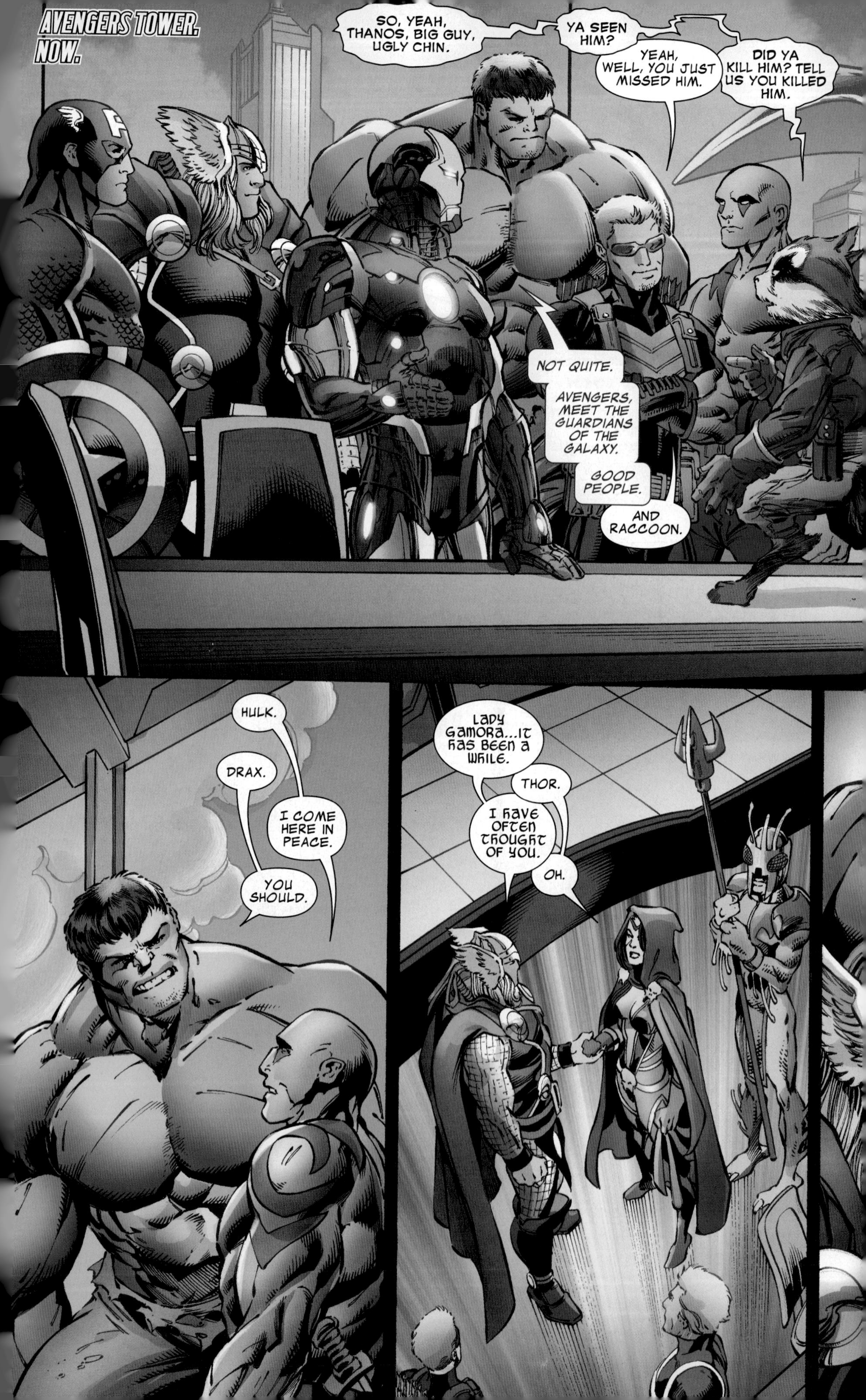
AVENGERS TOWER. NOW.
SO, YEAH, THANOS, BIG GUY, UGLY CHIN.
YA SEEN HIM?
YEAH, WELL, YOU JUST MISSED HIM.
DID YA KILL HIM? TELL US YOU KILLED HIM.
NOT QUITE.
AVENGERS, MEET THE GUARDIANS OF THE GALAXY.
GOOD PEOPLE.
AND RACCOON.
HULK.
DRAX.
I COME HERE IN PEACE.
YOU SHOULD.
LADY GAMORA...IT HAS BEEN A WHILE.
THOR.
I HAVE OFTEN THOUGHT OF YOU.
OH.

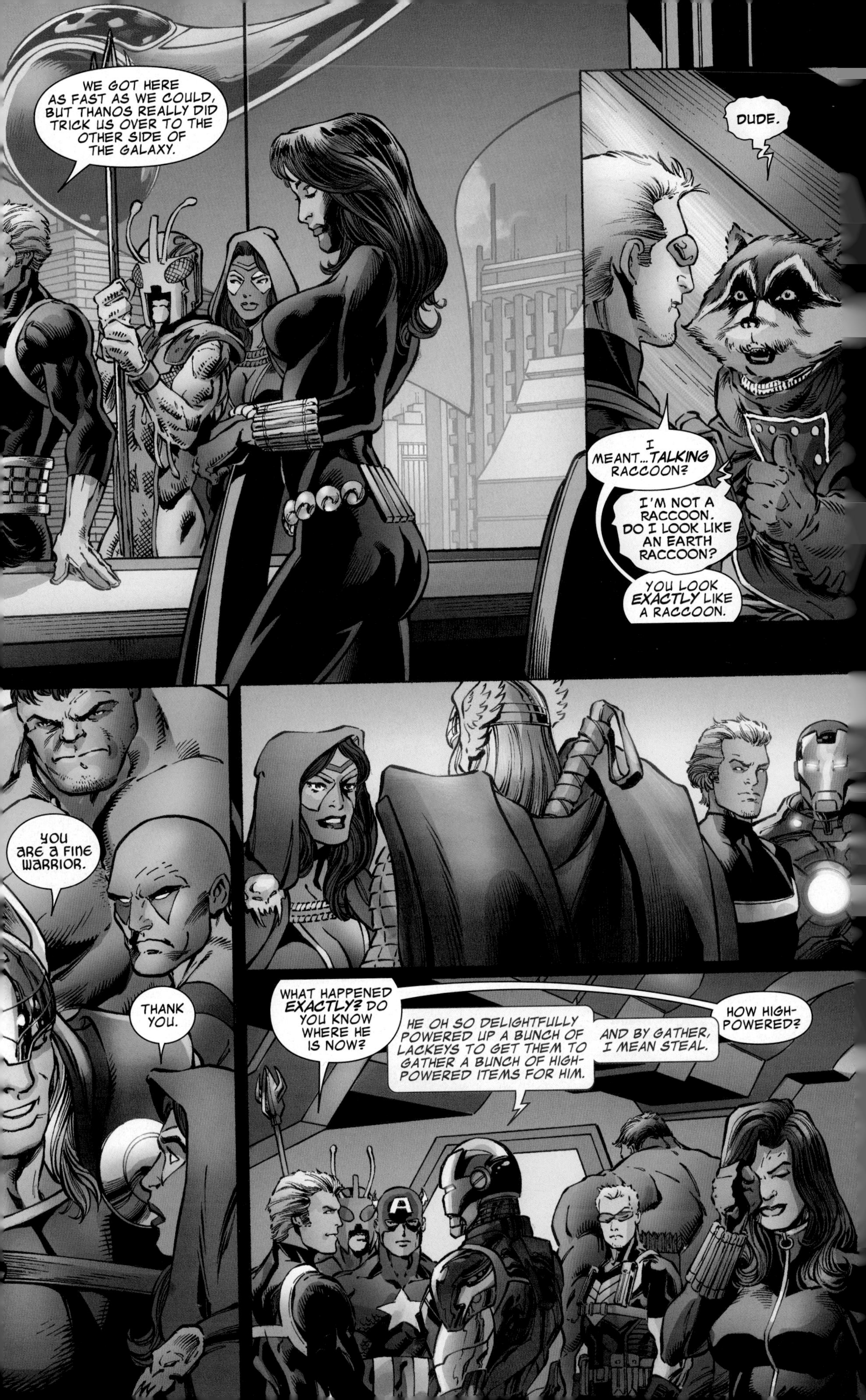
WE GOT HERE AS FAST AS WE COULD, BUT THANOS REALLY DID TRICK US OVER TO THE OTHER SIDE OF THE GALAXY.
DUDE.
I MEANT...TALKING RACCOON?
I'M NOT A RACCOON. DO I LOOK LIKE AN EARTH RACCOON?
YOU LOOK EXACTLY LIKE A RACCOON.
YOU ARE A FINE WARRIOR.
THANK YOU.
WHAT HAPPENED EXACTLY? DO YOU KNOW WHERE HE IS NOW?
HE OH SO DELIGHTFULLY POWERED UP A BUNCH OF LACKEYS TO GET THEM TO GATHER A BUNCH OF HIGH-POWERED ITEMS FOR HIM.
AND BY GATHER, I MEAN STEAL.
HOW HIGH-POWERED?

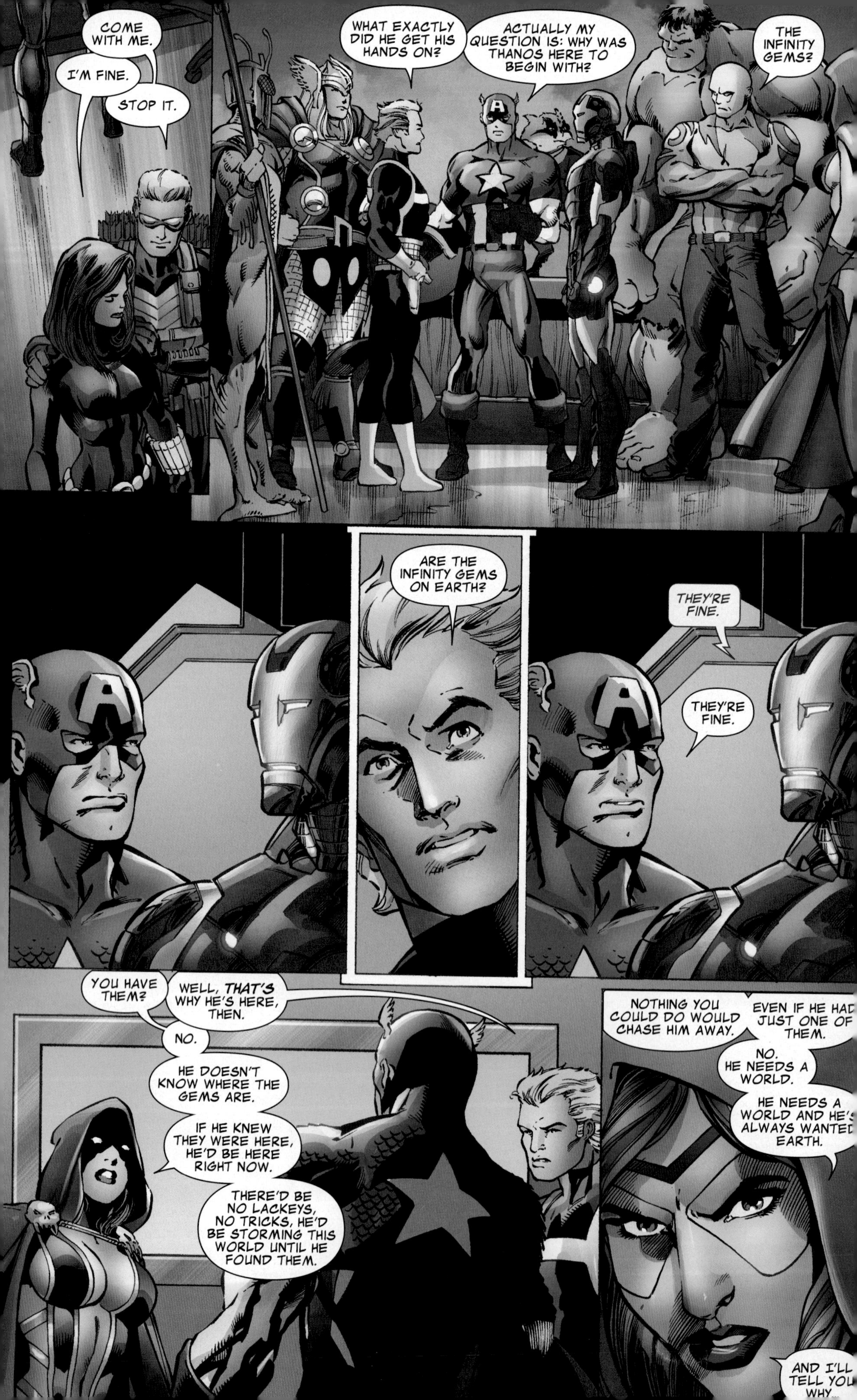
COME WITH ME.
I'M FINE.
STOP IT.
WHAT EXACTLY DID HE GET HIS HANDS ON?
ACTUALLY MY QUESTION IS: WHY WAS THANOS HERE TO BEGIN WITH?
THE INFINITY GEMS?
ARE THE INFINITY GEMS ON EARTH?
THEY'RE FINE.
THEY'RE FINE.
YOU HAVE THEM?
WELL, *THAT'S* WHY HE'S HERE, THEN.
NO.
HE DOESN'T KNOW WHERE THE GEMS ARE.
IF HE KNEW THEY WERE HERE, HE'D BE HERE RIGHT NOW.
THERE'D BE NO LACKEYS, NO TRICKS, HE'D BE STORMING THIS WORLD UNTIL HE FOUND THEM.
NOTHING YOU COULD DO WOULD CHASE HIM AWAY.
EVEN IF HE HAD JUST ONE OF THEM.
NO. HE NEEDS A WORLD.
HE NEEDS A WORLD AND HE'S ALWAYS WANTED EARTH.
AND I'LL TELL YOU WHY.

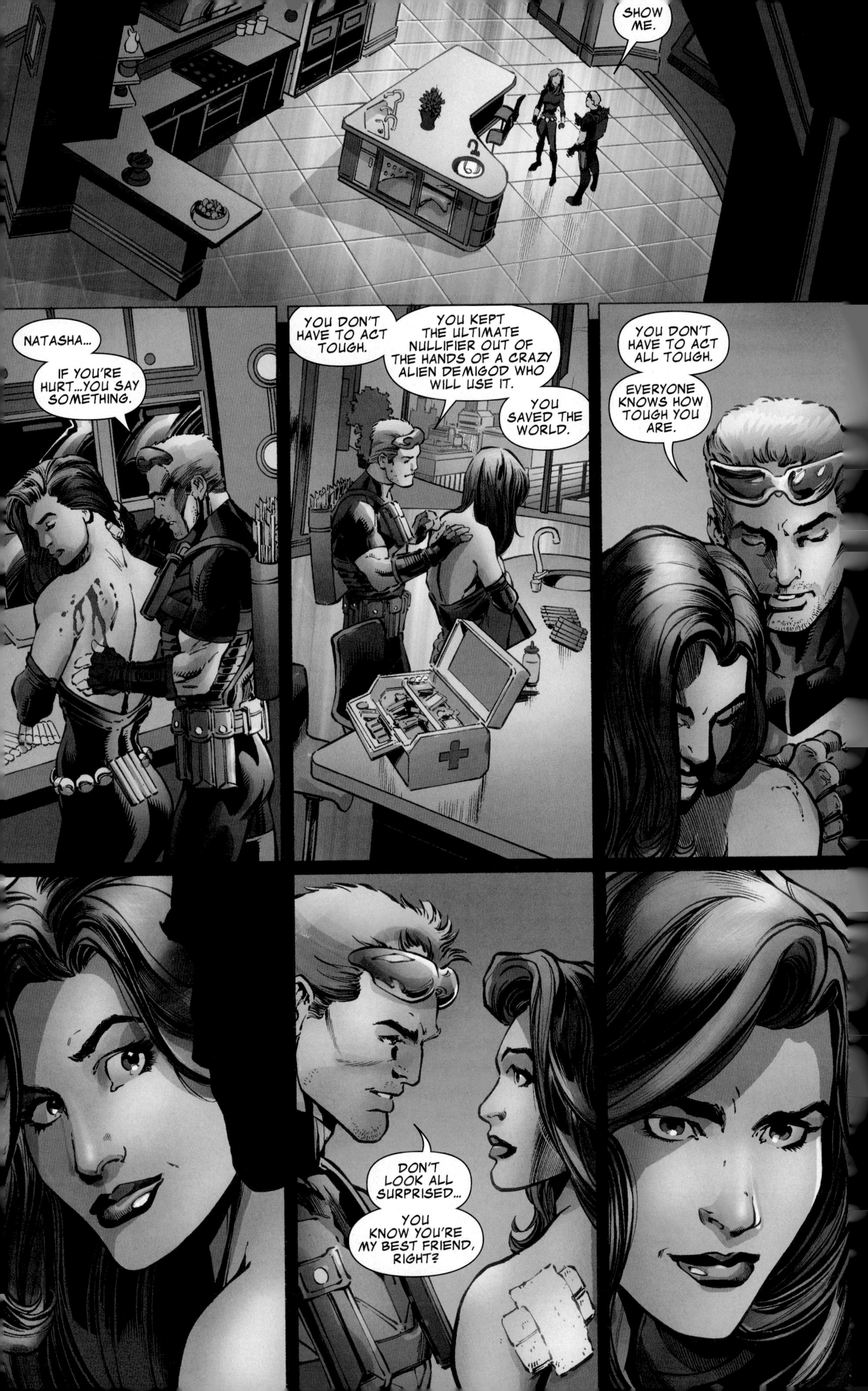
SHOW ME.
NATASHA...
IF YOU'RE HURT...YOU SAY SOMETHING.
YOU DON'T HAVE TO ACT TOUGH.
YOU KEPT THE ULTIMATE NULLIFIER OUT OF THE HANDS OF A CRAZY ALIEN DEMIGOD WHO WILL USE IT.
YOU SAVED THE WORLD.
YOU DON'T HAVE TO ACT ALL TOUGH.
EVERYONE KNOWS HOW TOUGH YOU ARE.
DON'T LOOK ALL SURPRISED...
YOU KNOW YOU'RE MY BEST FRIEND, RIGHT?

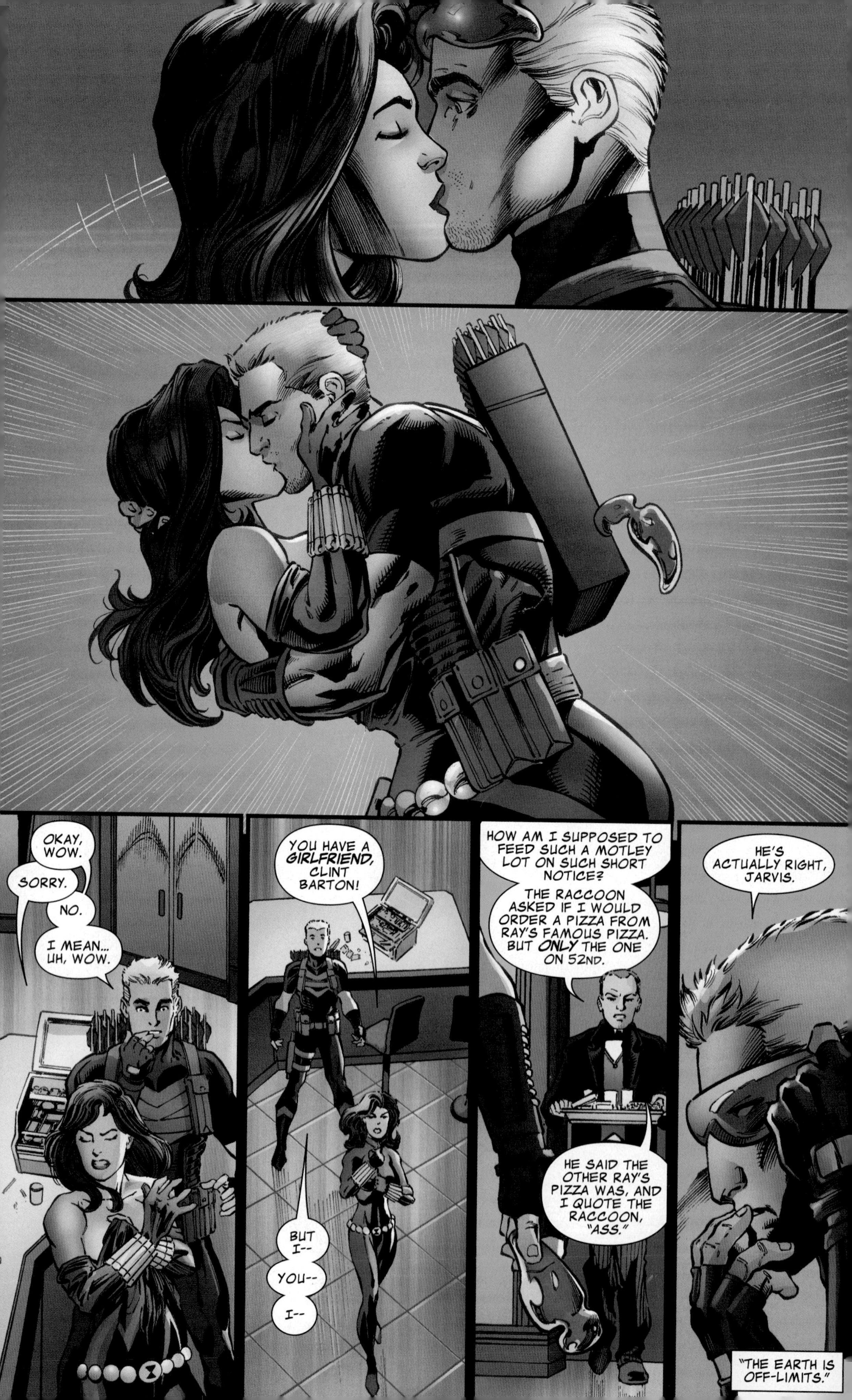
OKAY, WOW.
SORRY.
NO.
I MEAN... UH, WOW.
YOU HAVE A GIRLFRIEND, CLINT BARTON!
BUT I--
YOU--
I--
HOW AM I SUPPOSED TO FEED SUCH A MOTLEY LOT ON SUCH SHORT NOTICE?
THE RACCOON ASKED IF I WOULD ORDER A PIZZA FROM RAY'S FAMOUS PIZZA. BUT ONLY THE ONE ON 52ND.
HE SAID THE OTHER RAY'S PIZZA WAS, AND I QUOTE THE RACCOON, "ASS."
HE'S ACTUALLY RIGHT, JARVIS.
"THE EARTH IS OFF-LIMITS."

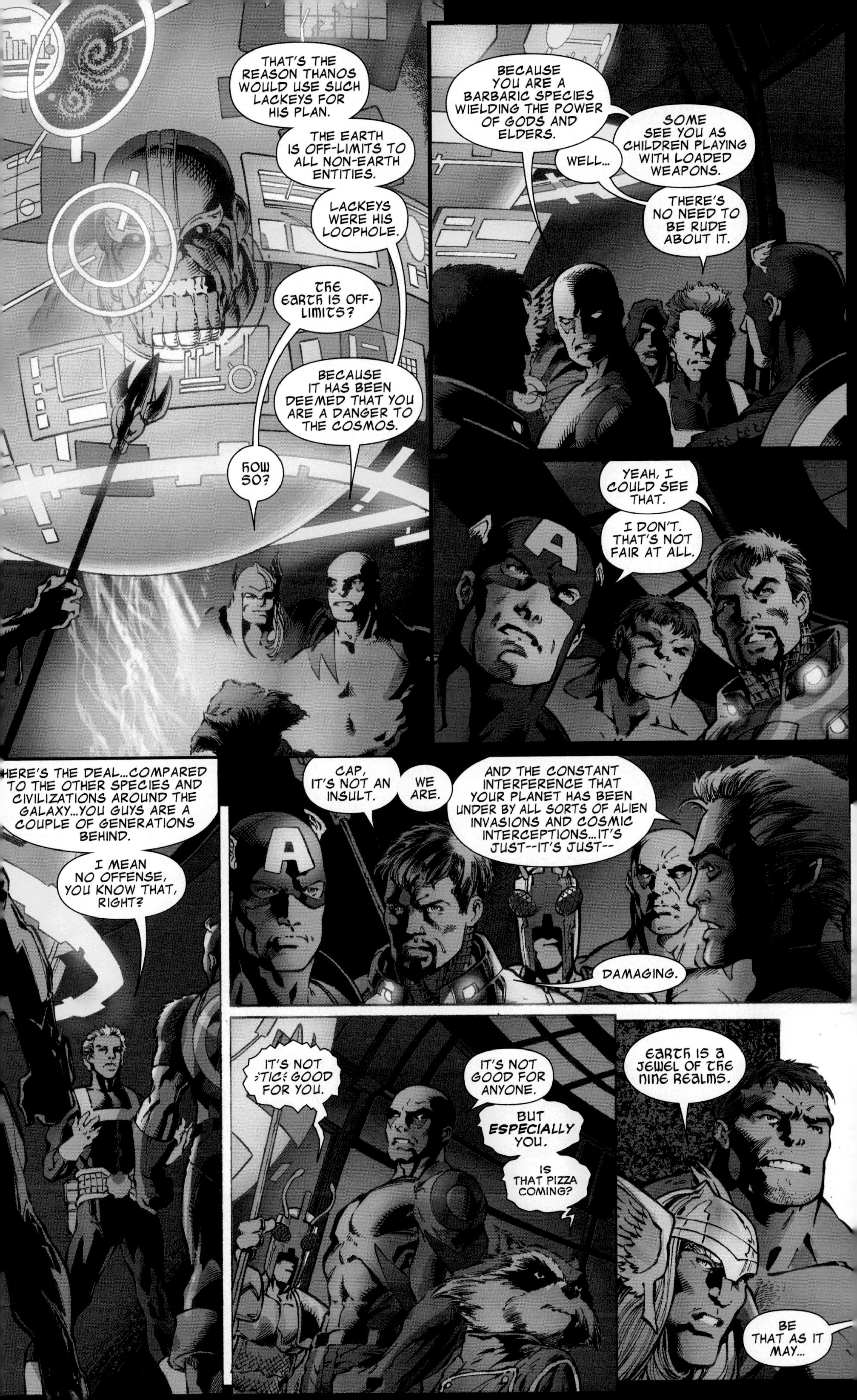
THAT'S THE REASON THANOS WOULD USE SUCH LACKEYS FOR HIS PLAN.
THE EARTH IS OFF-LIMITS TO ALL NON-EARTH ENTITIES.
LACKEYS WERE HIS LOOPHOLE.
THE EARTH IS OFF-LIMITS?
BECAUSE IT HAS BEEN DEEMED THAT YOU ARE A DANGER TO THE COSMOS.
HOW SO?
BECAUSE YOU ARE A BARBARIC SPECIES WIELDING THE POWER OF GODS AND ELDERS.
SOME SEE YOU AS CHILDREN PLAYING WITH LOADED WEAPONS.
WELL...
THERE'S NO NEED TO BE RUDE ABOUT IT.
YEAH, I COULD SEE THAT.
I DON'T. THAT'S NOT FAIR AT ALL.
HERE'S THE DEAL...COMPARED TO THE OTHER SPECIES AND CIVILIZATIONS AROUND THE GALAXY...YOU GUYS ARE A COUPLE OF GENERATIONS BEHIND.
I MEAN NO OFFENSE, YOU KNOW THAT, RIGHT?
CAP, IT'S NOT AN INSULT.
WE ARE.
AND THE CONSTANT INTERFERENCE THAT YOUR PLANET HAS BEEN UNDER BY ALL SORTS OF ALIEN INVASIONS AND COSMIC INTERCEPTIONS...IT'S JUST--IT'S JUST--
DAMAGING.
IT'S NOT -TIC- GOOD FOR YOU.
IT'S NOT GOOD FOR ANYONE.
BUT **ESPECIALLY** YOU.
IS THAT PIZZA COMING?
EARTH IS A JEWEL OF THE NINE REALMS.
BE THAT AS IT MAY...

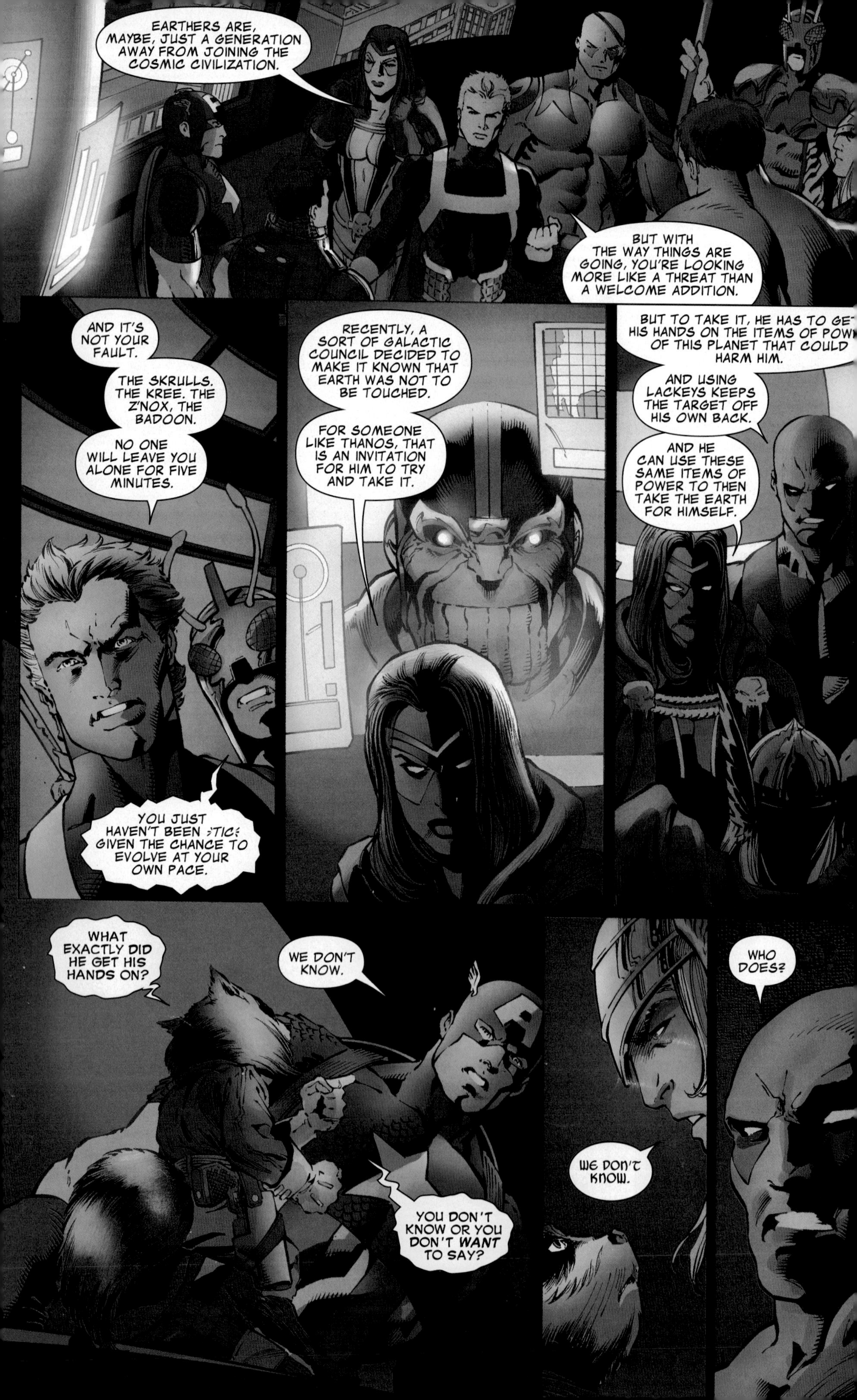
EARTHERS ARE, MAYBE, JUST A GENERATION AWAY FROM JOINING THE COSMIC CIVILIZATION.
BUT WITH THE WAY THINGS ARE GOING, YOU'RE LOOKING MORE LIKE A THREAT THAN A WELCOME ADDITION.
AND IT'S NOT YOUR FAULT.
THE SKRULLS. THE KREE. THE Z'NOX, THE BADOON.
NO ONE WILL LEAVE YOU ALONE FOR FIVE MINUTES.
YOU JUST HAVEN'T BEEN *TIC* GIVEN THE CHANCE TO EVOLVE AT YOUR OWN PACE.
RECENTLY, A SORT OF GALACTIC COUNCIL DECIDED TO MAKE IT KNOWN THAT EARTH WAS NOT TO BE TOUCHED.
FOR SOMEONE LIKE THANOS, THAT IS AN INVITATION FOR HIM TO TRY AND TAKE IT.
BUT TO TAKE IT, HE HAS TO GET HIS HANDS ON THE ITEMS OF POW OF THIS PLANET THAT COULD HARM HIM.
AND USING LACKEYS KEEPS THE TARGET OFF HIS OWN BACK.
AND HE CAN USE THESE SAME ITEMS OF POWER TO THEN TAKE THE EARTH FOR HIMSELF.
WHAT EXACTLY DID HE GET HIS HANDS ON?
WE DON'T KNOW.
YOU DON'T KNOW OR YOU DON'T *WANT* TO SAY?
WHO DOES?
WE DON'T KNOW.

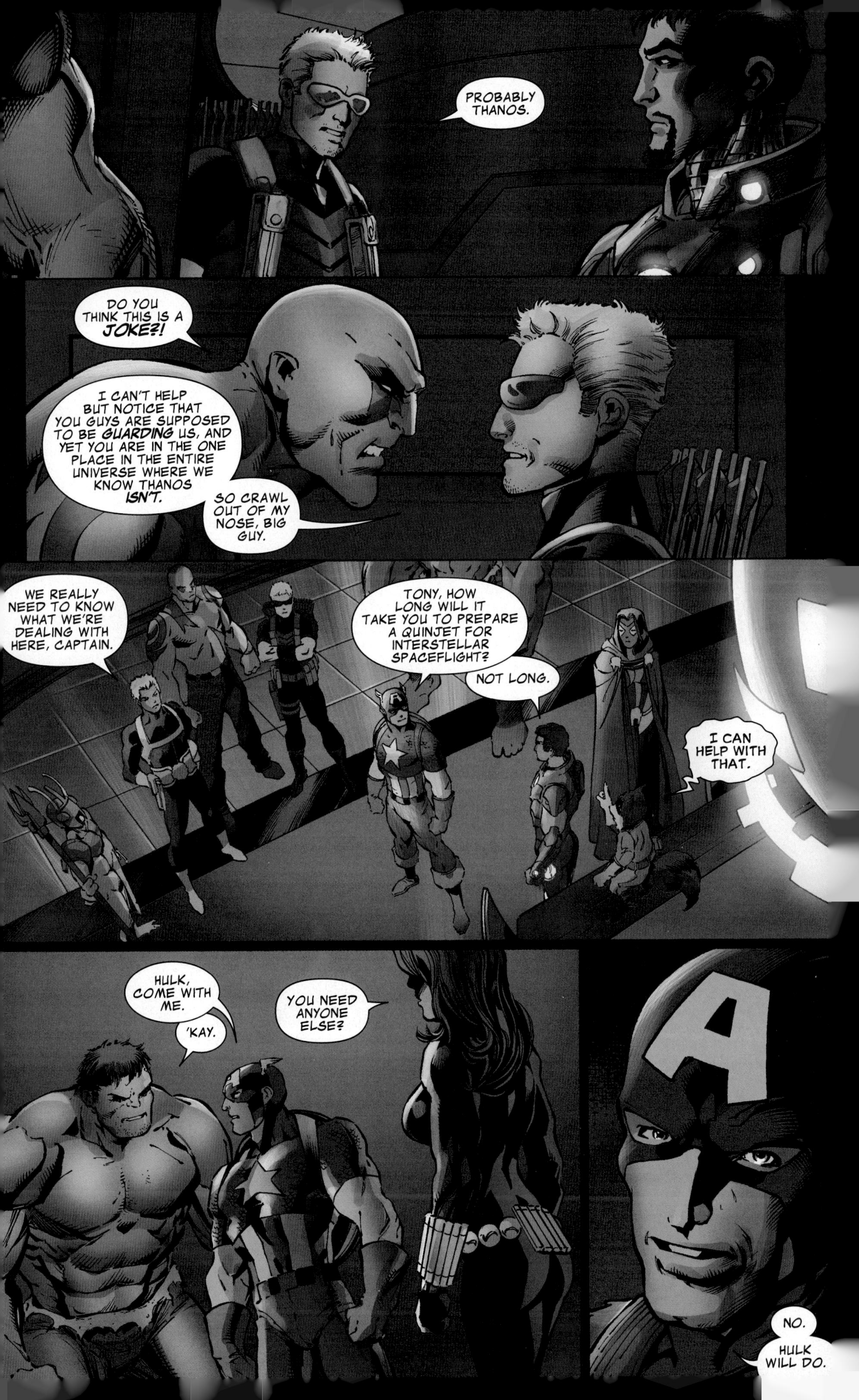

PROBABLY THANOS.
DO YOU THINK THIS IS A JOKE?!
I CAN'T HELP BUT NOTICE THAT YOU GUYS ARE SUPPOSED TO BE GUARDING US, AND YET YOU ARE IN THE ONE PLACE IN THE ENTIRE UNIVERSE WHERE WE KNOW THANOS ISN'T.
SO CRAWL OUT OF MY NOSE, BIG GUY.
WE REALLY NEED TO KNOW WHAT WE'RE DEALING WITH HERE, CAPTAIN.
TONY, HOW LONG WILL IT TAKE YOU TO PREPARE A QUINJET FOR INTERSTELLAR SPACEFLIGHT?
NOT LONG.
I CAN HELP WITH THAT.
HULK, COME WITH ME.
'KAY.
YOU NEED ANYONE ELSE?
NO.
HULK WILL DO.

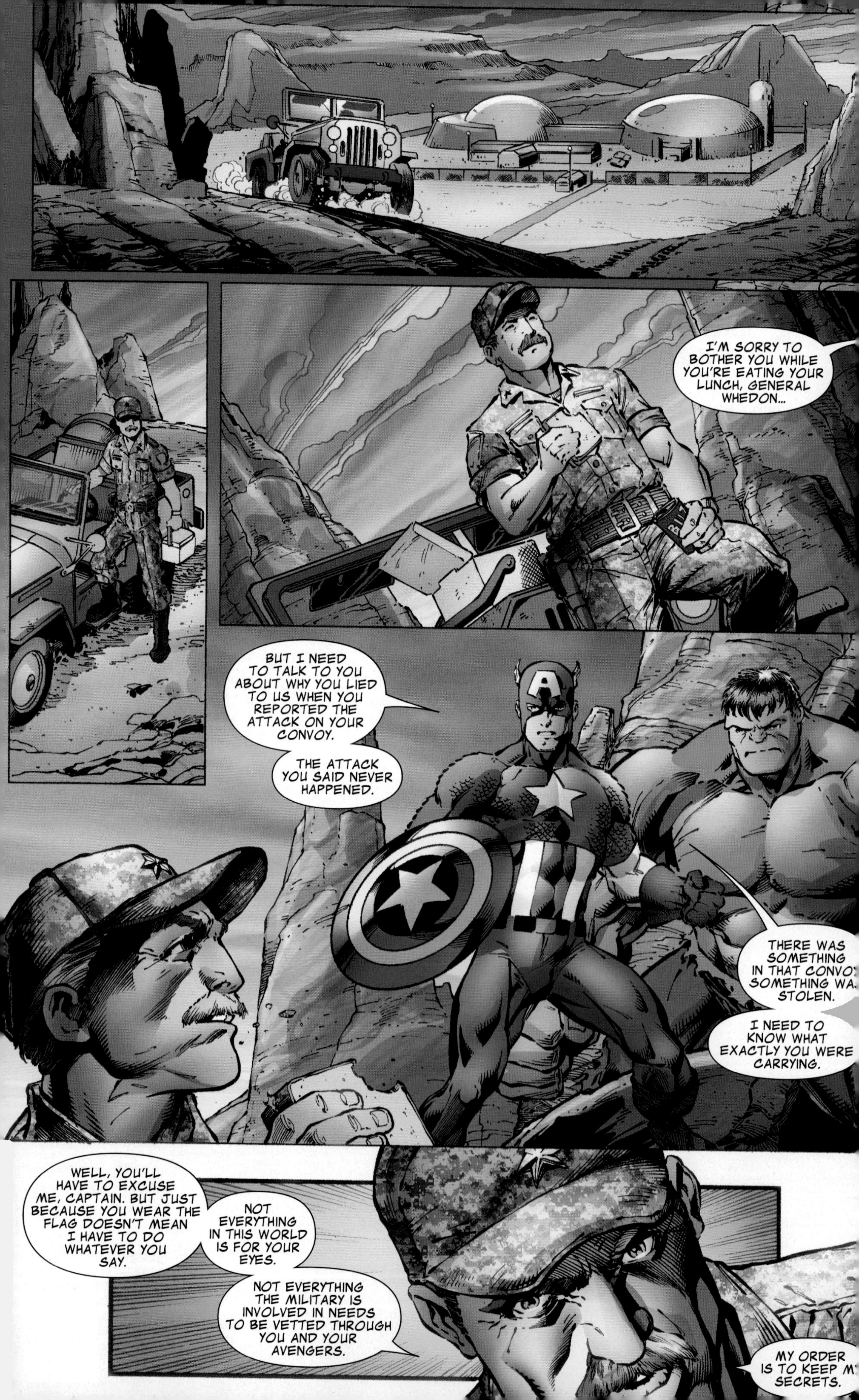

I'M SORRY TO BOTHER YOU WHILE YOU'RE EATING YOUR LUNCH, GENERAL WHEDON...
BUT I NEED TO TALK TO YOU ABOUT WHY YOU LIED TO US WHEN YOU REPORTED THE ATTACK ON YOUR CONVOY.
THE ATTACK YOU SAID NEVER HAPPENED.
THERE WAS SOMETHING IN THAT CONVO SOMETHING WA STOLEN.
I NEED TO KNOW WHAT EXACTLY YOU WERE CARRYING.
WELL, YOU'LL HAVE TO EXCUSE ME, CAPTAIN. BUT JUST BECAUSE YOU WEAR THE FLAG DOESN'T MEAN I HAVE TO DO WHATEVER YOU SAY.
NOT EVERYTHING IN THIS WORLD IS FOR YOUR EYES.
NOT EVERYTHING THE MILITARY IS INVOLVED IN NEEDS TO BE VETTED THROUGH YOU AND YOUR AVENGERS.
MY ORDER IS TO KEEP M SECRETS.

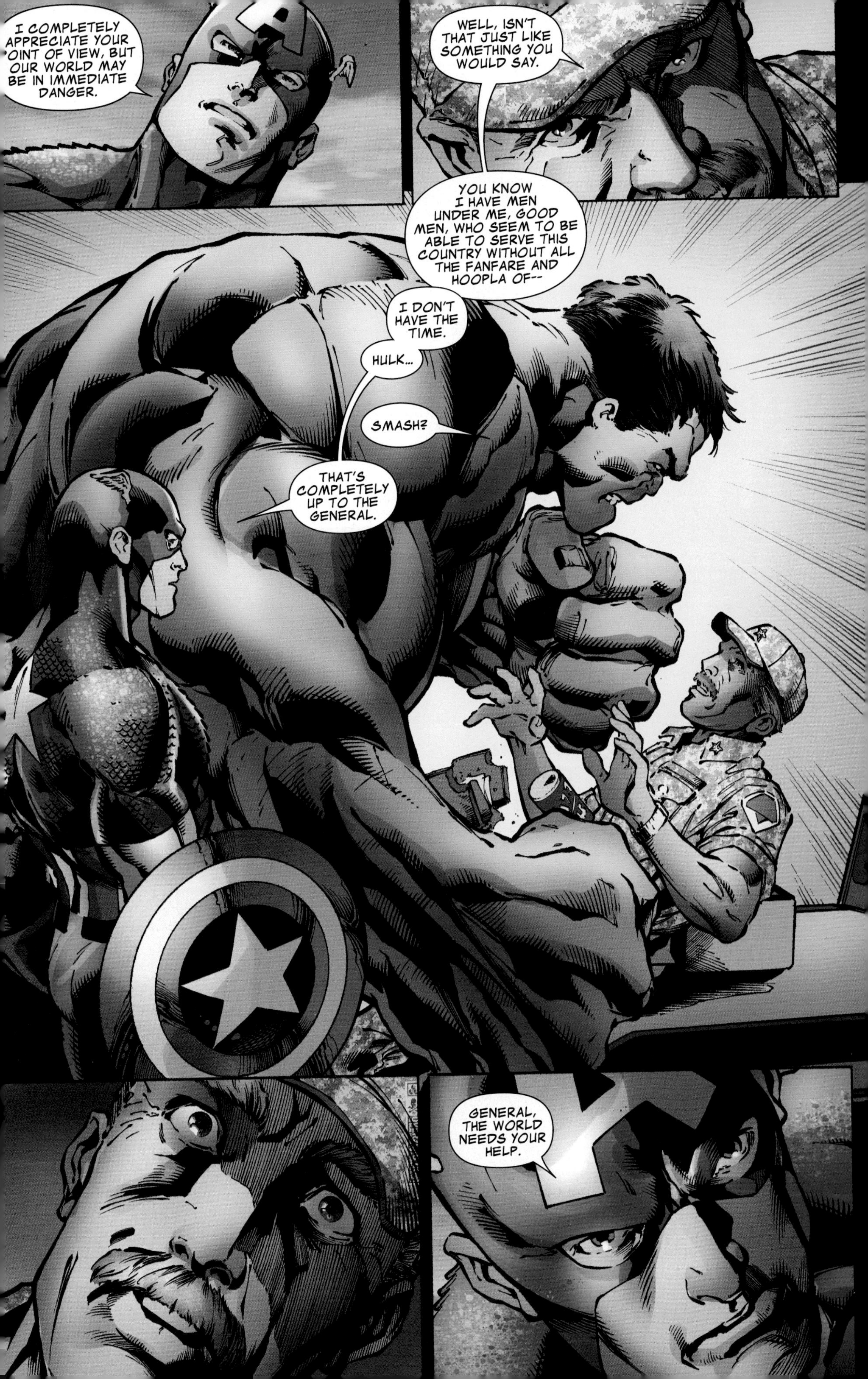
I COMPLETELY APPRECIATE YOUR 'OINT OF VIEW, BUT OUR WORLD MAY BE IN IMMEDIATE DANGER.
WELL, ISN'T THAT JUST LIKE SOMETHING YOU WOULD SAY.
YOU KNOW I HAVE MEN UNDER ME, GOOD MEN, WHO SEEM TO BE ABLE TO SERVE THIS COUNTRY WITHOUT ALL THE FANFARE AND HOOPLA OF--
I DON'T HAVE THE TIME.
HULK...
SMASH?
THAT'S COMPLETELY UP TO THE GENERAL.
GENERAL, THE WORLD NEEDS YOUR HELP.

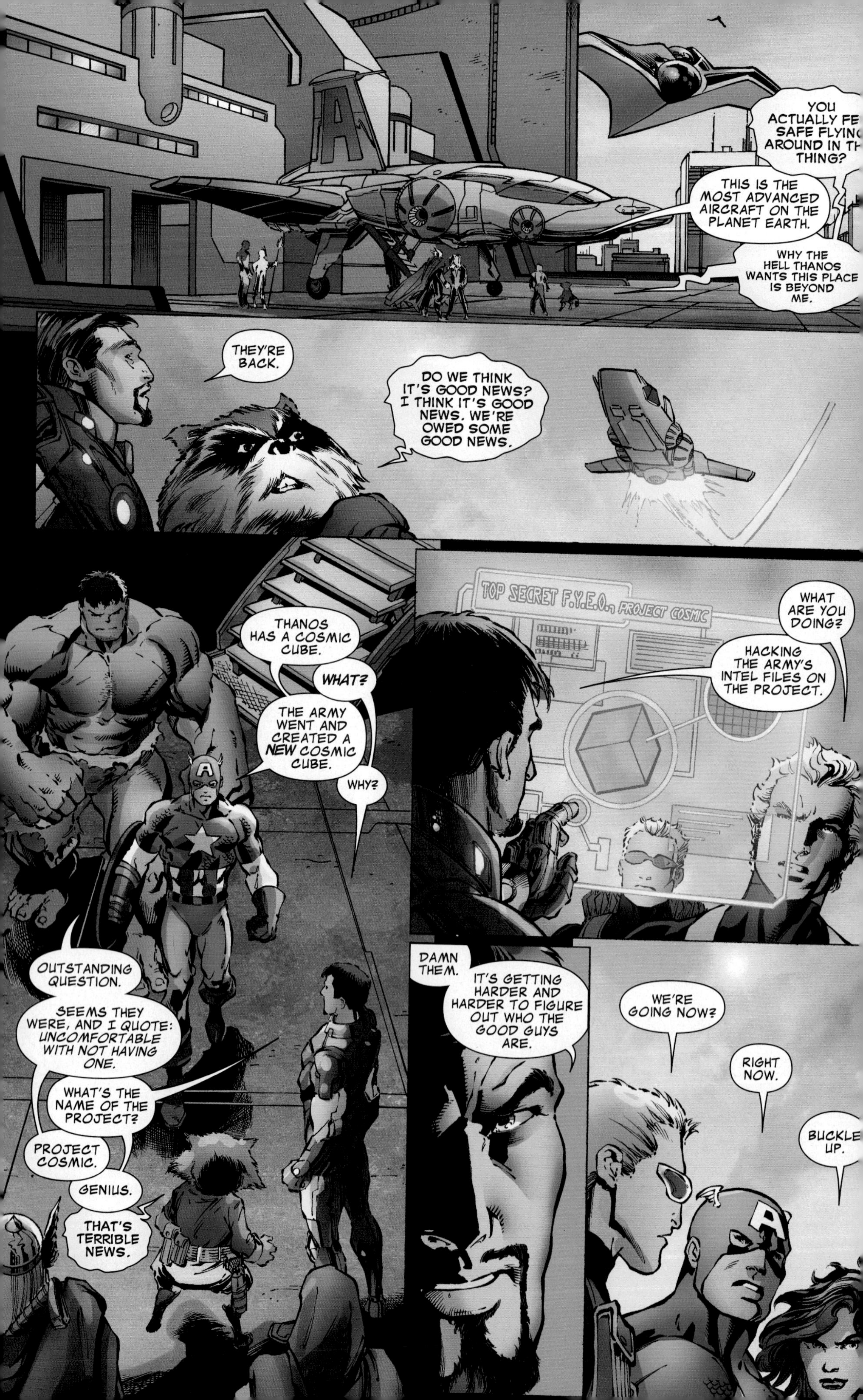
YOU ACTUALLY FE SAFE FLYIN AROUND IN TH THING?
THIS IS THE MOST ADVANCED AIRCRAFT ON THE PLANET EARTH.
WHY THE HELL THANOS WANTS THIS PLACE IS BEYOND ME.
THEY'RE BACK.
DO WE THINK IT'S GOOD NEWS? I THINK IT'S GOOD NEWS. WE'RE OWED SOME GOOD NEWS.
THANOS HAS A COSMIC CUBE.
WHAT?
THE ARMY WENT AND CREATED A NEW COSMIC CUBE.
WHY?
OUTSTANDING QUESTION.
SEEMS THEY WERE, AND I QUOTE: UNCOMFORTABLE WITH NOT HAVING ONE.
WHAT'S THE NAME OF THE PROJECT?
PROJECT COSMIC.
GENIUS.
THAT'S TERRIBLE NEWS.
TOP SECRET F.Y.E.O., PROJECT COSMIC
WHAT ARE YOU DOING?
HACKING THE ARMY'S INTEL FILES ON THE PROJECT.
DAMN THEM.
IT'S GETTING HARDER AND HARDER TO FIGURE OUT WHO THE GOOD GUYS ARE.
WE'RE GOING NOW?
RIGHT NOW.
BUCKLE UP.

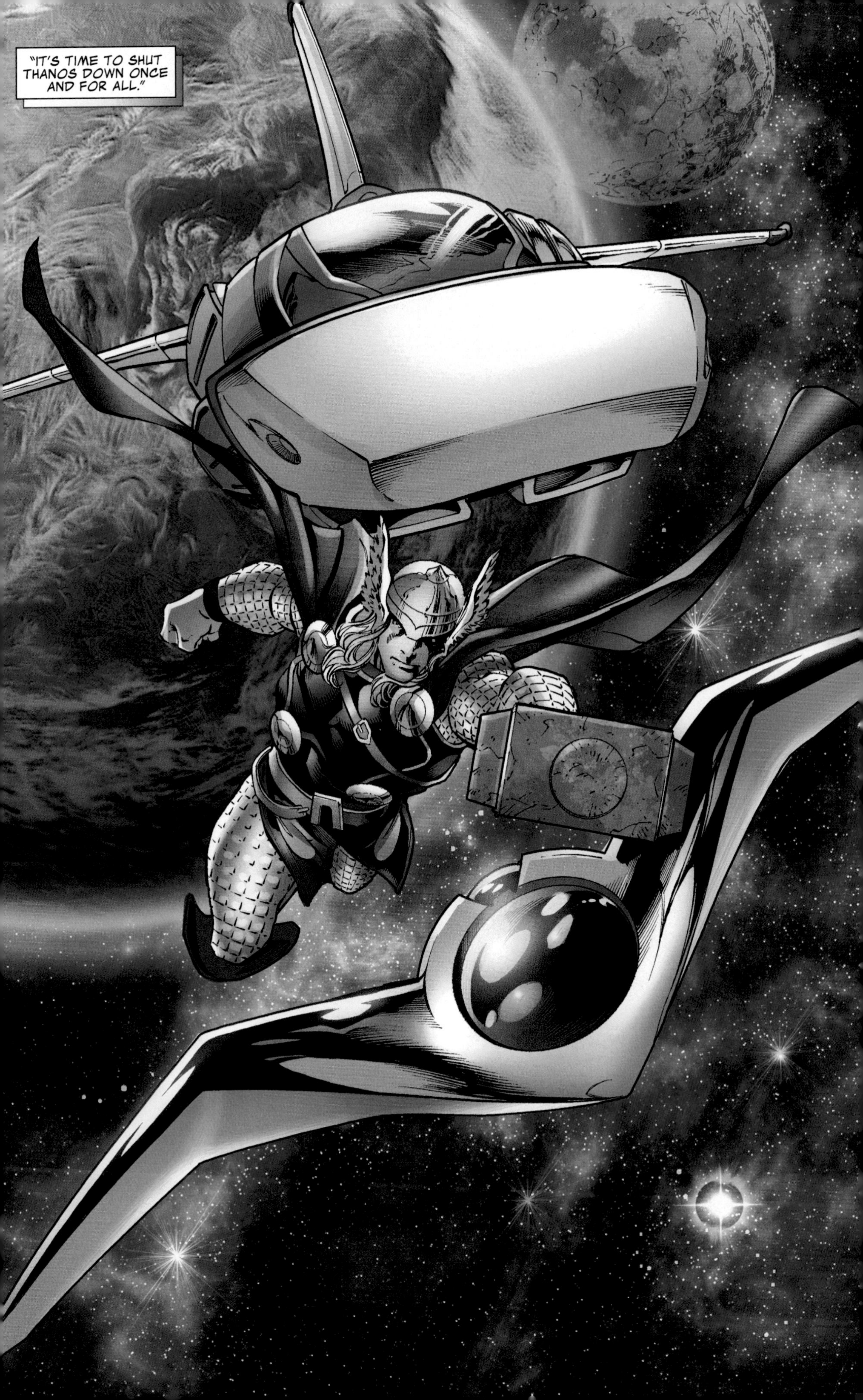
"IT'S TIME TO SHUT THANOS DOWN ONCE AND FOR ALL."

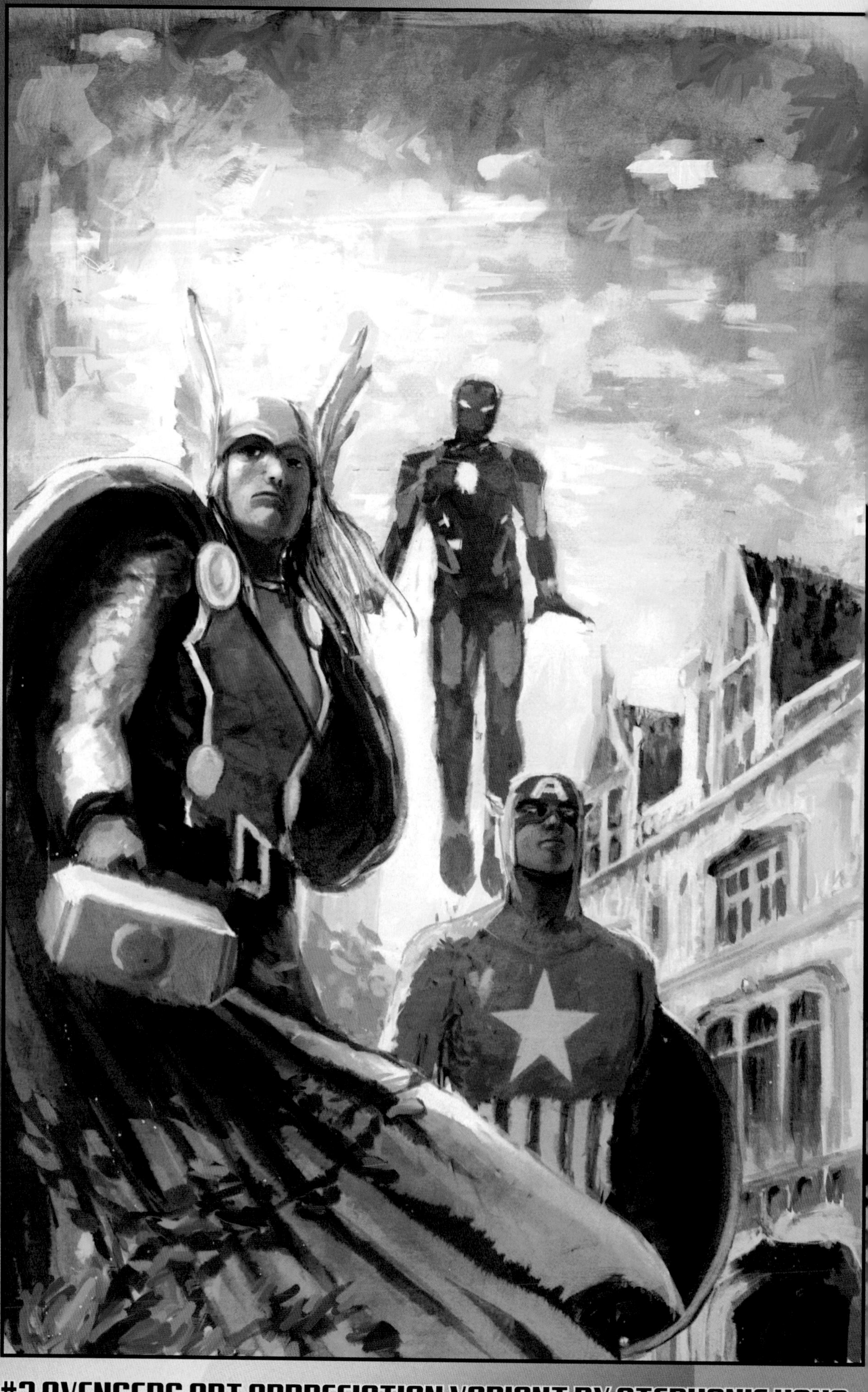

#2 AVENGERS ART APPRECIATION VARIANT BY STEPHANIE HANS

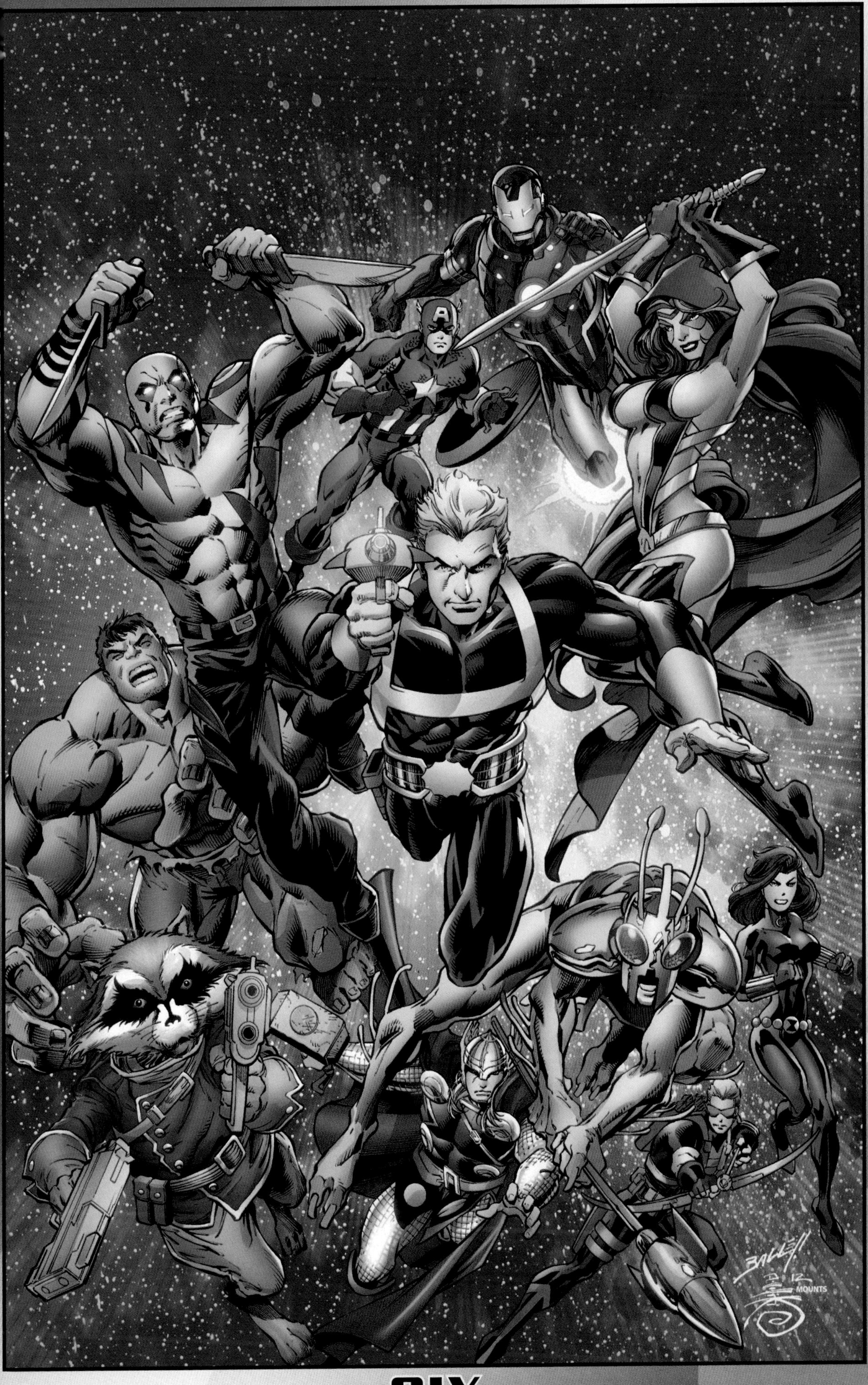
MOUNTS

SIX

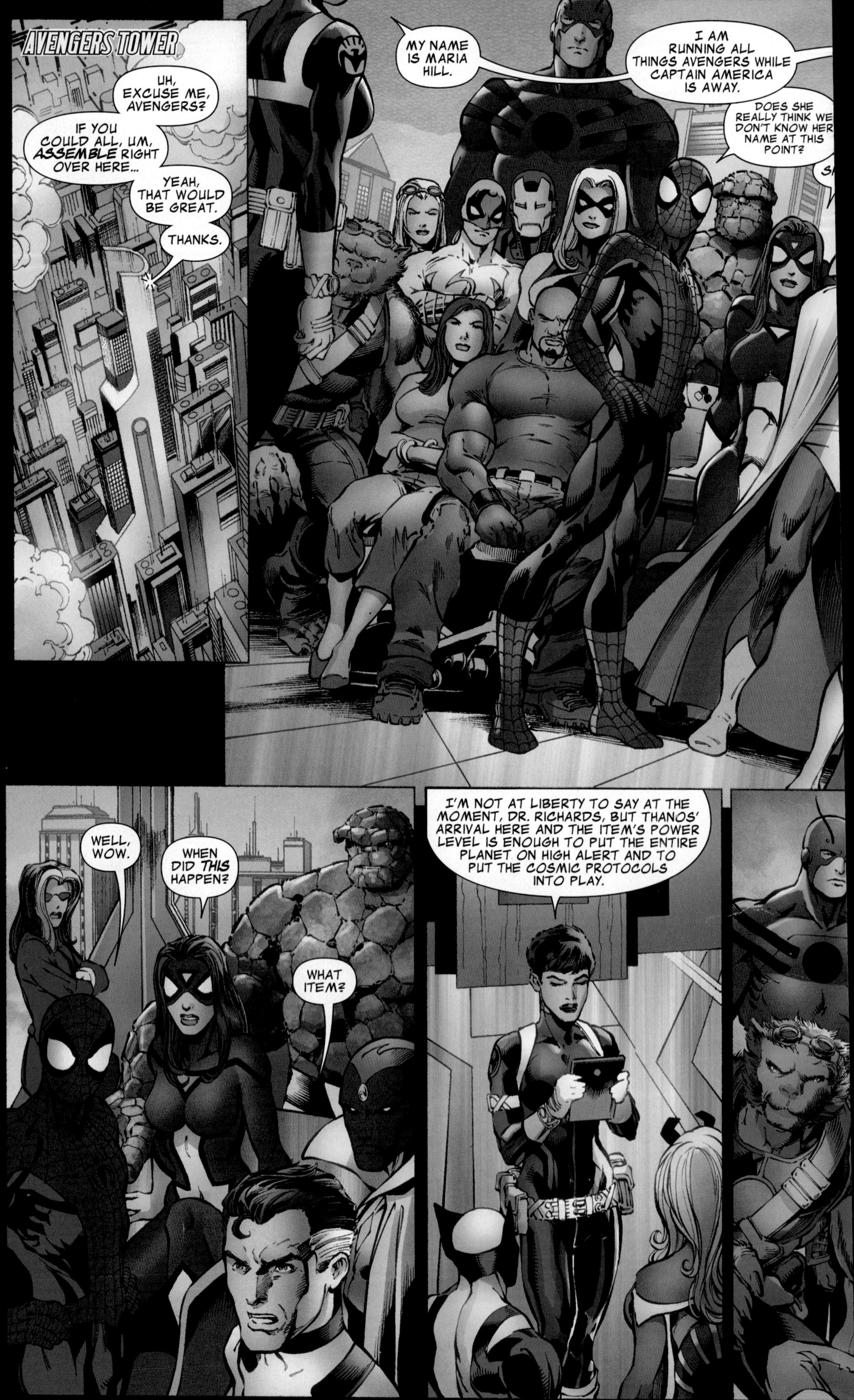
AVENGERS TOWER
UH, EXCUSE ME, AVENGERS?
IF YOU COULD ALL, UM, ASSEMBLE RIGHT OVER HERE...
YEAH, THAT WOULD BE GREAT.
THANKS.
MY NAME IS MARIA HILL.
I AM RUNNING ALL THINGS AVENGERS WHILE CAPTAIN AMERICA IS AWAY.
DOES SHE REALLY THINK WE DON'T KNOW HER NAME AT THIS POINT?
WELL, WOW.
WHEN DID THIS HAPPEN?
WHAT ITEM?
I'M NOT AT LIBERTY TO SAY AT THE MOMENT, DR. RICHARDS, BUT THANOS' ARRIVAL HERE AND THE ITEM'S POWER LEVEL IS ENOUGH TO PUT THE ENTIRE PLANET ON HIGH ALERT AND TO PUT THE COSMIC PROTOCOLS INTO PLAY.

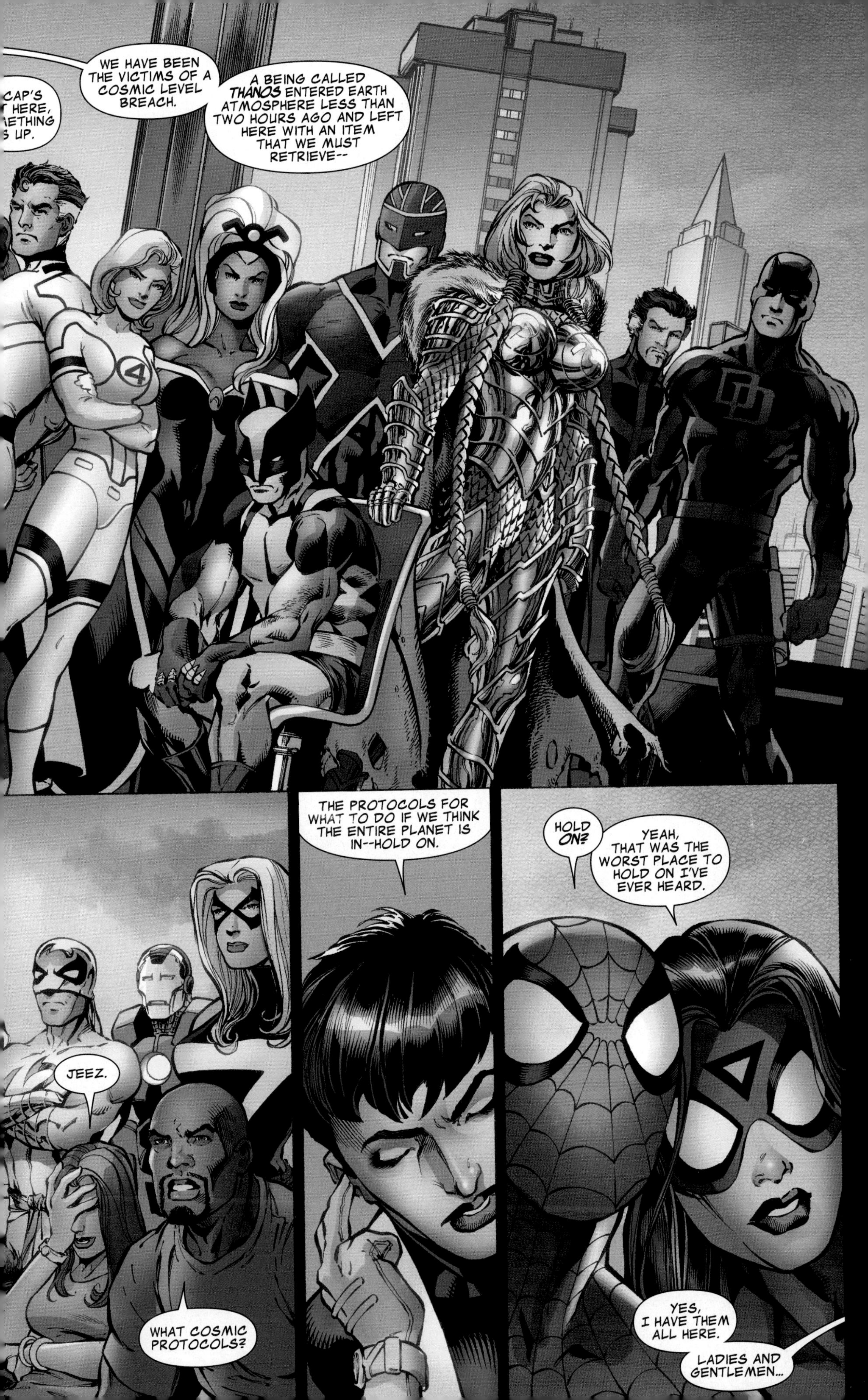
WE HAVE BEEN THE VICTIMS OF A COSMIC LEVEL BREACH.
A BEING CALLED THANOS ENTERED EARTH ATMOSPHERE LESS THAN TWO HOURS AGO AND LEFT HERE WITH AN ITEM THAT WE MUST RETRIEVE--
JEEZ.
WHAT COSMIC PROTOCOLS?
THE PROTOCOLS FOR WHAT TO DO IF WE THINK THE ENTIRE PLANET IS IN--HOLD ON.
HOLD ON?
YEAH, THAT WAS THE WORST PLACE TO HOLD ON I'VE EVER HEARD.
YES, I HAVE THEM ALL HERE.
LADIES AND GENTLEMEN...

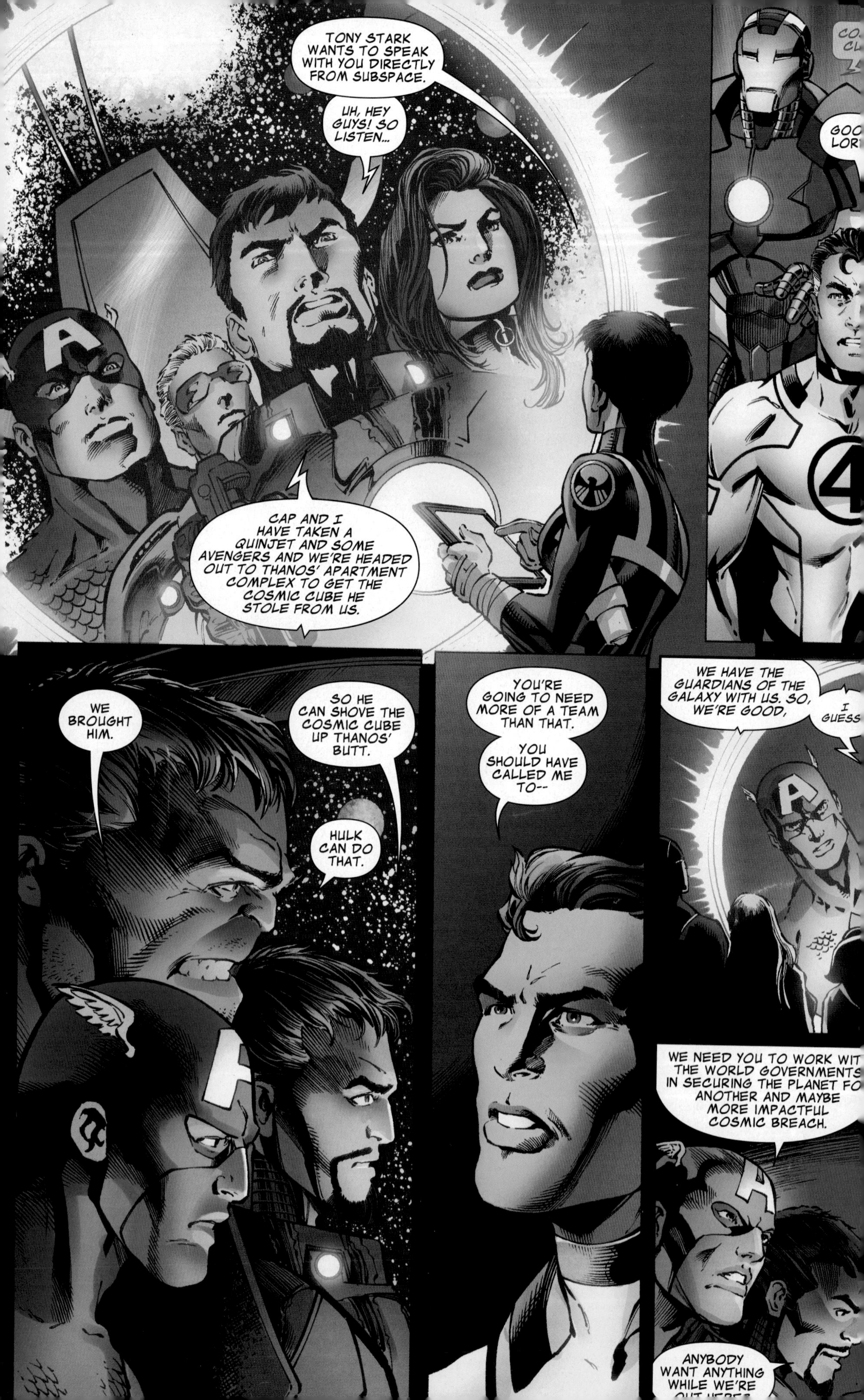
TONY STARK WANTS TO SPEAK WITH YOU DIRECTLY FROM SUBSPACE.
UH, HEY GUYS! SO LISTEN...
CAP AND I HAVE TAKEN A QUINJET AND SOME AVENGERS AND WE'RE HEADED OUT TO THANOS' APARTMENT COMPLEX TO GET THE COSMIC CUBE HE STOLE FROM US.
WE BROUGHT HIM.
SO HE CAN SHOVE THE COSMIC CUBE UP THANOS' BUTT.
HULK CAN DO THAT.
YOU'RE GOING TO NEED MORE OF A TEAM THAN THAT.
YOU SHOULD HAVE CALLED ME TO--
WE HAVE THE GUARDIANS OF THE GALAXY WITH US. SO, WE'RE GOOD,
I GUESS.
WE NEED YOU TO WORK WIT THE WORLD GOVERNMENTS IN SECURING THE PLANET FO ANOTHER AND MAYBE MORE IMPACTFUL COSMIC BREACH.
ANYBODY WANT ANYTHING WHILE WE'RE

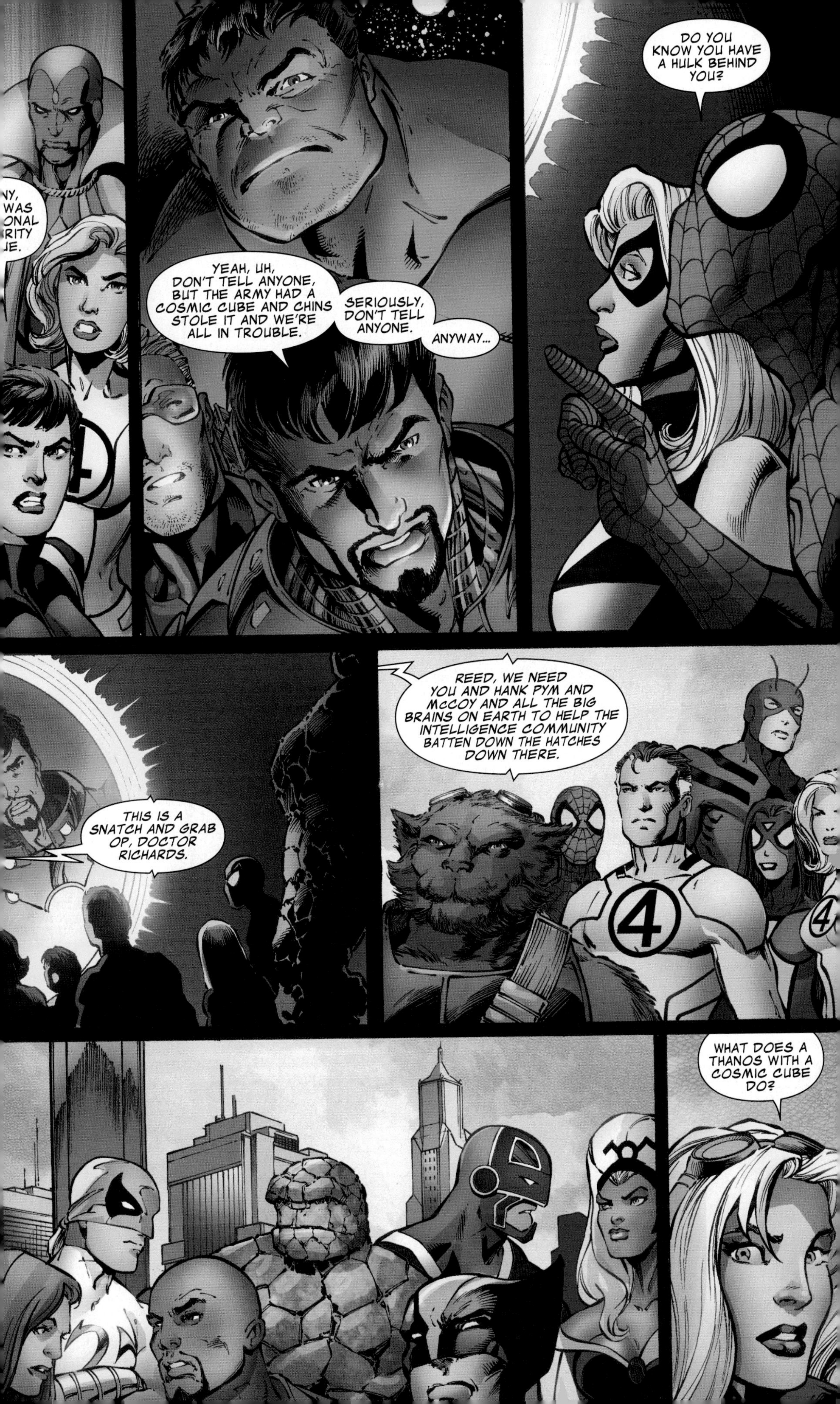

YEAH, UH, DON'T TELL ANYONE, BUT THE ARMY HAD A COSMIC CUBE AND CHINS STOLE IT AND WE'RE ALL IN TROUBLE.
SERIOUSLY, DON'T TELL ANYONE.
ANYWAY...
DO YOU KNOW YOU HAVE A HULK BEHIND YOU?
THIS IS A SNATCH AND GRAB OP, DOCTOR RICHARDS.
REED, WE NEED YOU AND HANK PYM AND McCOY AND ALL THE BIG BRAINS ON EARTH TO HELP THE INTELLIGENCE COMMUNITY BATTEN DOWN THE HATCHES DOWN THERE.
WHAT DOES A THANOS WITH A COSMIC CUBE DO?

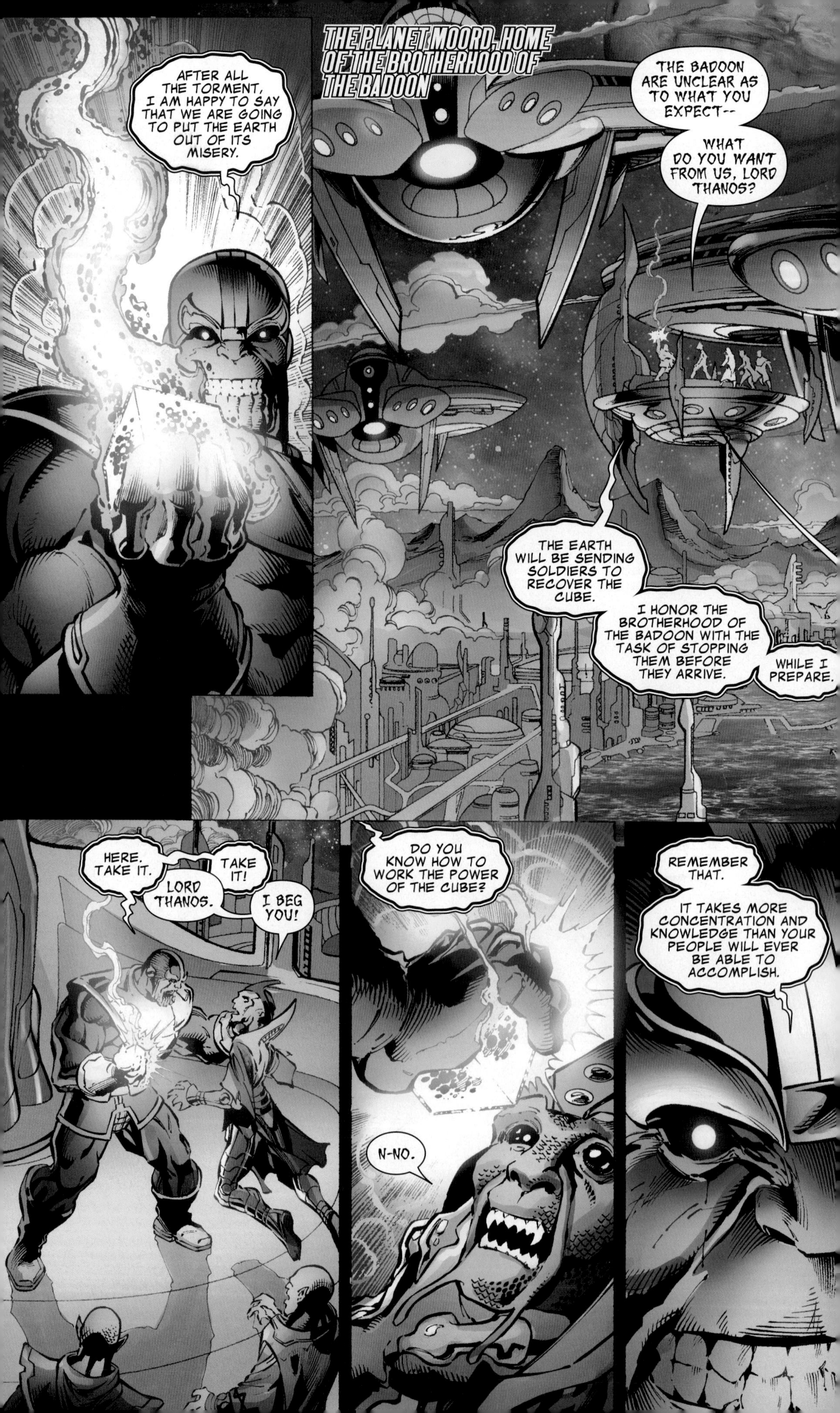
AFTER ALL THE TORMENT, I AM HAPPY TO SAY THAT WE ARE GOING TO PUT THE EARTH OUT OF ITS MISERY.
THE PLANET MOORD, HOME OF THE BROTHERHOOD OF THE BADOON
THE BADOON ARE UNCLEAR AS TO WHAT YOU EXPECT--
WHAT DO YOU WANT FROM US, LORD THANOS?
THE EARTH WILL BE SENDING SOLDIERS TO RECOVER THE CUBE.
I HONOR THE BROTHERHOOD OF THE BADOON WITH THE TASK OF STOPPING THEM BEFORE THEY ARRIVE.
WHILE I PREPARE.
HERE. TAKE IT.
LORD THANOS.
TAKE IT!
I BEG YOU!
DO YOU KNOW HOW TO WORK THE POWER OF THE CUBE?
N-NO.
REMEMBER THAT.
IT TAKES MORE CONCENTRATION AND KNOWLEDGE THAN YOUR PEOPLE WILL EVER BE ABLE TO ACCOMPLISH.

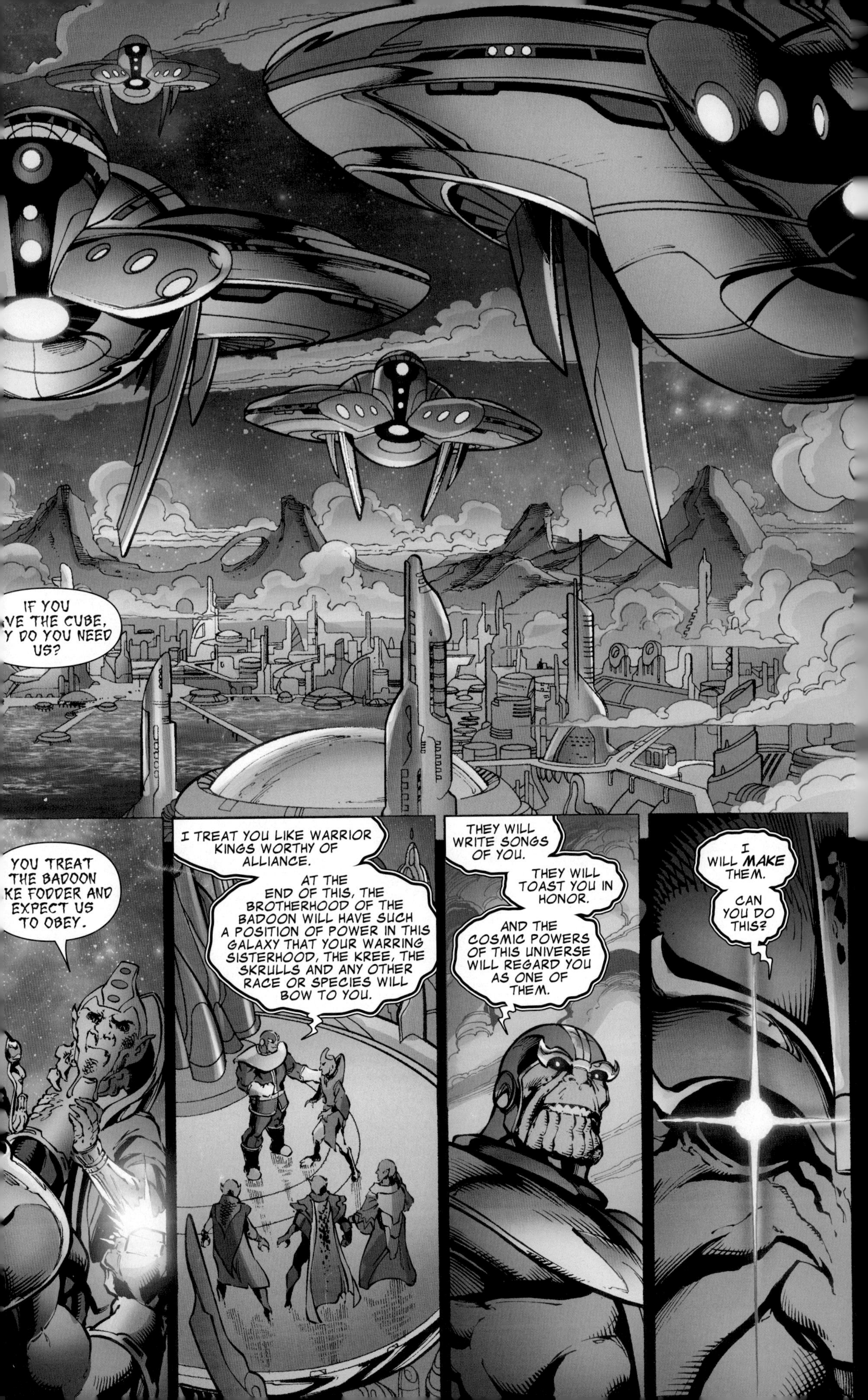
IF YOU
VE THE CUBE,
Y DO YOU NEED
US?
YOU TREAT
THE BADOON
KE FODDER AND
EXPECT US
TO OBEY.
I TREAT YOU LIKE WARRIOR KINGS WORTHY OF ALLIANCE.
AT THE END OF THIS, THE BROTHERHOOD OF THE BADOON WILL HAVE SUCH A POSITION OF POWER IN THIS GALAXY THAT YOUR WARRING SISTERHOOD, THE KREE, THE SKRULLS AND ANY OTHER RACE OR SPECIES WILL BOW TO YOU.
THEY WILL WRITE SONGS OF YOU.
THEY WILL TOAST YOU IN HONOR.
AND THE COSMIC POWERS OF THIS UNIVERSE WILL REGARD YOU AS ONE OF THEM.
I WILL *MAKE* THEM.
CAN YOU DO THIS?

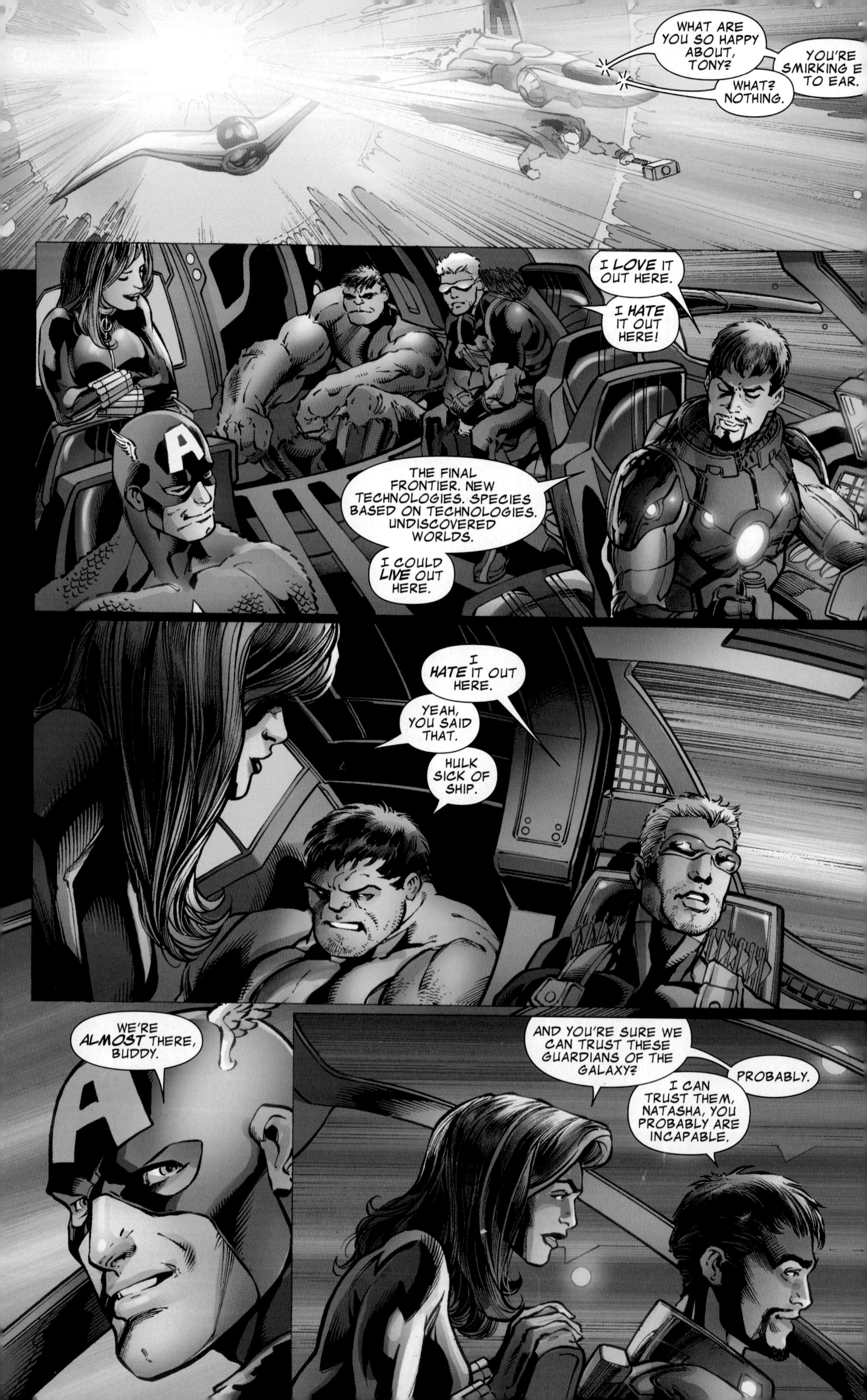

WHAT ARE YOU SO HAPPY ABOUT, TONY?
YOU'RE SMIRKING E TO EAR.
WHAT? NOTHING.
I LOVE IT OUT HERE.
I HATE IT OUT HERE!
THE FINAL FRONTIER. NEW TECHNOLOGIES. SPECIES BASED ON TECHNOLOGIES. UNDISCOVERED WORLDS.
I COULD LIVE OUT HERE.
I HATE IT OUT HERE.
YEAH, YOU SAID THAT.
HULK SICK OF SHIP.
WE'RE ALMOST THERE, BUDDY.
AND YOU'RE SURE WE CAN TRUST THESE GUARDIANS OF THE GALAXY?
PROBABLY.
I CAN TRUST THEM, NATASHA, YOU PROBABLY ARE INCAPABLE.

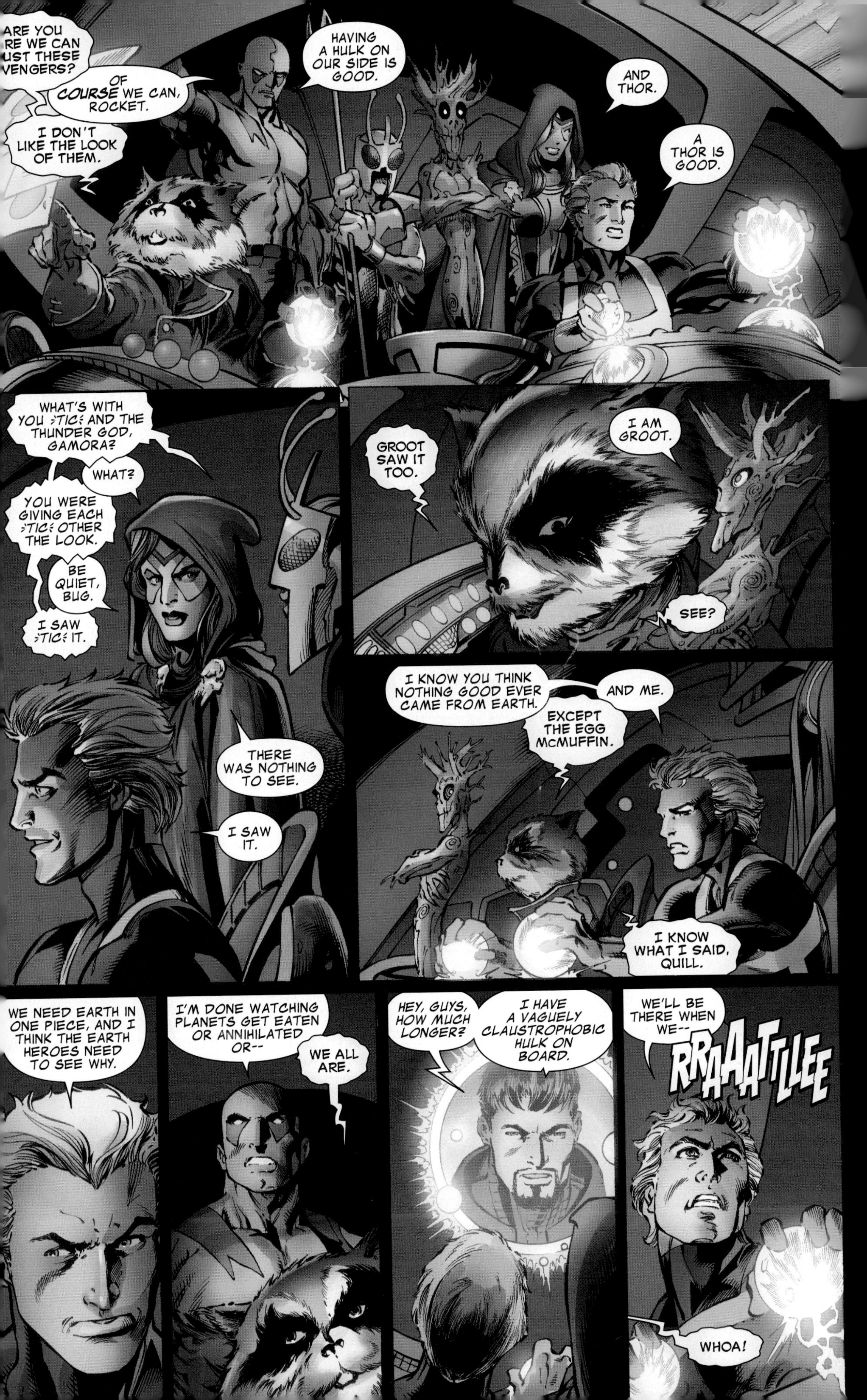
ARE YOU
RE WE CAN
UST THESE
VENGERS?
OF COURSE WE CAN, ROCKET.
HAVING A HULK ON OUR SIDE IS GOOD.
AND THOR.
A THOR IS GOOD.
I DON'T LIKE THE LOOK OF THEM.
WHAT'S WITH YOU *TIC* AND THE THUNDER GOD, GAMORA?
WHAT?
YOU WERE GIVING EACH *TIC* OTHER THE LOOK.
BE QUIET, BUG.
I SAW *TIC* IT.
THERE WAS NOTHING TO SEE.
I SAW IT.
GROOT SAW IT TOO.
I AM GROOT.
SEE?
I KNOW YOU THINK NOTHING GOOD EVER CAME FROM EARTH.
AND ME.
EXCEPT THE EGG McMUFFIN.
I KNOW WHAT I SAID, QUILL.
WE NEED EARTH IN ONE PIECE, AND I THINK THE EARTH HEROES NEED TO SEE WHY.
I'M DONE WATCHING PLANETS GET EATEN OR ANNIHILATED OR--
WE ALL ARE.
HEY, GUYS, HOW MUCH LONGER?
I HAVE A VAGUELY CLAUSTROPHOBIC HULK ON BOARD.
WE'LL BE THERE WHEN WE--
RRAAATTLLEE
WHOA!

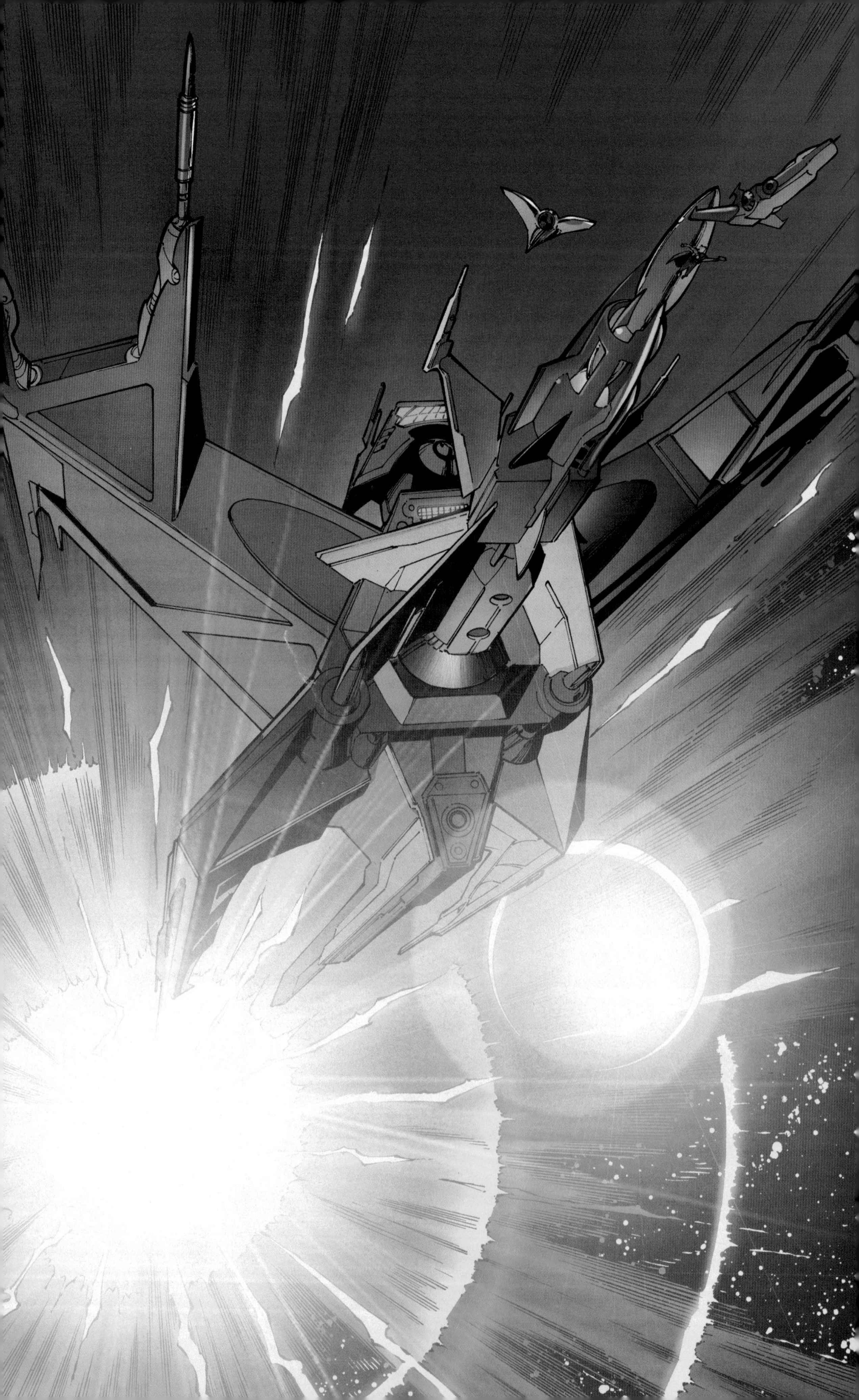

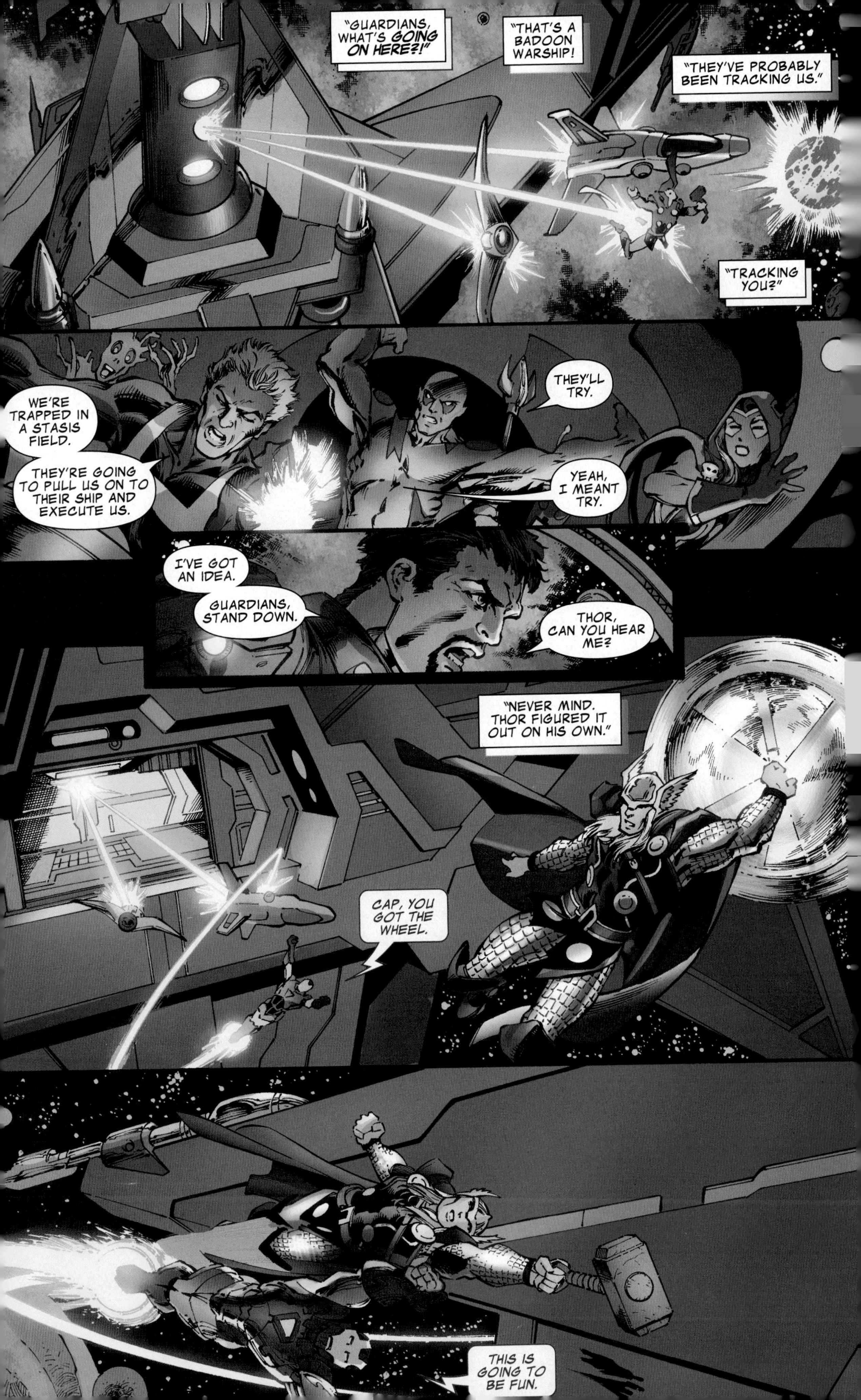
"GUARDIANS, WHAT'S GOING ON HERE?!"
"THAT'S A BADOON WARSHIP!
"THEY'VE PROBABLY BEEN TRACKING US."
"TRACKING YOU?"
WE'RE TRAPPED IN A STASIS FIELD.
THEY'RE GOING TO PULL US ON TO THEIR SHIP AND EXECUTE US.
THEY'LL TRY.
YEAH, I MEANT TRY.
I'VE GOT AN IDEA.
GUARDIANS, STAND DOWN.
THOR, CAN YOU HEAR ME?
"NEVER MIND. THOR FIGURED IT OUT ON HIS OWN."
CAP, YOU GOT THE WHEEL.
THIS IS GOING TO BE FUN.

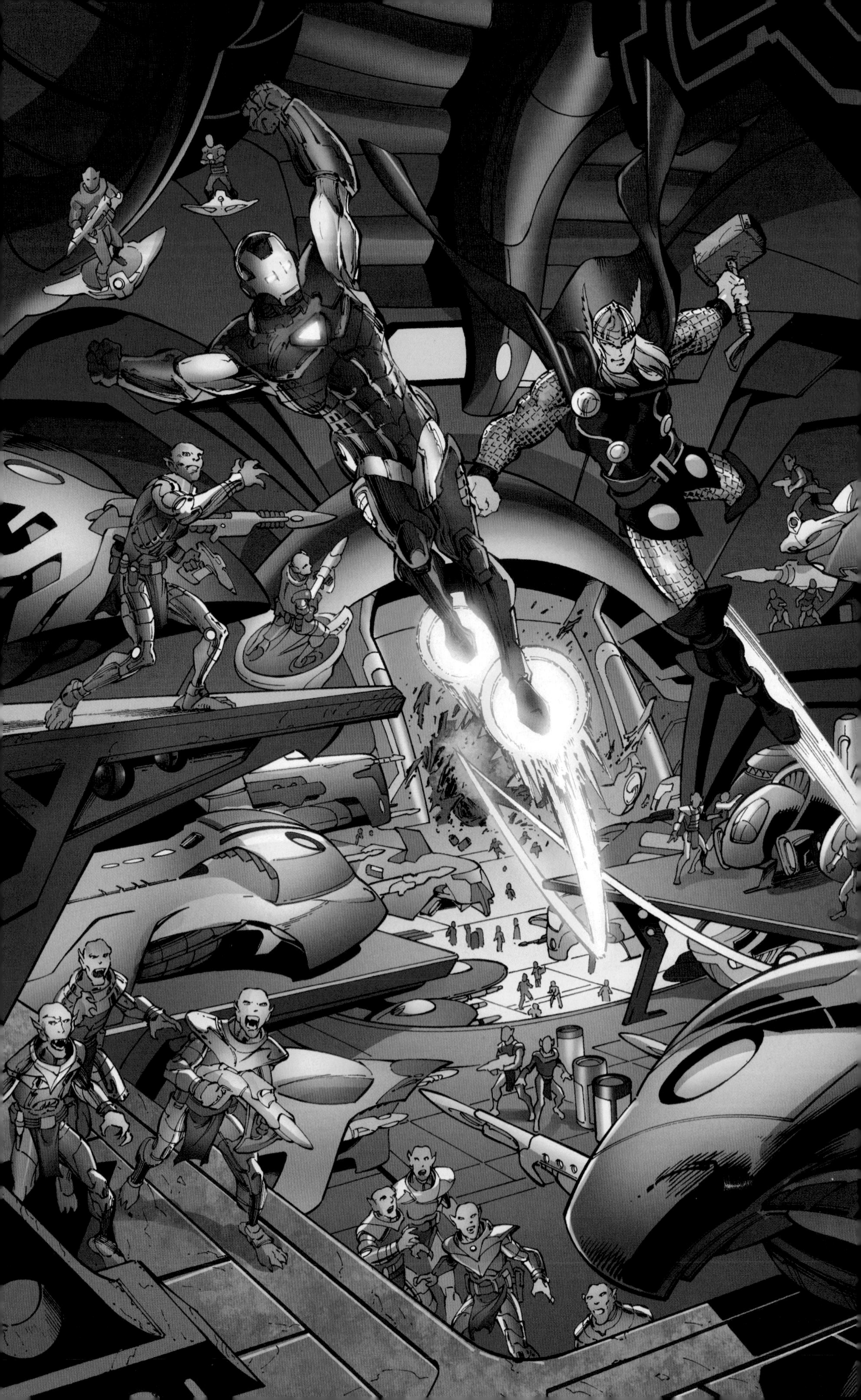

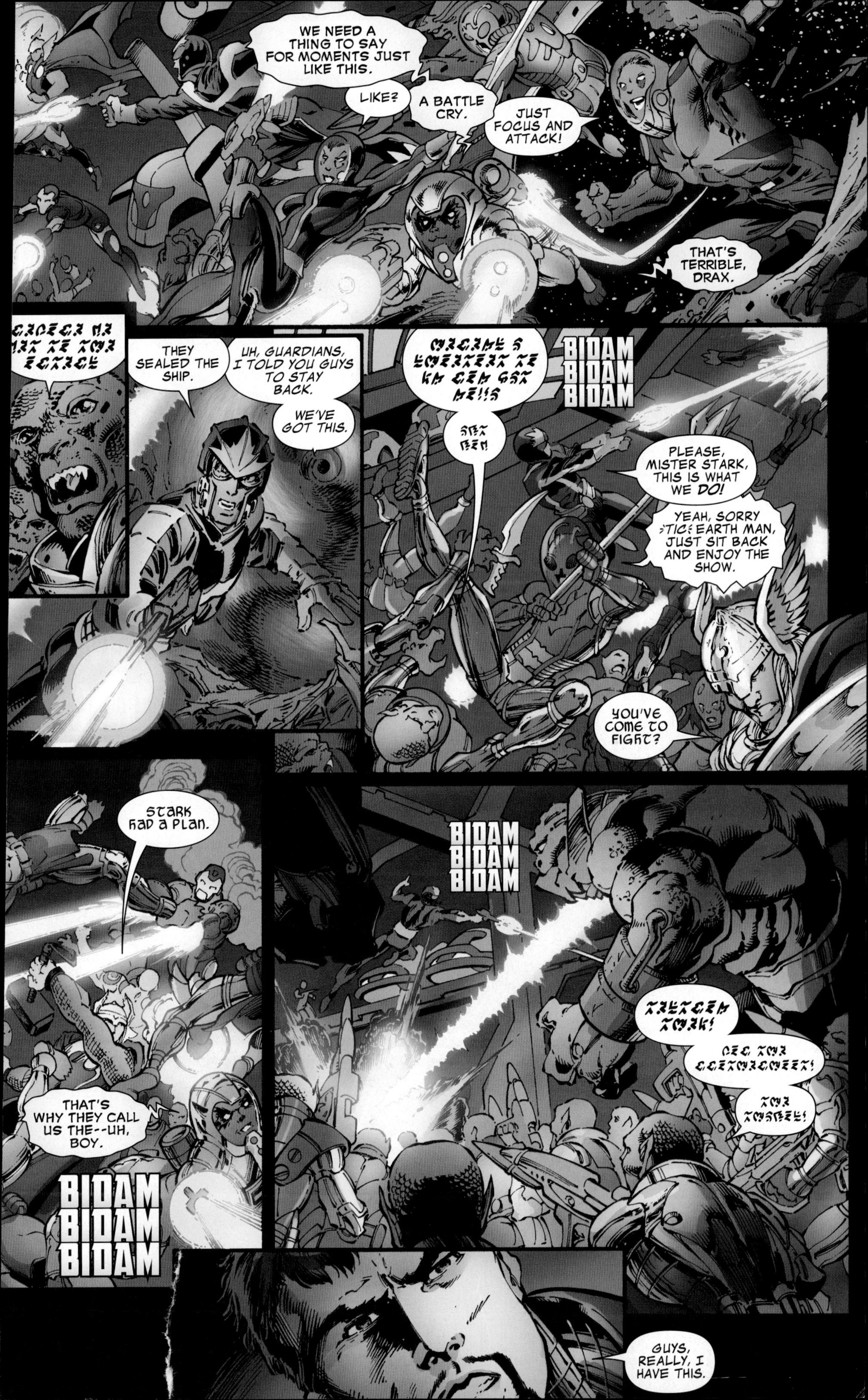

WE NEED A THING TO SAY FOR MOMENTS JUST LIKE THIS.
LIKE?
A BATTLE CRY.
JUST FOCUS AND ATTACK!
THAT'S TERRIBLE, DRAX.
THEY SEALED THE SHIP.
UH, GUARDIANS, I TOLD YOU GUYS TO STAY BACK.
WE'VE GOT THIS.
BIDAM BIDAM BIDAM
PLEASE, MISTER STARK, THIS IS WHAT WE DO!
YEAH, SORRY EARTH MAN, JUST SIT BACK AND ENJOY THE SHOW.
YOU'VE COME TO FIGHT?
STARK HAD A PLAN.
THAT'S WHY THEY CALL US THE--UH, BOY.
BIDAM BIDAM BIDAM
BIDAM BIDAM BIDAM
GUYS, REALLY, I HAVE THIS.

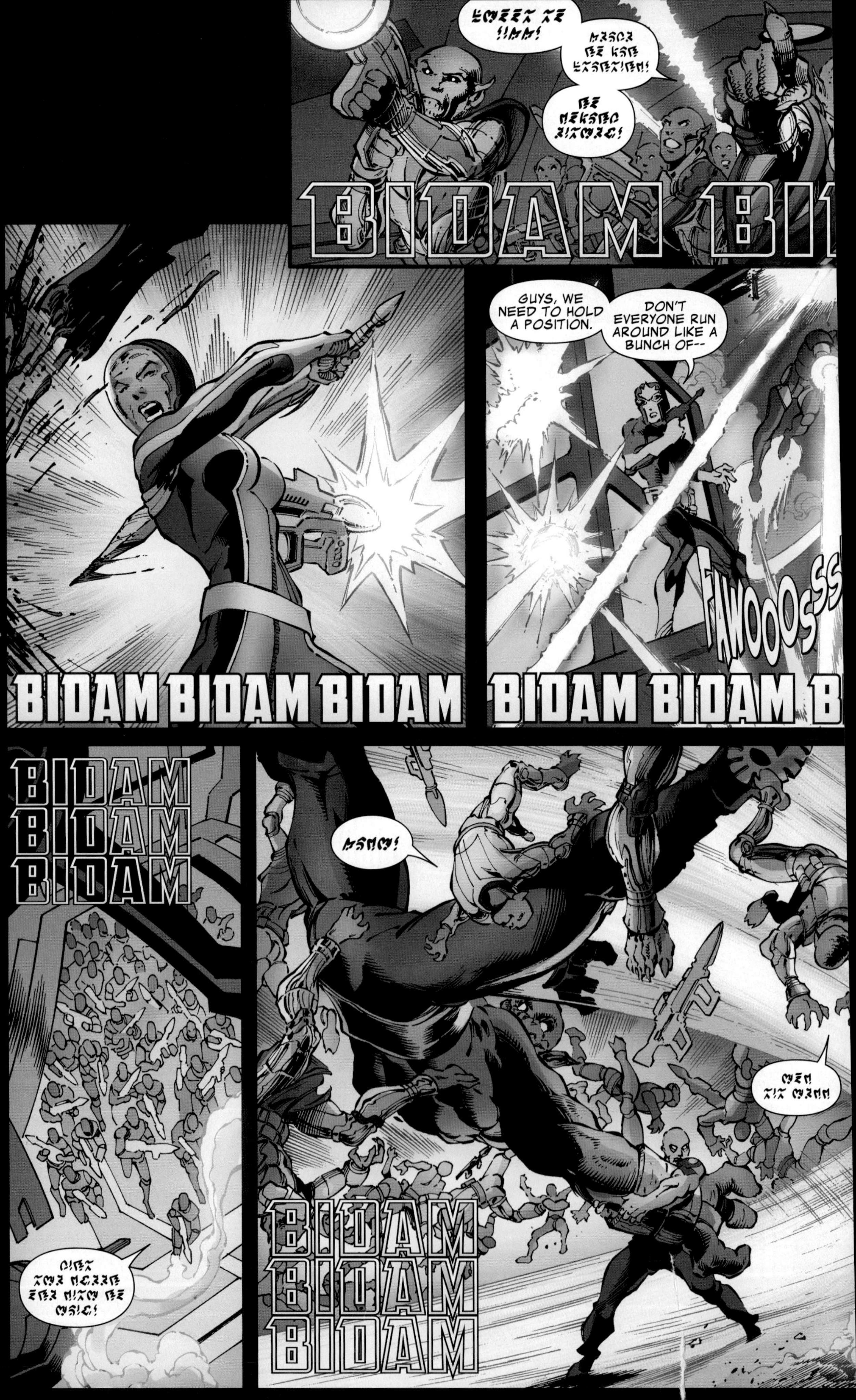
BIDAM BI
GUYS, WE NEED TO HOLD A POSITION.
DON'T EVERYONE RUN AROUND LIKE A BUNCH OF--
FAWOOOSSS
BIDAM BIDAM BIDAM
BIDAM BIDAM B
BIDAM
BIDAM
BIDAM
BIDAM
BIDAM
BIDAM

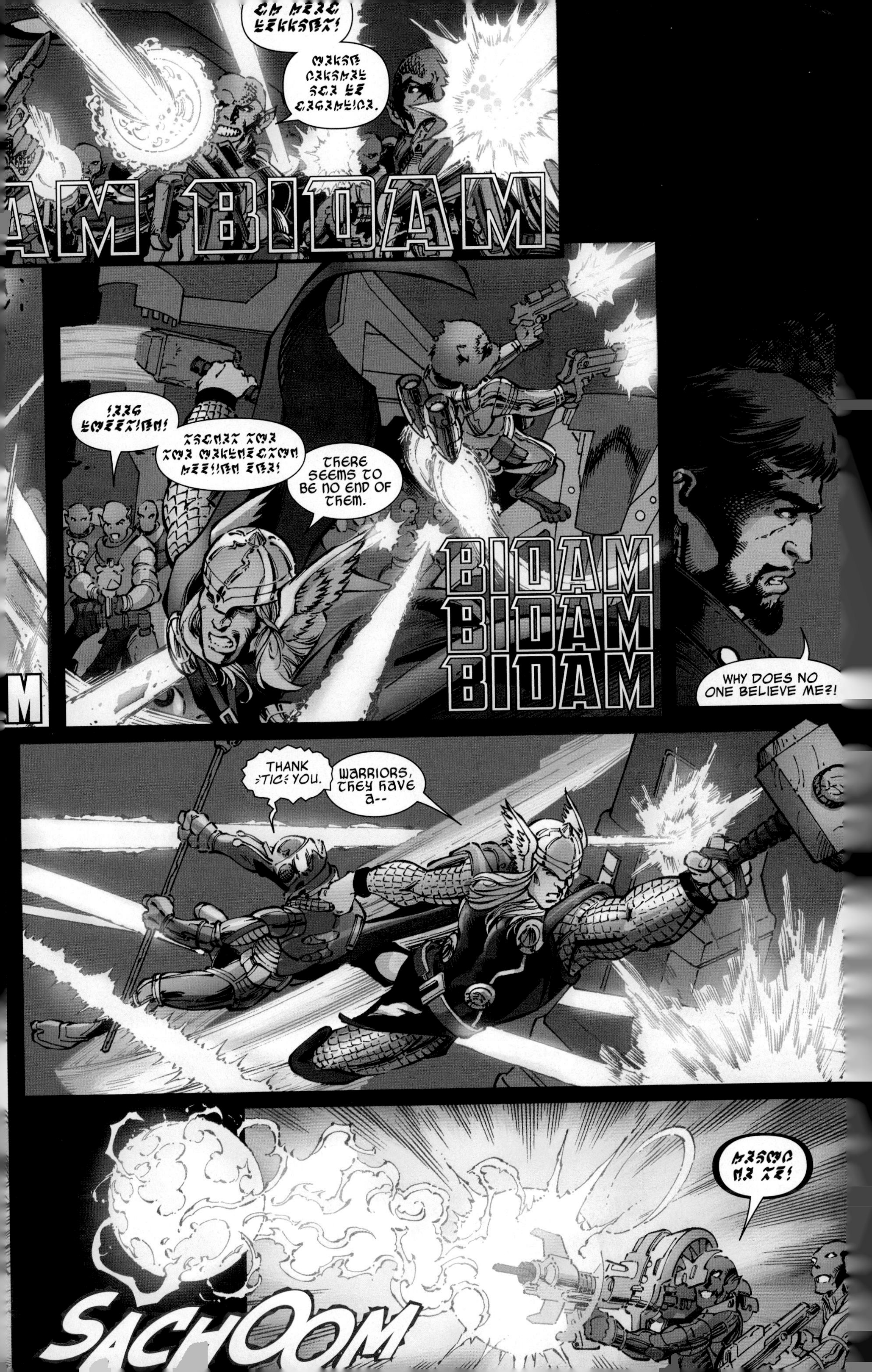
AM BIDAM
THERE SEEMS TO BE NO END OF THEM.
BIDAM BIDAM BIDAM
WHY DOES NO ONE BELIEVE ME?!
M
THANK YOU.
WARRIORS, THEY HAVE A--
SACHOOM

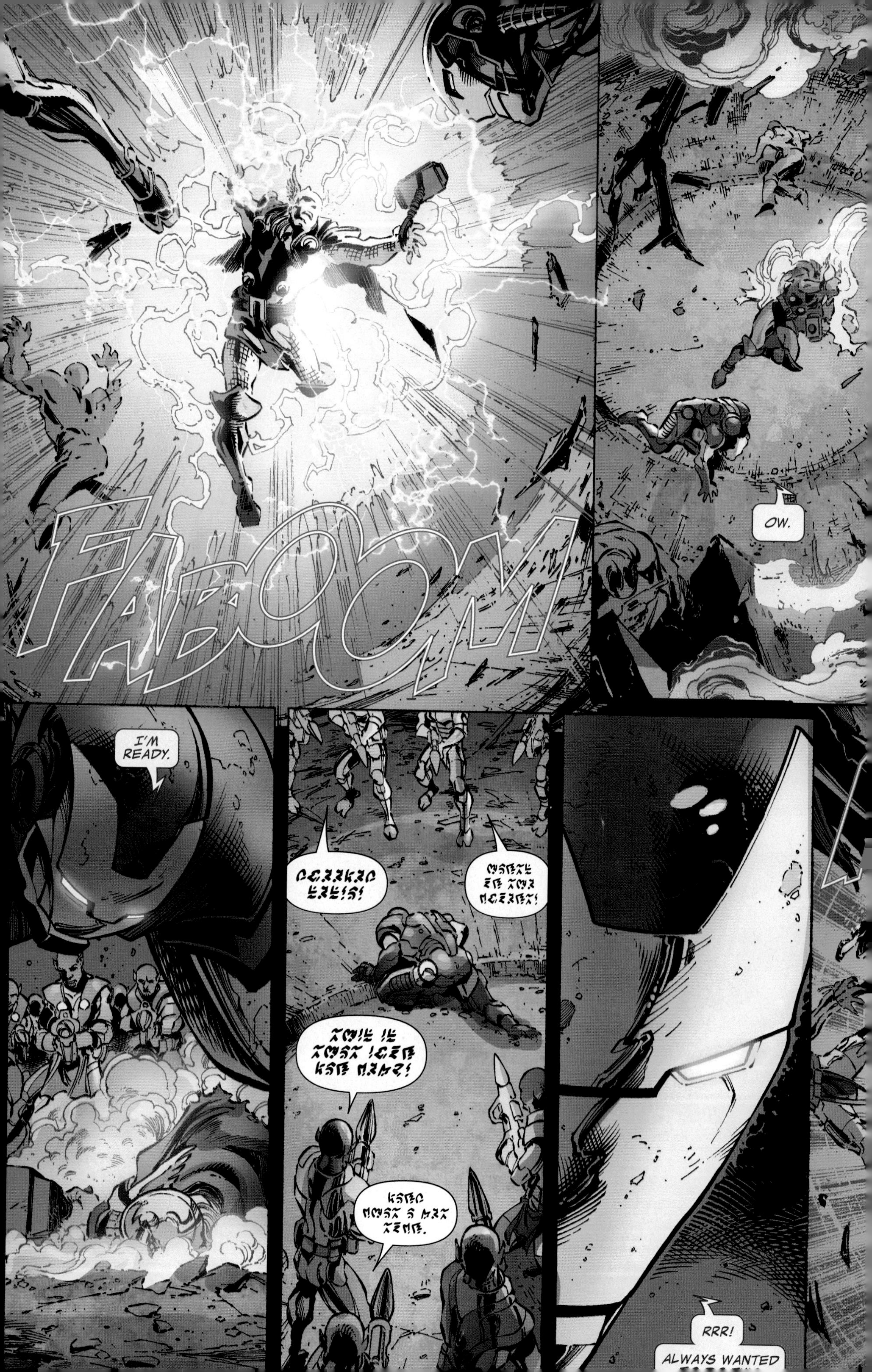
FABOOM
OW.
I'M READY.
RRR!
ALWAYS WANTED

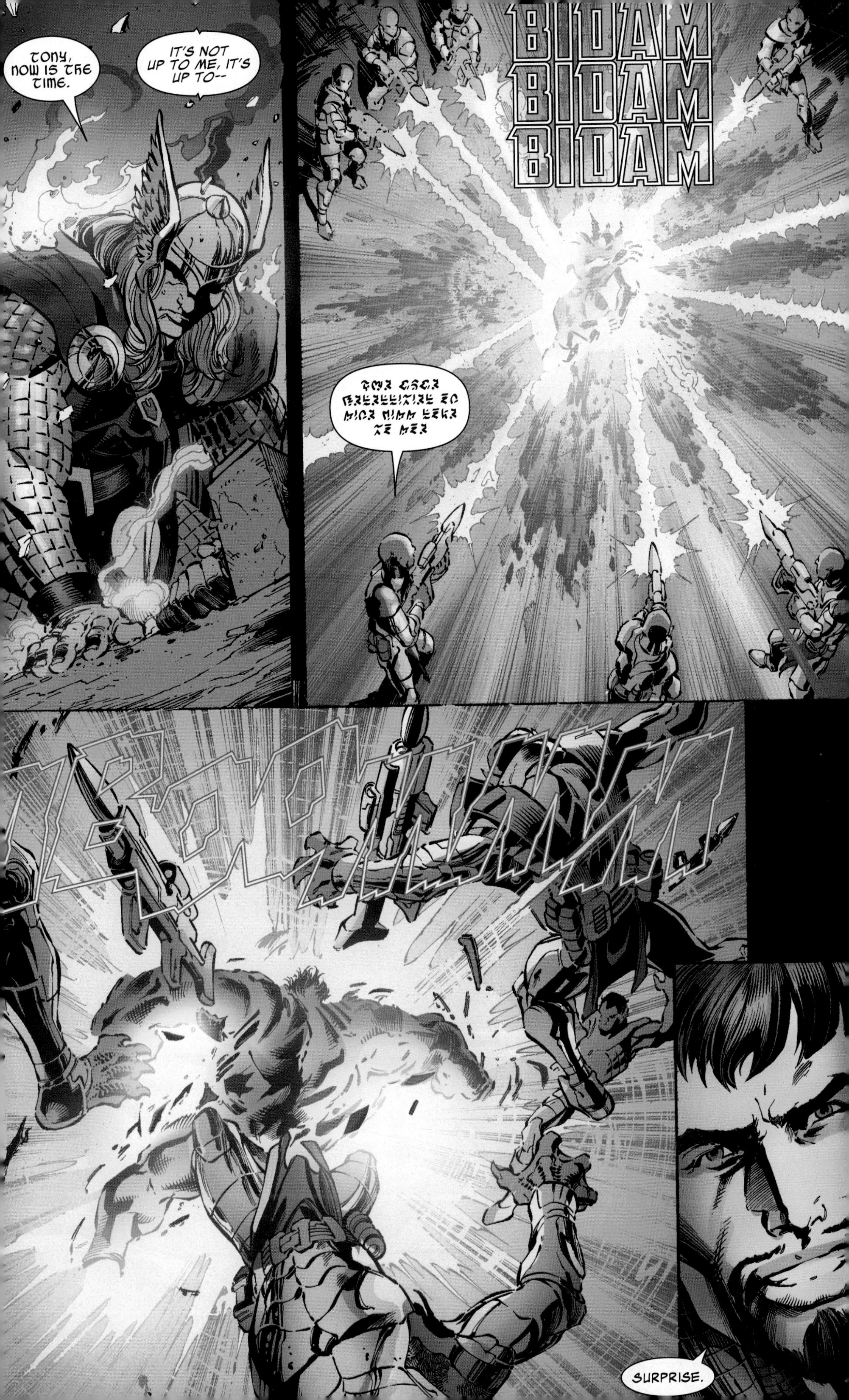
TONY, NOW IS THE TIME.
IT'S NOT UP TO ME, IT'S UP TO--
BIDAM BIDAM BIDAM
SURPRISE.

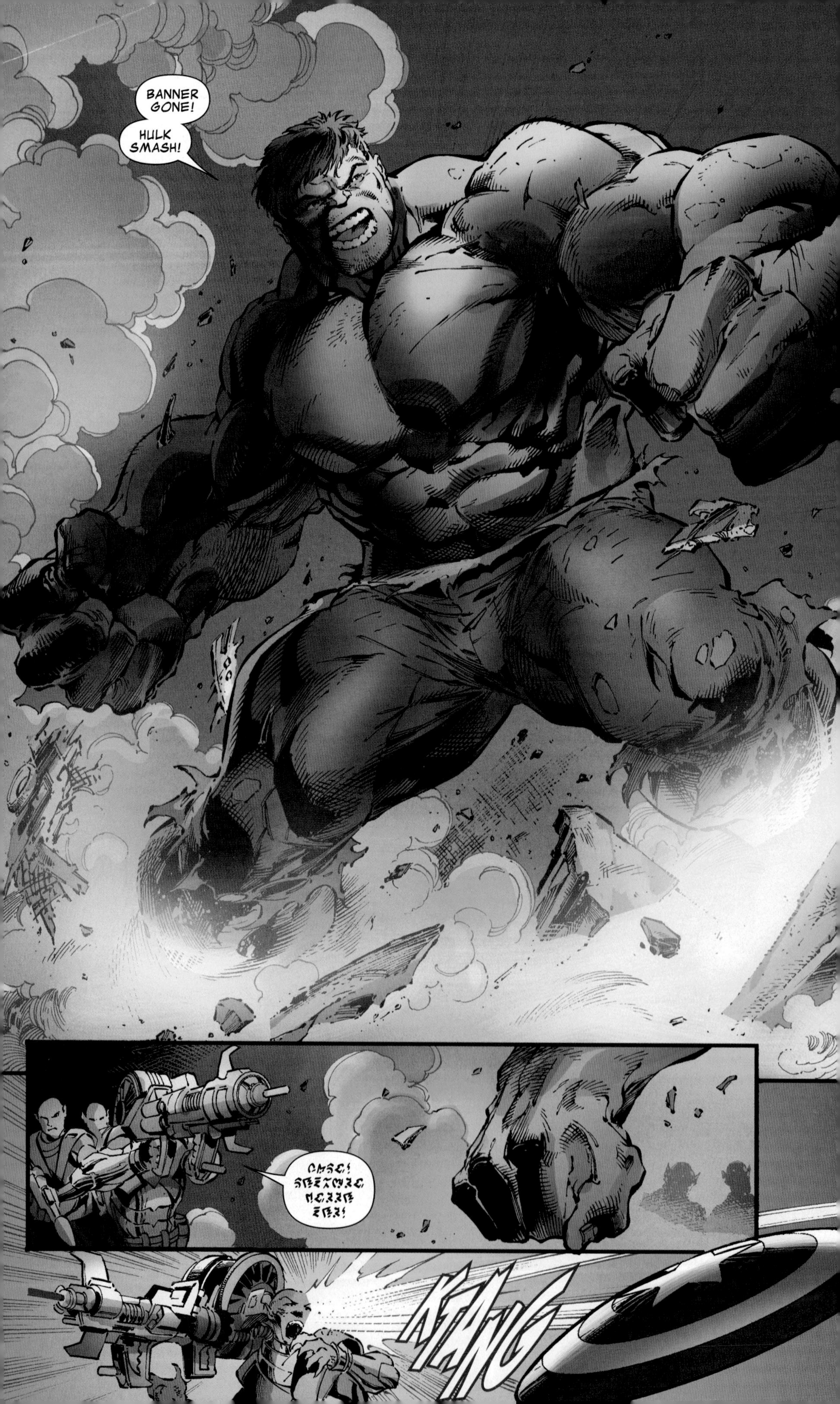
BANNER GONE!
HULK SMASH!

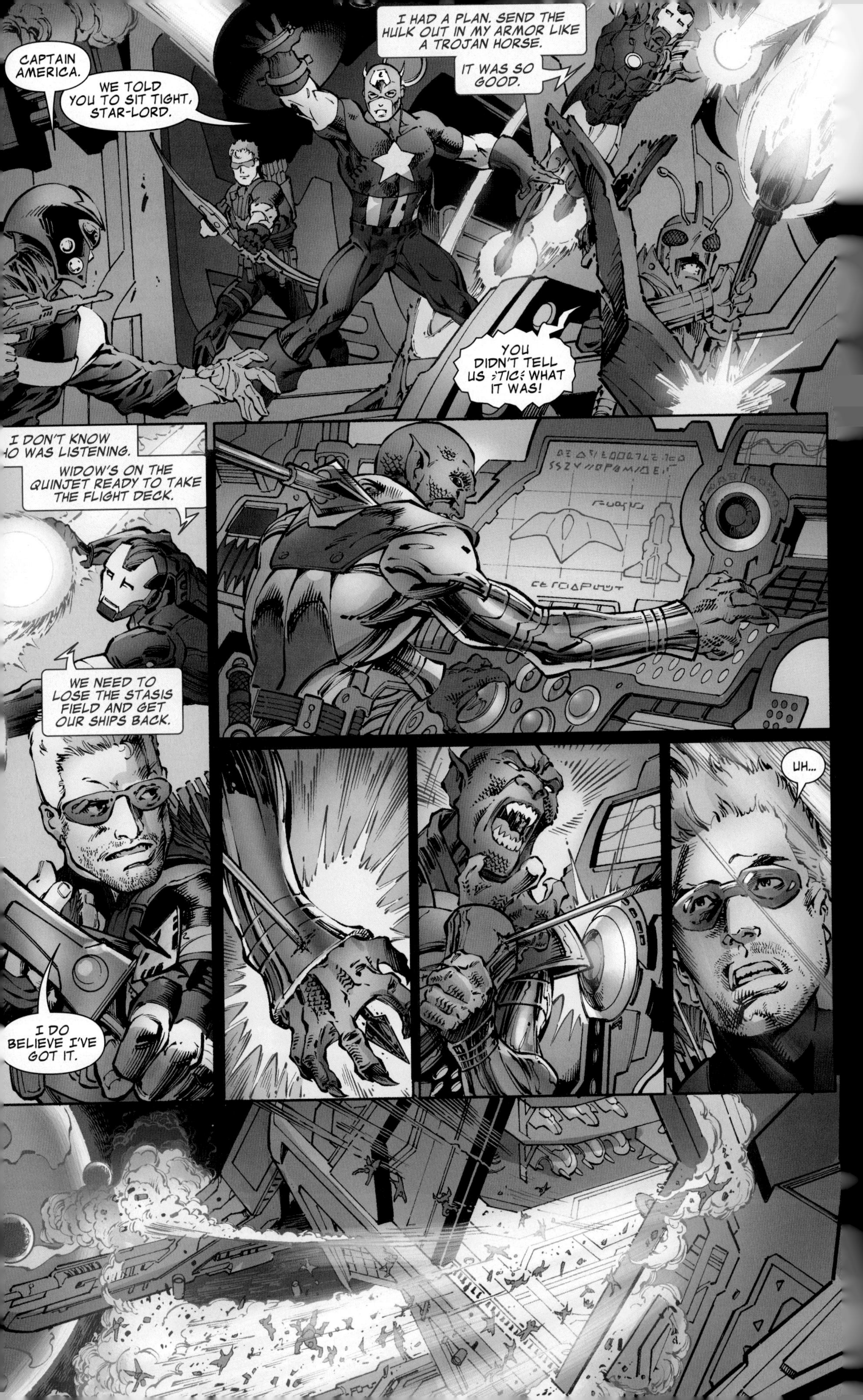

CAPTAIN AMERICA.
WE TOLD YOU TO SIT TIGHT, STAR-LORD.
I HAD A PLAN. SEND THE HULK OUT IN MY ARMOR LIKE A TROJAN HORSE.
IT WAS SO GOOD.
YOU DIDN'T TELL US ≠TIC≠ WHAT IT WAS!
I DON'T KNOW HO WAS LISTENING.
WIDOW'S ON THE QUINJET READY TO TAKE THE FLIGHT DECK.
WE NEED TO LOSE THE STASIS FIELD AND GET OUR SHIPS BACK.
I DO BELIEVE I'VE GOT IT.
UH...

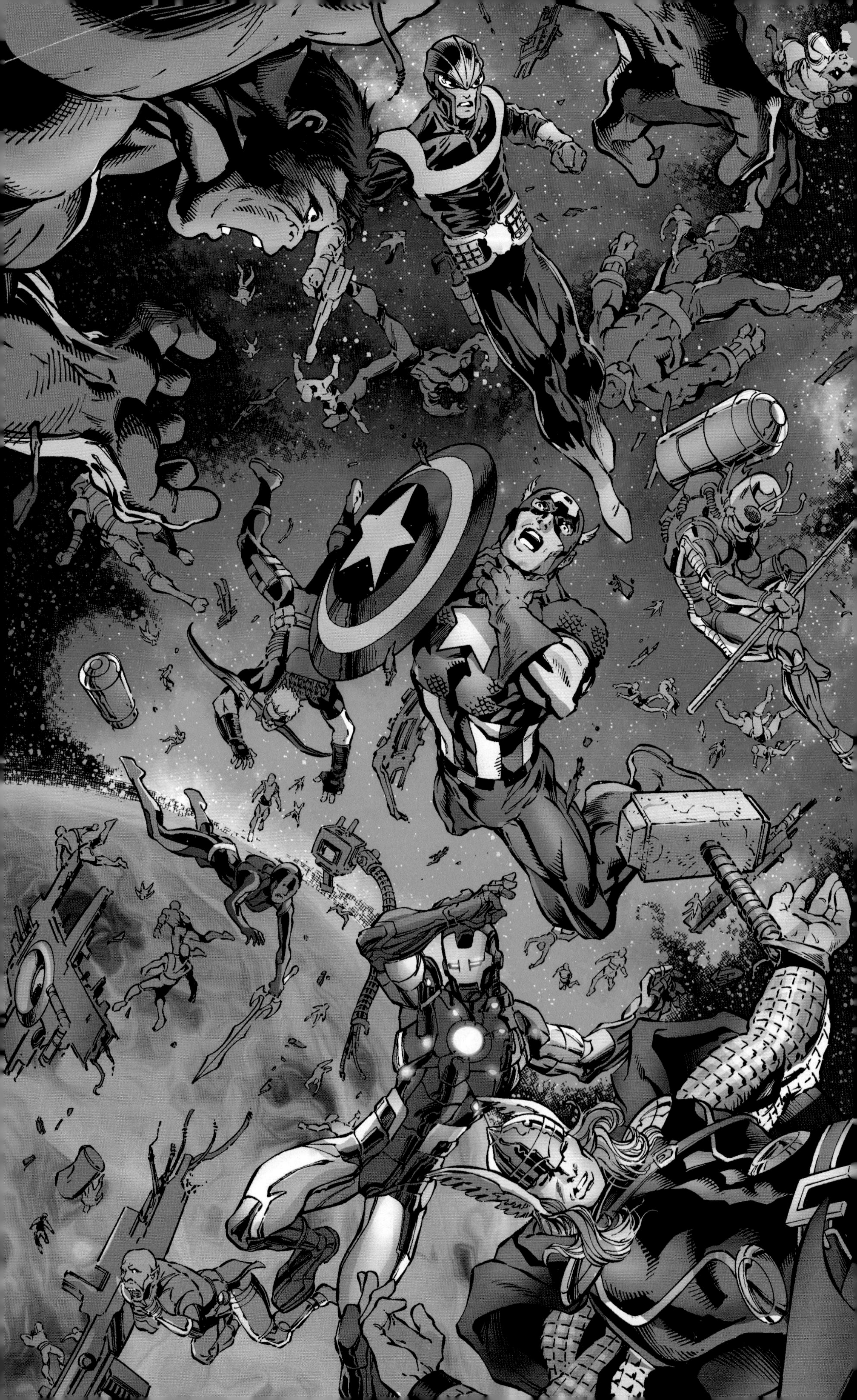

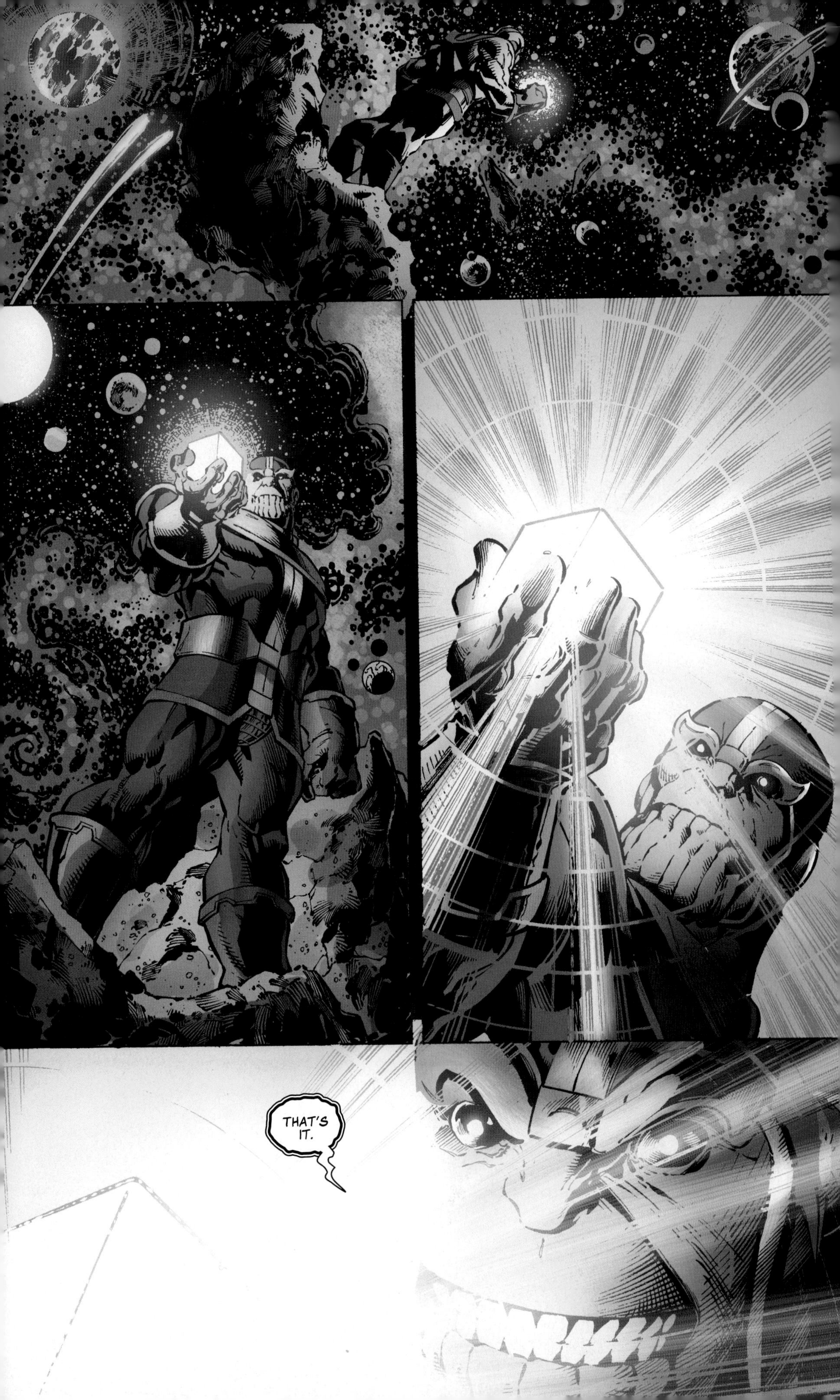
THAT'S IT.

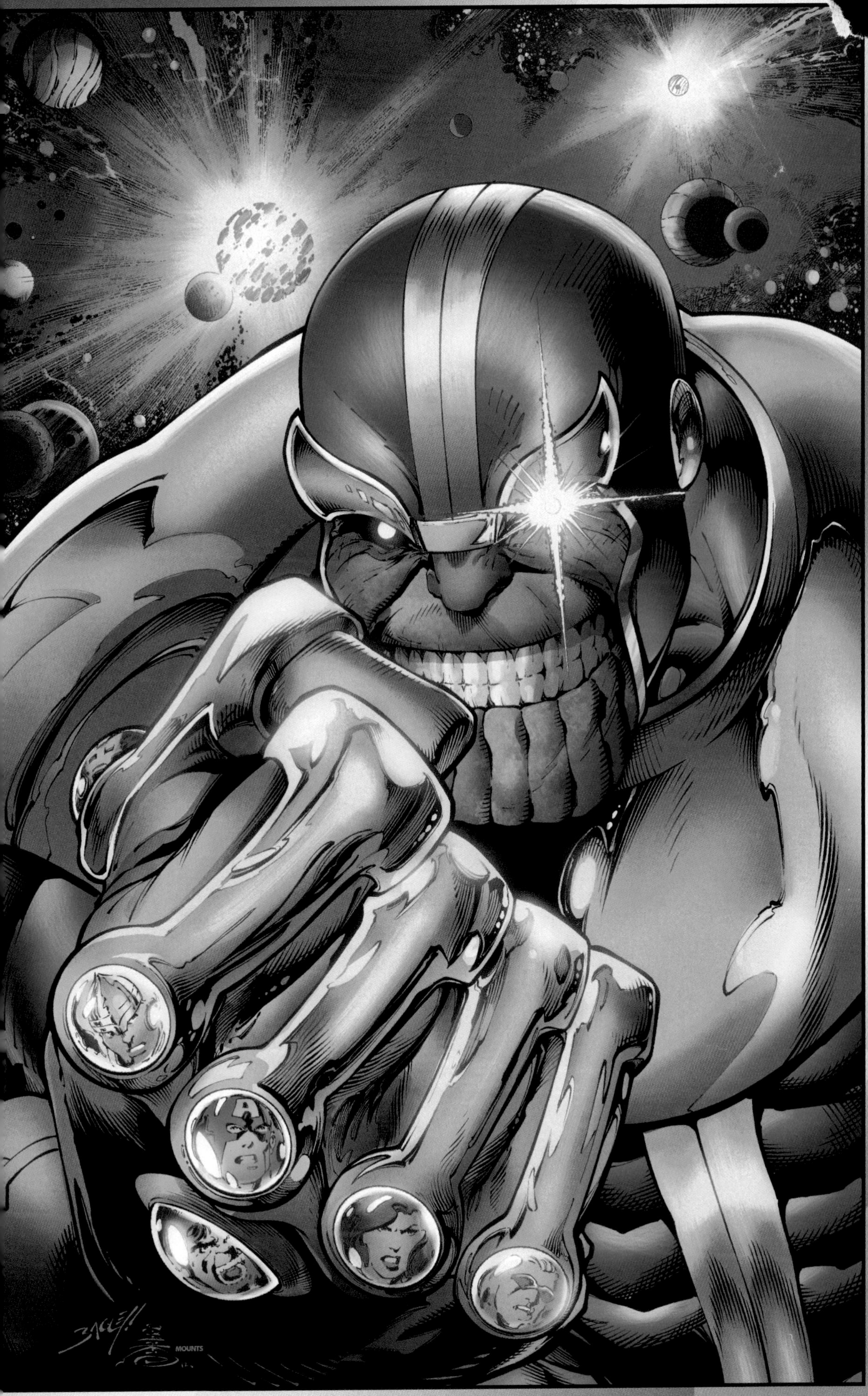
MOUNTS

SEVEN

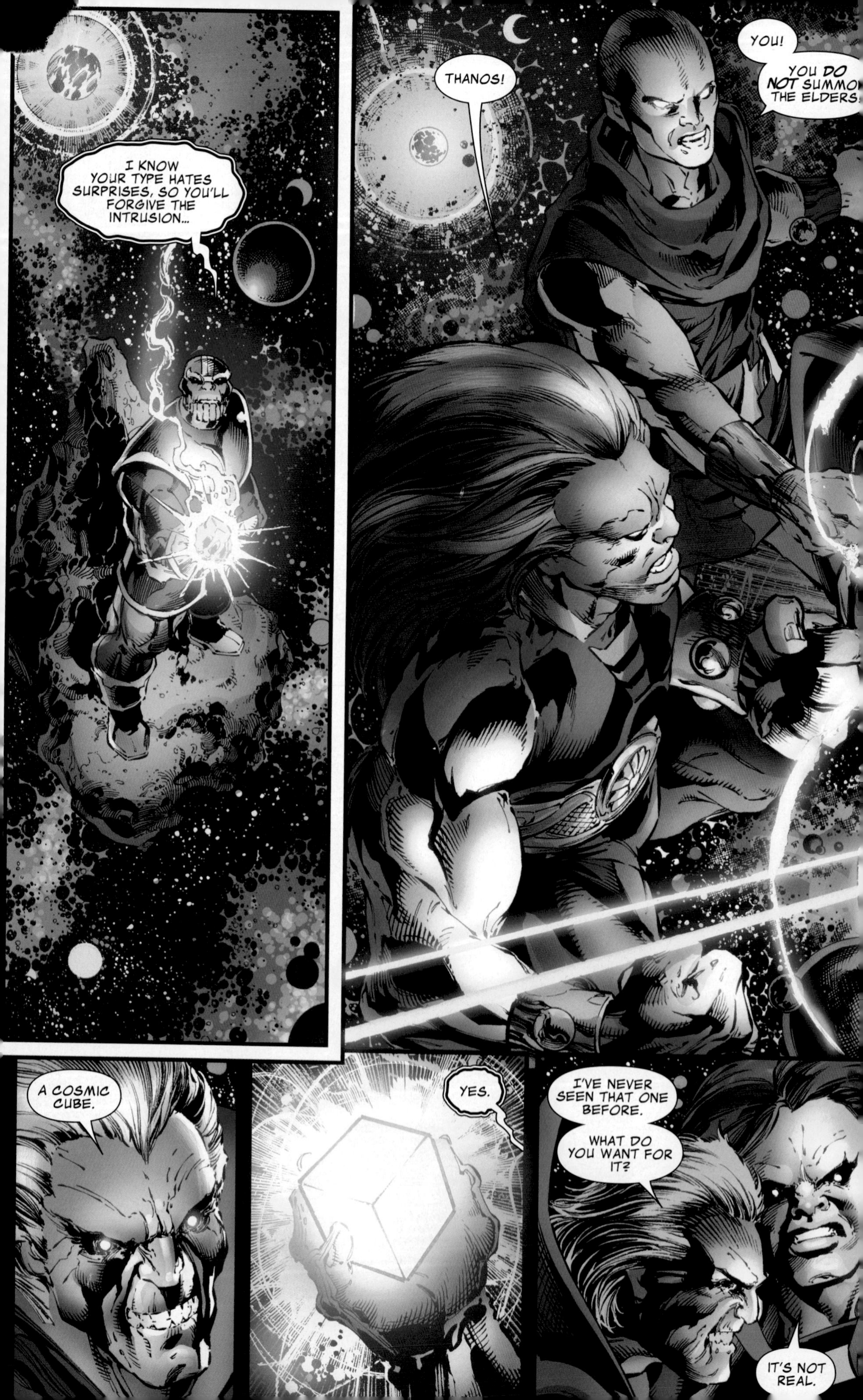
I KNOW YOUR TYPE HATES SURPRISES, SO YOU'LL FORGIVE THE INTRUSION...
THANOS!
YOU!
YOU DO NOT SUMMO THE ELDERS.
A COSMIC CUBE.
YES.
I'VE NEVER SEEN THAT ONE BEFORE.
WHAT DO YOU WANT FOR IT?
IT'S NOT REAL.

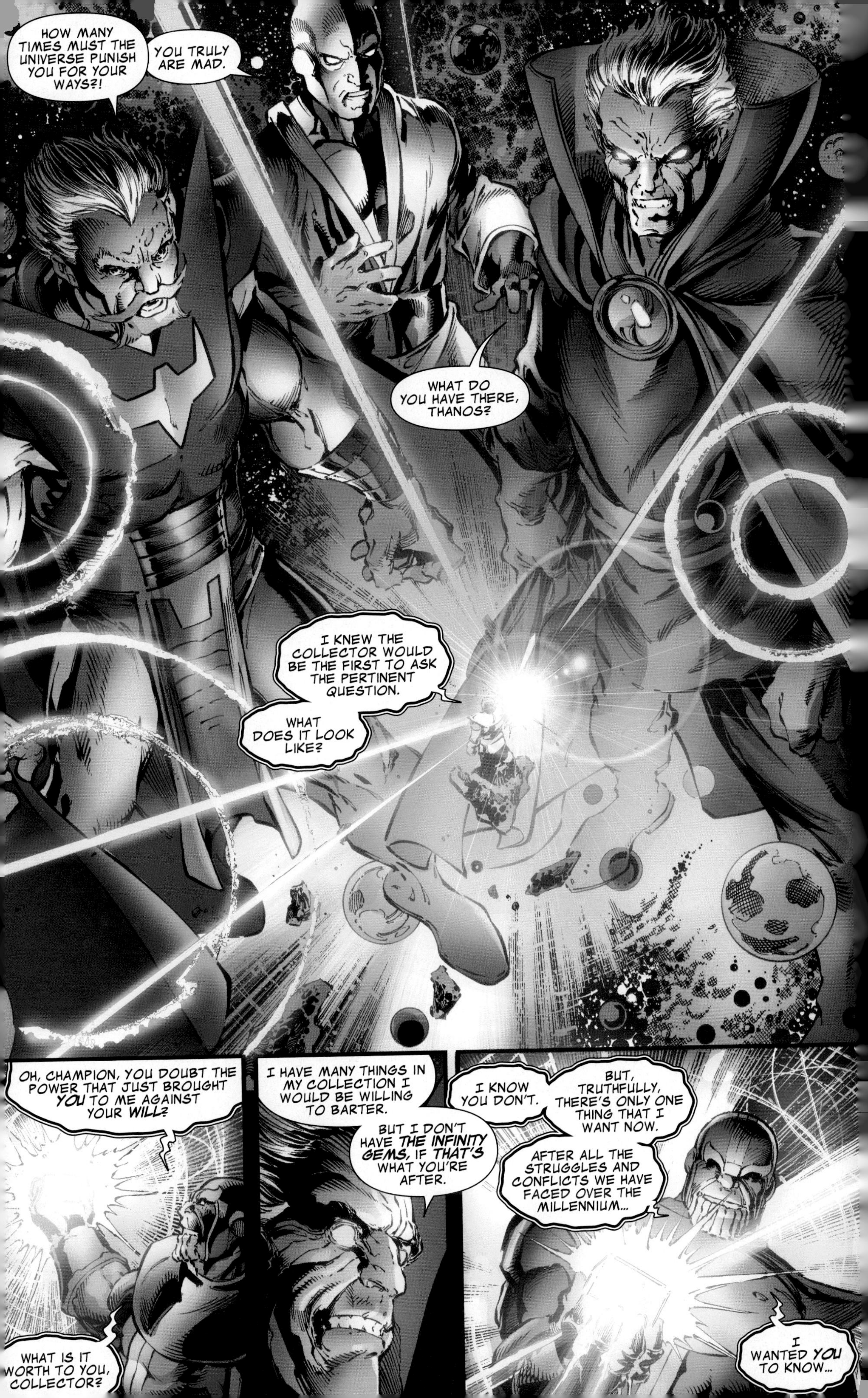
HOW MANY TIMES MUST THE UNIVERSE PUNISH YOU FOR YOUR WAYS?!
YOU TRULY ARE MAD.
WHAT DO YOU HAVE THERE, THANOS?
I KNEW THE COLLECTOR WOULD BE THE FIRST TO ASK THE PERTINENT QUESTION.
WHAT DOES IT LOOK LIKE?
OH, CHAMPION, YOU DOUBT THE POWER THAT JUST BROUGHT YOU TO ME AGAINST YOUR WILL?
WHAT IS IT WORTH TO YOU, COLLECTOR?
I HAVE MANY THINGS IN MY COLLECTION I WOULD BE WILLING TO BARTER.
BUT I DON'T HAVE THE INFINITY GEMS, IF THAT'S WHAT YOU'RE AFTER.
I KNOW YOU DON'T.
BUT, TRUTHFULLY, THERE'S ONLY ONE THING THAT I WANT NOW.
AFTER ALL THE STRUGGLES AND CONFLICTS WE HAVE FACED OVER THE MILLENNIUM...
I WANTED YOU TO KNOW...

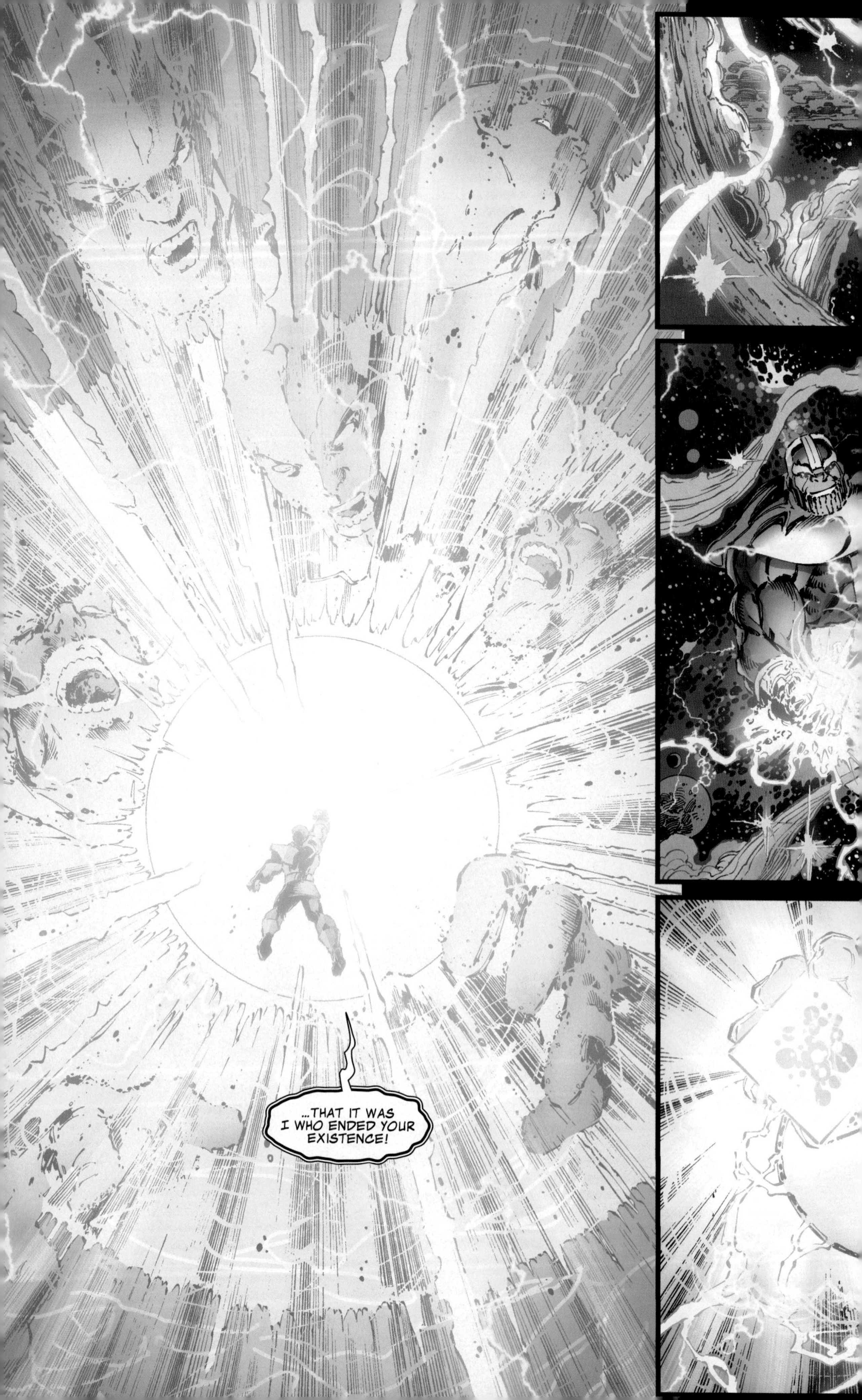
...THAT IT WAS I WHO ENDED YOUR EXISTENCE!

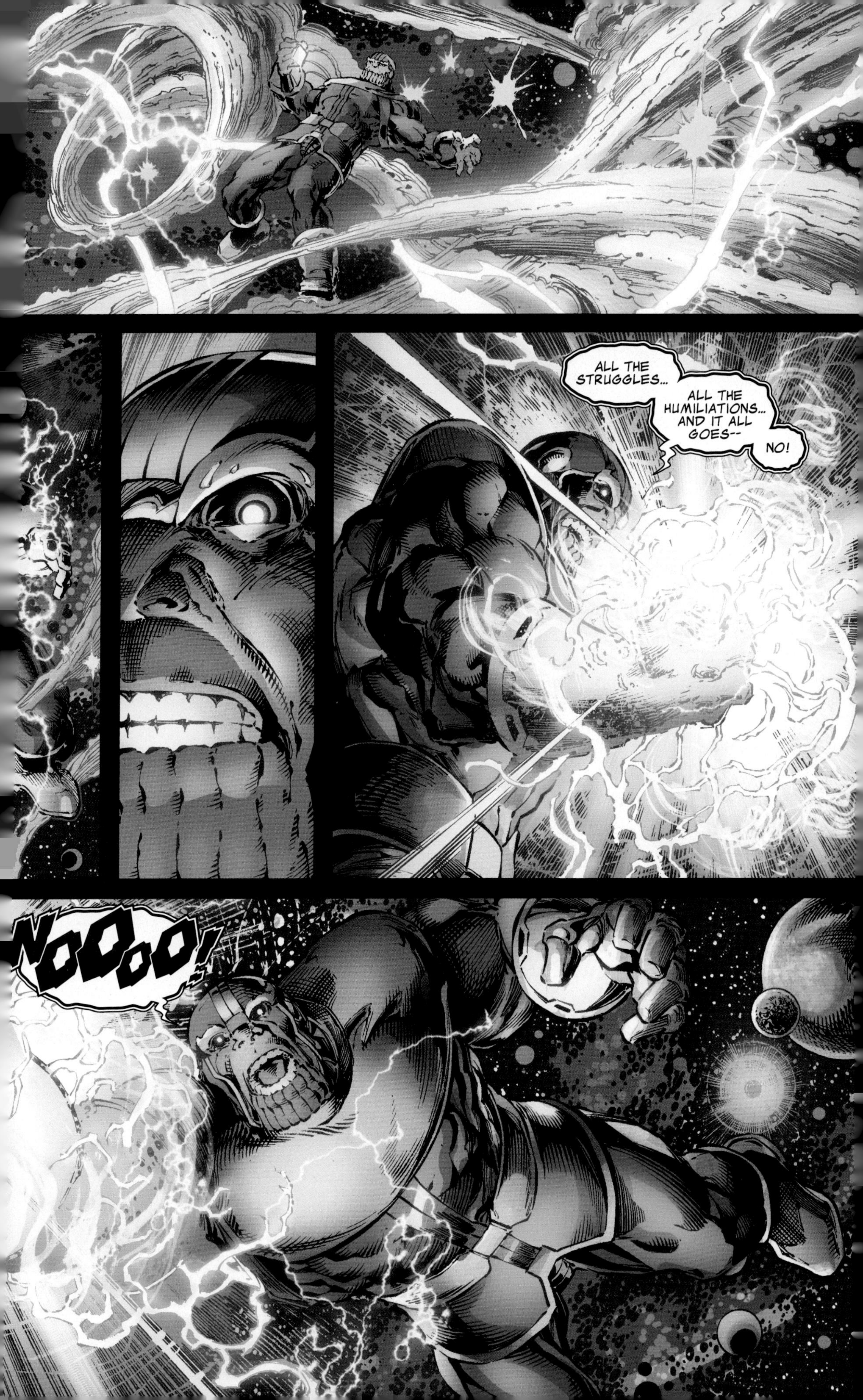
ALL THE STRUGGLES...
ALL THE HUMILIATIONS... AND IT ALL GOES--
NO!
NOOOOO!

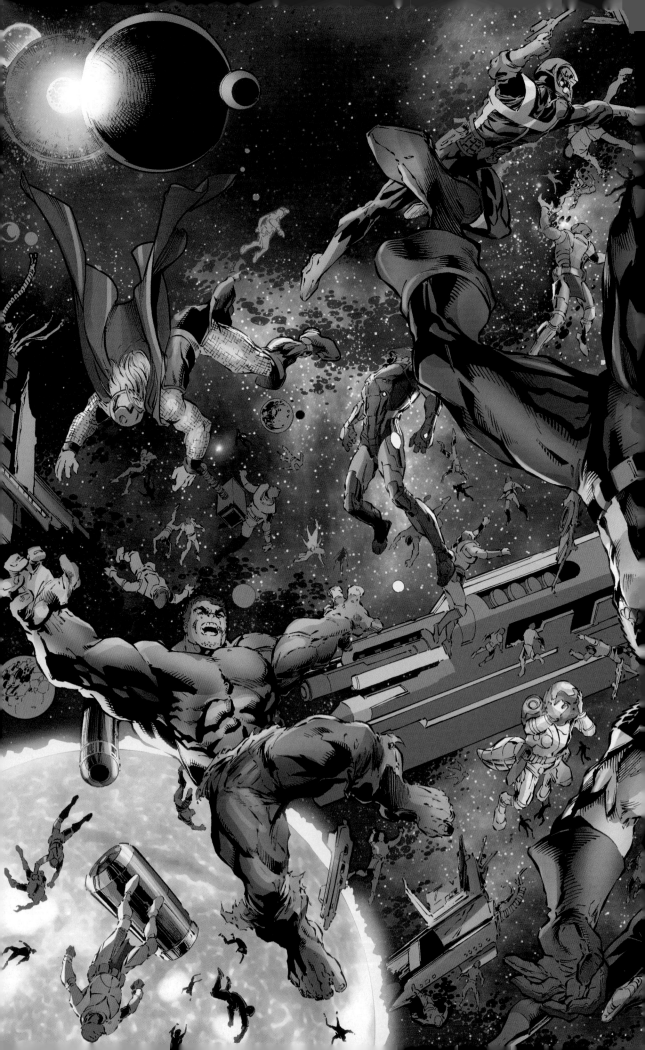

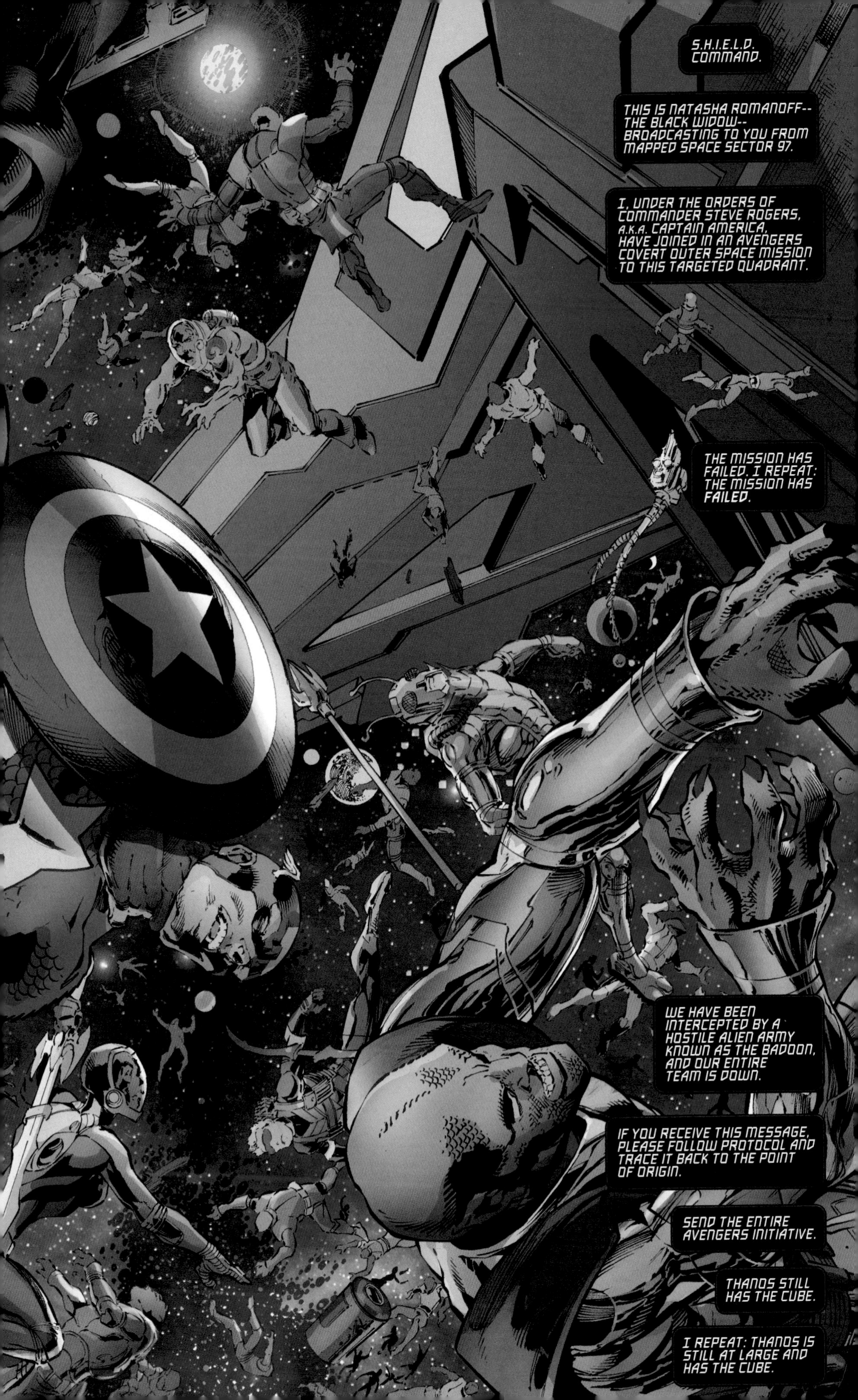
S.H.I.E.L.D. COMMAND.
THIS IS NATASHA ROMANOFF-- THE BLACK WIDOW-- BROADCASTING TO YOU FROM MAPPED SPACE SECTOR 97.
I, UNDER THE ORDERS OF COMMANDER STEVE ROGERS, A.K.A. CAPTAIN AMERICA, HAVE JOINED IN AN AVENGERS COVERT OUTER SPACE MISSION TO THIS TARGETED QUADRANT.
THE MISSION HAS FAILED. I REPEAT: THE MISSION HAS FAILED.
WE HAVE BEEN INTERCEPTED BY A HOSTILE ALIEN ARMY KNOWN AS THE BADOON, AND OUR ENTIRE TEAM IS DOWN.
IF YOU RECEIVE THIS MESSAGE, PLEASE FOLLOW PROTOCOL AND TRACE IT BACK TO THE POINT OF ORIGIN.
SEND THE ENTIRE AVENGERS INITIATIVE.
THANOS STILL HAS THE CUBE.
I REPEAT: THANOS IS STILL AT LARGE AND HAS THE CUBE.

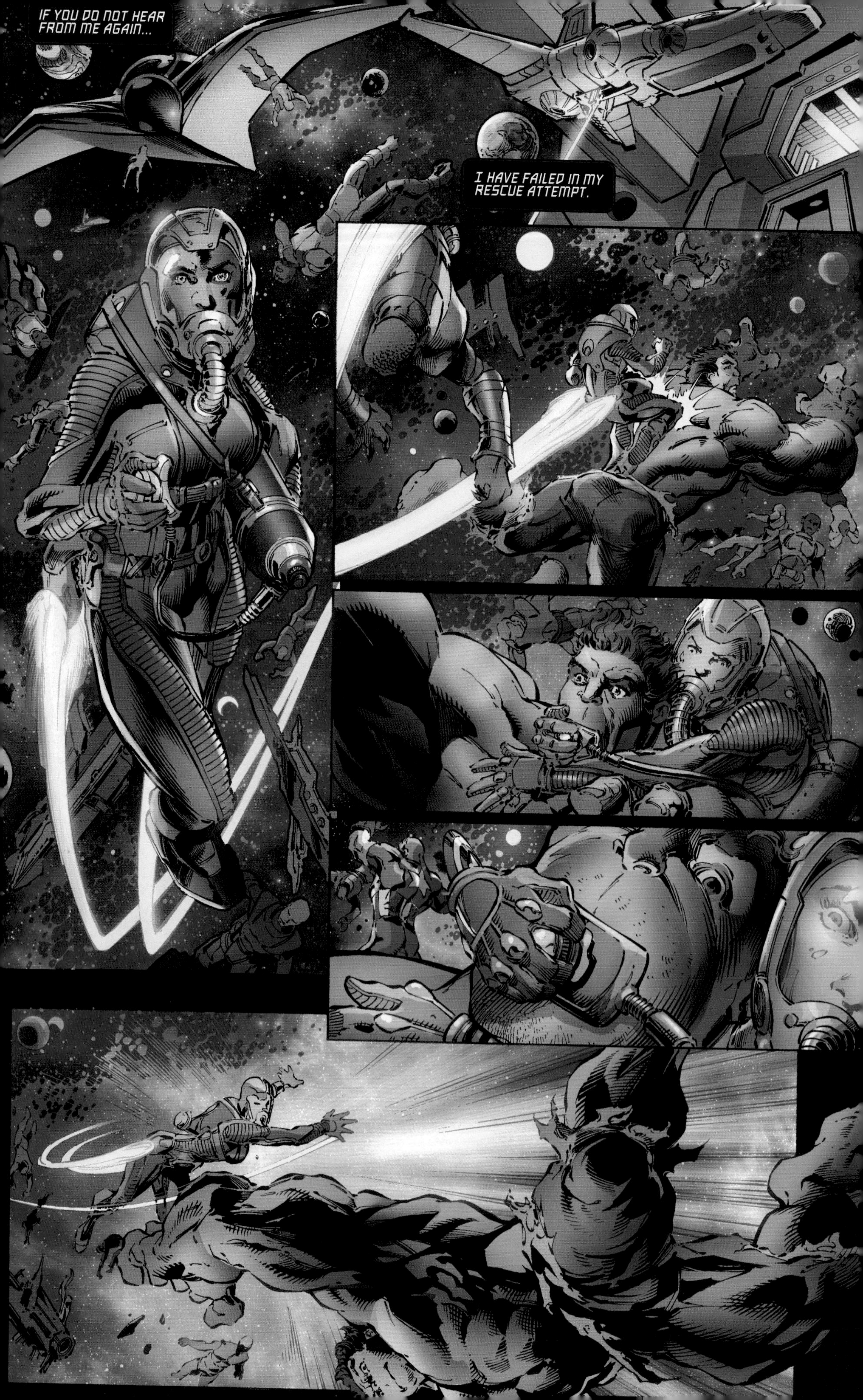
IF YOU DO NOT HEAR FROM ME AGAIN...
I HAVE FAILED IN MY RESCUE ATTEMPT.

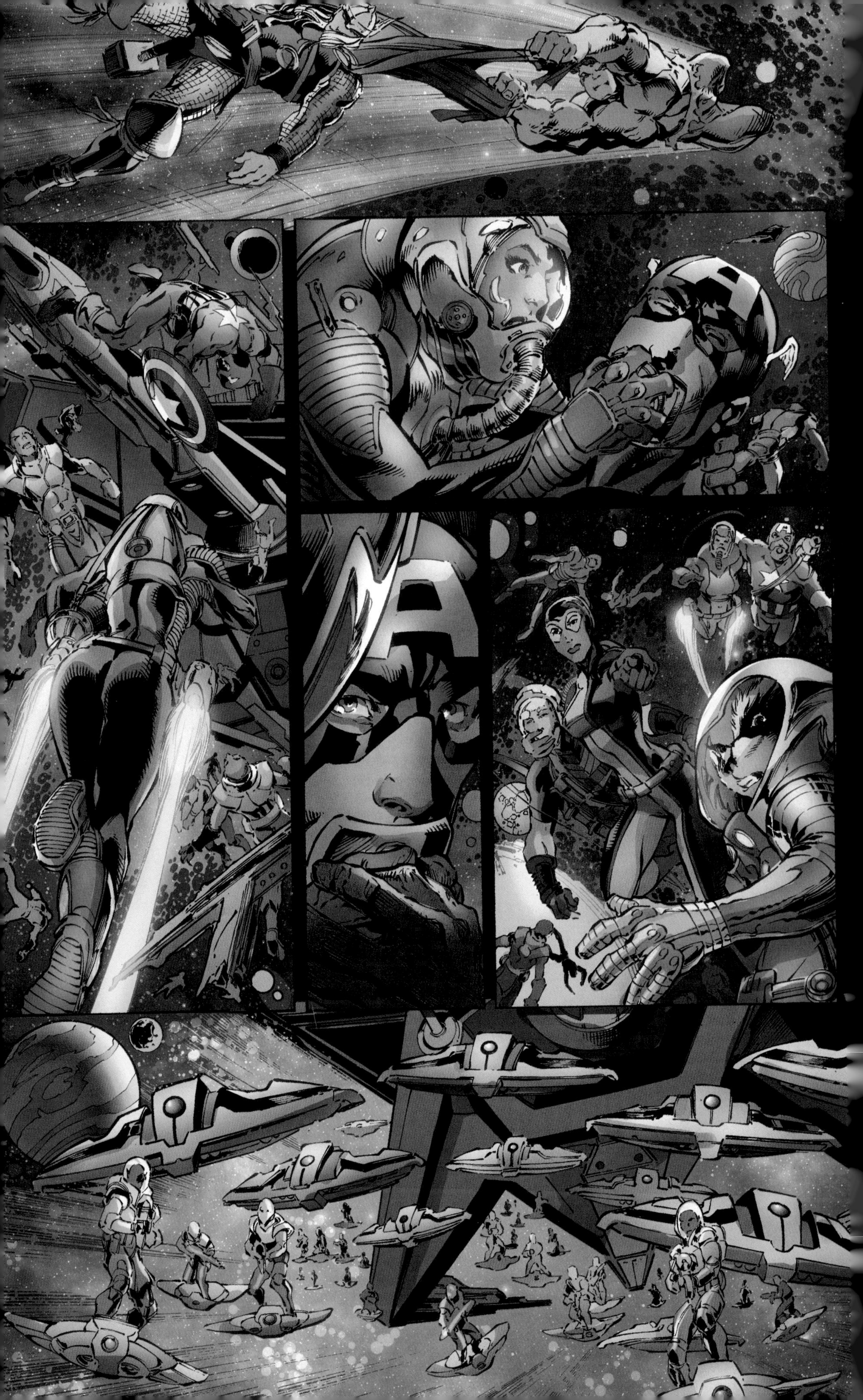

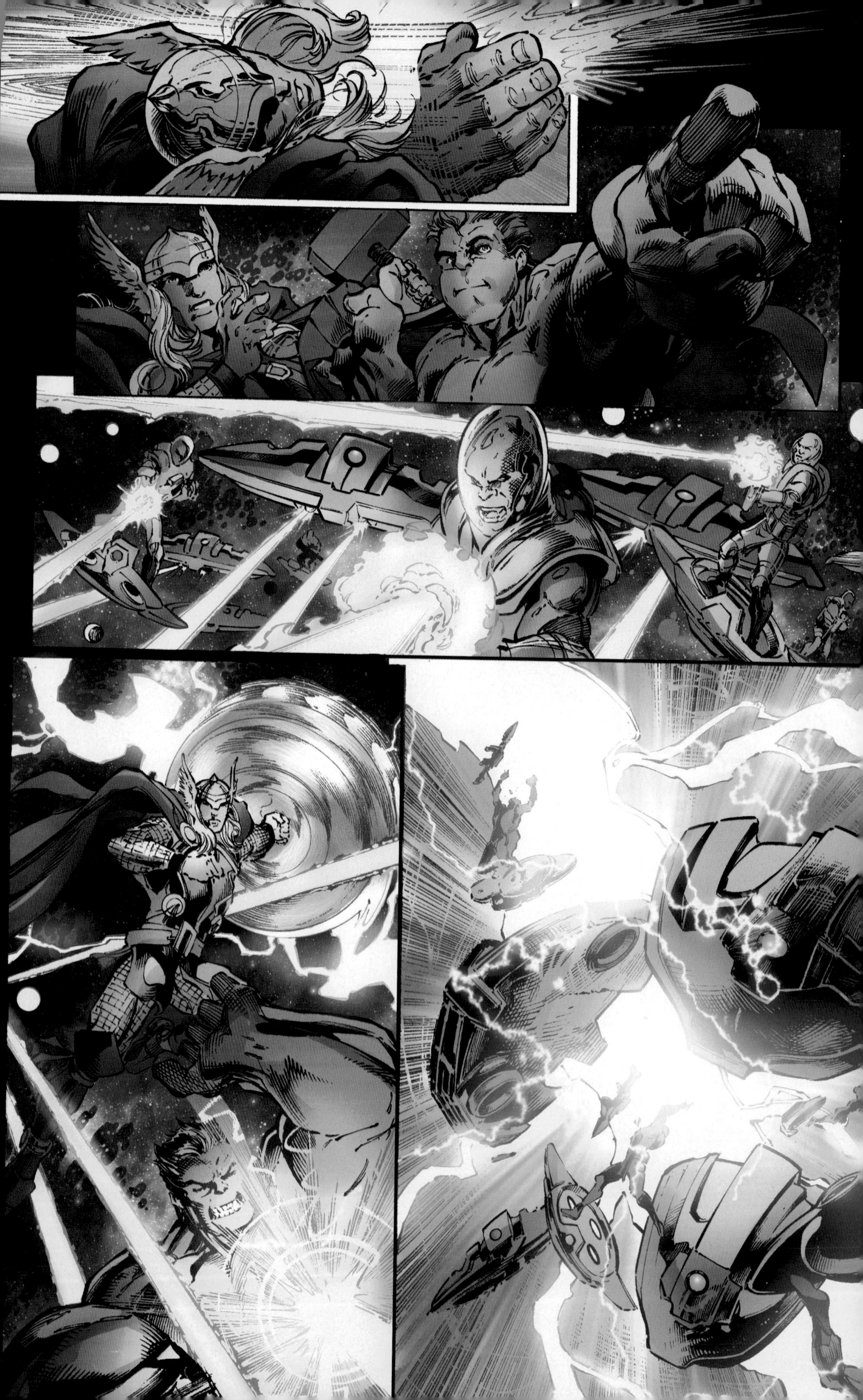

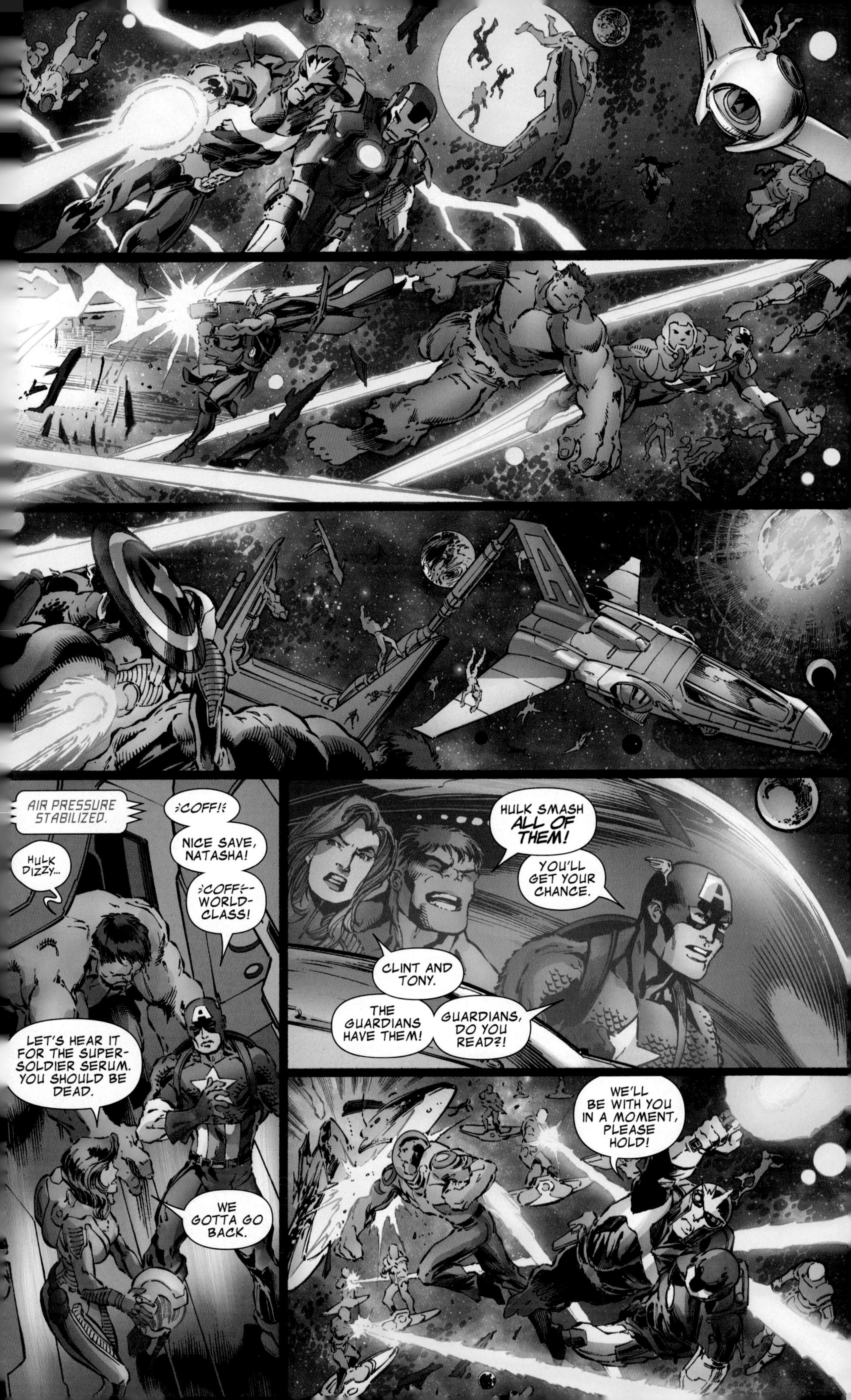
AIR PRESSURE STABILIZED.
HULK DIZZY...
COFF!
NICE SAVE, NATASHA!
COFF-- WORLD-CLASS!
LET'S HEAR IT FOR THE SUPER-SOLDIER SERUM. YOU SHOULD BE DEAD.
WE GOTTA GO BACK.
HULK SMASH ALL OF THEM!
YOU'LL GET YOUR CHANCE.
CLINT AND TONY.
THE GUARDIANS HAVE THEM!
GUARDIANS, DO YOU READ?!
WE'LL BE WITH YOU IN A MOMENT, PLEASE HOLD!

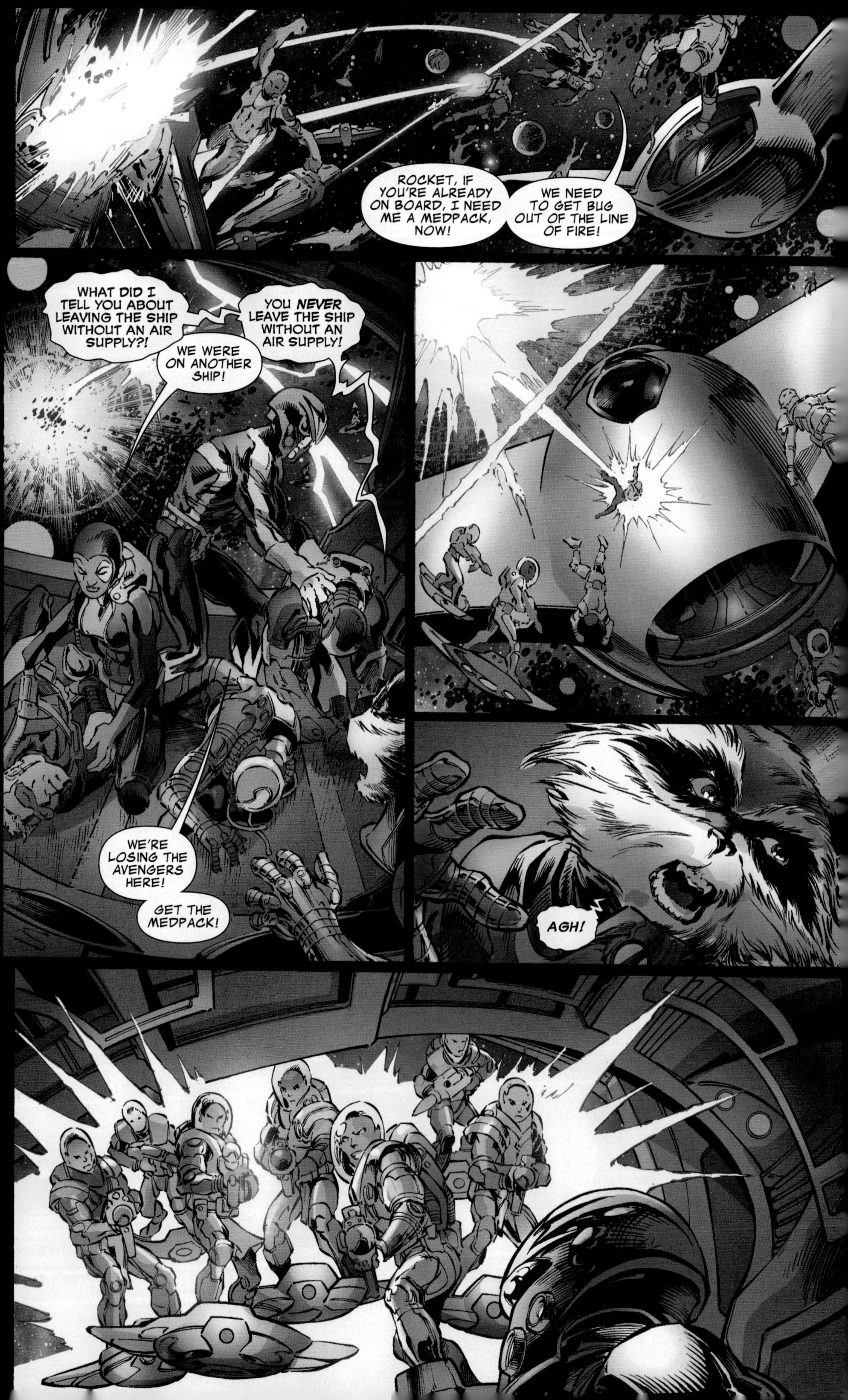
ROCKET, IF YOU'RE ALREADY ON BOARD, I NEED ME A MEDPACK, NOW!
WE NEED TO GET BUG OUT OF THE LINE OF FIRE!
WHAT DID I TELL YOU ABOUT LEAVING THE SHIP WITHOUT AN AIR SUPPLY?!
YOU NEVER LEAVE THE SHIP WITHOUT AN AIR SUPPLY!
WE WERE ON ANOTHER SHIP!
WE'RE LOSING THE AVENGERS HERE!
GET THE MEDPACK!
AGH!

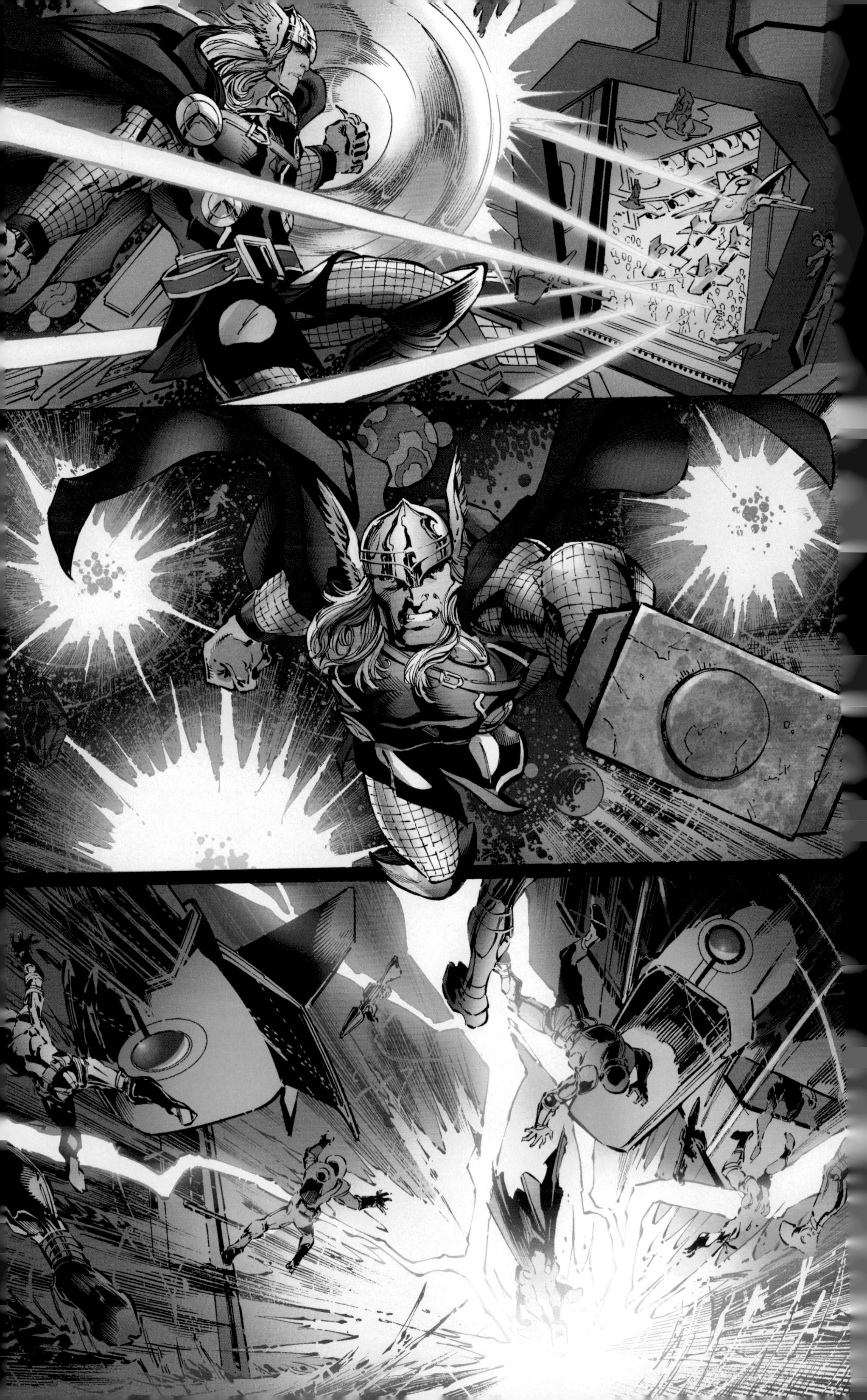

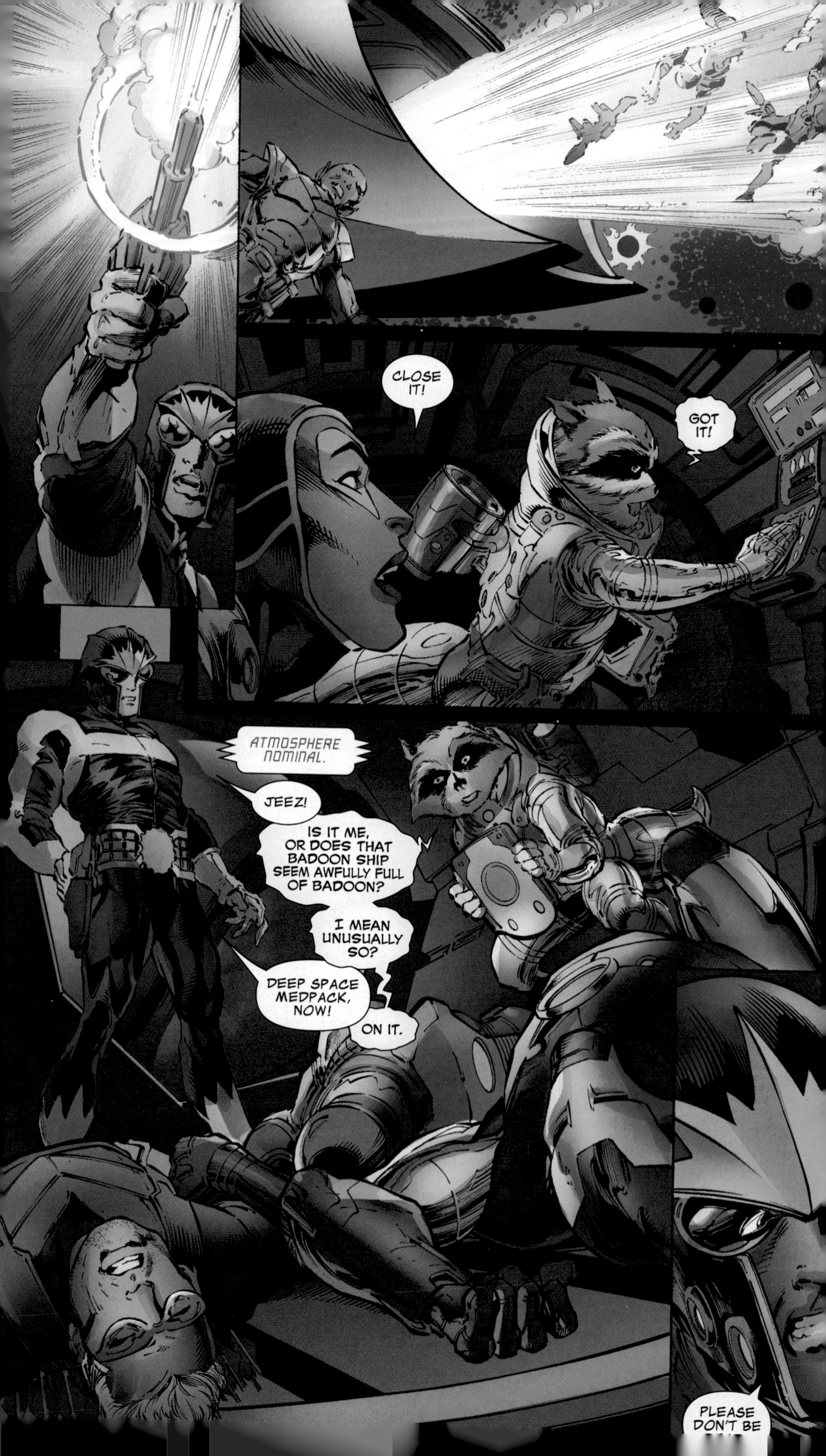
CLOSE IT!
GOT IT!
ATMOSPHERE NOMINAL.
JEEZ!
IS IT ME, OR DOES THAT BADOON SHIP SEEM AWFULLY FULL OF BADOON?
I MEAN UNUSUALLY SO?
DEEP SPACE MEDPACK, NOW!
ON IT.
PLEASE DON'T BE

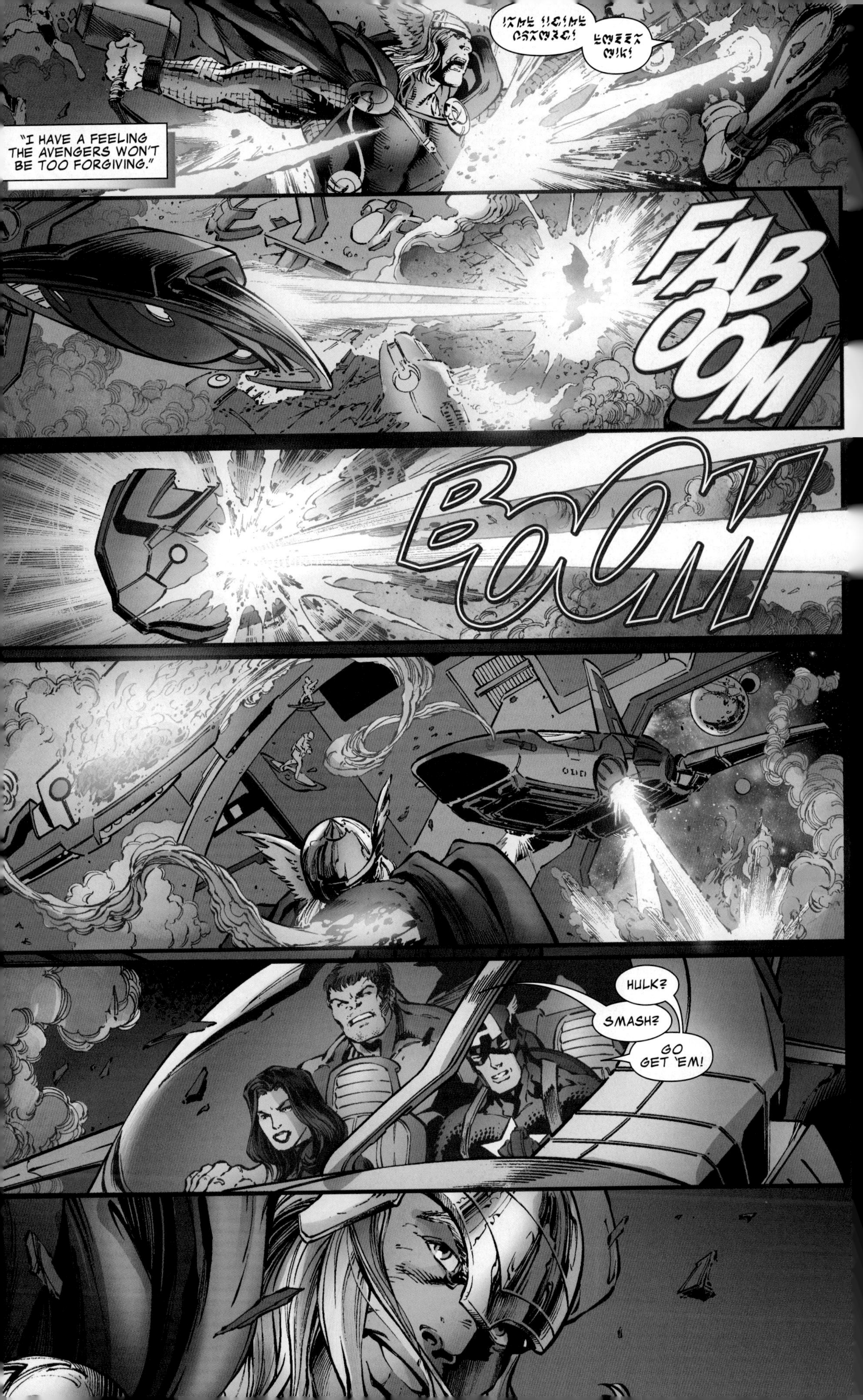
"I HAVE A FEELING THE AVENGERS WON'T BE TOO FORGIVING."
FABOOM
BOOM
HULK?
SMASH?
GO GET 'EM!

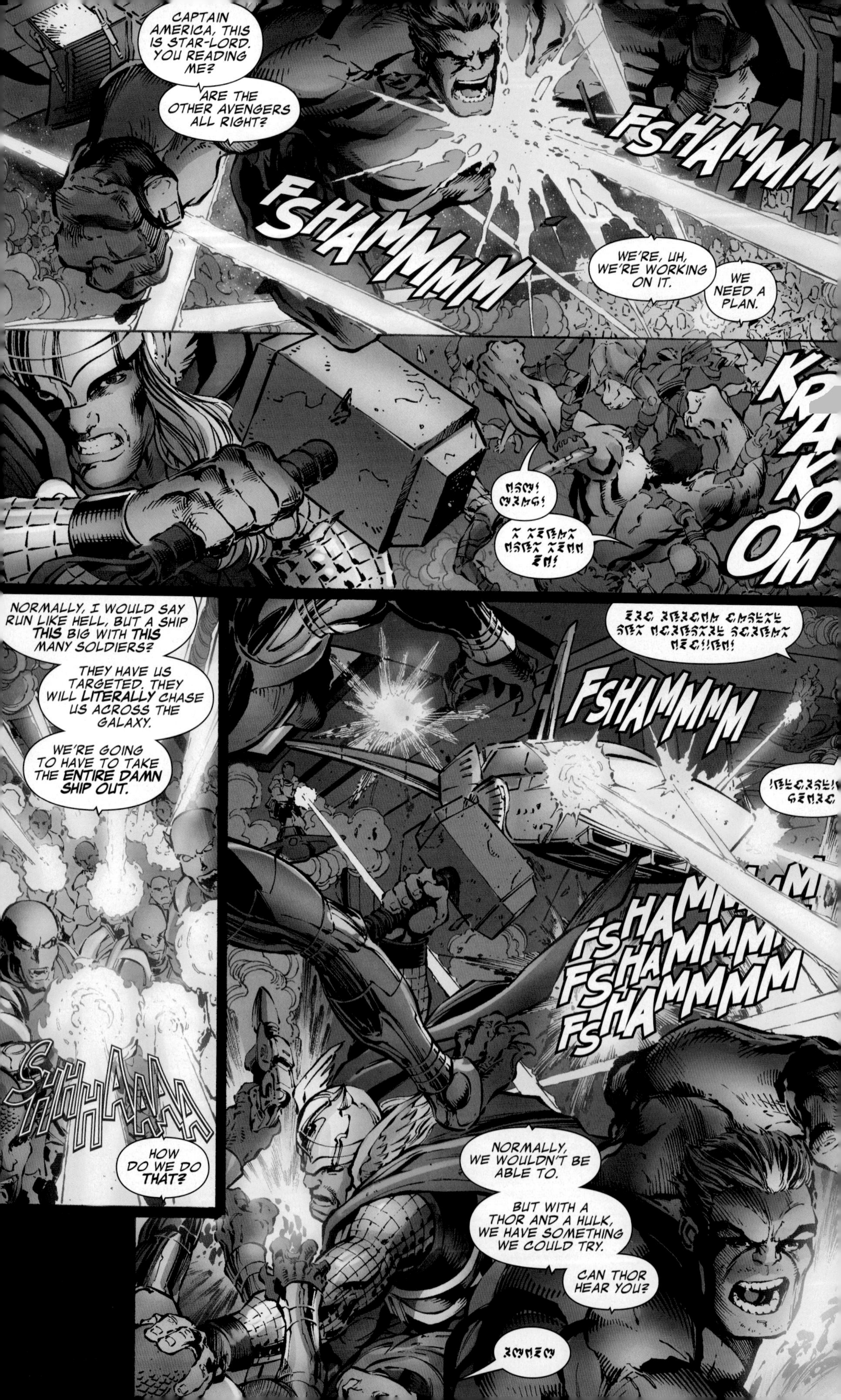
CAPTAIN AMERICA, THIS IS STAR-LORD. YOU READING ME?
ARE THE OTHER AVENGERS ALL RIGHT?
FSHAMMMMM
FSHAMMMM
WE'RE, UH, WE'RE WORKING ON IT.
WE NEED A PLAN.
KRAKOOM
NORMALLY, I WOULD SAY RUN LIKE HELL, BUT A SHIP **THIS** BIG WITH **THIS** MANY SOLDIERS?
THEY HAVE US TARGETED. THEY WILL **LITERALLY** CHASE US ACROSS THE GALAXY.
WE'RE GOING TO HAVE TO TAKE THE **ENTIRE DAMN SHIP OUT.**
SHHHAAAA
HOW DO WE DO **THAT?**
FSHAMMMM
FSHAMMMM
FSHAMMMM
FSHAMMMM
NORMALLY, WE WOULDN'T BE ABLE TO.
BUT WITH A THOR AND A HULK, WE HAVE SOMETHING WE COULD TRY.
CAN THOR HEAR YOU?

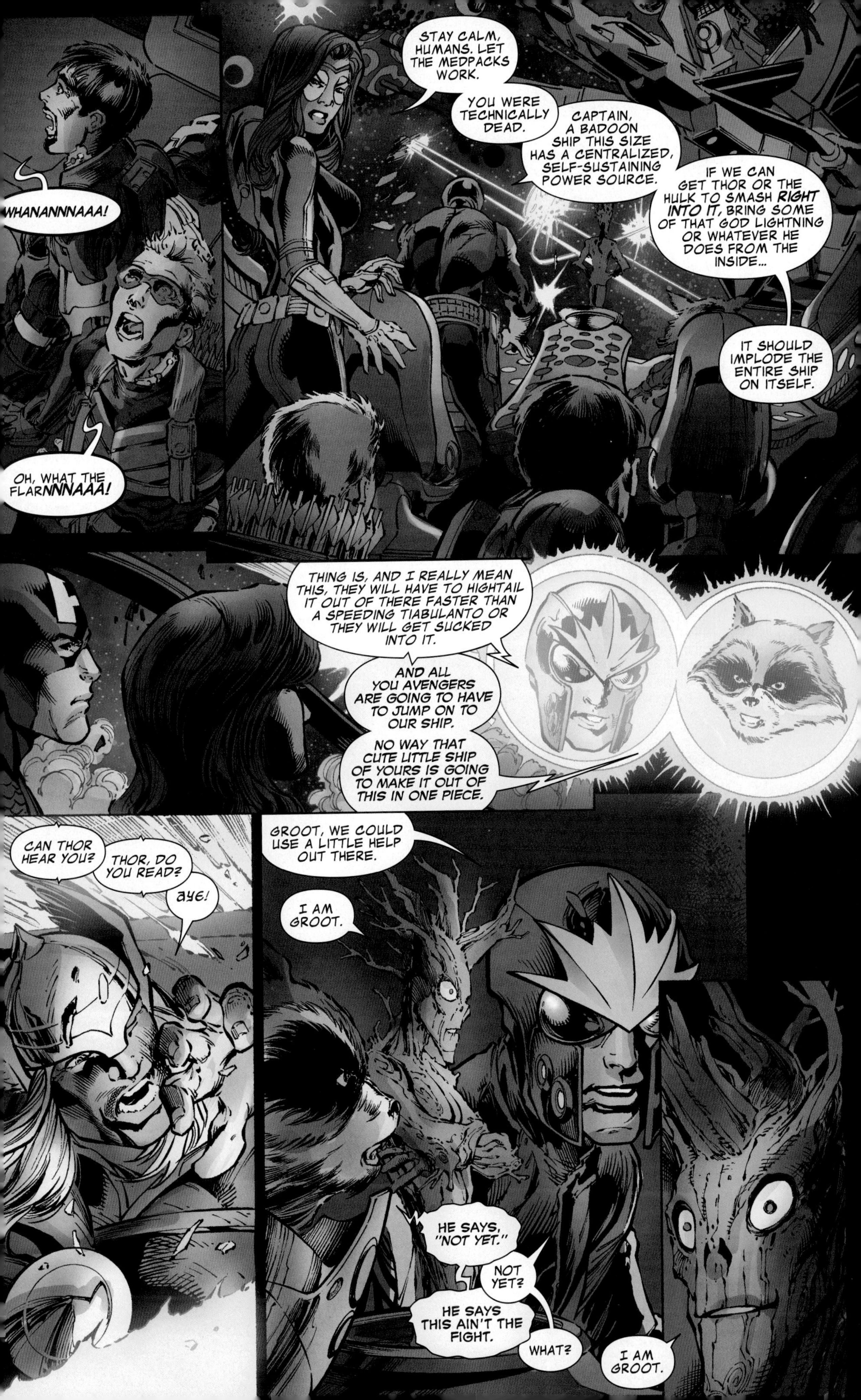
STAY CALM, HUMANS. LET THE MEDPACKS WORK.
YOU WERE TECHNICALLY DEAD.
WHANANNNAAA!
OH, WHAT THE FLARNNNAAA!
CAPTAIN, A BADOON SHIP THIS SIZE HAS A CENTRALIZED, SELF-SUSTAINING POWER SOURCE.
IF WE CAN GET THOR OR THE HULK TO SMASH RIGHT INTO IT, BRING SOME OF THAT GOD LIGHTNING OR WHATEVER HE DOES FROM THE INSIDE...
IT SHOULD IMPLODE THE ENTIRE SHIP ON ITSELF.
THING IS, AND I REALLY MEAN THIS, THEY WILL HAVE TO HIGHTAIL IT OUT OF THERE FASTER THAN A SPEEDING TIABULANTO OR THEY WILL GET SUCKED INTO IT.
AND ALL YOU AVENGERS ARE GOING TO HAVE TO JUMP ON TO OUR SHIP.
NO WAY THAT CUTE LITTLE SHIP OF YOURS IS GOING TO MAKE IT OUT OF THIS IN ONE PIECE.
CAN THOR HEAR YOU?
THOR, DO YOU READ?
AYE!
GROOT, WE COULD USE A LITTLE HELP OUT THERE.
I AM GROOT.
HE SAYS, "NOT YET."
NOT YET?
HE SAYS THIS AIN'T THE FIGHT.
WHAT?
I AM GROOT.

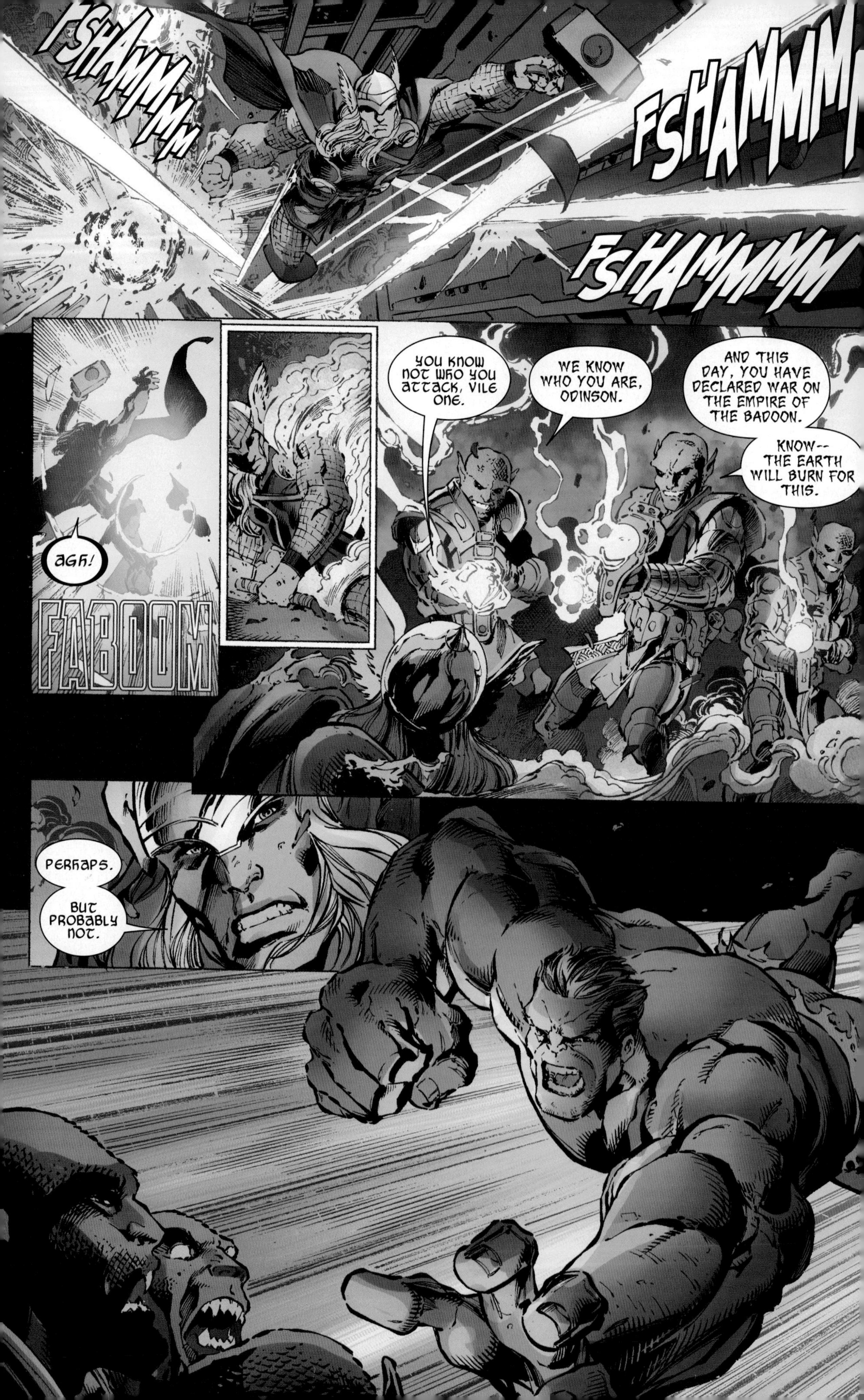
FSHAMMMM
FSHAMMM
FSHAMMMM
AGH!
FABOOM
YOU KNOW NOT WHO YOU ATTACK, VILE ONE.
WE KNOW WHO YOU ARE, ODINSON.
AND THIS DAY, YOU HAVE DECLARED WAR ON THE EMPIRE OF THE BADOON.
KNOW-- THE EARTH WILL BURN FOR THIS.
PERHAPS.
BUT PROBABLY NOT.

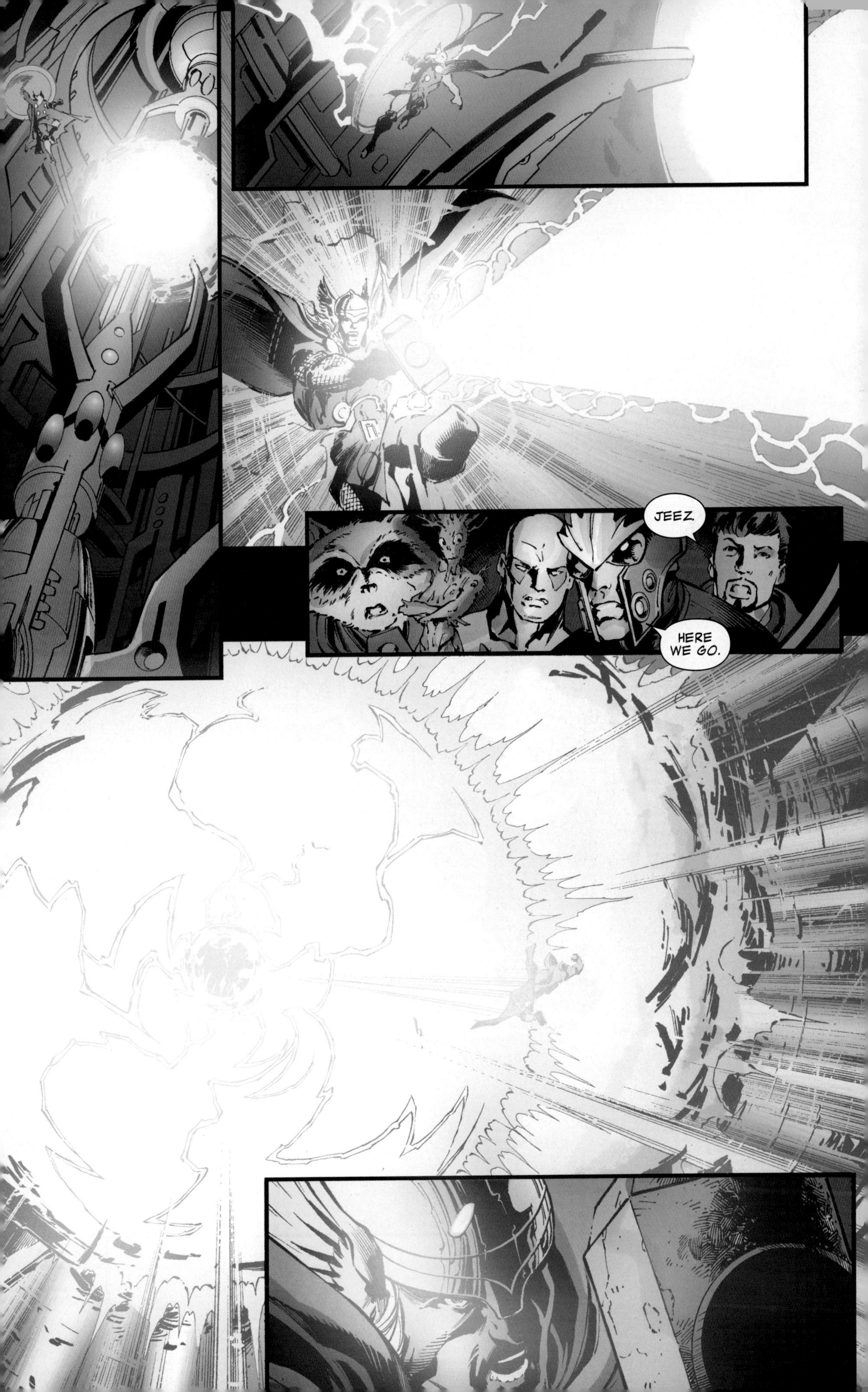
JEEZ.
HERE WE GO.

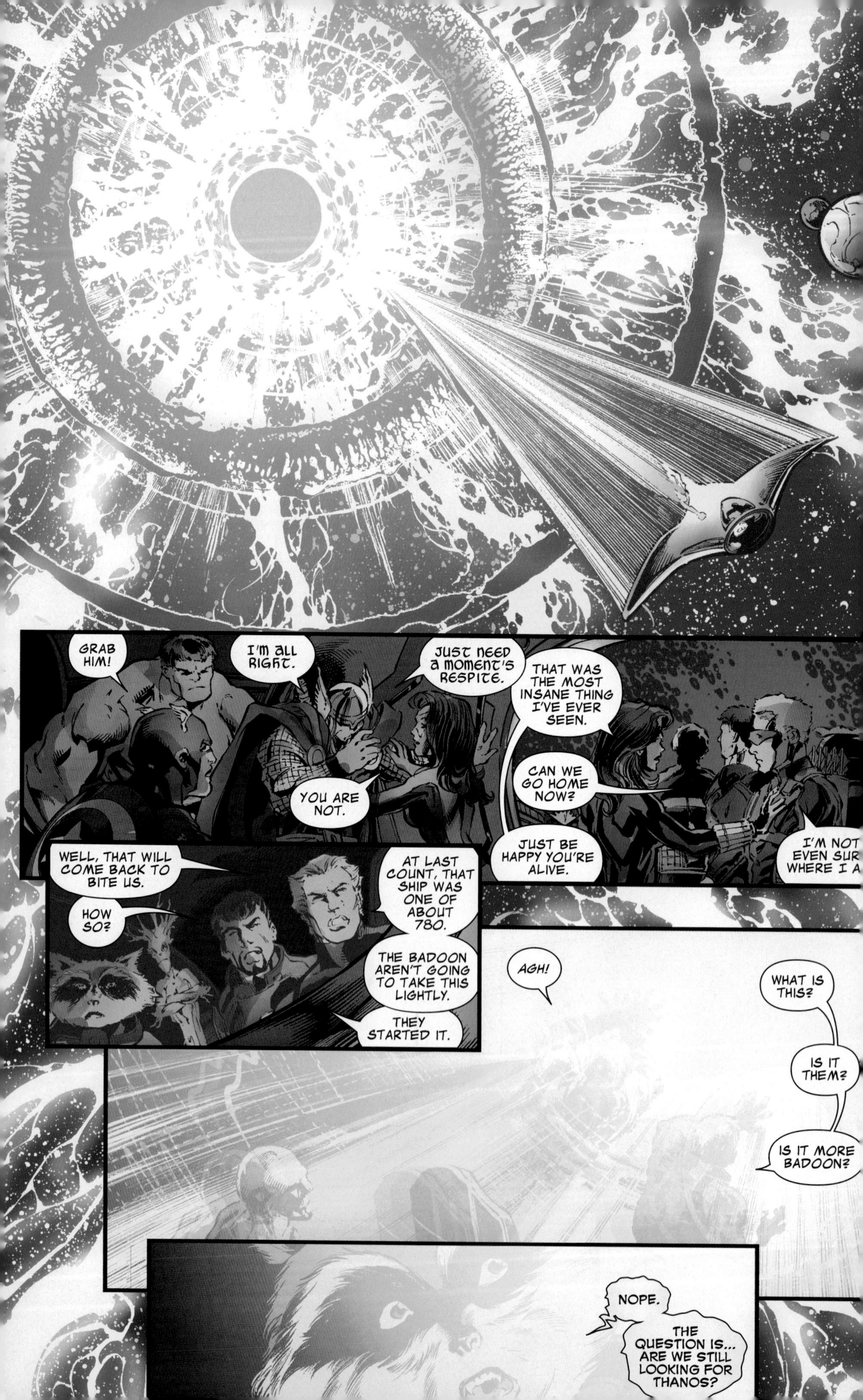
GRAB HIM!
I'M ALL RIGHT.
JUST NEED A MOMENT'S RESPITE.
YOU ARE NOT.
THAT WAS THE MOST INSANE THING I'VE EVER SEEN.
CAN WE GO HOME NOW?
JUST BE HAPPY YOU'RE ALIVE.
WELL, THAT WILL COME BACK TO BITE US.
HOW SO?
AT LAST COUNT, THAT SHIP WAS ONE OF ABOUT 780.
THE BADOON AREN'T GOING TO TAKE THIS LIGHTLY.
THEY STARTED IT.
AGH!
WHAT IS THIS?
IS IT THEM?
IS IT MORE BADOON?
NOPE.
THE QUESTION IS... ARE WE STILL LOOKING FOR THANOS?

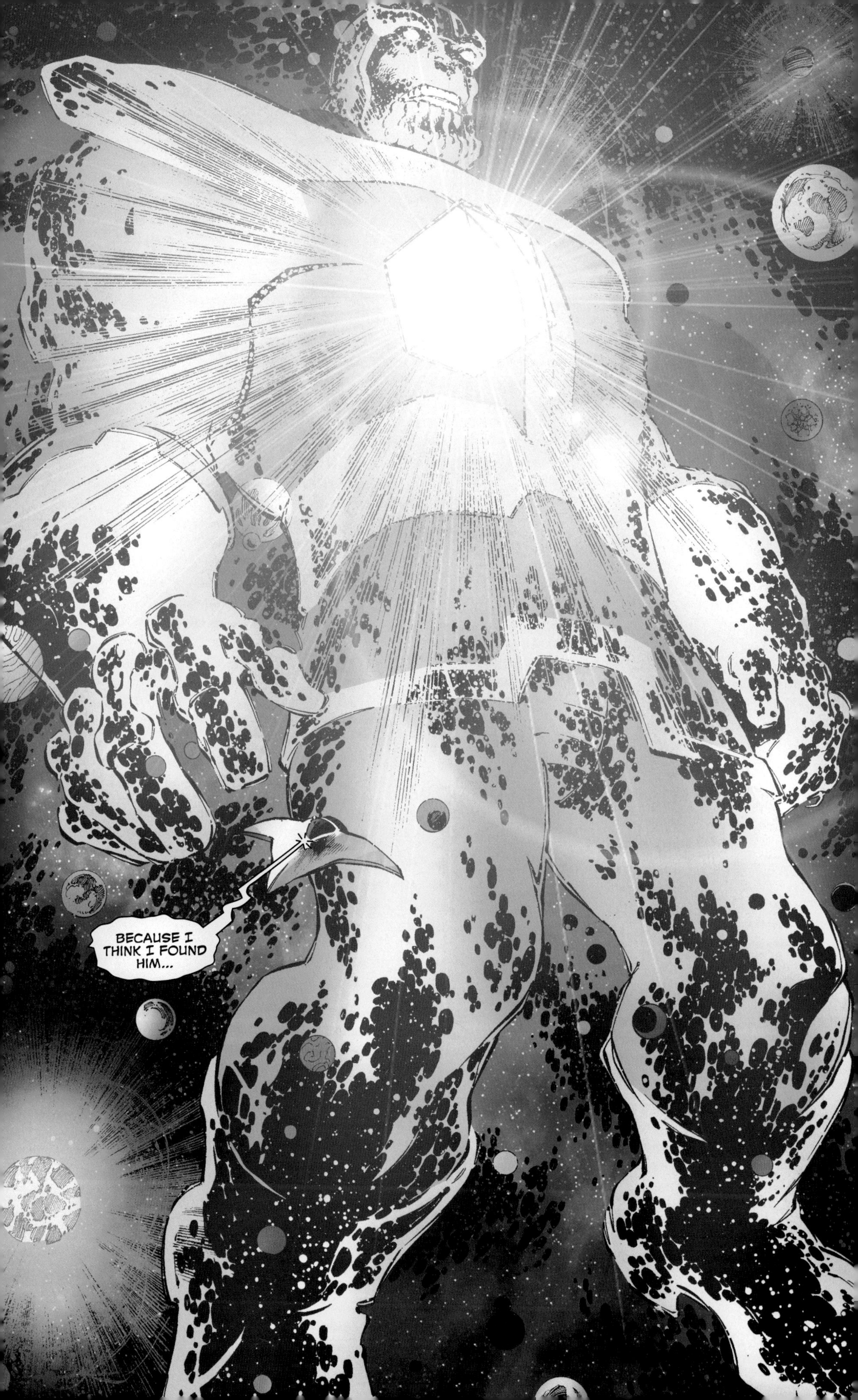
BECAUSE I THINK I FOUND HIM...

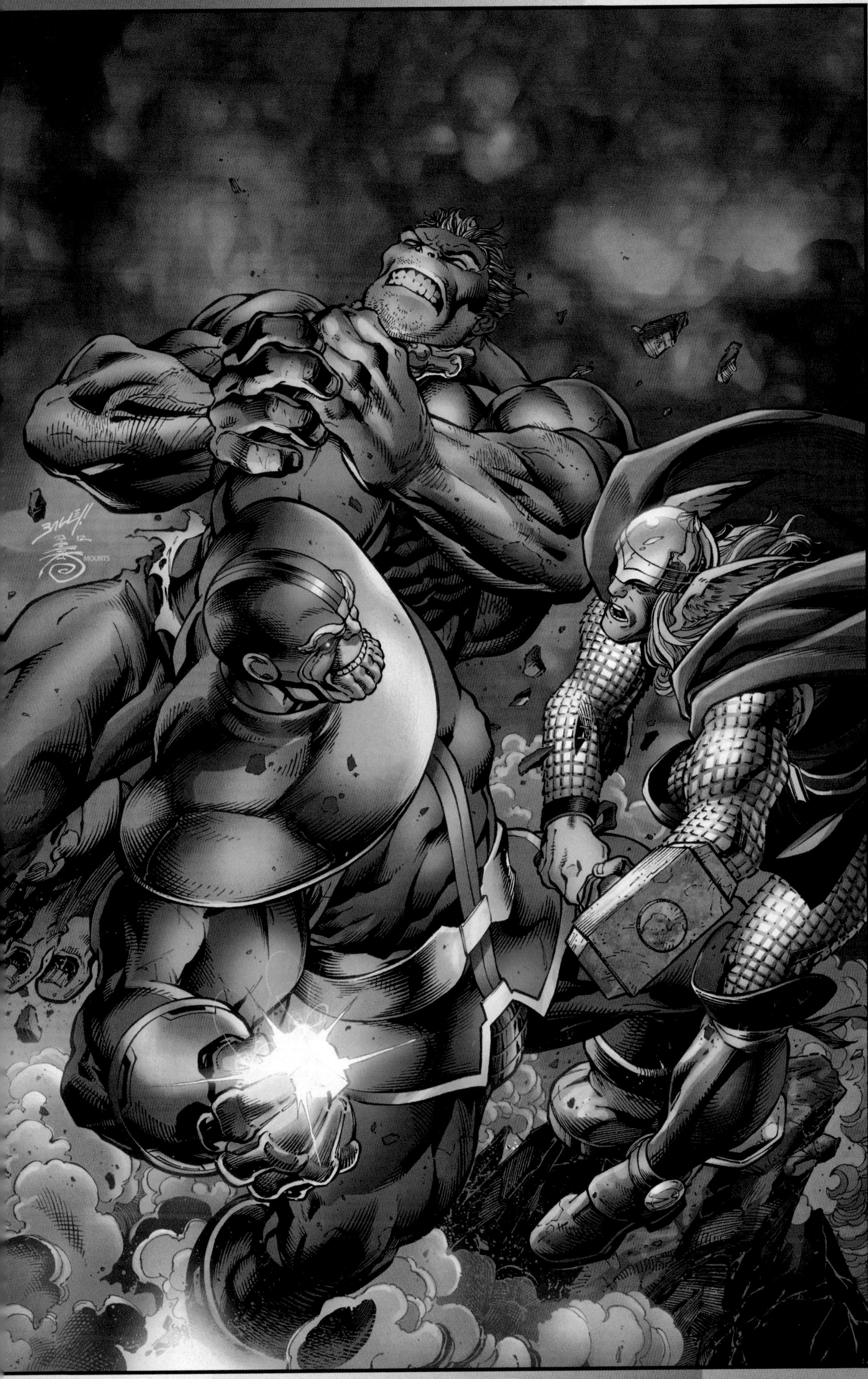

EIGHT

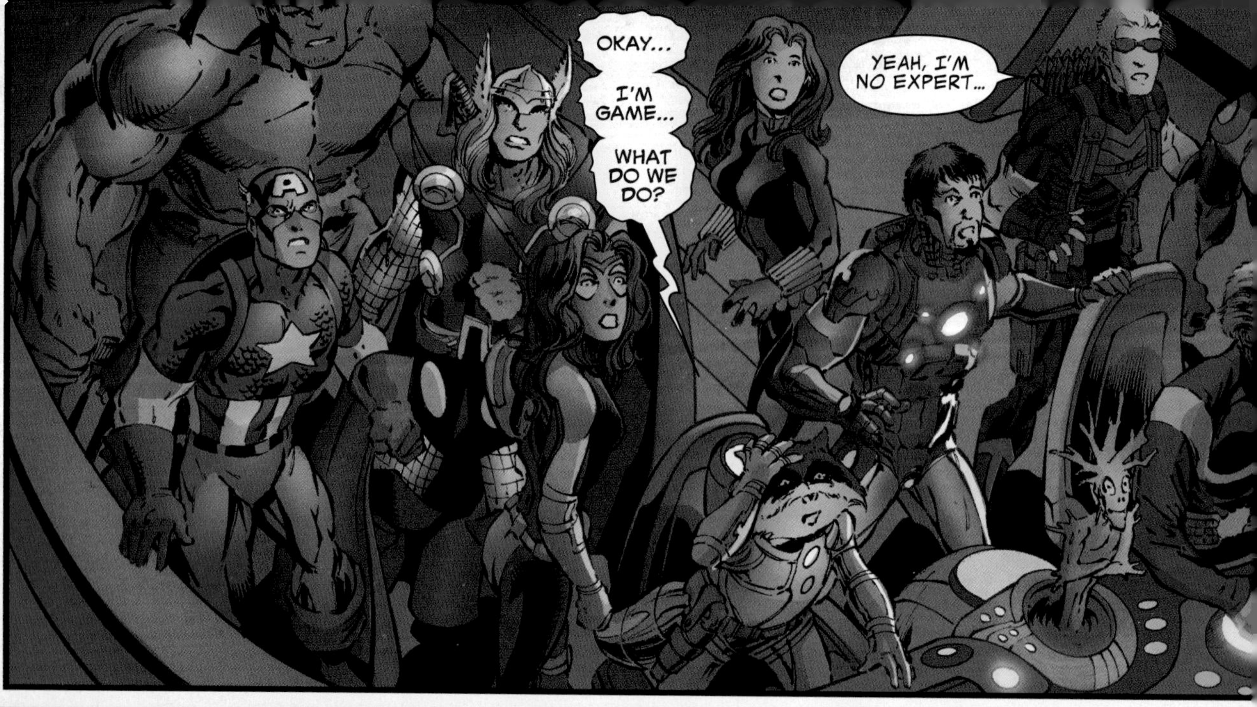
OKAY... I'M GAME... WHAT DO WE DO?
YEAH, I'M NO EXPERT...
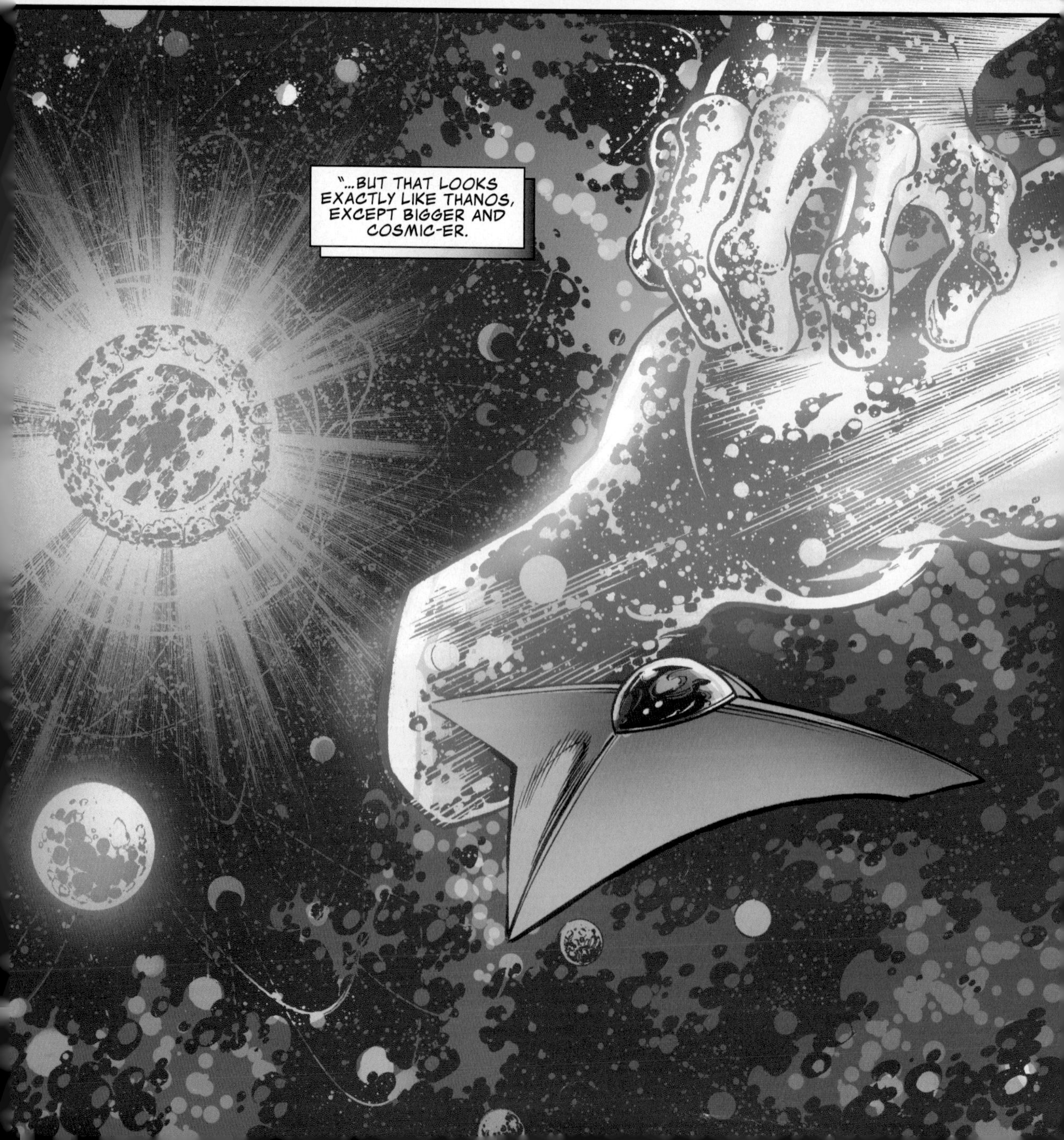
"...BUT THAT LOOKS EXACTLY LIKE THANOS, EXCEPT BIGGER AND COSMIC-ER.

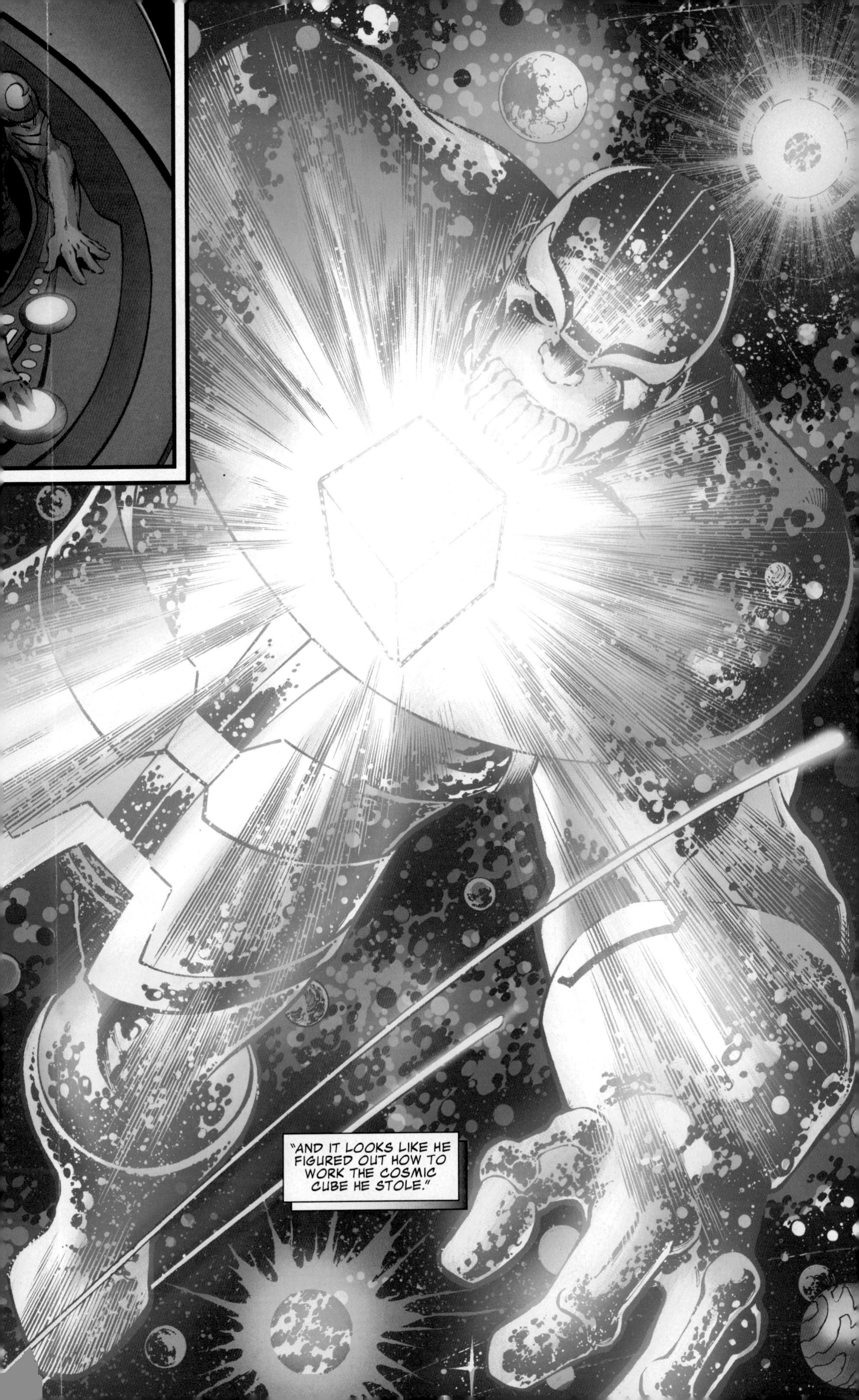
"AND IT LOOKS LIKE HE FIGURED OUT HOW TO WORK THE COSMIC CUBE HE STOLE."

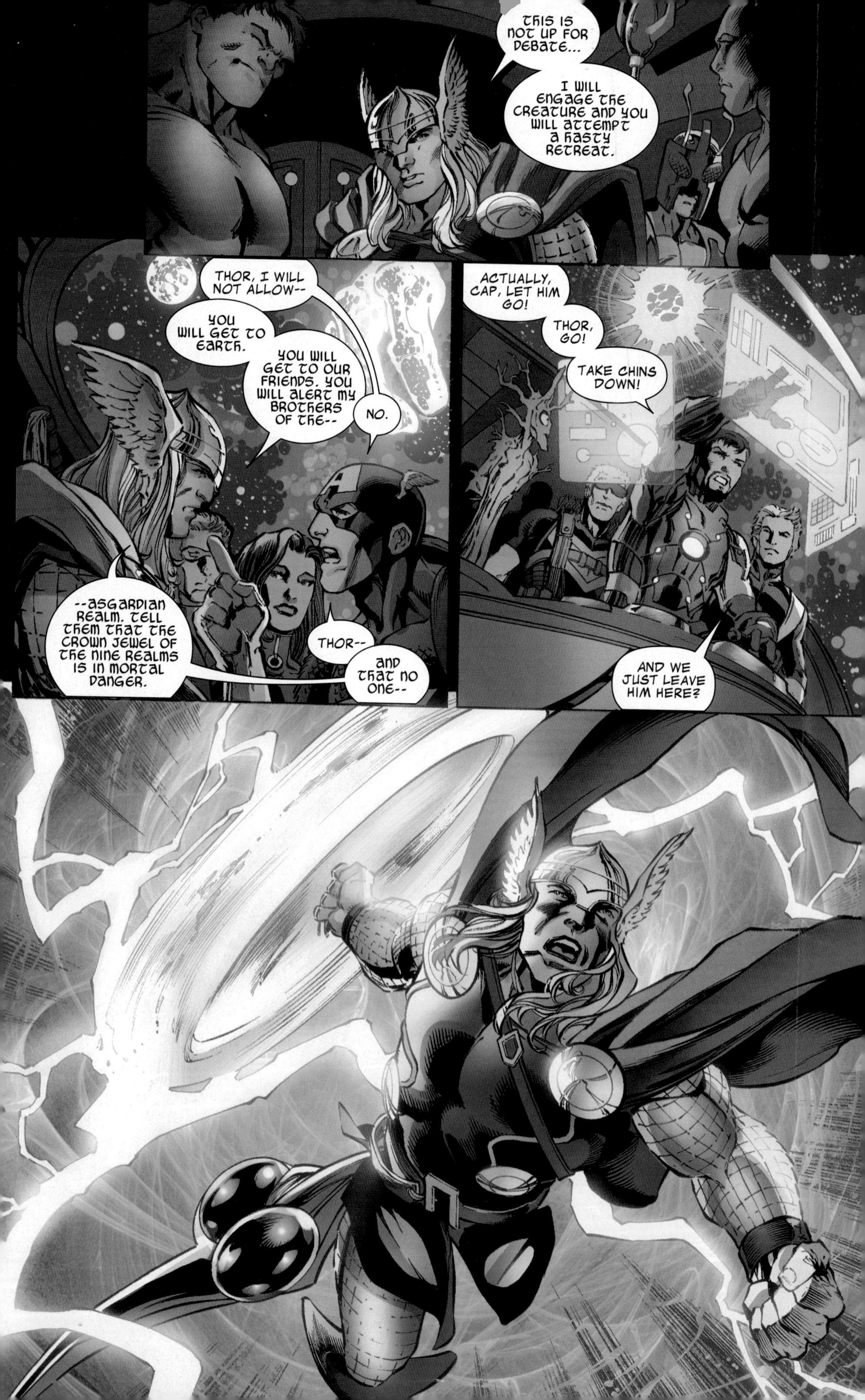
THIS IS NOT UP FOR DEBATE...
I WILL ENGAGE THE CREATURE AND YOU WILL ATTEMPT A HASTY RETREAT.
THOR, I WILL NOT ALLOW--
YOU WILL GET TO EARTH.
YOU WILL GET TO OUR FRIENDS. YOU WILL ALERT MY BROTHERS OF THE--
NO.
--ASGARDIAN REALM. TELL THEM THAT THE CROWN JEWEL OF THE NINE REALMS IS IN MORTAL DANGER.
THOR--
AND THAT NO ONE--
ACTUALLY, CAP, LET HIM GO!
THOR, GO!
TAKE CHINS DOWN!
AND WE JUST LEAVE HIM HERE?

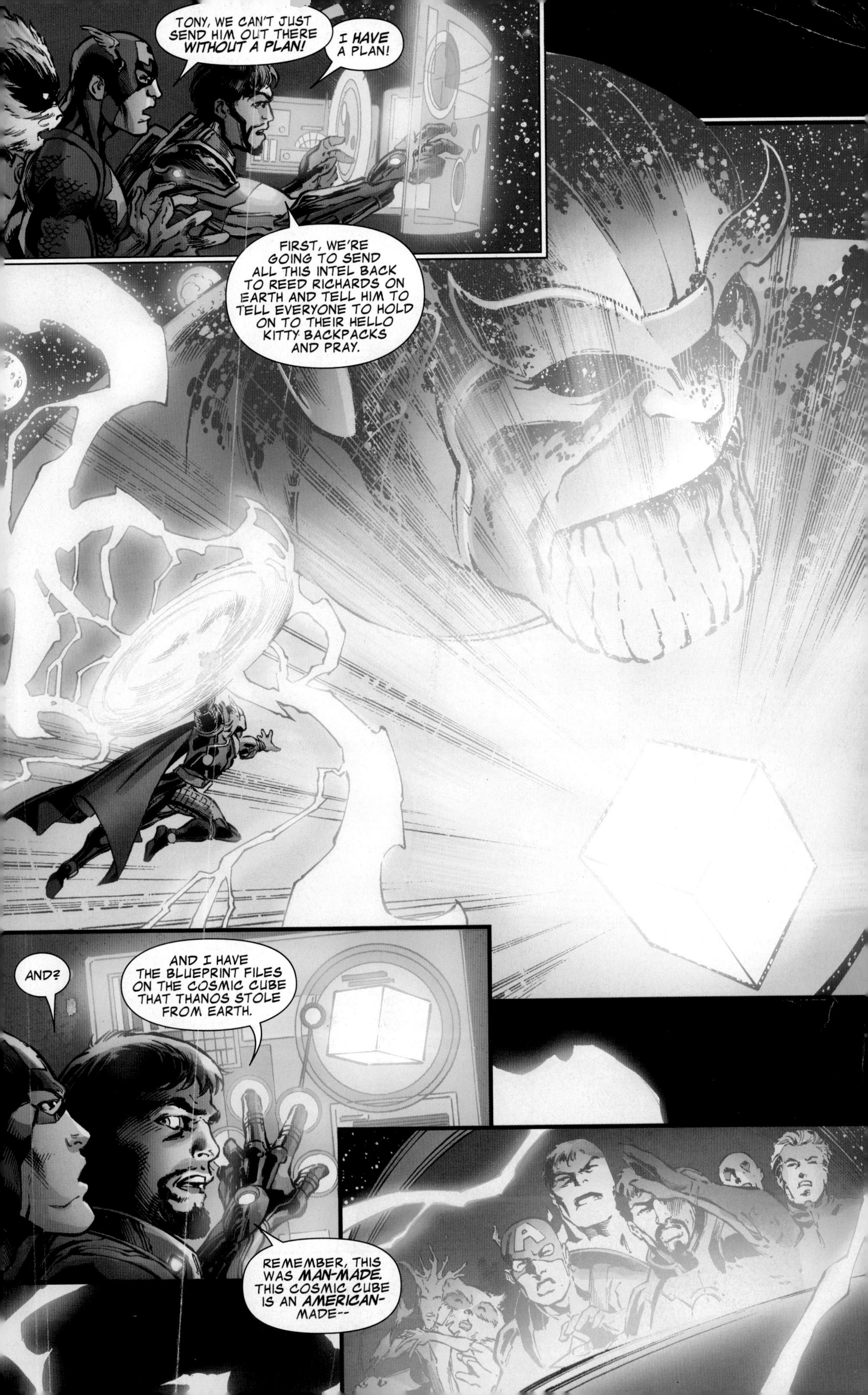
TONY, WE CAN'T JUST SEND HIM OUT THERE WITHOUT A PLAN!
I HAVE A PLAN!
FIRST, WE'RE GOING TO SEND ALL THIS INTEL BACK TO REED RICHARDS ON EARTH AND TELL HIM TO TELL EVERYONE TO HOLD ON TO THEIR HELLO KITTY BACKPACKS AND PRAY.
AND?
AND I HAVE THE BLUEPRINT FILES ON THE COSMIC CUBE THAT THANOS STOLE FROM EARTH.
REMEMBER, THIS WAS MAN-MADE. THIS COSMIC CUBE IS AN AMERICAN-MADE--

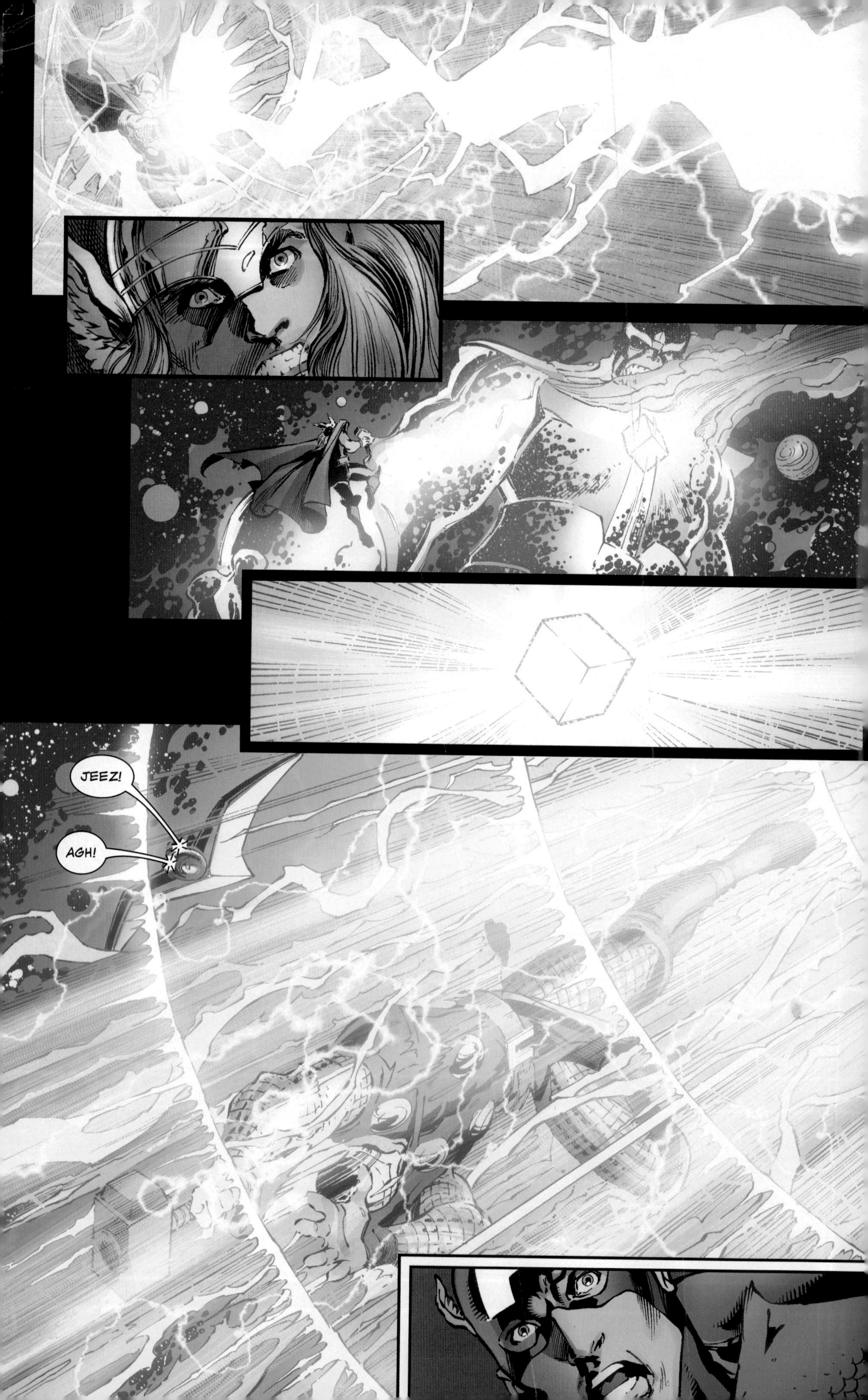
JEEZ!
AGH!

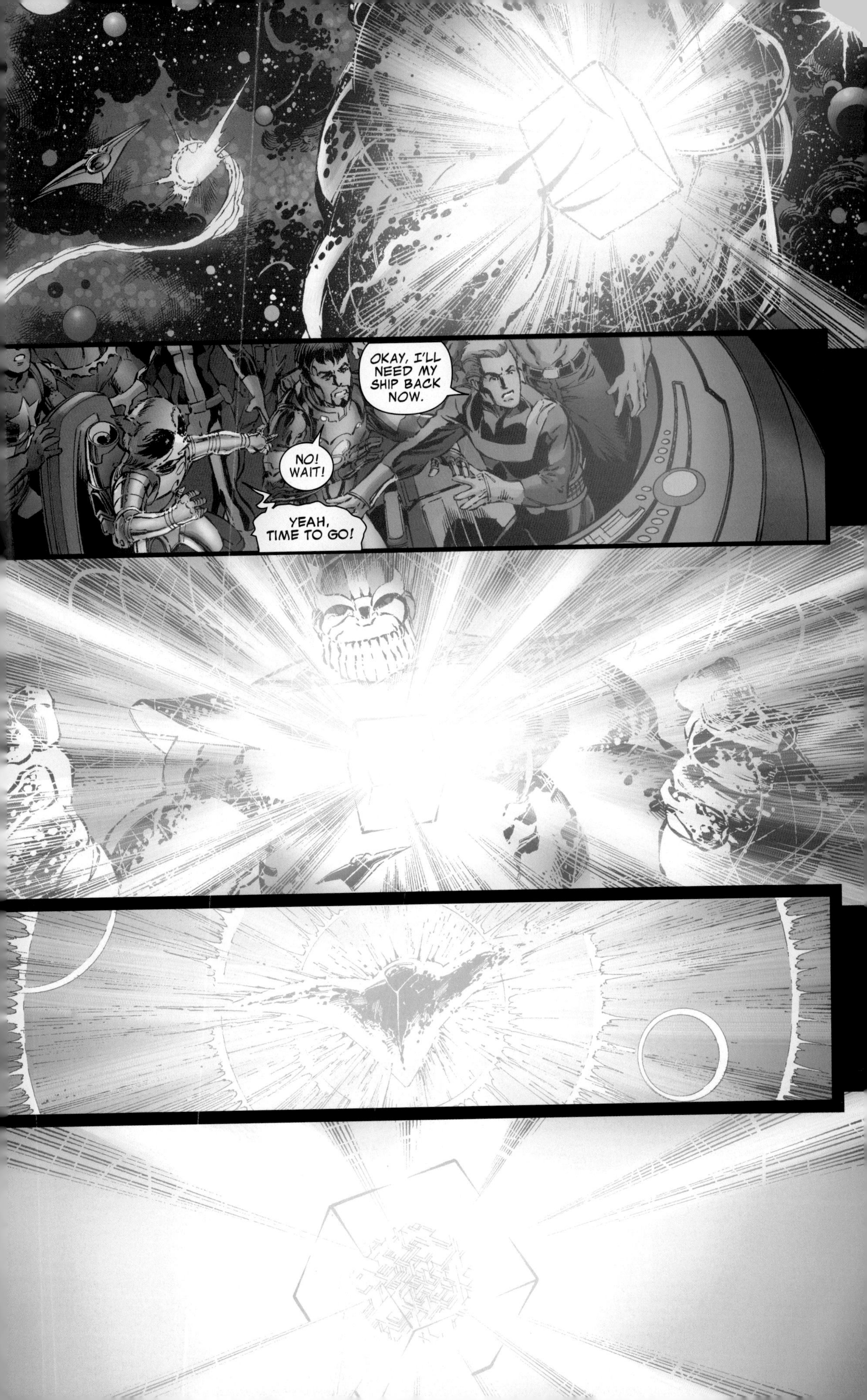
OKAY, I'LL NEED MY SHIP BACK NOW.
NO! WAIT!
YEAH, TIME TO GO!

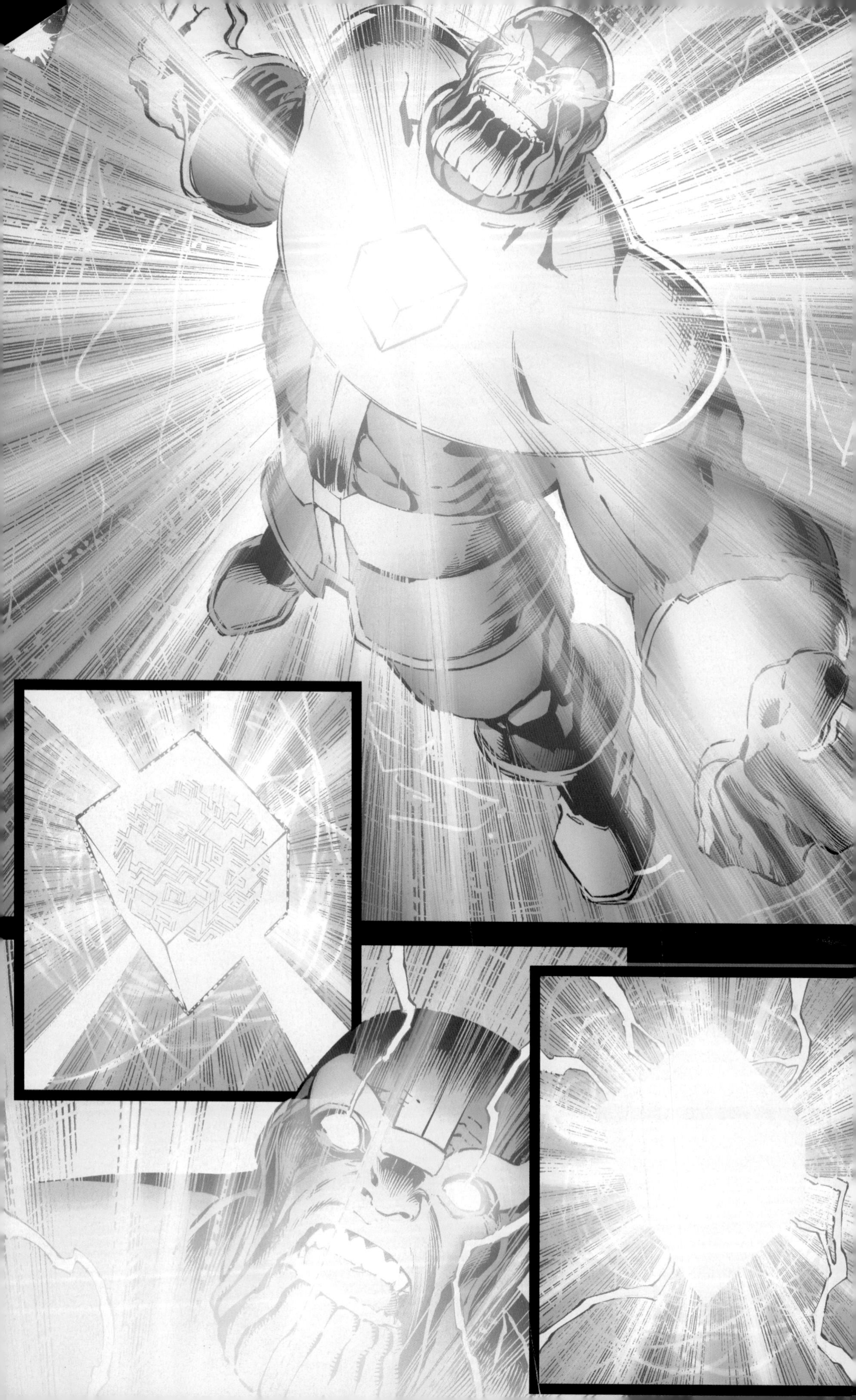

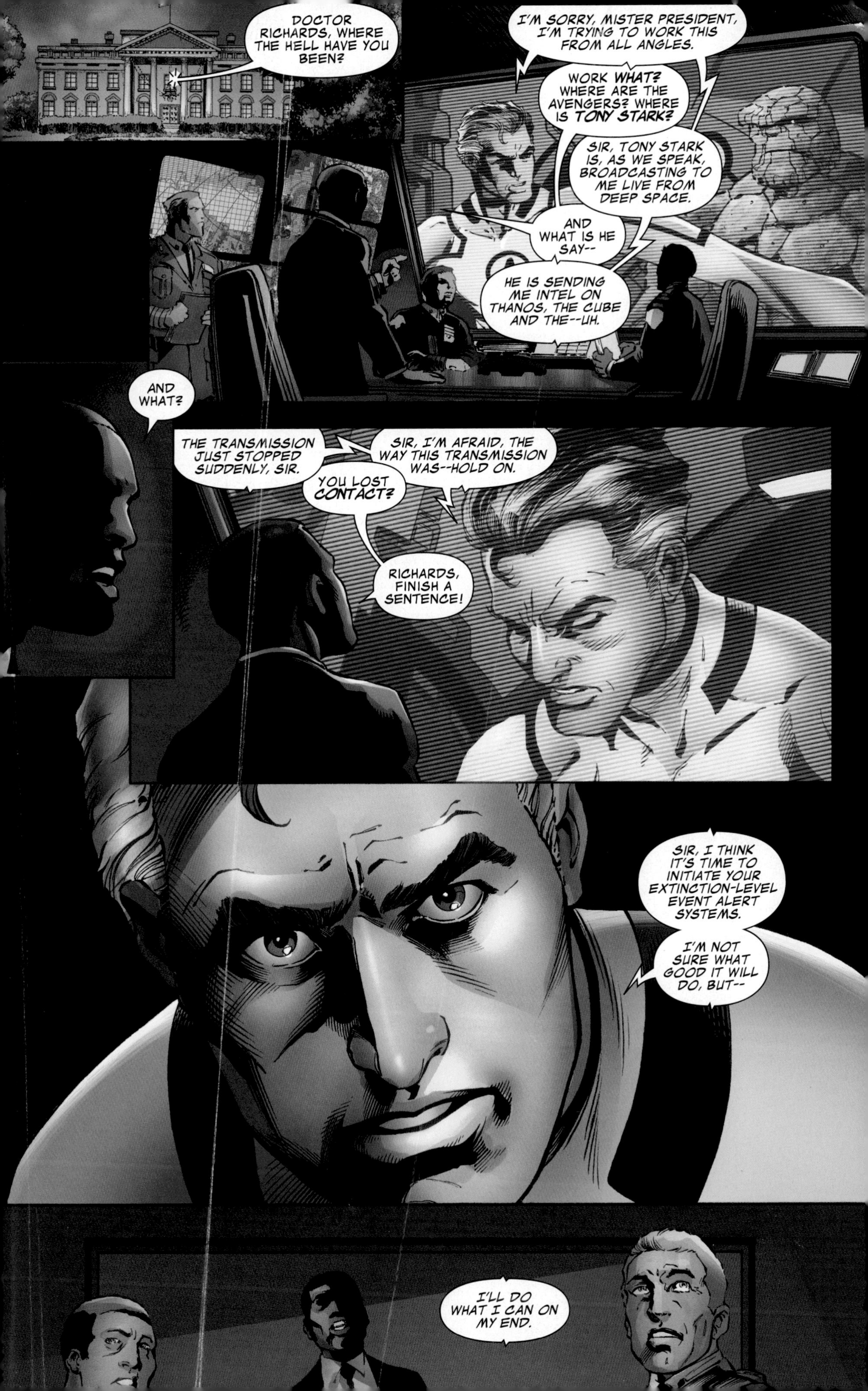
DOCTOR RICHARDS, WHERE THE HELL HAVE YOU BEEN?
I'M SORRY, MISTER PRESIDENT, I'M TRYING TO WORK THIS FROM ALL ANGLES.
WORK WHAT? WHERE ARE THE AVENGERS? WHERE IS TONY STARK?
SIR, TONY STARK IS, AS WE SPEAK, BROADCASTING TO ME LIVE FROM DEEP SPACE.
AND WHAT IS HE SAY--
HE IS SENDING ME INTEL ON THANOS, THE CUBE AND THE--UH.
AND WHAT?
THE TRANSMISSION JUST STOPPED SUDDENLY, SIR.
SIR, I'M AFRAID, THE WAY THIS TRANSMISSION WAS--HOLD ON.
YOU LOST CONTACT?
RICHARDS, FINISH A SENTENCE!
SIR, I THINK IT'S TIME TO INITIATE YOUR EXTINCTION-LEVEL EVENT ALERT SYSTEMS.
I'M NOT SURE WHAT GOOD IT WILL DO, BUT--
I'LL DO WHAT I CAN ON MY END.

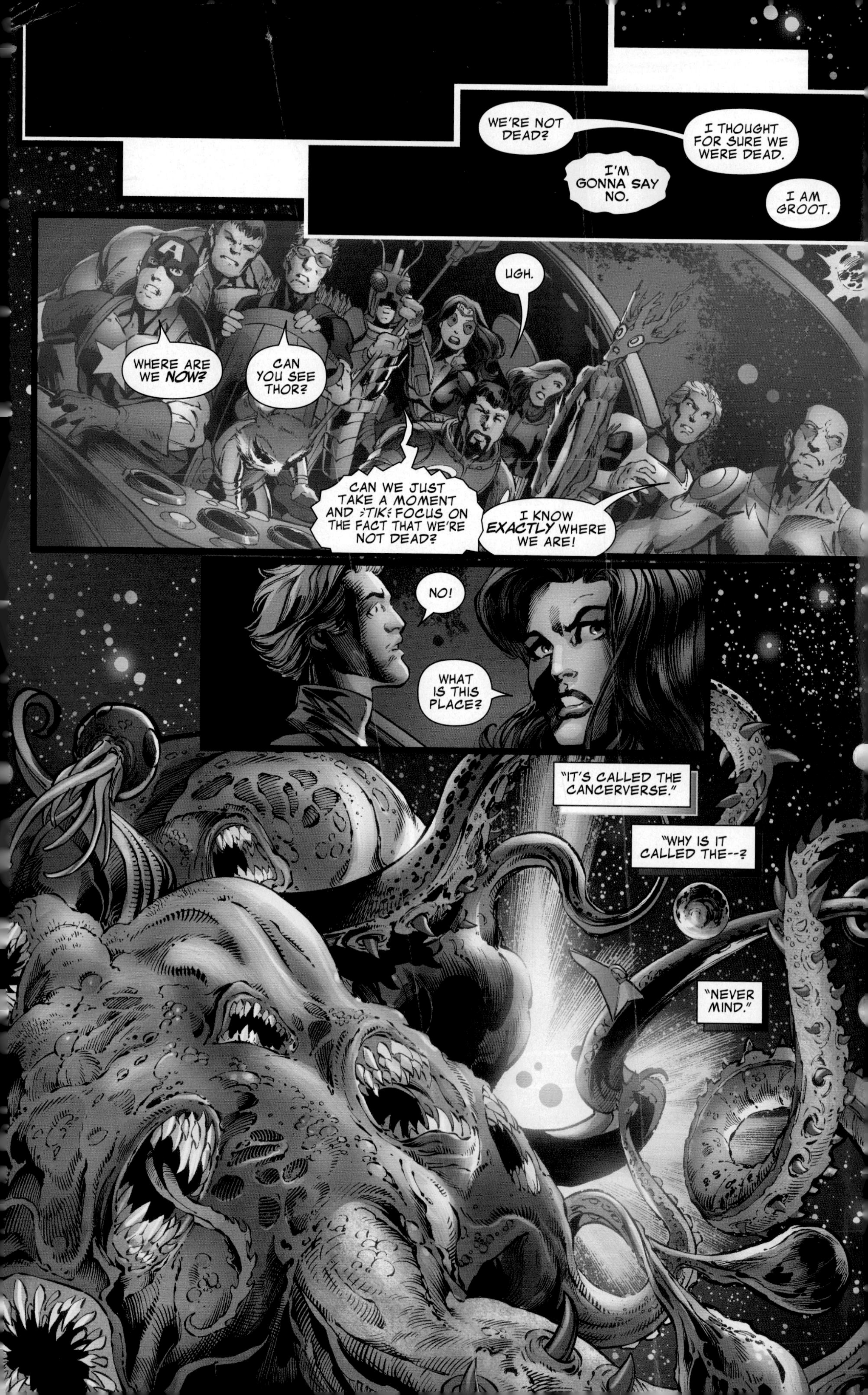
WE'RE NOT DEAD?
I THOUGHT FOR SURE WE WERE DEAD.
I'M GONNA SAY NO.
I AM GROOT.
UGH.
WHERE ARE WE NOW?
CAN YOU SEE THOR?
CAN WE JUST TAKE A MOMENT AND ;TIK; FOCUS ON THE FACT THAT WE'RE NOT DEAD?
I KNOW EXACTLY WHERE WE ARE!
NO!
WHAT IS THIS PLACE?
"IT'S CALLED THE CANCERVERSE."
"WHY IS IT CALLED THE--?
"NEVER MIND."

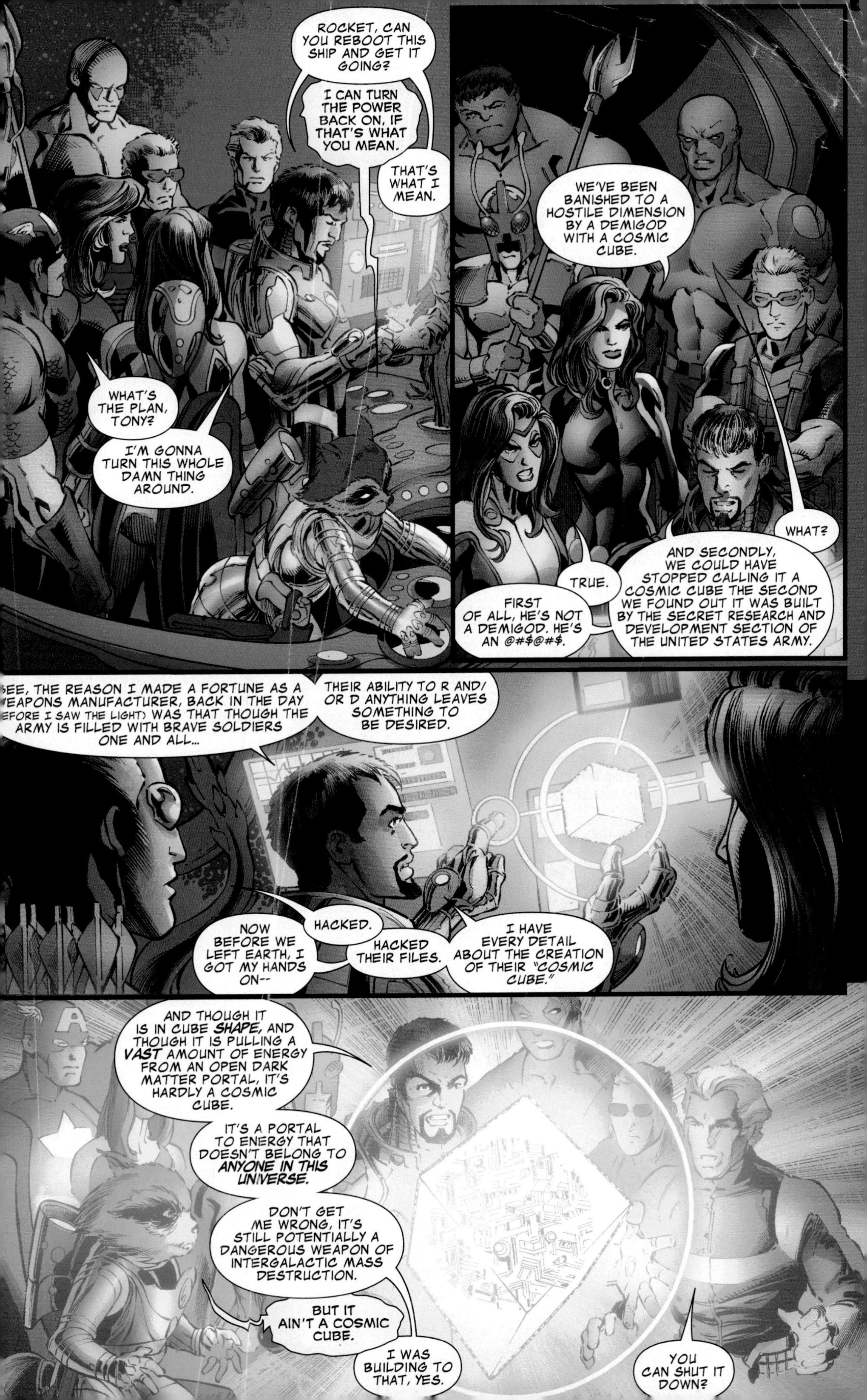
ROCKET, CAN YOU REBOOT THIS SHIP AND GET IT GOING?
I CAN TURN THE POWER BACK ON, IF THAT'S WHAT YOU MEAN.
THAT'S WHAT I MEAN.
WHAT'S THE PLAN, TONY?
I'M GONNA TURN THIS WHOLE DAMN THING AROUND.
WE'VE BEEN BANISHED TO A HOSTILE DIMENSION BY A DEMIGOD WITH A COSMIC CUBE.
FIRST OF ALL, HE'S NOT A DEMIGOD. HE'S AN @#$@#$.
TRUE.
AND SECONDLY, WE COULD HAVE STOPPED CALLING IT A COSMIC CUBE THE SECOND WE FOUND OUT IT WAS BUILT BY THE SECRET RESEARCH AND DEVELOPMENT SECTION OF THE UNITED STATES ARMY.
WHAT?
EE, THE REASON I MADE A FORTUNE AS A EAPONS MANUFACTURER, BACK IN THE DAY EFORE I SAW THE LIGHT) WAS THAT THOUGH THE ARMY IS FILLED WITH BRAVE SOLDIERS ONE AND ALL...
THEIR ABILITY TO R AND/OR D ANYTHING LEAVES SOMETHING TO BE DESIRED.
NOW BEFORE WE LEFT EARTH, I GOT MY HANDS ON--
HACKED.
HACKED THEIR FILES.
I HAVE EVERY DETAIL ABOUT THE CREATION OF THEIR "COSMIC CUBE."
AND THOUGH IT IS IN CUBE SHAPE, AND THOUGH IT IS PULLING A VAST AMOUNT OF ENERGY FROM AN OPEN DARK MATTER PORTAL, IT'S HARDLY A COSMIC CUBE.
IT'S A PORTAL TO ENERGY THAT DOESN'T BELONG TO ANYONE IN THIS UNIVERSE.
DON'T GET ME WRONG, IT'S STILL POTENTIALLY A DANGEROUS WEAPON OF INTERGALACTIC MASS DESTRUCTION.
BUT IT AIN'T A COSMIC CUBE.
I WAS BUILDING TO THAT, YES.
YOU CAN SHUT IT DOWN?

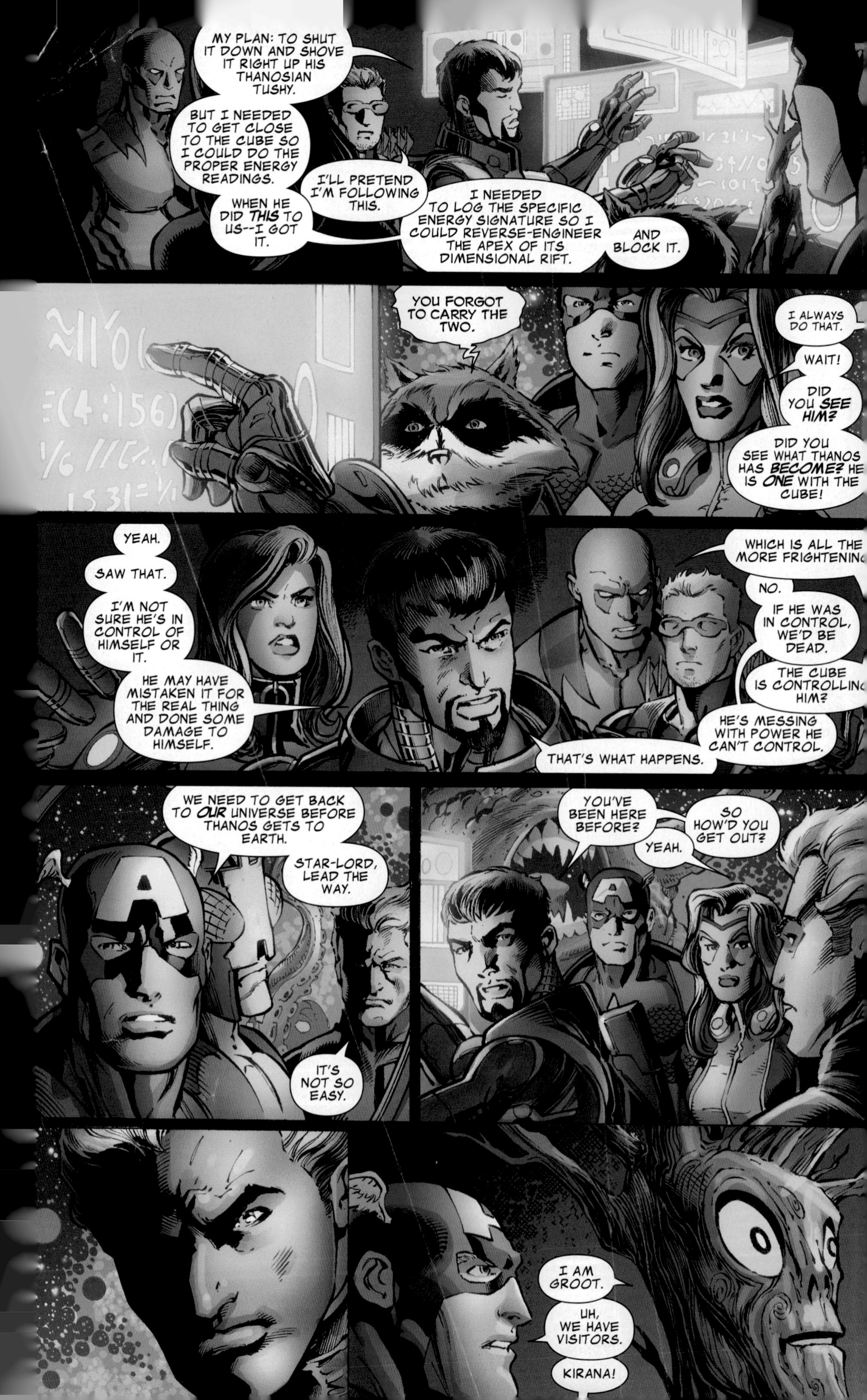
MY PLAN: TO SHUT IT DOWN AND SHOVE IT RIGHT UP HIS THANOSIAN TUSHY.
BUT I NEEDED TO GET CLOSE TO THE CUBE SO I COULD DO THE PROPER ENERGY READINGS.
WHEN HE DID THIS TO US--I GOT IT.
I'LL PRETEND I'M FOLLOWING THIS.
I NEEDED TO LOG THE SPECIFIC ENERGY SIGNATURE SO I COULD REVERSE-ENGINEER THE APEX OF ITS DIMENSIONAL RIFT.
AND BLOCK IT.
YOU FORGOT TO CARRY THE TWO.
I ALWAYS DO THAT.
WAIT!
DID YOU SEE HIM?
DID YOU SEE WHAT THANOS HAS BECOME? HE IS ONE WITH THE CUBE!
YEAH.
SAW THAT.
I'M NOT SURE HE'S IN CONTROL OF HIMSELF OR IT.
HE MAY HAVE MISTAKEN IT FOR THE REAL THING AND DONE SOME DAMAGE TO HIMSELF.
WHICH IS ALL THE MORE FRIGHTENIN
NO.
IF HE WAS IN CONTROL, WE'D BE DEAD.
THE CUBE IS CONTROLLIN HIM?
HE'S MESSING WITH POWER HE CAN'T CONTROL.
THAT'S WHAT HAPPENS.
WE NEED TO GET BACK TO OUR UNIVERSE BEFORE THANOS GETS TO EARTH.
STAR-LORD, LEAD THE WAY.
IT'S NOT SO EASY.
YOU'VE BEEN HERE BEFORE?
YEAH.
SO HOW'D YOU GET OUT?
I AM GROOT.
UH, WE HAVE VISITORS.
KIRANA!

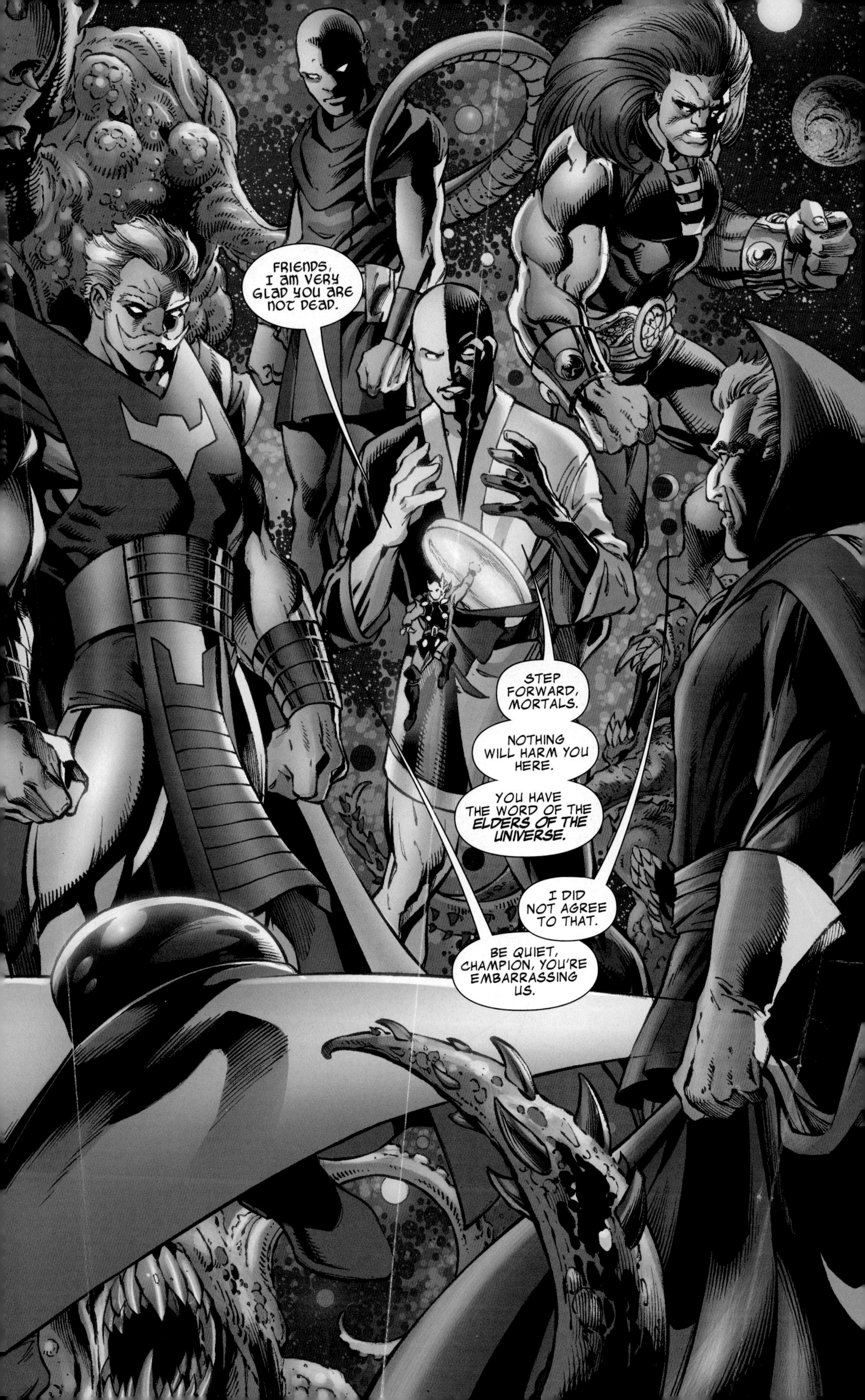

FRIENDS, I AM VERY GLAD YOU ARE NOT DEAD.
STEP FORWARD, MORTALS.
NOTHING WILL HARM YOU HERE.
YOU HAVE THE WORD OF THE *ELDERS OF THE UNIVERSE.*
I DID NOT AGREE TO THAT.
BE QUIET, CHAMPION, YOU'RE EMBARRASSING US.

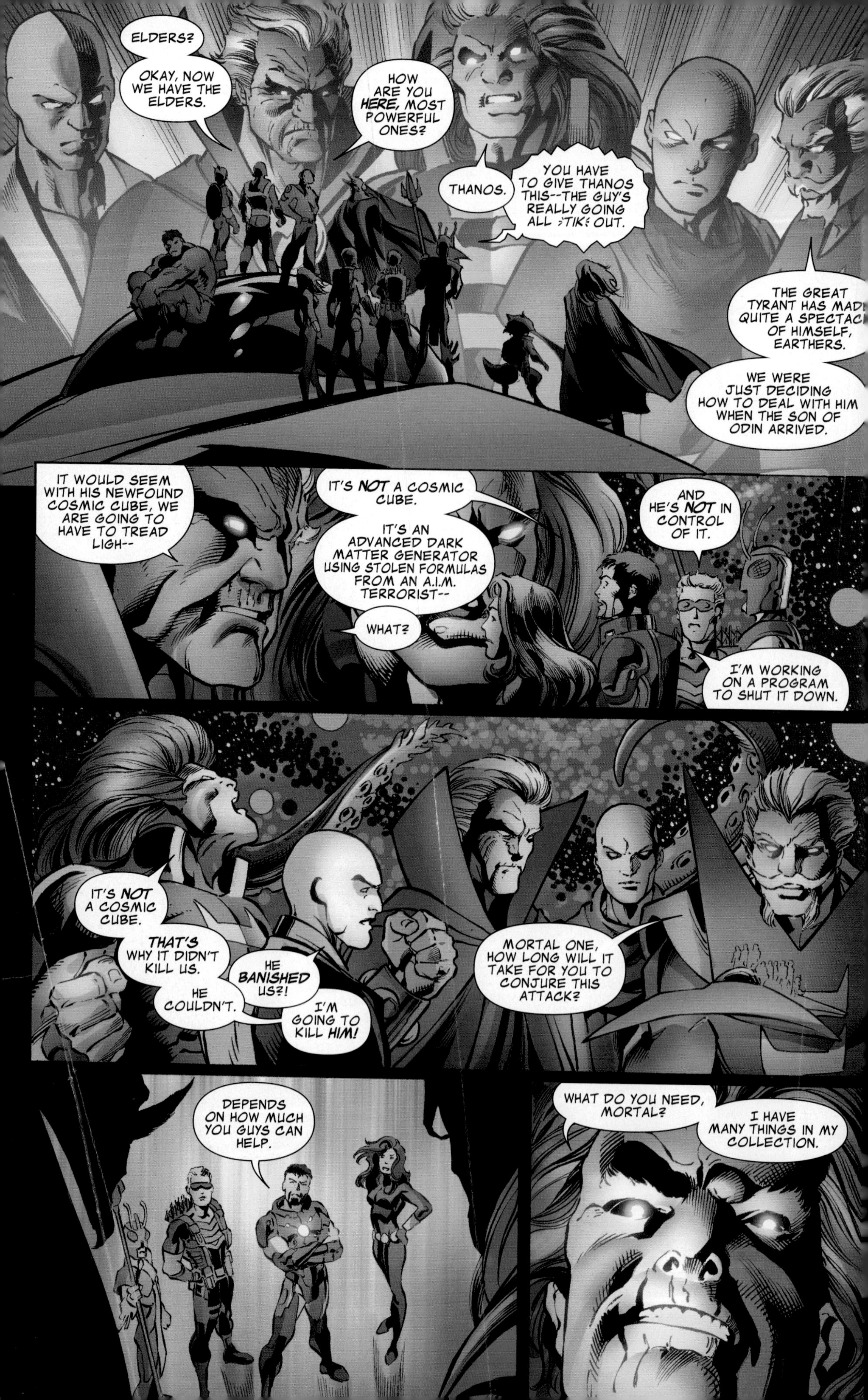
ELDERS?
OKAY, NOW WE HAVE THE ELDERS.
HOW ARE YOU HERE, MOST POWERFUL ONES?
THANOS.
YOU HAVE TO GIVE THANOS THIS--THE GUY'S REALLY GOING ALL ⚡TIK⚡ OUT.
THE GREAT TYRANT HAS MAD QUITE A SPECTAC OF HIMSELF, EARTHERS.
WE WERE JUST DECIDING HOW TO DEAL WITH HIM WHEN THE SON OF ODIN ARRIVED.
IT WOULD SEEM WITH HIS NEWFOUND COSMIC CUBE, WE ARE GOING TO HAVE TO TREAD LIGH--
IT'S NOT A COSMIC CUBE.
IT'S AN ADVANCED DARK MATTER GENERATOR USING STOLEN FORMULAS FROM AN A.I.M. TERRORIST--
WHAT?
AND HE'S NOT IN CONTROL OF IT.
I'M WORKING ON A PROGRAM TO SHUT IT DOWN.
IT'S NOT A COSMIC CUBE.
THAT'S WHY IT DIDN'T KILL US.
HE BANISHED US?!
HE COULDN'T.
I'M GOING TO KILL HIM!
MORTAL ONE, HOW LONG WILL IT TAKE FOR YOU TO CONJURE THIS ATTACK?
DEPENDS ON HOW MUCH YOU GUYS CAN HELP.
WHAT DO YOU NEED, MORTAL?
I HAVE MANY THINGS IN MY COLLECTION.

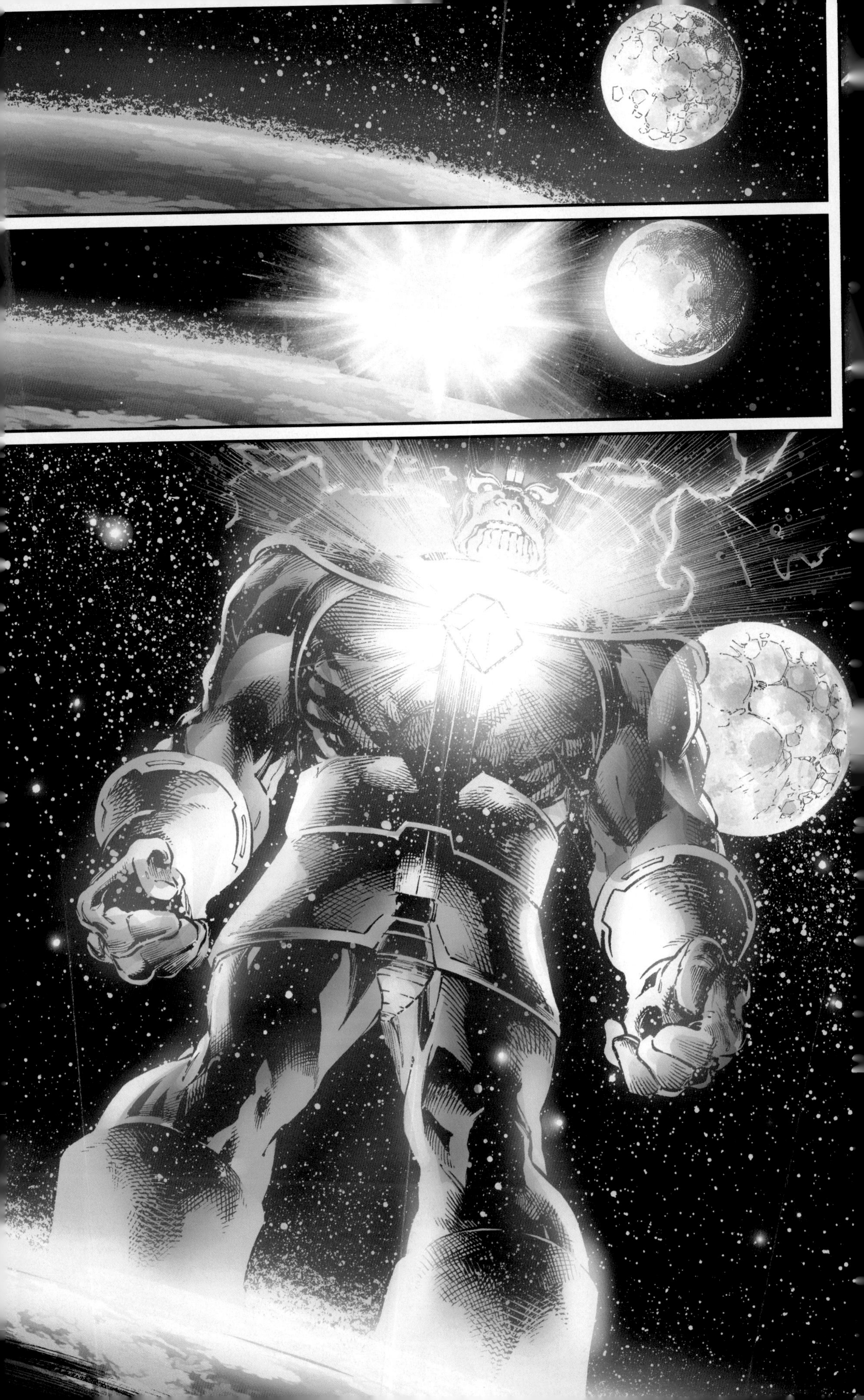

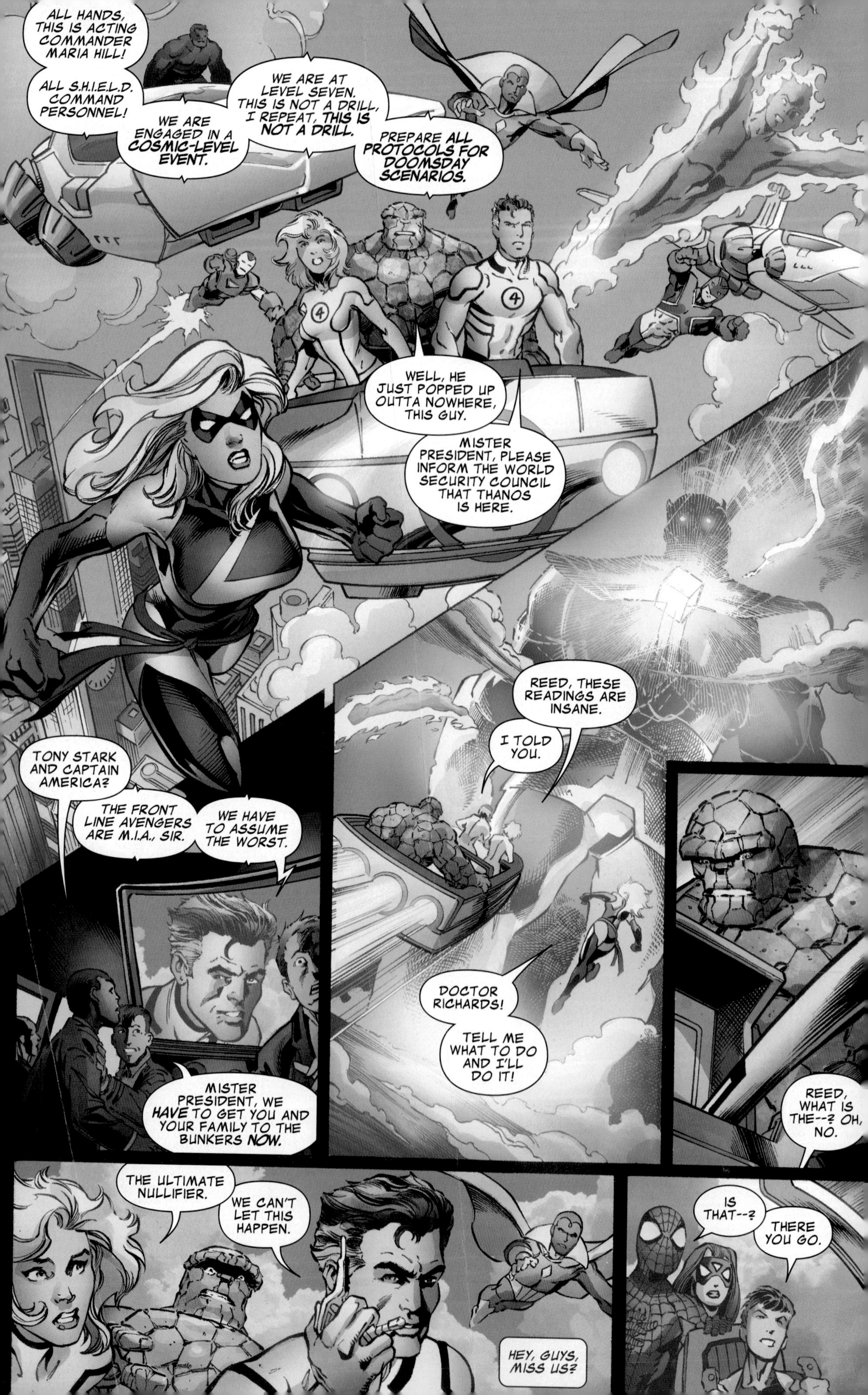
ALL HANDS, THIS IS ACTING COMMANDER MARIA HILL!
ALL S.H.I.E.L.D. COMMAND PERSONNEL!
WE ARE ENGAGED IN A COSMIC-LEVEL EVENT.
WE ARE AT LEVEL SEVEN. THIS IS NOT A DRILL, I REPEAT, THIS IS NOT A DRILL.
PREPARE ALL PROTOCOLS FOR DOOMSDAY SCENARIOS.
WELL, HE JUST POPPED UP OUTTA NOWHERE, THIS GUY.
MISTER PRESIDENT, PLEASE INFORM THE WORLD SECURITY COUNCIL THAT THANOS IS HERE.
TONY STARK AND CAPTAIN AMERICA?
THE FRONT LINE AVENGERS ARE M.I.A., SIR.
WE HAVE TO ASSUME THE WORST.
MISTER PRESIDENT, WE HAVE TO GET YOU AND YOUR FAMILY TO THE BUNKERS NOW.
REED, THESE READINGS ARE INSANE.
I TOLD YOU.
DOCTOR RICHARDS!
TELL ME WHAT TO DO AND I'LL DO IT!
REED, WHAT IS THE--? OH, NO.
THE ULTIMATE NULLIFIER.
WE CAN'T LET THIS HAPPEN.
HEY, GUYS, MISS US?
IS THAT--?
THERE YOU GO.

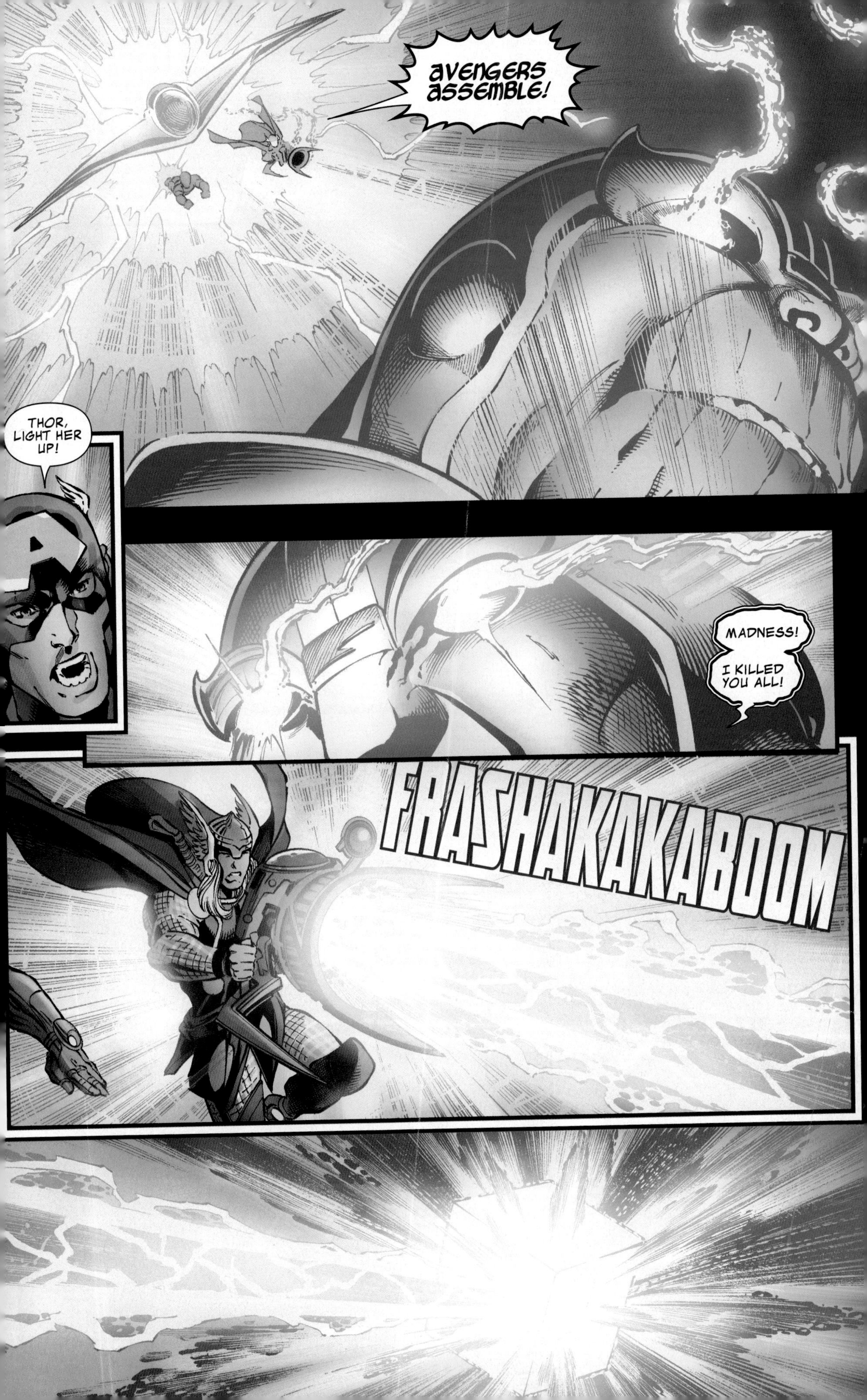
AVENGERS ASSEMBLE!
THOR, LIGHT HER UP!
MADNESS!
I KILLED YOU ALL!
FRASHAKAKABOOM

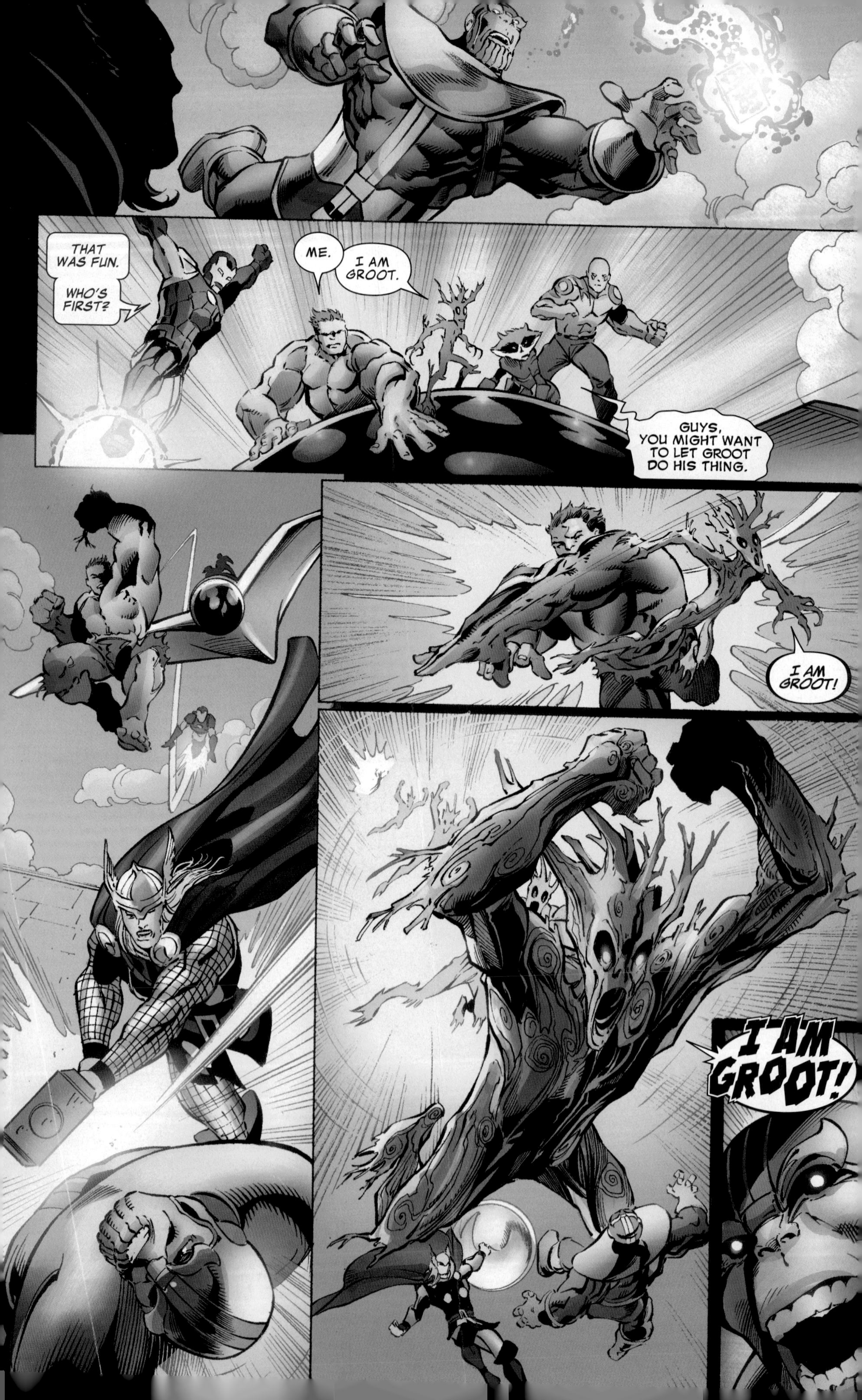
THAT WAS FUN.
WHO'S FIRST?
ME.
I AM GROOT.
GUYS, YOU MIGHT WANT TO LET GROOT DO HIS THING.
I AM GROOT!
I AM GROOT!

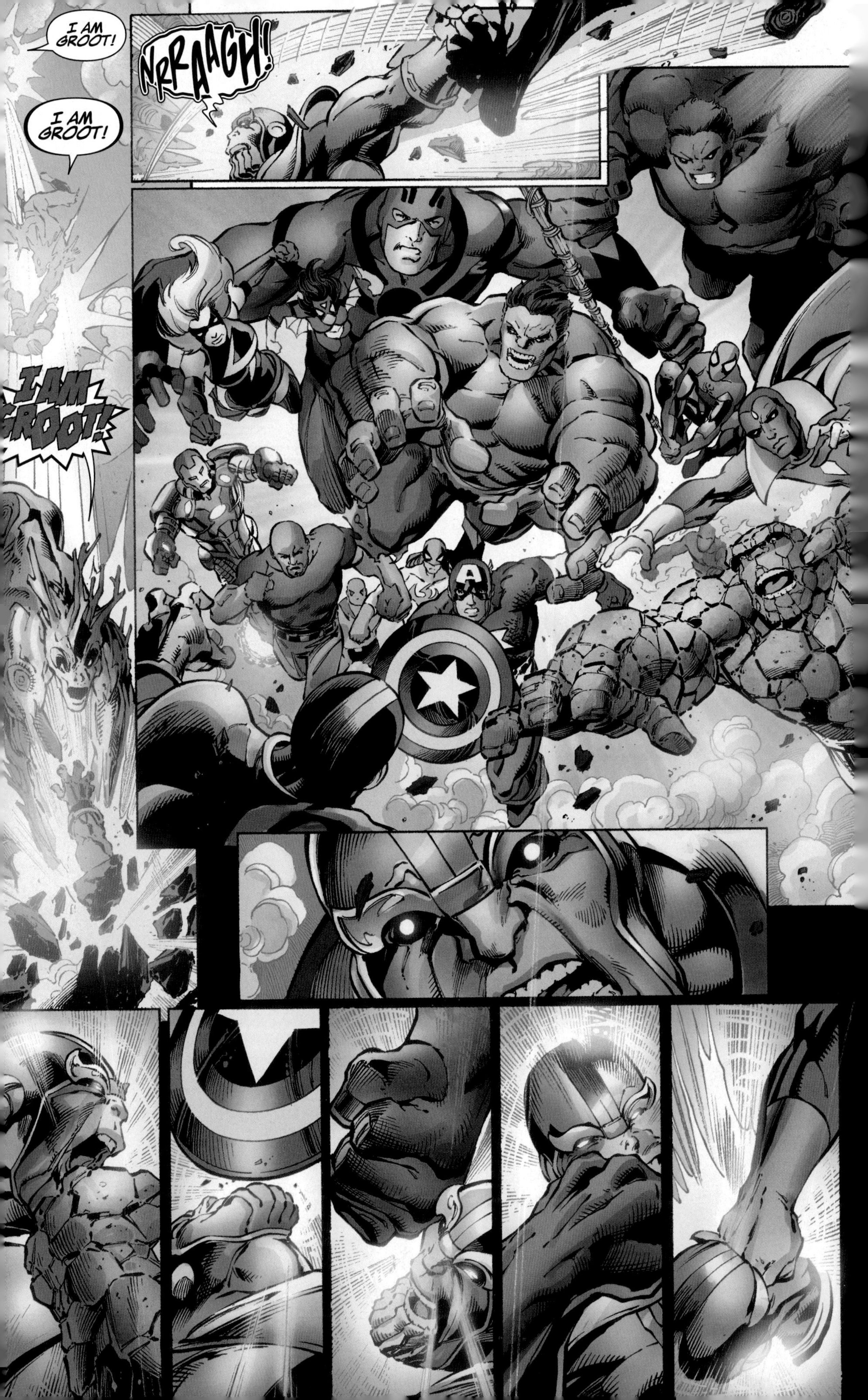
I AM GROOT!
NRRAAGH!
I AM GROOT!
I AM GROOT!

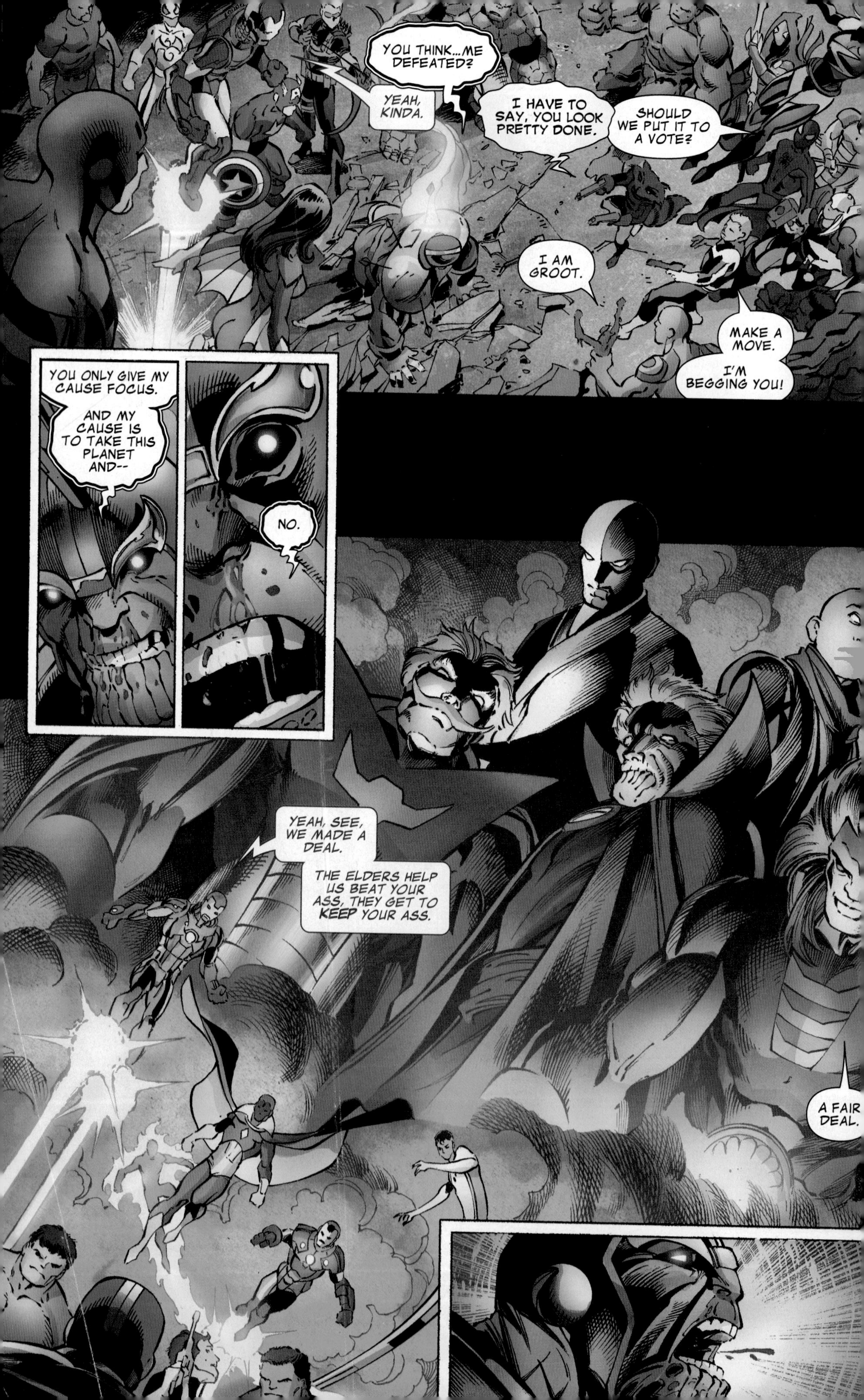
YOU THINK...ME DEFEATED?
YEAH, KINDA.
I HAVE TO SAY, YOU LOOK PRETTY DONE.
SHOULD WE PUT IT TO A VOTE?
I AM GROOT.
MAKE A MOVE.
I'M BEGGING YOU!
YOU ONLY GIVE MY CAUSE FOCUS.
AND MY CAUSE IS TO TAKE THIS PLANET AND--
NO.
YEAH, SEE, WE MADE A DEAL.
THE ELDERS HELP US BEAT YOUR ASS, THEY GET TO KEEP YOUR ASS.
A FAIR DEAL.

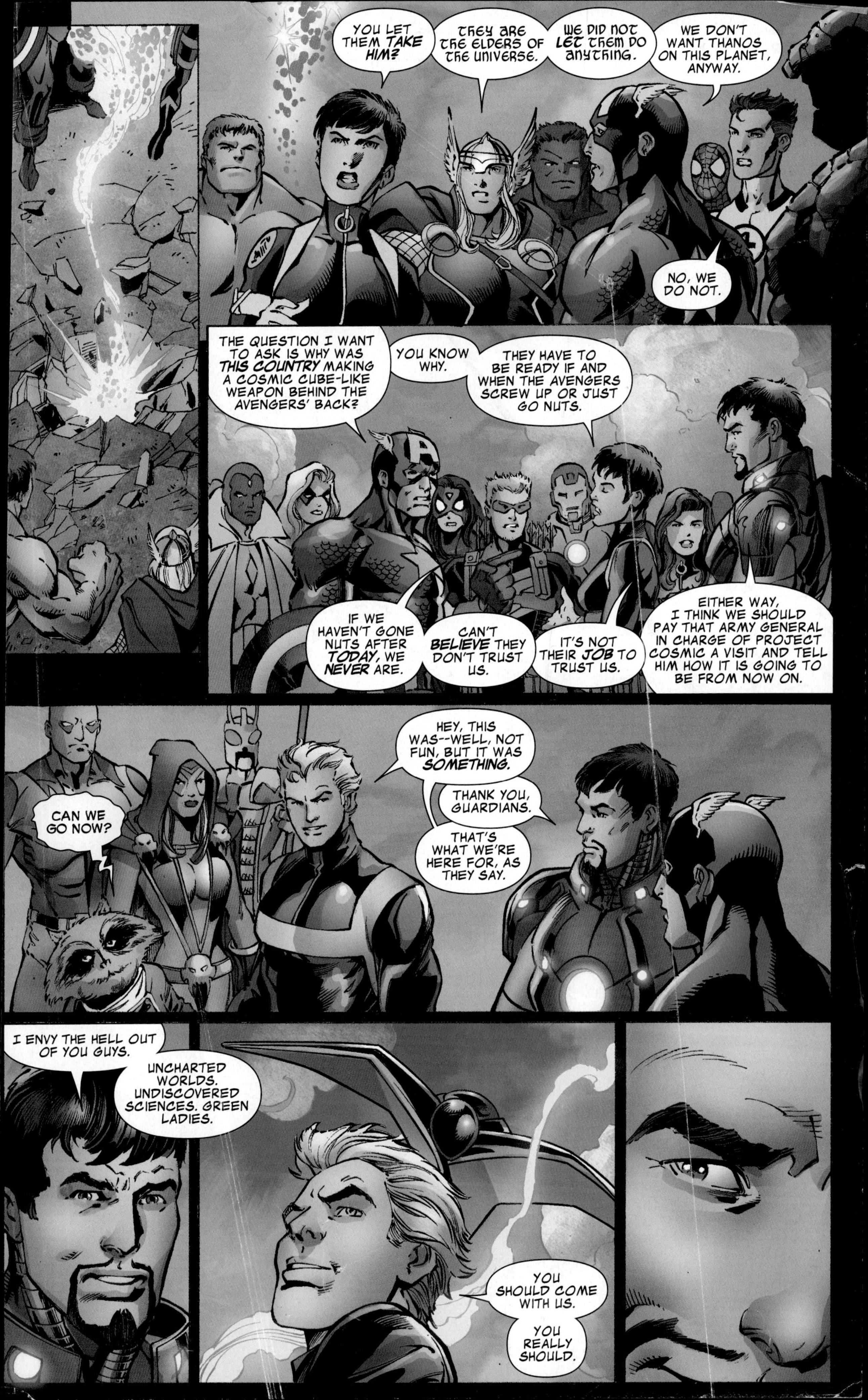

YOU LET THEM TAKE HIM?
THEY ARE THE ELDERS OF THE UNIVERSE.
WE DID NOT LET THEM DO ANYTHING.
WE DON'T WANT THANOS ON THIS PLANET, ANYWAY.
NO, WE DO NOT.
THE QUESTION I WANT TO ASK IS WHY WAS THIS COUNTRY MAKING A COSMIC CUBE-LIKE WEAPON BEHIND THE AVENGERS' BACK?
YOU KNOW WHY.
THEY HAVE TO BE READY IF AND WHEN THE AVENGERS SCREW UP OR JUST GO NUTS.
IF WE HAVEN'T GONE NUTS AFTER TODAY, WE NEVER ARE.
CAN'T BELIEVE THEY DON'T TRUST US.
IT'S NOT THEIR JOB TO TRUST US.
EITHER WAY, I THINK WE SHOULD PAY THAT ARMY GENERAL IN CHARGE OF PROJECT COSMIC A VISIT AND TELL HIM HOW IT IS GOING TO BE FROM NOW ON.
CAN WE GO NOW?
HEY, THIS WAS--WELL, NOT FUN, BUT IT WAS SOMETHING.
THANK YOU, GUARDIANS.
THAT'S WHAT WE'RE HERE FOR, AS THEY SAY.
I ENVY THE HELL OUT OF YOU GUYS.
UNCHARTED WORLDS. UNDISCOVERED SCIENCES. GREEN LADIES.
YOU SHOULD COME WITH US.
YOU REALLY SHOULD.

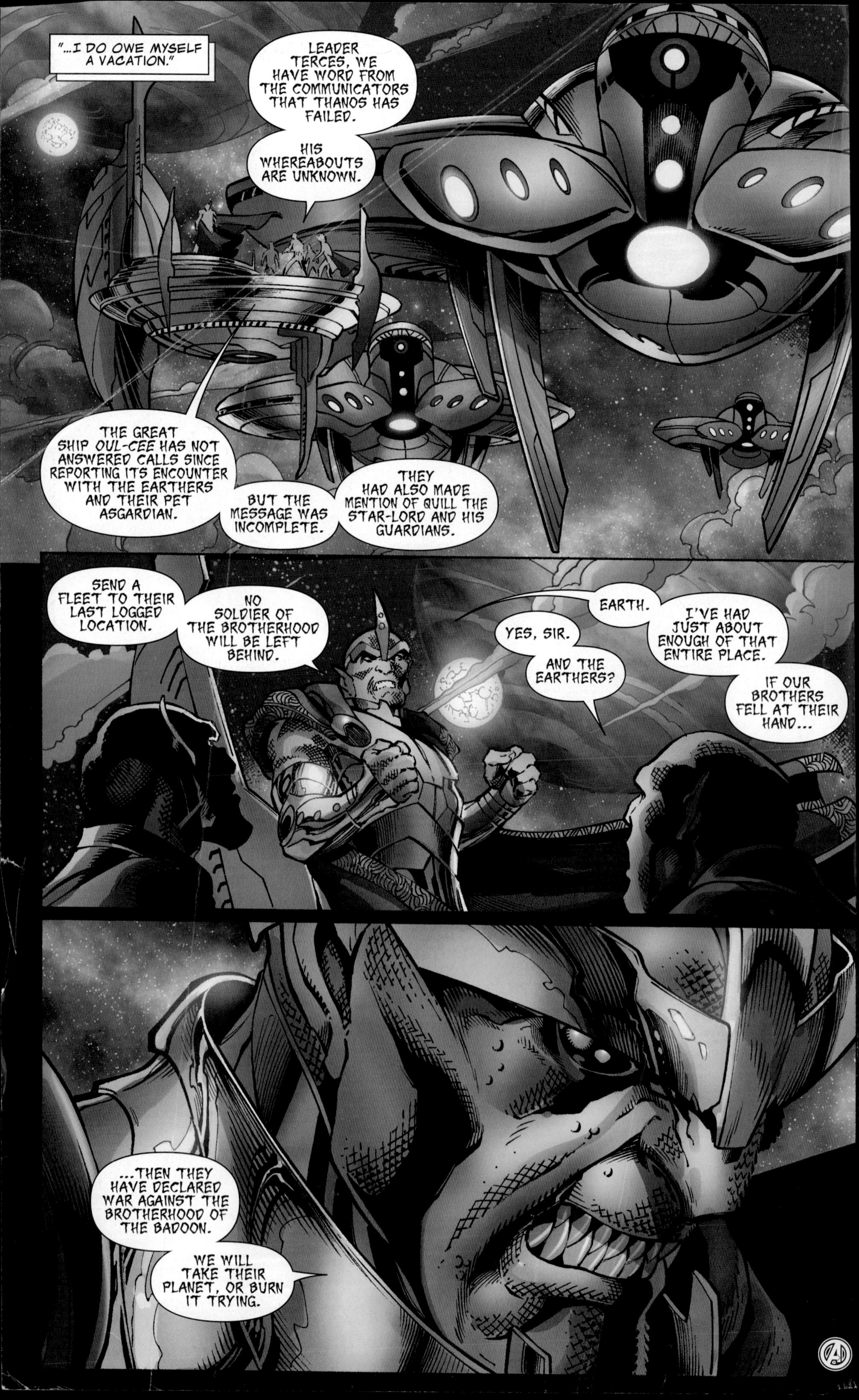
"...I DO OWE MYSELF A VACATION."
LEADER TERCES, WE HAVE WORD FROM THE COMMUNICATORS THAT THANOS HAS FAILED.
HIS WHEREABOUTS ARE UNKNOWN.
THE GREAT SHIP OUL-CEE HAS NOT ANSWERED CALLS SINCE REPORTING ITS ENCOUNTER WITH THE EARTHERS AND THEIR PET ASGARDIAN.
BUT THE MESSAGE WAS INCOMPLETE.
THEY HAD ALSO MADE MENTION OF QUILL THE STAR-LORD AND HIS GUARDIANS.
SEND A FLEET TO THEIR LAST LOGGED LOCATION.
NO SOLDIER OF THE BROTHERHOOD WILL BE LEFT BEHIND.
YES, SIR.
AND THE EARTHERS?
EARTH.
I'VE HAD JUST ABOUT ENOUGH OF THAT ENTIRE PLACE.
IF OUR BROTHERS FELL AT THEIR HAND...
...THEN THEY HAVE DECLARED WAR AGAINST THE BROTHERHOOD OF THE BADOON.
WE WILL TAKE THEIR PLANET, OR BURN IT TRYING.

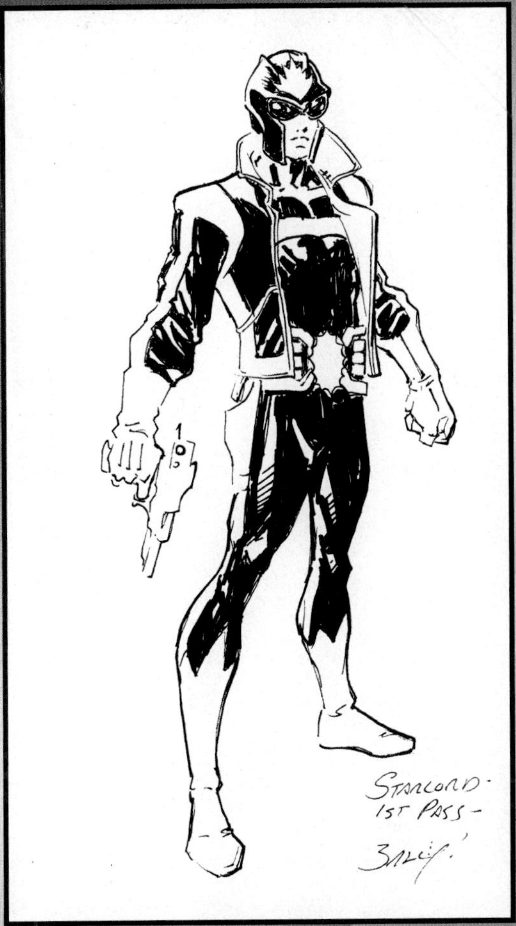
STARLORD-
1ST PASS-

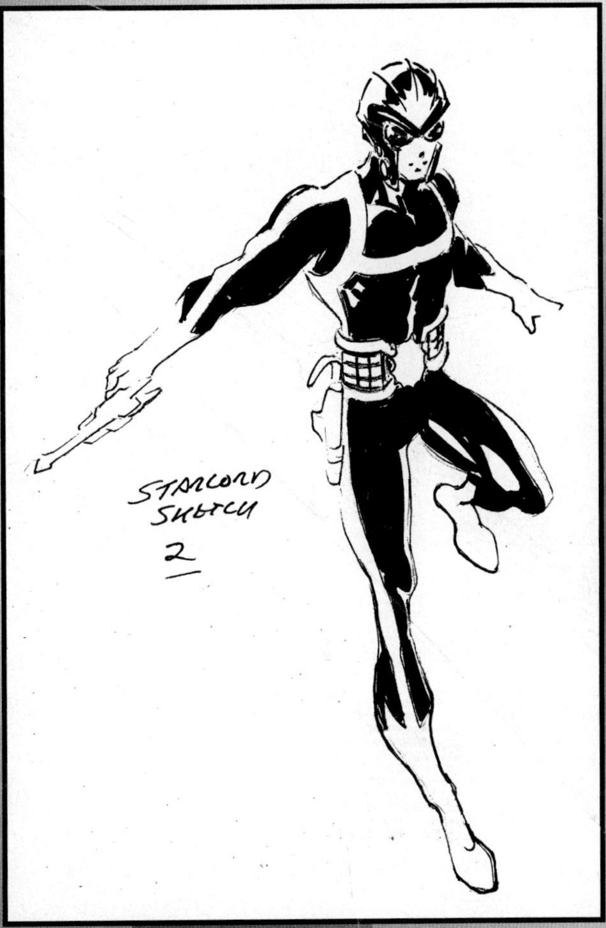
STARLORD
SKETCH
2

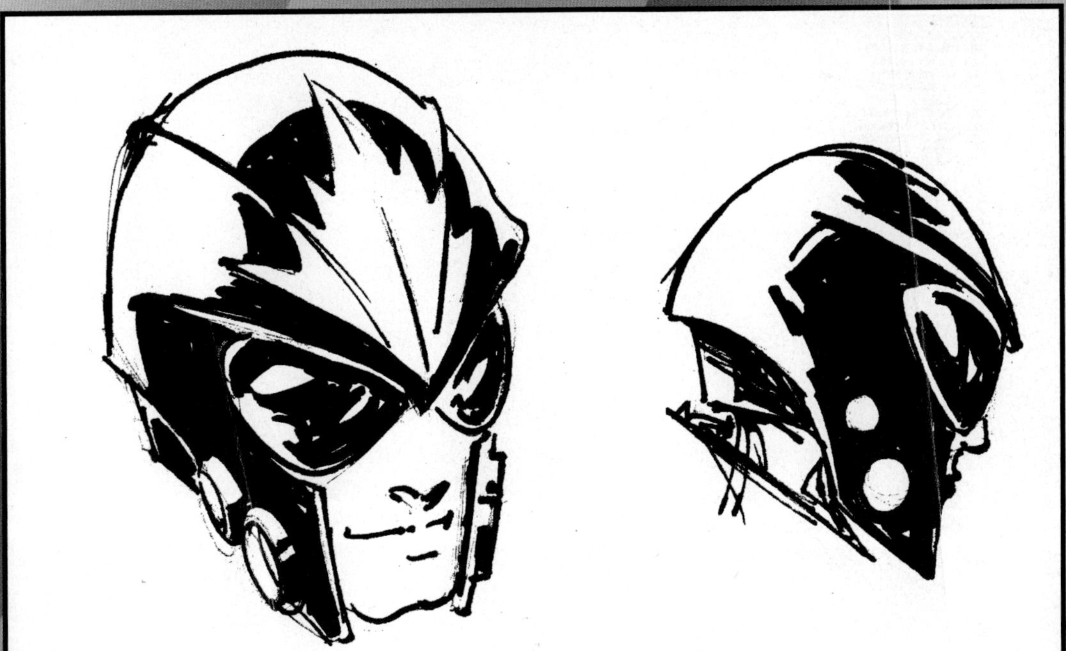
SLIGHTLY
TWEAKED
HELMET..

STARLORD DESIGNS BY MARK BAGLEY

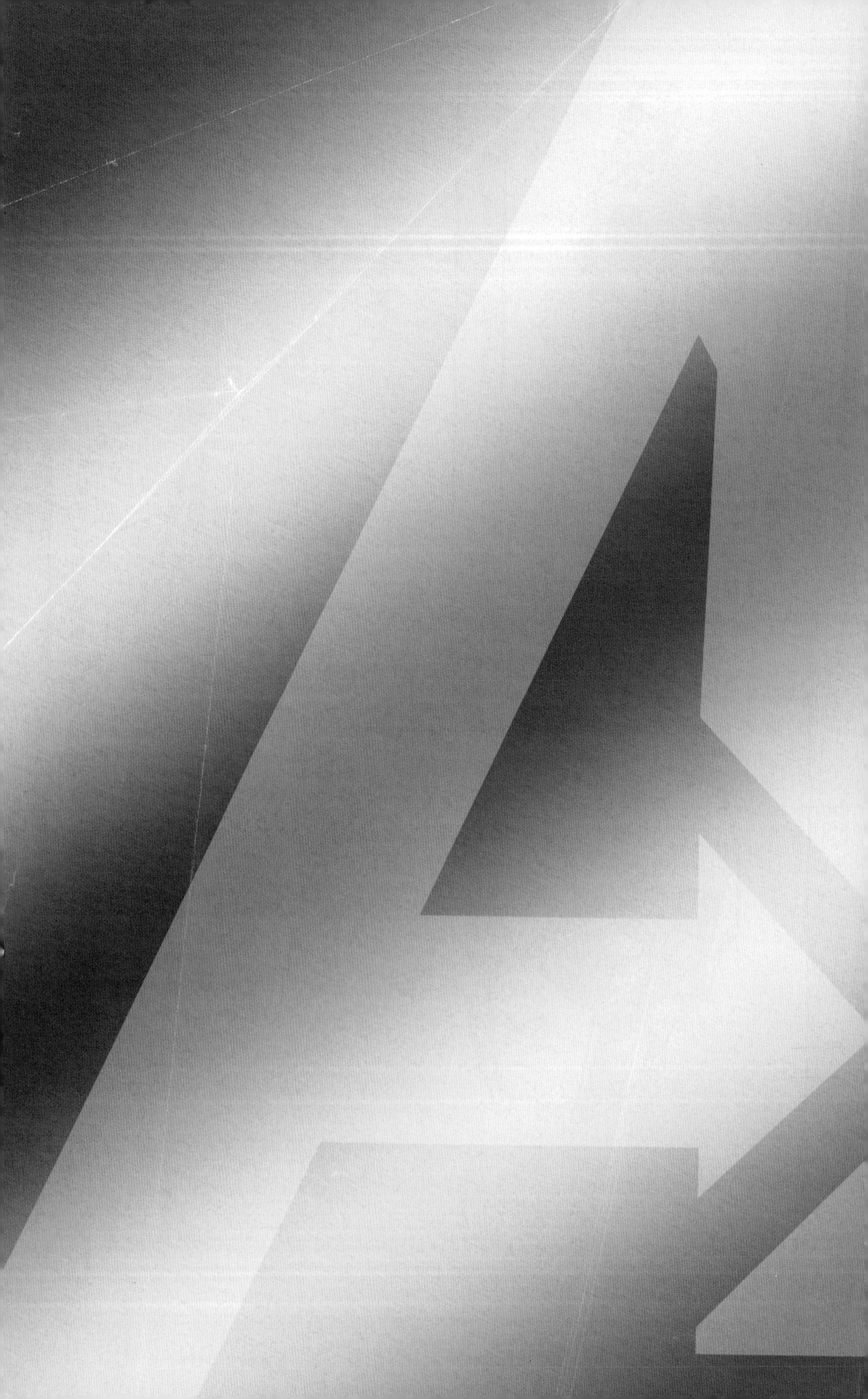